THE PRINCIPLES OF LITERATURE

A GUIDE FOR READERS AND WRITERS

CHRISTINA MYERS-SHAFFER, M.ED.

BARRON'S

Acknowledgments

The Life of Samuel Johnson, LL.D., (1964), by J. Boswell reproduced with the permission of McGraw-Hill Companies; "Liberty Hall" in *Round Up,* by Ring Lardner, © 1928 by Ellis A. Lardner; "Virga Vay & Allan Cedar" from *Cass Timberlane,* © 1945 by Sinclair Lewis, © Random House; "Barn Burning" from *Collected Stories of William Faulkner,* © 1939 by William Faulkner, © Random House; *Clerihew* and *Troilet* from *The New Princeton Encyclopedia of Poetry and Poetics,* © 1993 by Alex Preminger and T. V. P. Brogan, co-editors; "Pied Beauty" from *Poems of Gerard Manley Hopkins,* by Gerard Manley Hopkins, reprinted by permission of Oxford University Press; "Bell-tones," "Pity the Poor Raccoon," "Know Yourself," "Alphabet Soup," "Stressed and Unstressed," "Is It Euphemism or Euphony?," and "That Sound," © 1996 by Lillian E. Myers, all rights reserved; "Runaways", "An Encounter with Honey Bees," © 1999 by Lillian E. Myers and reprinted by permission of Lillian E. Myers, all rights reserved; definition of "air" from the *Merriam-Webster Dictionary,* © 1997 by Merriam-Webster, Incorporated; *The Great Code,* © 1982, 1981 by Northrop Frye, reprinted with permission of Harcourt, Inc; *Words With Power,* © 1990 by Northrop Frye, reprinted with permission of Harcourt, Inc.

All inquiries should be addressed to:
Barron's Educational Series, Inc.
250 Wireless Boulevard
Hauppauge, New York 11788
http: / /www.barronseduc.com

International Standard Book No. 0–7641–1240–6

Library of Congress Catalog Card No. 00-030400

Library of Congress Cataloging-in-Publication Data

Myers-Shaffer, Christina.
The principles of literature : a guide for readers and writers / Christina
Myers-Shaffer.
p. cm.
Includes index.
ISBN 0-7641-1240-6
1. Literature. 2. Authorship. I. Title.

PN45 .M94 2000
808--dc21
00-030400

Printed in the United States of America

9 8 7 6 5 4 3 2 1

Contents

▼

Part I
The Principles of Literature:
An Instructional Reference Guide
for Readers and Writers

▼

Part II
Putting the Principles of Literature to Work

▼

Preface

Would you be surprised to learn that H. G. Wells, author of *The War of the Worlds* and *The Time Machine,* held a degree in zoology and once worked as a draper's apprentice and as a schoolteacher? Daniel Defoe (author of *Robinson Crusoe*) was a hosiery merchant. Edgar Rice Burroughs (*Tarzan*) served as a soldier in the U.S. Cavalry. During the Civil War, Louisa May Alcott (*Little Women*) worked as a Union Army nurse. In addition to her successful writing career, poet, novelist, and short-story writer Frances E. W. Harper ("The Two Offers") worked as a nursemaid, seamstress, and teacher and actively participated in social and civic organizations on a national level. You may have seen a movie made in the late 1990s called *Riders of the Purple Sage;* the author of the book upon which the movie is based (Zane Grey) was a dentist.

These famous writers of British and American literature had to deal with meeting deadlines, going to school, getting to work on time, following orders, and making advantageous business deals, many of the same kinds of daily decisions, traumas, joys, and griefs that people have to face today. These experiences, in combination with their skillful use of the principles of literature, resulted in literary works that readers still can relate to and enjoy. Some life experiences, of course, vary from generation to generation. The principles of literature used by famous writers, however, are timeless and relevant to readers and writers in the twenty-first century, as well as in the past. You, too, can use them to become a more perceptive reader and expressive writer.

The principles of literature give writers a way to communicate their beliefs, feelings, and ideas. Understanding the principles of literature can help you, as a reader, to understand not only what the writer is saying, but also how he or she is expressing those ideas. As a result, your perception will increase, whether you are reading a great work of literature or the daily newspaper.

Do you sometimes think that your daily life lacks the adventure necessary to be an effective writer? Consider the young doctor named Sir Arthur Conan Doyle who used the quiet periods of time between seeing patients as opportunities to write about an exciting genius detective named Sherlock Holmes. Many parents make up stories to entertain their children. When Robert Louis Stevenson (educated to be a law advocate) wrote a story for his stepson, he named it *Treasure Island*. Be encouraged. There is nothing mundane enough about your life to prevent you from being the reader or writer you want to be.

Perhaps your life seems too difficult at times to pursue your writing. Anne Bradstreet, who has been called "America's first published poet," was married when she was sixteen years old and eventually had eight children. She expressed the experiences of her life in her writing, such as the elegies she wrote after the deaths of some of her children. Poet, playwright, and novelist William Wells Brown turned the adversities of his life as a slave in Kentucky into experiences that he shared with future generations through his writing.

Works of literature provide an opportunity to look into the hearts and minds of people who lived in a different time and place. However, you also can learn from these works the principles necessary to improve your communication skills today.

More About This Book

This book is a reference work and instructional guide written for people who want to learn to be more perceptive readers and expressive writers. If you are a writer, or aspire to be one, you can use this book to stimulate your thinking and further refine your work and skills. The instructional reference features of Part I should be especially helpful for literature and writing students engaged in independent study or classes, and Part II contains useful activities for instructors to use when planning a writing or literature curriculum. Regardless of your profession, you can use this book to enhance your enjoyment and appreciation of literature and to improve your writing skills.

In Part I, you will find the principles of literature. This instructional reference guide defines and illustrates five basic principles found in literature. Also, it examines some of the more complex, challenging, and interesting ways words can be used to communicate within those basic principles.

You can use this section to become acquainted with the principles of literature. Also, use Part I as you would any reference guide when you engage in reading and writing activities. Some of the terms in this section may be unfamiliar to you. These terms are included for reference purposes. The focus here, however, is on meaning rather than advanced terminology. In addition, you will notice that the instructional reference guide is generally aimed at examining the literary principles from the reader's perspective. Writers also can use Part I (in conjunction with Part II) to become sensitive to viewing their writing as readers might. For example, *aposiopesis* and *paraposiopesis* are two related terms (defined on pages 228 and 229) referring to when a speaker stops in mid-sentence. The terms may sound obscure; however, an awareness of these two literary devices can lead you to examine *why* a speaker stops in mid-sentence or to recognize the possible *effect* of that device. Is the speaker too scared to continue? Does the speaker stop to express emotion? Perhaps the speaker stops intentionally to comment directly on his or her own emotional state? In reading, these ideas are clues to help you determine the character of the speaker. In writing, they are techniques you can use to develop a fictional character.

Part II ("Putting the Principles of Literature to Work") provides you with specific ways you can use the principles of literature to improve your own reading and writing skills. It gives hands-on methods you can use to develop a reader-writer synergy. You will learn specific ways to become a more perceptive reader by recognizing how writers use the principles of literature to communicate their meanings. You can improve your effectiveness as a writer by learning how to examine and evaluate from a reader's perspective the role of the literary principles in your own writing. This concept changes the way you think as you read and write, regardless of the subject and purpose.

This book as a whole will enable you to understand and use effectively the principles of literature. Generally speaking, developing an interactive perspective is a gradual growth process that can become second nature to you. Becoming sensitive to the principles of literature described in this book encourages you to think, read, and write in these terms.

Why do readers return again and again to the literature of the past? The principles of literature allowed yesterday's writers to bridge time and speak to future generations. This book examines, illustrates, and explains these principles and shows how fresh and useful they are for the readers and writers of today.

The five literary principles for readers and writers are timeless. This book tells you what they are and how you can use them.

PART I

The Principles of Literature: An Instructional Reference Guide for Readers and Writers

Understanding Prose, Poetry, and Drama

Prose and Poetry

Prose is expression (whether written or spoken) that does not have a *regular* rhythmic pattern. Prose does have rhythm, but its rhythm lacks any sustained regularity and is not meant to be scanned.

Poetry is expression that is written in verse, often with some form of regular rhythm. The basis of poetic expression is a heightened sense of perception or consciousness.

Do all poems have regular rhythm? No. Do all poems take verse form? No. How, then, can you distinguish between prose and poetry? Both prose and poetry share many elements. As a result, prose and poetry can be seen as two levels or planes, each going in opposite directions, but partially overlapping at their common ends. Eventually prose pulls elements from poetry and poetry pulls elements from prose until each reaches a finite point at which prose becomes poetry and poetry becomes prose.

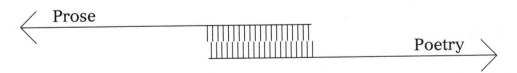

For example, look at this prose poem (a poem without traditional line divisions or lengths). Notice the prose elements at work, such as both left and right margin justification (each line starts and finishes at the same point) and paragraph indentation.

Bell-tones

Bells have been ringing and marking time in my life. Bells to come for and bells to go by. Bells to ring and bells to hear. Easy bell-tones turn to clattering bells ringing, finally becoming muted into many soft death knells.

I started with Tinker Bell, then listened to school bells between playing in fields of bluebells. Happy bells ringing; proms, parties, and dancing, playing happily and listening to the ringing of sleigh bells. Church bells comforting and confirming and wedding bells promising our love Always; such joy, bluebonnets and baby bonnets, with happy baby bells on baby booties.

Dinner bells called me; laundry bells startled me; cake timers beckoned me; liberty bells stirred me; jingle bells amused me until all the bells jangled and wrangled metallic as door bells and telephone bells ringing in pairs demanded me.

Then bells rang for help . . . time to get up, time to sleep, time to eat, time to leave, time to escape danger, time to come and time to go. Bells marked the hours and the times of my life. Now the beautiful bluebells in fields are calling me once again, mute bells singing soft notes as Church bells sound in blissful bell-tones, while we are waiting for the joyful ringing rapture of the Resurrection.

by Lillian E. Myers

Where would you place this prose poem on the diagram? Although visually made to look like prose, this prose poem contains such major poetic elements as personification ("bluebells . . . calling me"), onomatopoeia ("jangled and wrangled metallic"), and alliteration ("baby bells on baby booties") and the intensity of meaning characteristic of poetry, such as symbolism (the bell itself as a symbol of life's major events) and other uses of language such as the oxymoron ("mute bells"). The meaning is reflected and intensified by elements of rhythm throughout the work, such as the back-and-forth bell-like movement in "time to sleep, time to eat, time to leave . . . ."

Obviously, a clear-cut distinction between prose and poetry is difficult to establish, and you need to be constantly alert to the poet's use of prose techniques and the prose writer's borrowing of poetic devices.

How Language Saved a Nation

English prose is the result of the courage and far-sighted thinking of a young hero named Alfred the Great, the ninth-century King of Wessex. In the 870s, the Danes were vigorously attacking the English-speaking kingdoms. Should the Danes have overtaken them, there would not have been any English-speaking kingdoms left. The English language was in danger of extinction. King Alfred managed to push back the Danes from Wessex, but he knew that without the help of the Englishmen surrounding Wessex, the treaty King Alfred signed with the Danes would not save them. What could he do?

In a brilliant move to unify the kingdoms against the Danes, King Alfred consolidated the people on the basis of their "Englishness," with the English language at the heart of their new awareness of national identity. In a sense, King Alfred used the English language to establish and, at the same time, save a nation. When the people were united against the Danes, Alfred moved boldly ahead. He replaced Latin with English, had English chronicles written to give the people a sense of history, established a standardized English writing system, and earned for himself the title of "founder of English prose" by writing (in A.D. 887) the first example of completed English prose (*Handbook*).

Whereas the Danes were a threat to the English-speaking people and their language as a nation, Latin was a threat to English prose within the nation. Obviously, Alfred's promotion of English over Latin as an impetus for national unity did much to help English prose in its struggling stages. Even after English prose became more prevalent, however, its forms and syntax were significantly influenced by Latin.

Drama

Drama is a story intended to be acted out on a stage. Some critics include pantomime (silent acting), but others specify that drama requires dialogue. Drama also requires a plot, a setting, and characters.

Drama is divided into two very broad categories, each with its own characteristics:

1. *Comedy.* Generally, comedy refers to plays that amuse and/or have happy endings.

2. *Tragedy.* In a tragic play, the protagonist is disastrously overcome by some catastrophe.

The poet and prose writer can use dramatic elements (for example, elements of both comedy and tragedy can be found in prose fiction and in narrative poetry), and the dramatist can incorporate elements of prose and poetry within the development of the drama. Take the use of poetic forms in drama as an example. In Elizabethan drama, Marlowe's lowerclass characters speak in prose, but the "Good and Bad Angels" speak in blank verse (defined on page 67). Of William Shakespere's plays, a large number are written in blank verse. Shakespeare used poetic elements throughout his dramas to create moods, project character, develop plot, and signal the mechanical elements of the play. This technique can be seen in his ingenious use of couplets to cue entrances and to close scenes. A striking example is in Shakespeare's *The Tragedy of Julius Caesar.* Notice the dramatic impact of Shakespeare's use of couplet (two rhymed lines) at the moment when the struggle between Caesar and Marcus Brutus ends with Brutus committing suicide:

> Act V, Scene V
> **MARCUS BRUTUS.   Hence!   I will follow.**
> **[Exeunt CLITUS, DARDANIUS, and VOLUMNIUS.]**
> **I prithee, Strato, stay thou by the lord:**
> **Thou art a fellow of a good respect;**
> **Thy life hath had some smatch of honour in it:**
> **Hold, then, my sword, and turn away thy face,**
> **While I do run upon it. Wilt thou, Strato?**
> **STRATO. Give me your hand first: fare you well,**
> **my lord.**
> **MARCUS BRUTUS. Farewell, good Strato.—**
> **Caesar, now be still:**
> **I kill'd not thee with half so good a will.**
> **[*He runs on his sword, and dies.*]**

As you can see, many patterns and devices can be used within prose, poetry, and drama to accomplish, alter, or establish the purpose of the writer. Consequently, the *mixing and blending* of purpose, overall form, patterns of development, and literary techniques *is at the core of literary expression.*

An Overview of the Principles of Literature

Literature contains hidden treasures, filled with mysteries to be revealed and intrigues to be discovered. As a reader, you are an adventurer on a quest—to find what treasures are buried within each literary selection. Interpretive skills are the tools that are essential to finding these treasures, and the reader who develops and practices interpretive skills will uncover the many secrets of meaning and experience literature has to offer.

Interpretive skills involve learning to examine and analyze the literary principles that work together in a selection. These literary principles include meaning, form, voice and tone, charac-ter(ization), and language (uses and meanings).

One of the purposes of this book is to help you identify and explicate (explain in detail) each of the five principles of literature when they are at work in many different types of literary selec-tions. The following questions are grouped by literary principle and will give you an idea of the type of information you will be seeking when you analyze a literary selection.

Meaning:

- ▶ What is the work about? What is its theme?
- ▶ What effect or impression does the work have on the reader?
- ▶ What is the argument or summary of the work?
- ▶ What is the writer's intent?

Form:

- ▶ How has the writer organized the literary work to achieve the effect or express the meaning?
- ▶ How is the work structured or planned? As prose or poetry? As topics or scenes? As a long narrative, several short stories, or episodes?
- ▶ Into what genre (type or category) could the work be placed?
- ▶ What method of organization or pattern of development was used within the structure of the work?

Voice and Tone:

- ▶ Who is telling the story?
- ▶ How is the speaker or narrator characterized (his or her character revealed)? By action or description? Expressed or implied?
- ▶ From what perspective is the story told? By a person outside the story or by someone actually involved in the narrative?
- ▶ Is the speaker (the one telling the story) and the author or writer of the work the same person?
- ▶ If the writer and the speaker are two different individuals, are their attitudes toward the subject, events, and readers the same or different?
- ▶ What is the author's attitude toward the material, subject, or theme?
- ▶ What is the speaker's attitude (if different from the author) toward the material, subject, or theme? Toward the reader?
- ▶ Is the tone playful? Serious? Angry? Formal? Pleading? Joyful?
- ▶ What is the atmosphere of the work (the way in which the mood, setting, and feeling blend together to convey the prevailing tone)?

Character(ization):

- ▶ Who are the people in the work?
- ▶ How do dialogue (what he or she says) and action (what he or she does) reveal a character's personality traits?
- ▶ Is there a principal character?

▶ What is the character's motivation?
▶ Is the character's personality revealed directly by the speaker telling the reader or indirectly by the character's own words and deeds (requiring the reader to come to conclusions about the character based on dialogue and action)?
▶ In a nonnarrative work, how would you characterize the speaker or the writer? How would you characterize the work itself?

Language (Uses and Meanings):

▶ Does the selection include any imagery (the use of sensory images to represent someone or something)?
▶ What figures of speech does the writer use, and what effect do they have on the meaning of the selection?
▶ How does the writer use diction (word choice) to convey meaning?
▶ What is the impact of the words, phrases, and lines as they are used in the selection?
▶ Did the writer intend the words used to convey the meanings normally assigned to those words (the denotations)?
▶ Did the writer intend that some words would imply additional, associated meanings for the reader (connotations)?
▶ What is the significance of those implications to the meaning of the selection and the intent of the writer?
▶ How does the use of denotation, connotation, and syntax (how the words are structured and grouped to form meaningful thought units) relate to the style of the selection?
▶ Does the language of the selection include any elements of propaganda?

Literary Principles—Working Together for Unity

Have you ever tasted a well-made sweet-and-sour sauce? You can identify the sweet taste. You can identify the sour taste. Yet these two identifiable tastes join together and unify the sauce to produce a unique blend that is a flavor of its own. In much the same way, each of the literary principles can be identified individually; however, they also join together to unify the writing and to produce a blend that is unique to that particular work.

This guide defines and discusses, in a somewhat isolated manner, each of the literary principles. Literature, however, is not static. It is a dynamic marriage of concepts and ideas. Interpretation and critical analysis demand that readers and writers recognize the interrelatedness of these literary principles.

The literary principles contain concepts and functions that are shared. For example, an entire story can be an allegory, or allegory can be used as a literary technique within a story.

The interrelatedness and blending of use and form have led literary critics to vary considerably in defining not only the focus but also the scope each literary principle can and should entail. The principle of voice and tone is an excellent example of the wide range of interwoven definitions that these concepts can include.

Definitions of voice include:

▶ The speaker's attitude toward the reader/listener and toward the subject (therefore projecting a tone)
▶ The sense the reader gets of a writer's presence when the speaker's attitude and the writer's attitude toward the subject differ (in which case, the voice may disagree with the tone)
▶ The sense the reader gets of the writer's presence
▶ The point of view from which a selection is narrated
▶ The persona (mask-voice) of the writer (expressing the tone)
▶ A characteristic of a writer's style
▶ The thoughts of a poet to himself, the thoughts of a poet to the reader/listener, or the thoughts of a character in a poem
▶ A writer's style characterized by using active voice (I threw the ball) or passive voice (The ball was thrown to me) to project his or her point of view

Definitions of tone include:

▶ The speaker's attitude toward the reader/listener
▶ The writer's attitude toward the subject
▶ The writer's attitude toward the reader/listener
▶ The speaker's attitude toward the subject
▶ A device to develop mood and atmosphere (for example, the result of the use of figures of speech—use of language—in a selection)
▶ The musical elements (rhyme and rhythm) in literature
▶ How a literary selection is supposed to be read aloud, hence "tone of voice"

How language is figuratively used by a writer and what words mean in the context given are also elements of literary analysis that are difficult to define apart from one another. For instance, in the sentence, "John's attitude was a malignant growth spreading throughout the organization," the writer is comparing John's attitude to cancer. This type of comparison is a use of language called a metaphor. But how can the concept of metaphor (an implied comparison) be defined without recognizing the impact of the connotations (what the words mean in the specific context) that such a comparison brings to mind for the reader?

In fact, the same two comparisons can convey different connotations based on the context in which the comparisons are presented. Examine the simile (a comparison using *like* or *as*), "thin as a rail." In the first situation, a twenty-five-year-old man has recently lost 150 pounds on the advice and under the guidance of his doctor. He meets his aunt for lunch, and she laughingly exclaims upon seeing the healthy-looking young man, "Julio, you're as thin as a rail!" What are the connotations of this use of language, based on the context? In the second situation, a fifteen-year-old girl, 5 feet, 2 inches tall, has used starvation diets to reduce from 120 to 82 pounds. Her concerned mother takes her to see the family doctor. Upon seeing the girl enter the office, the nurse, who has known the girl since birth, gasps, "Young lady, you're as thin as a rail!" How has context changed the connotations of this use of language?

Time and Culture

Important clues to understanding literary selections are lost when the reader does not:

- ▶ Understand *historical references*
- ▶ Recognize *period motifs and conventions*
- ▶ Identify *regional, ethnic, and national accents or dialects*
- ▶ Realize how *words change in meaning over time and space*
- ▶ Appreciate *cultural differences*

Historical References

Understanding historical references in literature is the work of a lifetime. Yet, recognizing that both American and British literature have gone through definable periods, considering why the various works and authors are grouped within each period as they are, and seeking to find what events may have influenced the writers within the various periods can be very useful in developing interpretive skills.

Begin by looking at the sequence of the periods of American and English literature (since 1500) that are shown in the following chart. (Please note that dates may vary.)

LITERATURE AND WORLD EVENTS

1500

English Renaissance

- England's Golden Age Elizabeth I (1558–1603) (Shakespeare and Raleigh)

- Cortés conquers Aztecs (1521)
- Magellan sails around the world (1522)
- Counter-Reformation (1545)

1600

English Renaissance continues to 1660

- Jacobean Age of King James (1603–1625)
- Caroline Age (1625–1649)
- English Commonwealth Period (1649–1660)

- Thirty Years' War (1618)
- English Civil War (1642)

Restoration England: 1660–1700

- Neoclassicism in art and literature

American Colonialism

- Captain John Smith and Cotton Mather

- "Glorious Revolution" (1688)
- King William of Orange

- Jamestown colony (1607)
- Pilgrims arrive in America (1620)

1700

English Neoclassicism continues to 1798

- Augustan Age (1700–1745)— emphasis on Latin literature (Age of Pope)
- Age of Sensibility (1745–1798)
- Samuel Johnson

- Seven Years' War (1756–1763)
- French Revolution (1789)

American Colonialism Ends (1775);
Nationalism Begins
- Franklin and Jefferson

- American Revolution (1775)

1800

English Romantic Period to 1832
- Revolt against Neoclassicism in art and literature
- Wordsworth and Byron

- Napoleon defeated (1815)

American Transcendentalism and
Romanticism (1823–1865)
- Ralph Waldo Emerson
- Holmes and Poe

- Mexican War (1846–1848)
- American Civil War (1861–1865)

Victorian England (1832–1901)
- Emphasis on respectability
- Dickens, Browning, Rossetti

- German Empire established (1871)

American Realism (1865–1900)
- Art and literature mirror life
- Twain and Hawthorne

- Spanish-American War (1898)

1900

Edwardian England (1901–1910)
- Emphasis on elegance
- Yeats and Kipling

- World War I (1914–1918)
- Great Depression (1929)

American Naturalism to 1930
- Literature includes environmental realism

- Hitler in power (1933)
- American New Deal (1933)
- World War II (1939–1945)

England's Georgian Age to 1940
Modern Literature (1914–1965)
Postmodern Literature (1965–   )

- Berlin Wall (1961–1990)
- Kennedy assassinated (1963)
- King march on Selma, Alabama (1965)
- Vietnam War (1964–1975)

How do you think the events shown might have influenced writers at the time? For example, what effect might the Vietnam War have had on the literature written in the Counterculture Movement in America? What do you think the tone of the writing might be? Why might the impact of Vietnam have been different on writers in England than on those in the United States? How are events of today influencing your writing?

How does this knowledge increase your interpretive skills? An awareness of the events, thoughts, or conditions that may have influenced a writer helps you understand motivation and perhaps even purpose or meaning in what he or she has written. As the writer reveals attitudes, historical context and perspective put you in a better position to know where the writer is "coming from." For example, knowing that critics believe Spenser (a writer during the Renaissance) and Shelley (a Romantic writer) were influenced by the philosopher Plato might be very useful in understanding their attitudes, word choices, and references.

Also, sometimes writers refer to events, places, people, or other writers without explaining their significance—upon the assumption that the reader will understand the reference. When, in *The Vanity of Human Wishes,* Samuel Johnson writes:

> **In full-blown dignity, see Wolsey stand,**
> **Law in his voice, and fortune in his hand:**
>
> **(lines 99–100)**

he assumes that the reader knows that Thomas, Cardinal Wolsey was a powerful Lord Chancellor under King Henry VIII. Knowing the story of Wolsey, his rise and eventual fall, enables the reader to better understand Johnson when he writes:

> **Speak thou, whose thoughts at humble peace repine,**
> **Shall Wolsey's wealth, with Wolsey's end be thine?**
> **Or liv'st thou now, with safer pride content,**
> **The wisest justice on the banks of Trent?**
> **For why did Wolsey, near the steeps of fate,**
> **On weak foundations raise the enormous weight?**
> **Why but to sink beneath misfortune's blow,**
> **With louder ruin to the gulfs below?**
>
> **(lines 121–128)**

Likewise, what point is biographer James Boswell making in *The Life of Samuel Johnson, LL.D.,* when he writes "When I [Boswell] had him [Johnson] fairly seated in a hackney coach with me, I exulted as much as a fortune hunter who has got an heiress into a post chaise with him to set out for Gretna Green"? What is so special about Gretna Green? Gretna Green was a place in Scotland where couples could go to be married in a hurry by the local blacksmith or innkeeper—a place a fortune hunter would definitely want to take an heiress.

Boswell uses going to Gretna Green, a reference with which he assumes his readers are familiar, as part of a simile (a comparison using *like* or *as*) to show how intensely glad he was to have Johnson in the hackney coach with him. Earlier in the same account, Boswell wants a friend to invite Dr. Johnson to a dinner party to which his friend had planned to invite a notorious and controversial figure in Parliament named John Wilkes. Boswell writes:

> . . . I was persuaded that if I had come upon him with a direct proposal, "Sir, will you dine in company with Jack Wilkes?" he would have flown into a passion, and would probably have answered, "Dine with Jack Wilkes. Sir! I'd as soon dine with Jack Ketch."

Who is Jack Ketch? He was a public hangman, whose name was well-known to Boswell's learned contemporaries in 1791; but Boswell does not explain this reference to his twenty-first century readers. Likewise, authors today are writing about such people, places, and ideas as the Big Apple, John Glenn's return to space, *60 Minutes,* the Big Easy, the boob-tube, the Iron Curtain, the Berlin Wall, Cape Kennedy, and Oprah Winfrey. Will people two hundred years from now understand the significance of these references? Should a writer assume that the reader will have some background knowledge? What would happen to an author's style of writing if he or she tried to explain every reference used?

Period Motifs and Conventions

Different periods of literary history have brought with them identifiable motifs and themes, as well as conventions and traditions. Being able to recognize when these motifs and conventions are being used helps the reader form expectations and determine whether those expectations are being met.

First, examine motifs and themes. A *motif* is a figure or element that recurs in literary works; the *theme* of a work is its main idea or concept. (Theme will be discussed later.)

Some common motifs include:

▶ Loathly lady motif—an ugly girl turns out to be a beautiful woman; the ugly duckling becomes a beautiful swan in the children's tale (closely related to the Cinderella motif).

▶ *Ubi sunt* motif—the motif of mourning a lost past (sometimes used in lyric poetry). A poem might include the question "Where are . . . ?" (Latin: *Ubi sunt*), such as "Where are the carefree days of youth?" This motif is widely used in movies today. For example, *The English Patient* is a movie framed in the flashbacks of a severely burned man remembering and mourning his life and lost love of the past. Woven in and out of the movie is *carpe diem* (see next item) as his attending nurse, struggling with feelings that everyone she loves gets killed, learns to love again—to seize the day.

▶ *Carpe diem* motif—meaning "seize the day" because of the brevity of life. A well-known example of the *carpe diem* motif is Edmund Waller's *Song: Go, lovely rose!* (1645) in which the speaker compares a young girl to a rose to impress upon her that, like the rose, her youth and beauty have only a short time to live and be admired. He establishes the motif in the first stanza:

> **Go, lovely rose!**
> **Tell her that wastes her time and me**
> **That now she knows,**
> **When I resemble her to thee**
> **How sweet and fair she seems to be.**

▶ Magic spell motif—music makes the girl fall in love; an apple causes a princess to fall asleep.

▶ Wake-up motif—one lover urging the other to awake. This motif is found in an *aubade,* a song at dawn. For example, Shakespeare's *Hark, Hark! the Lark* ends with these lines:

> **With every thing that pretty is,**
> **My lady sweet, arise!**
> **Arise, arise!**

▶ Star-crossed lovers—a boy and girl fall in love but are doomed to tragedy because their families are feuding (*Romeo and Juliet,* the Hatfields and McCoys, and *Westside Story*).

Motifs may include a sense of formula. You can expect the princess to awake when kissed by her prince or the frog to become a prince when kissed by the beautiful girl.

Second, look at the role of conventions (plots and genres, characters, verse forms, styles, or literary devices that recur in literature) **and traditions** (a way to group literary works because they share themes or concerns).

Conventional plots and genres include many different forms, such as the romance in which girl falls in love with boy, boy is momentarily distracted by a heartless, conniving female, but boy realizes in the end that the heroine is the true love of his life. Although variations on conventional plots are seemingly endless, what cop-and-robber story can be complete without a chase scene or western without a barroom brawl? The reader knows what is going to happen—what to expect.

Conventional characters are often not difficult to identify: stock characters in fiction (types of characters that are usually found in certain literary forms—the tall, handsome leading man in a romance or the heart-of-gold saloon girl in a western). *Conventional forms* also can give the reader a sense of anticipation, such as in the epic poem. Three standard features of an epic poem are that the poet (1) moves right into the middle of the action and conflict without explaining the situation, (2) consults a muse for help, and (3) includes a superman-type epic hero whose fate is to overcome tremendous odds for the sake of a grand purpose. Sometimes a *conventional style or literary device* is used within a conventional form. An example would be the **epic epithet** (a description of character traits to identify a person) within an epic poem. Conventions within drama include the soliloquy in which a character speaks, but is "heard" only by the audience.

To identify a literary *tradition* is to attempt to group works that share themes or ideas. There are many possible ways to identify traditions, sometimes even by the way they employ certain conventions, as in the Courtly Love Tradition in which religious vocabulary is a convention used to put the object of affection "on a pedestal." A few traditions include Neoclassical, Pastoral, and Satiric Traditions, as well as the English, European, Western, and Modern Traditions.

Regional, Ethnic, and National Dialects

Word choices and dialects vary greatly not only between England and America, but also within England and America. A Texan, accustomed to ordering *soda water,* might get a moment's hesitation from a waiter in Ohio, where *pop* is the common usage. Not recognizing regional differences in dialect and vocabulary can lead to confusion and lack of communication, as demonstrated by the young couple who moved from the Midwest to Texas. They searched the classified ads in local newspapers for land for sale, but were disappointed that many places were described as having "tanks." Picturing large, above-ground water tanks, the couple did not even bother to look at these properties until they discovered that "tank" is the "Texas lingo" for pond or small lake. A building supply store chain is taking these regional differences in vocabulary so seriously that their advertising explains that "wallboard," "drywall," and "gypsum" refer to the same product. They might have included "Sheetrock" (trademark) and "plasterboard" as regional synonyms, also.

Many times writers will attempt to convey to the reader the dialect (the speech of a region) or accent (the ways words are actually pronounced) by use of vocabulary choices and spelling variations (to show pronunciation). Writers should exercise care that such uses do not confuse or offend readers or interrupt the flow of the dialogue.

What elements can determine a person's dialect or accent?

1. Ethnicity or nationality—a Frenchman speaking English with a "French accent"

2. Regional differences—an Oklahoma accent compared to a Brooklyn accent; use of *y' all* in the Southern United States, *you guys* in the Midwest, and *you 'uns* in the Ohio River Valley

In addition, authors also attempt to convey in writing ways of speaking and accents that are the result of:

3. Education—usually seen in word choice as well as in pronunciation; note the speech patterns of American journalist William F. Buckley, Jr.

4. Occupation—"buzzwords" or word choices peculiar to an occupation being a predominant feature of the dialect, including technical terminology called **jargon**

5. Time
   a. Periods of English—the Queen's English of Victorian England, for example, compared to Modern English

b. The "generation gap" illustrated by the speech of the Beat Generation, the hippies, the yuppies, and the preppies; compare the "surf talk" of Annette Funicello in the beach party movies of the late 1950s and 1960s to the "surf talk" of "Valley Girls" in the 1980s

Changes in Meanings of Words over Time and Space

Time is an element that helps shape a person's dialect. Linguistic scholars have identified English, a Germanic language, as part of the Indo-European family of languages. English language history is divided into periods: Old English, Middle English, Modern English from 1500 to 1800, and Modern English from 1800 to the present. Notice the progression and changes the English language has undergone since the Old English period.

The Old English Period (A.D. 449–1100)

British Celts, under attack by the Picts and Scots (Irishmen), called on fierce Germanic warriors when the Romans would not provide adequate help in A.D. 449. After driving out the Picts and Scots, these Germanic Angles, Saxons, and Jutes took over England and established the seven kingdoms of Kent, Essex, Sussex, Wessex, East Anglia, Mercia, and Northumbria (names that appear throughout English literature—even in those works written in Modern English).

The following poem, written in Old English, was penned sometime between A.D. 658 and 680 and illustrates how radically different the English of this period was compared to English today.

Cædmon's Hymn

Nu sculon herigean   heofonrices Weard
Meotodes meahte   and his modgeþanc
weorc Wuldor-Fæder   swa he wundra gehwæs
ece Drihten   or onstealde
He ærest sceop   ielda bearnum
heofon to hrofe   halig Scyppend
ða middangeard   moncynnes Weard
ece Drihten   æfter teode
firum foldan   Frea aelmihtig

The Middle English Period (A.D. 1100–1500)

Middle English began shortly after the Norman Conquest (William the Conqueror) in 1066. Naturally, the impact was felt in the language, especially in vocabulary. During this time, the dialect of London became a standard for English; however, writers continued to use their regional dialects (North, South, Kent, West Midland, and East Midland) almost until the end of the period.

Examine these lines of Chaucer's "General Prologue" to *The Canterbury Tales,* written in 1386.

> A good man was ther of religioun,
> And was a povre PERSOUN of a toun;
> But riche he was of holy thoght and werk.
> He was also a lerned man, a clerk,
> That Cristes gospel trewely wolde preche;
> His parisshens devoutly wolde he teche.

Modern English (A.D. 1500–1800)

The English language underwent important changes during this time, especially changes in pronunciation. Perhaps the most radical change is what linguists call "the Great Vowel Shift." Even though English was changing significantly in pronunciation, spelling in the 1500s was not keeping pace.

Notice the first sentence of a paragraph written by Bankkes in 1525 in a "botanical" book called *Herball.*

> **Rofemary.**

> This herbe is hote and dry/take the flowres and put
> them in a lynen clothe/ & fo boyle them in fayre
> clene water to ỹ halfe & coole it & drynke it/for it is
> moche worth agaynft all euylles in the body.

The earliest English dictionaries appeared in this period, with Robert Cawdrey's *A Tabel Alphabeticall* leading the way in 1604; however, English spelling and usage was not standardized until Samuel Johnson was commissioned in 1746 to write *A Dictionary of the English Language.* Note Johnson's definition of *enthusiasm:*

> ENTHU'SIASM. n. 1. A vain belief of private revelation; a vain confidence of divine favor or communication.
> *Enthusiasm* is founded neither on reason nor divine

> revelation, but rises from the conceits of a warmed
> or overweening brain. —*Locke*.

How has this word changed in meaning since the mid-1700s?

Modern English (1800 to Present)

In terms of form and structure of English, this period has seen little radical change, with forms of standardized English being sustained in both England (where British Standard is taught in schools) and in the United States (where American English is the offspring of the British-speaking colonists and explorers of the seventeenth century).

Surprising to some, words in American usage have found their way into the British vocabulary, partly as a result of advanced communications, commerce, and American technology. Even so, there are significant differences between British and American word choices even in Modern English (note the British *posh frock* and the American *fancy dress*) and, of course, pronunciation. Spelling is another area of difference, due in part to Noah Webster, who took the *u* out of *colour, armour,* and *neighbour,* changed *-re* to *-er* in *theatre, centre,* and *manouvre,* and changed the *c* to *s* in *defence,* to cite just a few of his influences.

British English and American English have undergone and continue to undergo tremendous changes in the denotative and the connotative values of English words. How and why do words change meanings and how are new words added to the English vocabulary? Here are a few of the more common ways:

▶ Words often have more than one meaning, and usage can add even more meanings. A case in point is the word *firebreak,* a fire-fighting term referring to a barrier (often a gap in combustible trees or vegetation) meant to stop a fire. The key players in the Nuclear Age, however, have extended this word, giving it an additional, new meaning: a barrier or gap separating conventional warfare and nuclear war, meant to stop nuclear confrontation.

Sometimes words gain so many meanings they become very generalized and no longer carry the preciseness of meaning that they once conveyed. Some people would use the word *love* as an example.

▶ Obviously, the meanings of a word can also be reduced, becoming rare, archaic, or even obsolete. *Buckle* (verb) is an example, as it appears in Webster's *New Twentieth Century Dictionary* (Unabridged).

In fact, an entire word form can become obsolete, such as *brut* in its verb form (meaning to browse) or *bruckled* (an adjective meaning grimy). Very rarely today is a little stream called a *brun*. And look at the word *corn:* corn once meant grain; then it came to mean Indian corn or maize in America, wheat in England, and oats in Scotland.

▶ Entirely new words can be coined or added to the language, often due to new technologies, explorations, or any circumstances in which a never-before-communicated idea must be expressed. Consider the word *Kodak,* which was "invented" by George Eastman in 1888.

▶ Words once thought to have negative connotations can be elevated in the public's perception and become respectable for use (*nice* once meant *ignorant*) or the opposite when words fall into disrepute (*hussy* once meant *housewife*).

▶ Words can come into use to avoid the negative connotations of harsher words. For example, the Irish began referring to *the little people* rather than saying *fairies.* The kinder, gentler word is called a *euphemism.* This genteelism is a significant factor in the language and literature of Victorian England, where, for instance, a piano *leg* was called the less-suggestive word *limb.*

▶ New uses of prefixes, suffixes, and compounding can add to a language's vocabulary. Note *panorama, snacketeria,* and *splashdown.*

▶ Words also can be added to a vocabulary by abbreviation or clipping (*exam* for *examination*), blending (*broasted* = *broiled* + *roasted*), and using acronyms (NOAA = National Oceanic and Atmospheric Administration).

▶ Borrowing from other languages has had a significant influence on English. These borrowings include such words as *fork* (*furca*) from Latin, *frankfurter* from German, *raffle* (*rafle*) from French, *spaghetti* from Italian, and *serape* from Mexican-Spanish.

Of how much importance is recognizing the changes English has undergone to understanding literature? Consider the use of the word *petty* in this statement written during the mid-1700s by Samuel Johnson in *A Dictionary of the English Language*:

> **Swift, in his *petty* treatise on the English language, allows that new words must sometimes be introduced, but proposes that none should be suffered to become obsolete. [emphasis added]**

What attitudes come to mind when Johnson calls Swift's treatise "petty"? *Petty* can mean *unimportant*; however, it can also mean *small* in size or length. How would this definition change the meaning of the statement?

Cultural Differences

When an American answers the telephone, he or she may utter any number of responses, ranging from a simple "hello" to stating his or her name and asking "May I help you?" In England, however, you may hear the person answering the phone recite (rapidly) the telephone number that has been rung. Recognizing such cultural differences enables the reader to understand plot and character better and allows the reader to form cultural expectations.

The word *culture,* for the purpose of literary analysis, can be defined as a body of concepts, skills, and institutions that make a particular people in a particular place and/or period of time an identifiable group or civilization. How significant is culture to literary analysis? The culture of the writer can shape the attitudes of an entire work; for example, the English devotion to the British monarchy.

Cultural contrasts can help sharpen perceptions, and sometimes identifying these contrasts is important to literary meaning. A case in point is Boswell's reference to a *turnspit* in *The Life of Samuel Johnson, LL.D.*

> **A man whom he had never seen before was employed one night to sit up with him. Being asked next morning how he liked his attendant, his answer was, "Not at all, Sir: the fellow's an idiot; he is as awkward as a turnspit when first put into the wheel, and as sleepy as a dormouse."**

In the Western American culture of the past century or so, readers are familiar with the image of a person carefully turning buffalo or beef over an open campfire. To Boswell's contemporaries, however, the image of a dog (usually a relative of a terrier), called a turnspit, running on a treadmill to turn a roasting-spit, was equally familiar. By using this reference, the writer makes a colorful point, for what could be more awkward than a dog just learning to run a treadmill?

Parenthetically, the value of identifying cultural points that are shared by peoples and time should also be noted. A relevant instance is found in lines 79–80 of Samuel Johnson's *The Vanity of Human Wishes* in which Johnson refers to the mid-1700s practice of morning receptions used by statesmen to grant interviews and to meet friends and political allies.

> **Love ends with hope, the sinking statesman's door**
> **Pours in the morning worshiper no more;**

A comparison can be made to the current American practice of politicians who routinely participate in breakfasts for the press and civic groups, where they can present their points of view under congenial and (hopefully) nonthreatening circumstances. Johnson here refers to the "sinking statesman's door"—a place where "the morning worshiper" no longer comes—a statesman who no longer draws the crowds of reporters and no longer receives invitations to address local civic groups, political party receptions, or crowds of admirers.

Overview in Summary

What method can you use to gain insights and clues to meaning in literary selections, clues that can help you develop interpretive reading and more expressive writing skills? First, *read extensively*. The more you read literary selections from the various periods and cultures, the better your ability to understand the people, events, and places of the times. Then, *reread* the selections, using the definition and discussion chapters that follow to examine individually each of the literary principles as you learn to be a more perceptive reader and effective writer.

Principle One: Determine the Meaning

Samuel Foote (1720–1777)

Charles Howard of Greystock published a silly book he called 'Thoughts'. He meets Foote at a coffee-house. 'And have you read my Thoughts?' says he. 'No,' replies the other, 'I wait for the second volume.'—'And why so?'—'Because I have heard', says Foote, 'that Second Thoughts were best.'

The purpose of writing is communication. Whether the literary selection is in the form of prose, poetry, or drama, the writer is communicating. That communication, that purpose on the part of the writer, forms an important part of the meaning of the work. One of the first steps, then, in determining meaning is to identify the writer's purpose.

There are four types of writing based on its purpose or function.

1. The Descriptive or Expressive Purpose

In description, the prose writer, poet, or dramatist attempts to "paint a picture with words." Description, however, is also an important way to convey abstract concepts. Description can be factual (describing, for example, the color and dimension of an object), or it can be impressionistic (such as expressing what love feels like). Although descriptive or expressive writing may make extended use of descriptive adjectives and be characterized by powerful action verbs, it is not necessarily "wordy." A tightly written work that makes use of carefully chosen figurative language can be *very* expressive. Notice the rich textures of meaning in these four lines from a poem by Percy Bysshe Shelley:

> **From thy nest every rafter**
> **Will rot, and thine eagle home**
> **Leave thee naked to laughter,**
> **When leaves fall and cold winds come.**

2. The Expository or Informative Purpose

The expository writer includes ideas and facts about the focus subject. Most instructional books, textbooks, and reference works are written with an expository purpose. Encyclopedias, newspapers, and business reports are all written to inform the reader.

3. The Narrative Purpose

A narrator tells a story. The story may focus on an incident or brief episode (as in an anecdote), chronicle a hero's adventurous relationship to the history of a nation (as in an epic poem), or follow the history of a family's generations (as in a saga). An important element of narration is time—events unfolding through time.

4. The Argumentative and/or Persuasive Purpose

Argumentation can be joined to persuasion, but it also can be distinguished from persuasion. A writer or speaker uses argumentation to convince readers or hearers of the truth (or falsehood) of a proposition. The purpose of persuasive writing, however, is to convince the reader or hearer that some action must be taken. The writer's purpose might be to convince you that what he or she is saying is true, such as that the spotted owl is an endangered species. But the writer's purpose may also include persuading you to take some action, such as pressuring your local representative to support legislation that would set aside protected habitats for the spotted owl. Expository or informative writing and argumentation focus on the subject, but persuasion focuses on the reader or listener.

Although a literary selection may be identified as predominately one of these four types of composition, seldom is a work exclusively one type. Generally, the writer uses elements of the other three types to aid in the development of the main purpose. For instance, description is frequently used in narration; describing details about oppressive heat, black water, and clinging leaches helps the narrator tell his or her story of convicts escaping a swamp-bound prison camp. An expository writer, aiming to "tell the facts," can narrate an anecdote (an episode or event) to help the reader better understand the information; and political writers often incorporate illustrative narration in their persuasive speeches.

A current trend among writers of informative articles in popular magazines is to begin their articles with anecdotes designed to capture the reader's interest before presenting the facts of the topic. The topics range from the humorous to the serious; the anecdotes range from abbreviated personal experiences of the writer to complex incidences in the lives of others.

Determining the meaning of a work involves looking at its *effect*. The emotional impact, the impression the work leaves on the reader, is part of its effect. Skillful writers will plan a certain effect—perhaps drawing from the reader's feelings of anger, aversion, joyful laughter—by careful use of the literary principles and the techniques available to the writer within those principles. Yet, sometimes an effect happens unintentionally, without the writer's deliberate plan or even conscious knowledge, because meaning is a two-sided concept. On one side you have the writer, someone with a topic to discuss, a point to make, an agenda to fulfill. When you look for the purpose in a work, you are looking at the writer's intent. On the other side of meaning is the reader, someone who often comes to the work without preknowledge of the writer's intent, but someone who does generally have some preconceived thoughts or opinions. For the reader, the focus is on the work itself and what effect the work has on him or her. Read this poem by William Oldys.

The Fly

An Anacreontic

Busy, curious, thirsty fly,
Gently drink, and drink as I;
Freely welcome to my cup,
Could'st thou sip, and sip it up;
Make the most of life you may,
Life is short and wears away.
Just alike, both mine and thine,
Hasten quick to their decline;
    Thine's a summer, mine's no more,
Though repeated to threescore;
Threescore summers when they're gone,
Will appear as short as one.

William Oldys

What is the effect of this poem on you? How might the reader's age affect his or her views of this poem and the speaker's meaning? (*Anacreontic* means in the easy style of the Greek poet Anacreon.)

Notice the relationships in the poem that work together to establish the poem's meaning: Why does the speaker fondly welcome the fly to drink from his cup? Because the fly's life is short. Why does the speaker care that the fly's life is short? Because the speaker's life also seems short. What is the effect (emotional impact) of this comparison on the poem's meaning? It establishes, in relation to the life cycle, a similarity between the speaker and the fly: whether life lasts a summer or "threescore summers," life is relatively short.

Another way to determine the meaning of a literary work is to look for different *levels* of meaning. Some levels of meaning follow:

▶ **The literal meaning** This level of meaning is based on taking the work at its "face value"—without examining any figurative levels.

▶ **The allegorical meaning** At the allegorical level, particularly in narrative works, each object, person, place, and event represents something else, with the characters of the narrative personifying abstract qualities. An entire work may be allegorical (for example, in *Pilgrim's Progress,* the man named Christian meets Mr. Worldly Wiseman—in this story people and places represent the qualities after which they are named), or a literary selection may have or incorporate a few allegorical elements.

▶ **The symbolic meaning** Symbols have dual meaning, the literal or face value meaning and a representative meaning—the symbol stands for something else. "Old Glory, Mother, and apple pie" are symbols of down-home American patriotism. A symbol represents something else, but in a less structured way than an allegory.

▶ **The figurative meaning** At the figurative level, the writer strives for a special meaning other than the standard or literal meaning of the words. These special meanings (tropic meanings) are brought about by the use of tropes. Some tropes include simile (a comparison using "like" or "as"— lips as red as a rose) and metaphor (an implied comparison—rose-red lips). Tropes will be examined in more detail in a later section in this book.

These four levels of meaning, and possibly other levels as well, can, depending on how they are used, affect in a very narrow sense the meaning of specific elements of a work, or they can affect the meaning of the entire selection.

Read the following poem by Tennyson.

Dark House

line   Dark house, by which once more I stand
        Here in the long unlovely street,
        Doors, where my heart was used to beat
    So quickly, waiting for a hand,

(5)   A hand that can be clasped no more—
        Behold me, for I cannot sleep,
        And like a guilty thing I creep
    At earliest morning to the door.

    He is not here; but far away
(10)   The noise of life begins again,
        And ghastly thro' the drizzling rain
    On the bald street breaks the blank day.

Alfred, Lord Tennyson

What is the literal meaning of this poem? The speaker is standing by a dark house on a rainy morning.

Do you see any symbolic meanings in the poem? What might the "dark house" represent? Could it symbolize death? Are there any other symbolic, figurative, or allegorical levels of meaning? Consider the possibility:

Why do you think that the speaker isolates "Doors" in line 3? What do the doors represent? How does this use relate to "door" in line 8? What is ironically significant in the speaker's inability to sleep (line 6)? Why does the speaker emphasize "hand" in lines 4 and 5? What might the hand represent? What other words and phrases do you see that carry levels of meaning in addition to the literal meaning?

"What is the meaning?" can be answered by determining:

▶ The author's purpose,
▶ The effect of the work on the reader or listener, and
▶ The level(s) of meaning working within the selection.

Another way meaning can be determined is by recognizing that a literary selection is made up of parts. These parts may be external structure (such as chapters in a novel, stanzas in a poem, acts and scenes in a play), or they may be internal (such as plot in a narrative). Each of these parts can have meaning independent of or contributing to the meaning of the work as a whole. Sometimes the meaning of a work is the sum of its parts; sometimes the meaning can be determined by a key portion of the work. You may want to determine the meaning of an entire selection or of just a portion of that selection. You may try to identify how the meaning of each part contributes to the whole or how it contrasts that meaning.

Meaning in Prose
Fiction

Prose fiction is often narrative, generally in the form of a novel or short story. In such works, the writer sometimes makes a statement (called the *theme*) that is intended to summarize or assert to the reader some main point, doctrine, or generalization about life, love, religion, the condition of the world, and so forth. Occasionally, the writer will state the theme, but more often it is implied in plot development and characterization. Unlike topic (the subject of the story, such as war, love, business, or children), the theme is what the story is about, its plot, setting, and character blended with the writer's perceptions to make a statement about the subject.

In some prose fiction, the theme can be seen as the "moral of the story." To cite an instance, *Aesop's Fables* are noted for the concise nature of their theme statements. Also, theme is referred to as "the message" of the story. The narrative, then, exemplifies or makes concrete an otherwise abstract idea.

Some topics or subjects are so popular that you will see themes developed within them over and over again. Here are just a few examples.

Survival   In these stories, an individual, family, or group of people must survive such disasters as shipwrecks on deserted islands, plane crashes into swamps, earthquakes, tidal waves, floods, volcanoes, and attacks by wild animals, as well as getting lost in mountains and being stranded in unfamiliar territory. Emphasis is usually placed on the elements of human behavior that are often revealed in life-threatening situations, such as bravery, cowardice, loyalty, and ingenuity. Some famous works written on this topic include *Robinson Crusoe* and *Swiss Family Robinson*.

Children raised by animals   This subject is a very old topic in literary history. A child is somehow lost, abandoned, or in some other way separated from parents and civilization and is adopted and raised by animals, often wolves or apes. A well-known example is the *Tarzan of the Apes* series of novels. The stories often portray the children (who may become adults in the story) as having great integrity or innocence in contrast to those raised in civilization.

UFO invasions and abductions   Stories in which Earth is contacted by other-world beings generally take one of two directions: the aliens are characterized as evil invading forces who want to destroy humans or as kindly, misunderstood visitors that are targets for people who want to destory them out of fear or ignorance. The UFO story is represented by *War of the Worlds*.

Lost pets   In stories based on this subject, a family pet (usually a dog or cat, but occasionally a larger animal, such as a horse) is lost or stolen and must undergo grand adventures and display remarkable courage and seeming intelligence as it overcomes and escapes captors, natural elements, and other such obstacles to return home. Family values and loyalty are important elements in these stories. The *Lassie* series included many examples of this popular topic.

End of the world   Seen in a variety of contexts, these stories usually involve a man-made disaster (ecological, biological, or nuclear) in which only a few people survive and must face the horrors of a world in which civilization and its amenities are destroyed.

Good versus evil   This is another very old concept that has been addressed in an almost endless variety of ways. A common form is the law versus the lawless. In this variation, the law is often represented by law enforcement officers, for example the Canadian Mounted Police, and the lawless are represented by criminals ranging from train robbers in Western genres to drug dealers in more modern stories. These plots usually involve chases that culminate in a final battle in which often (but not always) the law prevails.

War stories   Writers have been developing themes within this subject since early times: real battles of ancient history, imaginary wars of mythological proportions, and conflicts that are local, regional, national, global, and intergalactic. The stories can revolve around, for example, specific men (such as Napoleon), battles (the Battle of Hastings), events (explosion of the atom bomb in World War II), political positions (Vietnam protests), levels of conflict (the Cold War), and injustices (the Trail of Tears). Interactions of people in extraordinary circumstances are at the heart of most war stories. A modern example is Steven Spielburg's *Schindler's List*.

Nonfiction

The theme, the central idea of the work, is also called the *thesis* in nonfiction prose. The thesis refers to the writer's position on the subject. The thesis may be directly stated or implied; it might lead off the first paragraph of the selection or the author might "build" his or her main points to a concluding thesis. How a thesis is developed relates directly to the writer's purpose (descriptive, informative, narrative, or argumentative/persuasive).

In argumentation, the writer's main purpose is not just to explain something but to convince the reader that his or her thesis—or *proposition*—is true. Although the writer might use elements of exposition, narration, or description to support the proposition, the main purpose is to "argue the point." Consequently, the thesis or proposition is a statement of the generalization that the writer is attempting to prove or is a statement of the conclusion the writer wants you to make.

<u>Meaning in Poetry</u>

What does a poem "mean"? Answers to this question vary; however, here are some of the ways you can look for to identify meaning in a poem.

1. Poets used to write a prose paraphrase summarizing the plot or stating the meaning of the poem. Such a statement is called the *argument* of the poem. Modern poets may not provide an argument for a poem, but writing a prose summary and perhaps even a paraphrase in some cases will help you determine meaning.

2. Try to identify the poem's:
▶ Subject or topic, such as love, death, or birth.
▶ Theme (how the poet treats the subject). You might summarize (write a one- or two-sentence summary) a paraphrase of the poem (the line-by-line or stanza-by-stanza meaning of the poem expressed or explained in your own words) to establish the theme; for example, a simple life is best or unrequited love can make you sick.

▶ Motifs (if any)—elements that recur in poetry, such as carpe diem ("seize the day") themes.

▶ Use of poetic devices, such as rhythm and rhyme, as they relate to and affect the meaning.

As a practical application, read the following poem by Walt Whitman and (1) identify the subject, (2) write a paraphrase, and (3) identify the theme.

A Noiseless Patient Spider

line	
	A noiseless patient spider,
	I marked where on a little promontory it
	stood isolated,
	Marked how to explore the vacant vast sur-
	rounding,
	It launched forth filament, filament, filament,
	out of itself,
(5)	Ever unreeling them, ever tirelessly speeding
	them.
	And you O my soul where you stand,
	Surrounded, detached, in measureless oceans
	of space,
	Ceaselessly musing, venturing, throwing,
	seeking the spheres to connect them,
	Till the bridge you will need be formed, till
	the ductile anchor hold,
(10)	Till the gossamer thread you fling catch
	somewhere, O my soul.

The Subject

At first glance, the subject is a spider—on a literal level. But is a spider *really* the poet's subject, or is a spider the means he uses to metaphorically approach another, more abstract subject? You can examine the following paraphrase for clues.

The Paraphrase

Lines 1–5 The speaker watched a spider spin a web. Lines 1–2—The speaker saw a spider standing alone on a promontory. Line 3—The spider checked out its surroundings. Lines 4–5—It spun a web.

Lines 6–10   The speaker's soul is detached and is seeking to be attached. Lines 6–7—The speaker's soul is standing detached in space. Line 8—His soul is checking out his surroundings. Lines 9–10—His soul is seeking to become attached to something.

Now, based on the paraphrase, what is the subject? It can be stated many ways: "anchoring of the soul," "isolation," or perhaps stated simply "the soul."

The Theme

Based on the paraphrase, the theme is a product of a structural metaphor. In the first stanza, the speaker describes how a spider is isolated in space, spinning a web. This description forms the basis for the metaphor, the implied comparison. In the second stanza, he describes how the soul is isolated in space, attempting to fling "the gossamer thread"—to become attached (like a spider spinning its web). The spider spinning its web is a *vehicle*; the soul seeking attachment is the *tenor* of the metaphor. (These terms will be discussed in detail on pages 208–210.)

What is one possible statement of the theme of this poem? The soul, like a spider, is isolated and detached, trying to make connections with its surroundings.

Meaning in Drama

In drama written for television and movies, the main idea (the literal meaning) is a summary statement called a "hook." In *Close Encounters of the Third Kind,* the hook is aliens telepathically contacting humans, with the narrative culminating in an actual encounter. Hooks may revolve around any number of topics, ranging from social issues to famous personalities. But to find the meaning in literary drama, the hook serves only as a starting point. The action, setting, and character work with the plot to establish meaning in drama.

As with poetry, sometimes the writer provides an argument, a plot summary or statement of meaning; but most often the reader or audience is left to draw meaning from the performance itself.

At the center of literary drama and its meaning is conflict. This conflict (the good guys versus the bad guys, the obstacles to overcome, the love to win, and so forth) will naturally affect the meaning of the play.

The meaning may result from how the characters deal with the conflict. For instance, think about a play in which the hook is two ghetto-born brothers who each must face and deal with a legacy of abuse and poverty. One brother strives for immediate gratification by joining street gangs and drug dealers, eventually being killed by an overdose of drugs. The other brother exercises self-discipline and works his way through college to become a successful businessman and father. At this point, the meaning might be that the way to overcome a life of abuse and poverty is through perseverance and self-discipline. What if, however, the play continues and the successful brother returns to the ghetto to do community service work and is killed by a senseless, drive-by shooting? Now meaning is being affected not by how the characters deal with the conflict but by how the setting and forces within the plot structure work together with the conflict to overcome the characters. In this case, the meaning changes to be a very pessimistic view that regardless of the struggle, the forces of poverty and abuse cannot be overcome (an example of dramatic irony).

When trying to find meaning in a dramatic selection, remember that a play is intended to be performed. Consequently, you should first find the hook, then look for meaning.

Questions to Apply the Literary Principles

Ask these questions to help you identify and understand meaning.

1. What is the author's purpose: descriptive/expressive purpose, expository/informative purpose, narrative purpose, or argumentative and/or persuasive purpose?

2. Does the writer use any of the other types of writing to convey meaning more effectively?

3. What is the work about? (Express in a phrase or in a statement.)

4. What does the writer hope to achieve?

5. What is the effect of the work?

6. What is the literal, "face value" meaning of the selection?

7. Can you identify any other levels of meaning in this selection?

8. How does the meaning of the parts contribute to the meaning of the whole selection?

9. If the work is prose fiction, what is the topic (subject)? the theme?

10. If the work is prose nonfiction, what is the topic (subject)? the thesis?

11. In an argument, what is the writer's proposition?

12. Has the poet included a statement of argument?

13. If the work is a drama, what is its hook?

14. How do the actions, settings, and characters work with the plot of the drama to influence the meaning?

Additional Points to Remember

▶ Look for extensive use of symbolic levels of meaning in the works written in mid-nineteenth-century America. (For instance, Walt Whitman, Henry David Thoreau, and Ralph Waldo Emerson used romantic symbolism.)
▶ Be alert to the different forms of meaning. Sometimes a single word or phrase can sum up the topic of the selection (for example, marriage, death, persecution, loyalty). Meaning may include a statement of the theme (the thesis or statement of the propositions). Also, look for the various levels of meaning at work in a selection.
▶ When looking for the theme in narrative fiction, be alert for possible subthemes (generalizations that can be drawn from or supported by the story but are not the main theme; subthemes may support the main theme or may be independent of it). Also, watch for motifs (such as conventional situations).
▶ In an epic poem, look for the speaker to begin his or her narration with a statement of argument (the epic theme) just before asking a muse for inspiration and asking an epic question.

Principle Two: Establish the Form

Lines Written in Ridicule of Certain Poems

Wheresoe'er I turn my view,
All is strange, yet nothing new;
Endless labor all along,
Endless labor to be wrong;
Phrase that time has flung away,
Uncouth words in disarray,
Tricked in antique ruff and bonnet,
Ode, and elegy, and sonnet.

by Samuel Johnson

Ode . . . elegy . . . sonnet—their misuse in poorly executed
works led Samuel Johnson to write these critical lines about
"Phrase that time has flung away" and about "Uncouth words." Yet,
when well written, these forms of literary expression can stir emotions from deep within the reader or hearer.

Meaning might be called the "what?" (as in "What is the
writer trying to say?") in a literary selection, and form can surely
be called the "how?" ("How does he or she say it?"). Form includes
many different patterns of development and methods of organization—ways in which the writer attempts to achieve his or her pur-
pose(s). These purposes generally include (1) expressing oneself,
(2) providing information, (3) persuading, and (4) entertaining (or
creating a literary work). As a result, the basic organizing principles of form are governed to a greater or lesser degree by purpose.
The reason for this is easy to explain: some forms of writing communicate certain meanings better than others. There can be more

than one level of meaning; consequently, the form of a literary selection can be viewed from different perspectives.

Perspective One: Organizing Principles

How does the writer develop his or her thoughts as they relate to the purpose? The following summary sets forth in a very simplified manner some of the organizing principles commonly used by writers.

Basic Organizing Principle	Definition	Example
Analogy	Comparisons using the known to explain or clarify the unknown	Fried frog legs (the unknown) taste a lot like fried chicken (the known).
Cause and effect (causal analysis)	Establishing a relation between outcomes and the reasons behind them	She fired him (effect) because he drank on the job (cause).
Comparison/ contrast	Pointing out similarities and differences of subjects	His management style is bold, like Kennedy's (comparison), but less organized (contrast).
Definition	Clarifying by using synonyms or by pointing out uniqueness within a general class	Mucilage, liquid glue (synonym), was used to hold the inlaid pieces of the mosaic—a picture (general class) that's made of inlaid pieces (unique feature).
Description	Using words to convey sensory impressions or abstract concepts	The temperature was −32°F (objective description), with a frigid wind blowing blankets of snow over the ice (subjective description).

Analysis and classification (division)	Dividing a subject into parts (analysis) or grouping information by class	The elements of Earth's crust are mostly oxygen and silicon (analysis). Gold, silver, and copper, which are all found in the ground, have been known to man for many years (classification).
Example	Using illustrations to clarify, explain, or prove a point	A case in point is this column of this summary.
Induction	Reasoning that arrives at a general principle or draws a conclusion from the facts or examples	He was late for supper, late for our wedding, and even a late delivery when he was born (examples)—that man is habitually late (conclusion).
Deduction	Reasoning that uses a syllogism (two premises and a conclusion)	Premise 1: When it rains over 5 inches, the river floods. Premise 2: It has rained 6 inches. Conclusion: The river is overflowing its banks.
Narration	Telling what happened or is happening in chronological order (recounting events or telling a story)	I walked to the refrigerator, opened the door, pulled out the turkey, and spilled an open carton of milk.
Process (analysis)	Explaining how something happened or happens (works)— sometimes instructional in purpose	First, cream the sugar and butter. Next, add eggs and milk; then blend in the flour and baking powder. Finally, pour into the cake pan and bake at 350° for 50 minutes.

Also, as you identify and study the organizing principles being used in a literary work, give attention to *sequence* or *order* of presentation. Here are some of the most common ways writers sequence their work:

- ▶ Chronological sequence—tells what happened according to time
- ▶ Climactic order—arranged from the least important to the most important
- ▶ Deductive order—arrangement based on deductive reasoning (from the general to the specific)
- ▶ Inductive order—arrangement based on inductive reasoning (from the specific to the general)
- ▶ Problem-solving sequence—presents a problem and then suggests or explains the solution
- ▶ Spatial sequence—describes a location
- ▶ Topical order—presents ideas by topics
- ▶ Mixed order—arrangement that is a blend of patterns

Prose writers and poets, as well as dramatists, can use these basic organizing principles and sequence patterns. How they are used sometimes will determine the paragraph and chapter divisions of the prose work, the stanzas of a poem, or the scenes and acts of a play.

Literary Form and the Reader

You probably are aware of whether you are a visual learner who appreciates a hands-on approach or an auditory learner who benefits most from lectures and verbal communication. In addition, each person has talents, skills, experiences, and personal interests that directly and indirectly affect comprehension and learning (interests that may result from the joy experienced in exercising a particular ability or skill or that may result from the pleasure found in meeting a challenge to that ability or skill).

As you read different literary selections, can you see ways the writers use form to appeal more effectively to their readers? Perhaps a use of prose rhythm enhances the work's auditory appeal (a very effective device in rhetorical writing), or the use of an outline for a plan of action within a persuasive essay provides a visual structure. Does the writer appeal to any of your talents, skills, experiences, or personal interests within the body of the work?

Perspective Two: Structure and Genre

The organizing principles discussed in perspective one weave in and out of the writer's craft in varying amounts and to differing degrees, but the elements of the second perspective of form (structure and genre) work to make the literary selection a whole. Structure provides unity; genre provides labels for identification and a basis for certain expectations.

Structure is sometimes used as a synonym for form. For some, structure is an integral part of style. Regardless, structure refers to the plan, the framework of the writing. Often the structure can be identified by an outline or by the verse form. The formal study of structure (whose basis has been identified as binary or binomial) can, however, become very complex, particularly when investigating the Structuralism Movement that incorporates elements of structural linguistics and structural anthropology into the study of structure. (If you find structuralism interesting, there are many books on the subject, including *Structuralism in Literature: An Introduction* by Robert Scholes, 1974.) *Structure* as used in this book, however, refers to the general plan of a work of literature.

Genre, on the other hand, refers to identifying literary selections by (1) structure, (2) technique and use of organizing principles, and (3) subject matter.

These groupings and their resulting labels are very useful as descriptive devices for identification, particularly the genre classifications that contain anticipated characteristics that give clues to meaning, character, and the other literary principles.

Like so many other interdependent aspects of literary study, however, a work is often a blend of genres; you may not be able to wrap a literary selection in one tidy package and label it "genre: western," for example. Remember the "singing cowboy" movies starring Roy Rogers and Dale Evans? These westerns also incorporated elements of romance (boy gets girl at end of movie), musicals (both of the lead players sang), and comedy (generally a "sidekick" who acted as a "comic relief" to the drama). Many long-running television sitcoms (situation comedies) address social and family issues by blending elements of comedy and drama (note *Family Matters* and the *Bill Cosby Show*). You may have no difficulty identifying *The Perry Mason Movies* and *Murder, She Wrote* as belonging to the murder-mystery genre, but where would you place *Northern Exposure?*

An excellent example of this blending of genres can be found in the writing of Dick Gregory. *Dick Gregory's Natural Diet for Folks Who Eat: Cookin' with Mother Nature* (Harper & Row, Publishers, 1973) sounds like a cookbook, and indeed it does contain some recipes. However, the book mainly concerns the benefits of health principles, fasting, and vegetarianism (the food and nutrition genre). In addition, the book contains sample menus (the how-to genre), anecdotes about the author's life (autobiography), and social commentary, all written in an amusing style (the humor genre).

Form in Prose
Nonfiction

Here is a listing of a few of the genres written in nonfiction with brief descriptions of their characteristic structures, techniques, and subject matters. As you read a literary work, make note of what structures, techniques, and organizing principles have been utilized that are characteristic of that genre.

Genre: Essay

Characteristics

- ▶ Defined as a brief prose composition
- ▶ Restricted topics
- ▶ Purpose: discussion or persuasion
- ▶ Often contains a thesis statement
- ▶ Addressed to general audience
- ▶ Two types:
  Formal essay—serious tone, scholarly, organized
  Informal essay—intimate tone, everyday topics, humor, less structure

Examples

The French writer Montaigne's *Essais* appeared in 1580, and Francis Bacon began the English essay in 1597. *Essays,* especially the enlarged 1612 and 1625 editions, include many **aphorisms** (concise statements intended to make a point). For examples of periodical essays, go to Joseph Addison and Sir Richard Steele (*Tatler* and *Spectator*—eighteenth century). Keep alert for their use of humor and satire. Other important British essayists include

Jonathan Swift, Thomas Fuller, Abraham Cowley, John Locke, William Cowper, Robert Burton, Sir Thomas Browne, John Milton, Sir William Temple, John Dryden, Daniel Defoe, and Anthony Ashley Cooper (Earl of Shaftesbury). Be sure to include some American essayists in your examination of the essay. Washington Irving's *Sketch-Book* (1820) and Thoreau's *Walden* provide excellent examples for comparison and contrast of styles. William F. Buckley, Jr., is a prolific modern essayist, and you can go to such magazines as *The New Yorker* and *Scientific American* as well as to other magazines and newsletters for essays on a wide range of topics.

Genre: Biography

Characteristics

- ▶ Defined as the story of a person's life
- ▶ Word first used by Dryden (1683) and defined as "the history of particular men's lives"

Examples

To see how the biography genre changed over the years, compare the first English biography (William Roger's *Life of Sir Thomas More*) written in the sixteenth century with Boswell's use of **anecdote** (using brief narration of single episodes to tell about interesting events in Johnson's life) and **ana** (gossip). The Pulitzer Prize has had a category for biographers and autobiographers since 1917.

Another genre that can be explored is **the character.** These short character sketches describe the ideal or sometimes less than ideal of humanity as demonstrated or embodied by the person being described. They often have such titles as "A Wise Man" or "A Glutton." These were very popular in the early part of the seventeenth century. Richard Aldington's *A Book of Characters* (1924) anthologizes the character, and you can find examples among the writings of Bishop Joseph Hall.

Genre: Autobiography

Characteristics

- ▶ Defined as the story of one's own life
- ▶ Subtypes of autobiography:
  Diaries—an intimate account of day-to-day life, including thoughts

Journals—chronological logs of day-to-day events (also, some scholarly periodicals such as *The Journal of Medicine*)

Letters—notes and epistles; correspondence from one person to another

Memoirs—recollections that center around certain other persons or events

Confessions—autobiographical recollections of matters that are normally held private

Examples

Autobiographies and memoirs are written to be published; diaries, journals, and letters are more personal, with (in the case of letters especially) perhaps only a few people at most reading them. You may, in addition to looking at the most obvious autobiographies, such as those of Franklin and Adams, be interested in some letters written during various periods of literary history or written by noted writers (such as those of Charles Dickens or Lord Byron and perhaps the diary of Samuel Pepys).

Genre: Criticism

Characteristics

- ▶ Defined as studies that analyze and comment upon works of art and literature
- ▶ Rhetoric and diction were the subject of critics in Renaissance England

Examples

In the sixteenth century, a battle raged between English scholars (called purists), who would not allow any borrowing from other languages to contaminate English diction, and the Inkhornists, who extensively favored incorporating Latin and Greek words into the English vocabulary. Criticism often reflects the moods and trends of the period in which it is written, and literary critics (those who write criticisms) sometimes polarize into "schools" or groups that subscribe to various theories or that prefer certain methods of critical analysis. Historically, Dr. Benjamin Johnson in the eighteenth century and Matthew Arnold in the nineteenth century wrote critical essays. A noted twentieth-century critic is Northrup Frye.

Genre: Informational Text

Characteristics

> ▶ Factual
> ▶ Structured by topical outline (if subject allows)
> ▶ Can include examples, analogies, and descriptions, but most organizing principles can be effectively used

Examples

Instructional writing and textbooks rely heavily on process analysis for the purpose of the reader following instructions. Reference works (dictionaries, encyclopedias, directories, guides) and news articles can be informational and instructive.

Also, note the importance of the **chronicle** to the body of English literature. These forerunners of our modern history genre were significant since the time of King Alfred and provided rich resource materials for Shakespeare and other writers (note, for example, *Mirror for Magistrates*). Chronicles that record events year by year are called **annals.** Some "histories" have been awarded the Pulitzer Prize (such as Carl Sandburg's *Abraham Lincoln: the War Years* and Stanley Karnow's *In Our Image: America's Empire in the Philippines*). There also has been a Pulitzer Prize category for "General Nonfiction" since 1962.

Fiction

Fiction is an imaginative literary narrative that can be in the form of prose, poetry, or drama. Most prose fiction falls into one of several types based primarily on length:

> ▶ **Novel**   An extended prose narrative that is fiction. The first English novel was *Pamela; or, Virtue Rewarded* by Samuel Richardson. (Generally, novel-length works are divided into chapters.)
> ▶ **Novelette**   Shorter than the novel, more tightly structured. Sometimes called a short novel, it generally consists of about 15,000 to 50,000 words.
> ▶ **Short story**   Ranges from 500 (in the short-short story) to 15,000 words. The short story is very tightly structured with a formal development.
> ▶ **Anecdote**   A narrative of a single episode (an incident).

Once referring simply to gossip, today *anecdote* refers to any episodic narrative and is very popular among magazine article writers as an attention-getting device to introduce their subject. Also, political speech writers use the anecdote to enliven what might be otherwise "dull," issue-based speeches; and, if the narrative is about someone with whom the audience can identify, they use the anecdote as a means of persuasion.

Perhaps the single most important structural element in narrative fiction is **plot**—a summary of the action of the story, including the words and deeds of the characters.

What precipitates this action? Why do readers care about the words and deeds of the characters? Conflict. The motivating, driving force that involves both characters and (if written well) readers in the narrative is conflict. Conflict means opposition: person versus person, person versus group, person versus environment, person versus nature, or person versus self. Generally, as you read a narrative, you begin to anticipate the conflicts in the plot, select a "side" that you think is "right," evaluate the characters to see which "side" each is on, identify which character(s) you want to "win," and eventually even begin to identify with that character. The plot, then, with conflict as its driving force, provides unity for the work as a whole.

In its simplest, most predictable form, a narrative plot might look like this:

3. Climax
(The "high point"
when you know how conflict
will be resolved)

2. Complication
(Developing conflict)

4. Dénouement
(Resolution of
the conflict)

1. Exposition
(Introduction of
characters and
setting)

How can the plot line for a narrative be summarized? In a stereotypical "paperback romance" it might be: Jasmine is a beautiful, single professional woman on vacation in Hawaii (*Exposition*). She meets Roberto, the dark, handsome, rich sugar baron who sweeps her off her feet until Susan, Jasmine's rival for Roberto's affections, causes a misunderstanding that makes Roberto doubt Jasmine's love (*Complication*—developing conflict that obviously is the longest part of the narrative). Roberto discovers Susan's treachery while Jasmine is headed in a taxi to the airport to leave his life forever (*Climax*—you know how this is going to end). Roberto races to the airport and reconciles with Jasmine just in time to live happily ever after (*Dénouement*). Some genres have very predictable plot lines. For example, how would you summarize the plot line for a standard cop-and-robber movie? Or a typical western? (Such a plot summary is sometimes called an **epitome**, and each section of the narrative is an **episode**.)

Predictable narrative story lines are sometimes called formula plots. They consist of variations on the same plot line story after story. As you read narrative fiction, however, watch for departures from the expected plot line. Sometimes writers will depart from the usual plot structure in order to achieve a specific effect. In fact, most plots (whether they are traditional or departures from the usual) will aim to create some effect. Five significant examples of effects that are the result of plot follow.

1. **Tragedy**   In a tragic narrative, humans do not and cannot overcome inevitable failure, although they may demonstrate grace and courage along the way.

2. **Comedy**   A comic effect is produced when the plot leads the characters into amusing situations, ridiculous complications, and a happy ending.

3. **Satire**   A narrative is satiric when it makes a subject look ridiculous. The subjects being derided can range from an individual to all mankind and society. (Swift's *Gulliver's Travels,* written in 1726, is an example of indirect satire.)

4. **Romance**   A romantic narrative (called a *prose romance*) has clear distinctions between the "good guys" and the "bad guys," an adventurous plot, and events that occasionally demand that readers believe the otherwise unbelievable. (For instance,

Wuthering Heights, written by Emily Brontë in 1847 is a famous romance.)

5. **Realism**   A realistic narrative is in contrast to the romance. It tries to mirror real life, not present life as one thinks or wishes it could be. In realism, the leading characters are not necessarily beautiful or handsome, rich or talented. The plot revolves around events that people face every day in a real world.

In narrative fiction, the writer uses **genre** (a narrative identified by *structure*, technique, and subject matter) to achieve a tragic, comedic, satiric, romantic, or realistic effect. The genres available to writers are numerous. The following listing highlights the characteristics of some of the more common fictional narrative *genres* and provides some examples.

Genre: Picaresque

Characteristics

- ▶ Autobiographical—first person narrative
- ▶ A rascal as main character who does not change
- ▶ Adventurous episodes
- ▶ Main character lives by wits
- ▶ Generally lacks formal structure
- ▶ Main character called a picaroon (picaro)

Examples
The Adventures of Tom Sawyer, Fielding's *Jonathan Wild,* and Daniel Defoe's *Moll Flanders* fit this genre.

Genre: Stream of Consciousness

Characteristics

- ▶ Major technique: interior monologue
- ▶ Reports the nonverbalized flow of thoughts of the character(s)
- ▶ Thoughts are erratic, illogical
- ▶ Introspection
- ▶ Focus: inner consciousness

Examples
Freudian psychology influenced the more modern examples.

Examples of stream of consciousness are in the writings of James Joyce, Virginia Woolf, and Laurence Sterne.

Genre: Bildungsroman

Characteristics

- ▶ German for "novel of formation"
- ▶ Once called "apprenticeship novel"
- ▶ Account of growing up
- ▶ Called *Künstlerroman* when the protagonist is an artist or writer

Examples

James Joyce's *A Portrait of the Artist as a Young Man* and Dickens's *Great Expectations* are examples.

Genre: Regional

Characteristics

- ▶ Setting (including regional dialects) has significant impact on character and on plot *structure*

Example

Some of the works of William Faulkner and Thomas Hardy fit this genre. Also, notice the way such writers as Mark Twain combine the Regional Novel with other forms.

Genre: Social

Characteristics

- ▶ Plot centers on social environment
- ▶ Plot incorporates persuasive language—calls for social reform

Examples

The Lost Generation during the decade after World War I ended produced many social novelists, such as John Steinbeck.

Some other genres include the following:

- ▶ **Detective** Also called crime stories, murder mysteries, and who-dunnits, the plot focuses on solving a crime, often murder (Sir Arthur Conan Doyle, Agatha Christie).

- ▶ **Psychological** Plot tells not only what happens, but also why it happens, concentrating on motivation.
- ▶ **Problem** Plot centers on solving a problem.
- ▶ **Novels** of . . .
   a. **Sensibility** Plot focuses on emotion.
   b. **Character** Plot focuses on character.
   c. **Manners** Plot focuses on a social class.
   d. **Incident** Plot focuses on episodes.
   e. **The Soil** Plot focuses on rural regional struggle to survive.
- ▶ **Sociological** A type of problem novel, it purports to have the solutions for specified problems in society.
- ▶ **Propaganda** Plot is subordinated to the role of a vehicle to put forth a particular doctrine.
- ▶ **Western** "Dime novels" set in the American West.
- ▶ **Gothic** Plot centers on ghostly castles, medieval settings, and romantic knights bound by chivalry.
- ▶ **Epistolary** Plot is carried out through a series of letters between or among the characters.
- ▶ **Science Fiction** Plot centers on science fantasy, such as time machines, aliens, or mutants.
- ▶ **Suspense** Also called "edge of your seat" stories. The plot keeps the reader in a somewhat sustained sense of suspense or anticipation. In serials in which there is a break in the plot between episodes, the reader or viewer may be left at a cliffhanger—a point at which the suspense level is high, thus encouraging the reader or viewer to continue the story to see what happens. (A famous twentieth-century television cliffhanger is the "Who Shot J.R.?" episode in the American soap opera *Dallas*.)
- ▶ **Utopia** Plot depends upon a fictional, perfect world. (Contrast Utopia with Dystopia, wherein the fictional world is far less than perfect, as in Orwell's *1984*.)

As previously mentioned, writers often blend elements (including the structure, technique, and subject matter) of more than one genre to create the desired effect(s) and to fulfill their purpose(s). Generally speaking, however, the shorter narratives require tighter, more economical structures. Examples of some shorter genres follow.

- ▶ **Tales** center on an outcome. As a result of this focus, the tale may not be as tightly structured as some of the other short narrative genres. Look to O. Henry's work for some example tales.

▶ **Tall tales** center on the exaggerated feats of (generally) American heroes. Examples include such characters as Paul Bunyan and Davy Crockett (although some tall tales have been written in other countries).

▶ **Fables** center on a moral. The moral is often stated in an **epigram** put forth by the writer or one of the characters at the end (called a beast fable when the characters in the fable are talking animals). Examples include the famous fables of Aesop.

▶ **Folktales** are narratives that originally were transmitted orally. Elements of the folktale are commonly found in tall tales and fables.

▶ **Parables** teach a lesson by using very tightly structured allegory. As pointed out by Professors William Harmon and the late C. Hugh Holman of the University of North Carolina at Chapel Hill in *A Handbook to Literature* (Macmillan Publishing Company, 1992), the most famous parables are those of Jesus Christ (such as the "Prodigal Son," the "Parable of the Sowers," and the "Parable of the Workers").

▶ **Legends** relate the life of a hero or a person whose life is of legendary proportions.

▶ **Myths** once were believed to be true, but are now accepted as fiction. These stories are generally of anonymous origin and include supernatural elements.

Form in Poetry

Form in poetry can be seen on two levels. On one level, poetry, like prose, can be grouped into many different genres or types based to a great extent on structural techniques (organizing principles) and subject matter. But because of the intensity of poetry (intensity of meaning, sound, and form), each poem should also be examined on a second level by identifying the elements of form that are unique to that individual poem.

Each poem's meaning is to a greater or lesser degree affected by its form. Because economy of language and the other parameters within which the poet must work have such impact on the poem's form, and conversely, the poem's form can so greatly affect its language and meaning, this individualized approach is both necessary and greatly desirable.

Four common areas that you can examine to determine a poem's form as it relates to and affects meaning are (1) rhythm, (2) rhyme scheme, (3) physical form, and (4) genre (defined by patterns of rhythm, rhyme, physical form, and subject).

Rhythm

Poetry has rhythm—a variation of stressed and unstressed sounds that has some type of regular pattern. Generally, the stressed sounds or syllables (accents) recur *regularly* and, almost as a natural consequence, cause *grouping* of the stressed sounds into units. In music, these units are often counted aloud by the piano student learning rhythm and are fundamental to the driving beat of hard rock, the toe-tapping cadence of a Texas two-step, and the slow rhythm of the blues. Rhythm can directly affect moods (and perhaps perceptions?), and different people prefer and enjoy or avoid and dislike different rhythms.

The musical unit became a "signature" of the late bandleader Lawrence Welk (whose program, *The Lawrence Welk Show,* has been syndicated on the Public Broadcasting System for many years). He would begin directing his orchestra to begin with a smile, a raised swirl of his baton, and "a-one-and-a-two-and-a. . . ."

The emphasis on musical units continued with the reggae music of 1970s Jamaica and the rap music begun in the 1980s in New York City. Notice the strong regularity of this rap-style work:

> **So ya' wanna do your best,**
> **But ya' need a little rest.**
> **So your friends, they won't be knowin'**
> **To the party, you'll be goin'.**

As you examine poetic rhythm patterns, however, you will also encounter variation. Sometimes the variation simply breaks the monotony of the "beat." Sometimes it changes the mood and consequently affects the meaning. But at times, variation is used counter to the regular rhythm to the point that it becomes "unrhythmical."

Determining the rhythm in a poem is somewhat different from determining the accented syllables in everyday speech patterns. Natural rhythms of speech depend greatly upon such individual considerations as regional dialects. Prose rhythm is determined largely by the accents of the words as they would normally be spoken and by rhetorical accent, the emphasis placed on words and syllables because of their meaning. An example of rhetorical accent might be: "Roger is <u>so</u> popular. . . . <u>Everybody</u> knows Roger!" In "She gave the keys to <u>you</u>?", the rhetorical accent implies that the speaker is surprised at who is the recipient of the keys. Compare "She <u>gave</u> the keys to you?", which questions whether she really did give the keys, and "<u>She</u> gave the keys to you?", which questions who actually gave the keys. But *metrical accent,* the rhythm patterns found in poetry, is influenced by the varying levels of both syntax (word choice) and concepts that work within the tightly woven elements of poetic form.

Several factors will influence which syllables are stressed or accented in a line of poetry. These include the normal accents associated with the word, particularly in polysyllabic words, such as *es-tab-lish* or *stee-ple* (when the poet uses context to change the normal accent of a word, it is called *wrenched accent*); the grammatical function of the words (prepositions and articles are generally not stressed as strongly as nouns and verbs); rhetorical accents (stresses based on meaning); and metrical accents (stresses established in the context of the poem). The study of the rhythms and sounds of poetry is called **prosody;** the system used to describe rhythm is called **scansion.** When you **scan** a line of poetry, you first identify which kind of **foot** is being used. A foot is the unit formed by a strong stress or accent and the weak stress(es) or unaccented syllable(s) that accompany it. You identify the type or kind of foot that is being used as you "walk" along the individual line of poetry.

To illustrate, *scan* the first stanza of "The Wife of Usher's Well."

> **There lived a wife at Usher's Well,**
> > **And a wealthy wife was she;**
> **She had three stout and stalwart sons,**
> > **And sent them o'er the sea.**

The first step in scanning is to determine the accented or stressed sounds. This is done by placing an accent mark over each stressed syllable. (Remember that you are finding the "beat" of the poem.)

>   /   /   /   /
> **There lived a wife at Usher's Well,**
> >   /   /   /
> > **And a wealthy wife was she;**
>   /   /   /   /
> **She had three stout and stalwart sons,**
> >   /   /   /
> > **And sent them o'er the sea.**

Next, identify the unstressed syllables by placing an X over each.

<pre>
    X   / X   / X / X   /
There lived a wife at Usher's Well,
      X X   / X   /   X   /
    And a wealthy wife was she;
  X   /   X   /   X / X   /
She had three stout and stalwart sons,
      X   / X   / X   /
    And sent them o'er the sea.
</pre>

Now look for a pattern. In this poem, there seems to be a pattern of an unstressed syllable followed by a stressed syllable. Divide the groups of unstressed and stressed syllables into *feet* by using a slash mark (called a *virgule*).

<pre>
    X   /   X / X /   X   /
There lived / a wife / at Ush / er's Well,
     X X   / X   /   X   /
    And a weal / thy wife / was she;
  X   /   X   /   X   /   X   /
She had / three stout / and stal / wart sons,
     X   /   X   /   X   /
    And sent / them o'er / the sea.
</pre>

At this point, you can identify what kind of foot is used in the poem. There are many different kinds of feet, but the most common to English poetry are illustrated by Lillian E. Myers in the following five stanzas called "Stressed and Unstressed":

Stressed and Unstressed

Iambic foot (X /) unstressed, stressed
<pre>
  X   /X / X / X /
  Iambic is a line of verse,
       X   / X / X   /
      That first is weak, then strong.
  X / X   /   X / X /
  If this light rhyme you do rehearse,
        X   / X / X   /
      You're sure to do no wrong.
</pre>

Anapestic foot (X X /) unstressed, unstressed, stressed

<pre>
X X   / X X   / X   X / X X /
</pre>
With two weak and a strong we will learn anapest,
<pre>
 X X / X   X   /   X X /
</pre>
As we take this small verse right along.
<pre>
X X   /   X X   / X X / X X   /
</pre>
Feel the beat, mark the stress, anapest is the best,
<pre>
 X X / X   X / X X /
</pre>
With a rhythm that can be a song.

Trochaic foot (/ X) stressed, unstressed
<pre>
 /   X   /   X   /   X / X
</pre>
Strong then weak should bring no terror—
<pre>
 /   X / X / X
</pre>
Verse that is trochaic.
<pre>
 /   X   /   X   / X / X
</pre>
Up then down—you will not error—
<pre>
 / X / X / X
</pre>
Never be prosaic!

Dactylic foot (/ X X) stressed, unstressed, unstressed
<pre>
 /   X   X   / X X / X   X   / X X
</pre>
He could write verses like Alfred, Lord Tennyson,
<pre>
 / XX /   X   X   /   X   X / X X
</pre>
Dactylic foot that could march clear to Dennison.
<pre>
 /   X X /   X X /   X X / X X
</pre>
Rhythms he kept and to rhyme he was dutiful—
<pre>
 /   X X /   X X /   X X / XX
</pre>
That's why his work was so strong and so beautiful.

Spondaic foot (/ /) stressed, stressed
<pre>
 X / X / X / X /
</pre>
When two successive syllables
<pre>
 X / X   X   / X   X / X /
</pre>
with equal strong stresses occur in verse,
<pre>
 /   /   / X /
</pre>
Strong, strong, spondee foot
<pre>
 /   X / X /
</pre>
comes to mind at first.

Pyrrhic foot (X X) unstressed, unstressed: Although not basic meters, spondaic and pyrrhic feet generally occur as *variants* from the standard feet. For example, in the preceding stanza spondaic foot is used as a defining device, not as the rhythm for the entire stanza. Used in this way, spondaic foot is a method for the writer to call attention to meaning in prose rhythms as well as poetic forms. Some experts in scanning argue that a true pyrrhic foot does not exist because every foot must have an accented syllable.

Because the stanza from "The Wife of Usher's Well" is predominately groups of unstressed, then stressed syllables, *it is written in iambic foot.*

After determining the type of foot, you need to identify how many feet are *in each line.* Traditionally:

one foot   = monometer
two feet   = dimeter
three feet = trimeter
four feet = tetrameter
five feet = pentameter
six feet   = hexameter
seven feet = heptameter
eight feet = octameter

Look at the first line of "The Wife of Usher's Well":

There lived / a wife / at Ush / er's Well,

There are four feet in this line: tetrameter. Consequently, the *meter* or *metrical pattern* of line one is iambic tetrameter. Notice the metrical patterns of the entire stanza:

Iambic tetrameter   There lived/ a wife/ at Ush/er's Well,
Iambic trimeter   and a weal/ thy wife / was she;
Iambic tetrameter   She had / three stout/ and stal/wart sons,
Iambic trimeter   and sent/ them o'er/ the sea.

Because iambic and anapestic meters end on a high stress, they are often referred to as the **rising meters** or rhythms; and dactylic and trochaic are **falling meters** or rhythms. The meter used, the metrical pattern, can directly affect the mood, the tone, and/or the meaning.

What are some specific instances in which the metrical pattern is used to affect meaning and/or tone of a *verse* (a literary work written in meter)? Some examples follow.

1. Poems in which the poets use the metrical pattern to contribute to a *comic effect*:

Anapestic foot (X X /)
Iambic tetrameter (X / four times)

I Do Not Love Thee, Dr. Fell

I do not love thee, Dr. Fell,
The reason why I cannot tell;
But this I know, and know full well,
I do not love thee, Dr. Fell.

by Tom Brown

Trochaic (/ X) line that ends with an unstressed syllable

2. Pauses that affect the "pace" of a poem. When a poem has a very long pause within a line, it is called *caesura* (shown as / / in scansion).

3. Use of substitute feet. When a line scans predominately, for example, iambic, but the poet substitutes some other foot somewhere within the line. The poet then returns to iambic (or whatever the predominate foot is) until he or she again substitutes another foot. The effects can vary. For instance, when the predominate beat carries you along like a waltz, the substitute might be jarring—or at the very least might get your attention.

4. The direct use of meter to contribute to meaning. Notice how the bold use of spondee adds intensity to these lines of Tennyson's "Break, Break, Break."

Break, break, break,
On thy cold gray stones, O Sea!
And I would that my tongue could utter
The thoughts that arise in me.

Now, examine Richard Lovelace's "Going to the Wars" to see how he uses rhythm to affect meaning. What follows is one way this poem could be scanned. Note that some poems are scanned differently by different critics. For example, the very first line might also be scanned:

/　X　/　　/　X　/　X　/
Tell me not (Sweet) I am unkind.

Going to the Wars

line   X / X   / X / X /
Tell me not (Sweet) I am unkind,
      X   /   X   /   X /
That from the nunnery
  X /   X   /   X   / X
Of thy chaste breast, and quiet mind,
     X / X / X /
(4)   To war and arms I fly.

    / X X /   X / X /
True; a new mistress now I chase,
      X   / X / X   /
The first foe in the field;
  X   / X /   X   /   X   /
And with a stronger faith embrace
     X   / X   / X   /
(8)   A sword, a horse, a shield.

    X / X / X / X   /
Yet this inconstancy is such,
      X   / X   / X   /
As you too shall adore;
  X   /   X   / X   / X   /
I could not love thee (Dear) so much,
     X / X / X   /
(12)   Loved I not honour more.

Lines 1, 3, 5, 7, 9, and 11 are iambic tetrameter; lines 2, 4, 6, 8, 10, and 12 are iambic trimeter. Each line ends with a strong stress, called a **masculine ending**. (A line that ends with a weak stress is a **feminine ending**.)

Notice the natural pauses in both thought and reading at the ends of lines 1, 3, and 4 in the first stanza, lines 5, 6, and 8 in the second, and lines 9, 10, 11, and 12 in the third stanza. Lines such as these are called **end-stopped**. On the other hand, examine how the lack of natural pause at the end of line 2 pulls the reader to line 3. This movement of thought and rhythm is called a **run-on line**. Line 7 also is a run-on line (called **enjambement** in French). Can you spot any significant departures or breaks in the rhythm of this poem? Look at line 5. The poet uses two devices that break the rhythm; the semicolon is a clue to a very strong, lengthy pause—a *caesura*. Also, the usual iambic foot has been inverted to form a trochee (trochaic foot). Such a dramatic change in an otherwise predictable rhythm is a definite clue to a shift in thought—a change in meaning. The speaker uses a break in tempo in line 5 to suggest that he is shifting from a defensive to an offensive position.

Have you ever argued a position using a *negative* drone of words until you break the tension with "Yes! I feel this way because . . . "? Were you able to "feel" the startled response such a shift makes?

In the first stanza, the speaker is being defensive—he is "not . . . unkind" (line 1). But the second stanza's change in rhythm, his abrupt "True; a new mistress now I chase," (line 5) marks a dramatic and somewhat startling shift in the tone of his position: Yes! I must leave . . . I have an honorable reason to go. (Also, startlingly enough, he has "a new mistress.")

Before leaving this poem, look at line 8. Can you see any subtle differences between this line and the last lines of the first and last stanzas (lines 4 and 12)—differences that might contribute to meaning? The pauses (use of *caesura,* as described on page 57) change the pace and mark a shift in emphasis.

One final word about rhythm. Scanning a poem for its metrical patterns is very useful; however, do not forget that a poem is a literary work and as such also should be read and enjoyed as a whole. You may be surprised by the depth of meaning and reflections of tone a whole-work approach can reveal. You also may find that practicing using poetic elements (such as rhythm and rhyme) in writing your own poetry and prose is very beneficial to your skill development. As stated by William Cowper in "The Task,"

> **There is a pleasure in poetic pains**
> **Which only poets know . . . .**

"What should I write about?" you ask. You may find many subjects in your daily life—some serious or some light, as is John Fletcher's "Do Not Fear to Put Thy Feet":

> **Do not fear to put thy feet**
> **Naked in the river sweet;**
> **Think not leech, or newt or toad**
> **Will bite thy foot, when thou hast troad;**
> **Nor let the water rising high**
> **As thou wad'st in, make thee cry**
> **And sob, but ever live with me,**
> **And not a wave shall trouble thee.**

Rhyme Scheme

Rhyme as it relates to and influences form is when two or more words have a sound in common or echo one another. The degree to which words "rhyme" is affected, of course, by pronunciation because pronunciations have changed over time, differ nationally between American English and British English, and differ regionally. Essentially, the point is summarized by the questions, "Did you pick a 'tomato' [long *a*] or 'tomawto' from your garden?" and "Is your mother's sister your 'aunt' [pronounced as *ant*] or your 'awnt'?" Rigidity in opinion concerning what constitutes "correct" pronunciation of words can greatly affect the enjoyment of a poem. Differences can be subtle as in *quinine* (American *kwinin* with long *i* in both syllables, British *kwin-en* with short *i* in the first syllable and long *e* in the last) or striking as in *clerk* (American pronunciation usually rhyming with *work*; British pronunciation usually rhyming with *lark*), which was used by John Donne in "And though fowl now be scarce, yet there be clerks, The sky not falling, think we may have larks."

End rhymes occur when the rhyming words fall at the ends of two or more lines of verse:

> **But were some child of yours alive that *time*,**
> **You should live twice—in it, and in my *rhyme*.**

Echo verse employs a form of end rhyme used commonly in the 1500s and 1600s in which the closing syllables of a line are repeated to form the next line, as in these final lines of William Barnes's "The Echo":

> **The vaice did mock our neames, our cheers,**
> **Our merry laughs, our hands' loud claps,**
> **An' mother's call "Come, come my dears"**
> > **—my dears;**
> **Or "Do as I do bid, bad chaps"**
> > **—bad chaps.**

In some echo poems, the echo's repeated syllables serve to answer a question posed in the previous line:

> **For the Candidate**
> > **Echo!   How can I show my support**
> > **to devote it?**
> > ***Vote it.***

Internal rhymes are two or more rhyming words within a line of verse:

> **You'll be right when you see the light;**
> **Another day will bring a fresh new way.**

Here is another example: "My *wealth* is *health* and perfect ease . . . ."

Masculine rhyme is rhyme of a single stressed syllable that generally is forceful: *look, cook; sing, bring; sob, rob; sweet, treat.*

Feminine (or *double*) **rhyme** is rhyme of a stressed then unstressed syllable and, as a result, is softer than masculine rhyme: *looking, cooking; feature, creature.*

Compound rhyme is rhyme of both pairs of compound components: *fishbroth, dishcloth; corkscrew, pork stew.*

Triple rhyme is rhyme of a stressed followed by two

unstressed syllables: *bacteria, diphtheria.* (Take note of the way rhyme blends with rhythm for a pleasing effect in such words

/ XXX   / X X X

as *mandatory* and *obligatory.*)

Perfect rhyme (also called true or pure rhyme) is an exact alignment of sounds, whereas **imperfect rhyme** (also called partial, slant, or half rhyme) is only a close alignment:

> **And when he'd ride in the *afternoon***
> **I'd follow with a hickory *broom,***

Eye rhymes (also called **visual rhymes**) look like they should rhyme (and at one time perhaps did) but do not, such as *horse, worse* or as in the first two lines of this poem:

> **Shall a woman's virtues *move***
> **Me to perish for her *love?***
> **Or, her well-deserving known,**
> **Make me quite forget mine own?**

Rime riche (also called **identical rhyme**) consists of words that sound the same but have different spellings and meanings: *seas, sees; hare, hair; their, there; heart, hart. Rime riche* is sometimes identified as one of the many ways writers can make a "play on words," and *rime riche* lies at the heart of a pun.

Notice Shakespeare's use of *rime riche* as an internal rhyme in these lines from *The Rape of Lucrece:*

> That for his prey to pray he doth begin,
> As if the heavens should countenance his sin.

Historical rhymes are words that once rhymed, but due to pronunciation shifts no longer rhyme. For example, *tea* once rhymed with *day.*

Forced rhymes are those that are "invented" by the poet. Along with eye rhyme and imperfect rhyme, forced rhymes are examples of **poetic license**—when a poet departs from the usual use of rhyme, diction, syntax, and other such conventions.

Pity the Poor Raccoon

> Pity the poor raccoon.
> He could run fast 'cause he stayed slim and trim;
> But one day right at noon he heard a loon's tune
> That bedazzled and mystified him.
> "What's that sound?" he bemused, for he felt quite
>   amused
> 'Til a hound heard the sound when Raccoon left the
>   ground.
> He was trapped! He was cornered! But he wasn't
>   forlornered.
> The hound saw a flash and his teeth he did gnash
> For the prey he had treed just turned tail and fleed.

by Lillian E. Myers

Notice the pairing of "cornered" with "forlornered" and of "treed" with "fleed" in "Pity the Poor Raccoon."

After you have identified the poet's use of rhyme, you can then work out the **rhyme scheme** or pattern of the end rhyme of each line. To illustrate determining the rhyme scheme of a poem, examine Robert Browning's "Meeting at Night":

Line 1: *The gray sea and the long black land;*
    The line ends with the word "land" and is assigned the letter **a.**
Line 2: *And the yellow half-moon large and low;*
    Because "low" does not rhyme with "land," it is given the letter **b.**
Line 3: *And the startled little waves that leap*
    "Leap" does not rhyme with "low" or "land," so it is given the letter **c.**

Line 4: *In fiery ringlets from their sleep,*
　　"Sleep" and "leap" do rhyme; therefore, "sleep" is given the letter **c**, also.

Line 5: *As I gain the cove with pushing prow,*
　　Line 5 picks up the rhyme of line 2 ("prow" and "low"—eye-rhyme) and is consequently labeled **b**.

Line 6: *And quench its speed i' the slushy sand.*
　　This last line of the first stanza ends with "sand," rhyming with line 1. Give this line the letter **a**.

The rhyme scheme, then, of the first stanza is **a b c c b a**.
　　Now look at the second stanza.

Line 7: *Then a mile of warm sea-scented beach;*
　　Since "beach" does not rhyme with "land" (the **a** rhyme), with "low" (the **b** rhyme), or with "leap" (the **c** rhyme), line 7 is given the letter **d**.

Line 8: *Three fields to cross till a farm appears;*
　　"Appears" does not rhyme with any of the previous lines, so it is also given a new letter, **e**.

Line 9: *A tap at the pane, the quick sharp scratch*
　　Again, "scratch" does not rhyme with any other line, so it is given the letter **f**.

Line 10: *And blue spurt of a lighted match,*
　　Return to a rhyme with "scratch" and give the line the letter **f**.

Line 11: *And a voice less loud, through its joys and fears,*
　　"Fears" and "appears" (line 8) rhyme so line 11 is given an **e**.

Line 12: *Then the two hearts beating each to each!*
　　The final line of the second stanza picks up the rhyme of line 7 ("beach" and "each") and is assigned the letter **d**.

The rhyme scheme of the last stanza is **d e f f e d**.
　　The complete rhyme scheme of "Meeting at Night" is:

First stanza		Second stanza	
. . . land	a	. . . beach	d
. . . low	b	. . . appears	e
. . . leap	c	. . . scratch	f
. . . sleep	c	. . . match	f
. . . prow	b	. . . fears	e
. . . sand	a	. . . each	d

What effect does an **abccba deffed** rhyme scheme have on the reader (or listener)? Because the third and fourth lines of each stanza introduce rhyme to the poem's structure (form), the reader may pause (perhaps even imperceptibly) or have a sense of anticipation of a new direction that will either complement or contrast the first two lines. In the pattern of "Meeting at Night," however, a new direction is *not* taken as you return in the fifth line to rhyme with the second line and in the last line of the stanza to rhyme with the first line.

What are some of the possible effects? Emphasis . . . unity of thought . . . perhaps using the rhyme scheme to contribute to the tone. Subliminally, the cyclical nature of the rhyme scheme may give the reader a sense of movement and expectation—an expectation that is fulfilled—that is emotionally satisfying in the first stanza when the speaker comes ashore and the last stanza when he is reunited with the one waiting for him.

In this poem, the relationship of lines 1–4 to lines 5–6 and of lines 7–10 to lines 11–12 reflect the speaker's progression from challenge to attainment. Notice in lines 1–4 that the speaker is in a challenging situation: at sea surrounded by "startled little waves that leap in fiery ringlets"; however, he "gain[s] the cove" and makes it ashore in lines 5–6. This progression from challenge to attainment is mirrored in the second stanza as he is challenged to cross the beach and fields and to gain the attention of the one lighting the match in lines 7–10; he finally attains reunion in lines 11–12.

How do you determine the rhyme scheme in a poem when the pronunciations of one or more of the end-line words are unfamiliar to you due to regionalisms or changes in pronunciation over time or when the rhyme is imperfect? How do such situations affect the rhyme scheme? Here is a stanza from Shakespeare's "The Phoenix and the Turtle":

> **Let the priest in surplice white**
> **That defunctive music can,**
> **Be the death-divining swan,**
> **Lest the requiem lack his right.**

"White," "can," "swan," and "right" seem to be an **abca** rhyme scheme. When you look at the next two stanzas, however, the rhyme scheme appears to be somewhat different. (Because the rhyme schemes of individual stanzas are being compared in this illustration, the first line of each stanza begins with **a**.)

And thou treble-dated crow,	a
That thy sable gender makest	b
With the breath thou givest and takest,	b
Mongst our mourners shalt thou go.	a
Here the anthem doth commence:	a
Love and constancy is dead;	b
Phoenix and the turtle fled	b
In a mutual flame from hence.	a

You might surmise, based on the context of the rhyme scheme of the other stanzas, that the poet intends "can" and "swan" to rhyme for an **abba** pattern. When dealing with possible historical rhyme, eye rhyme, or imperfect rhyme, you need to look first at the context (the established rhyme scheme of the poem—a process called **correspondence**) and then at the meanings of the lines in which the rhyme appears. A word search in the *Oxford English Dictionary* or in some other etymological dictionary might reveal a change in pronunciation due to time or a difference in pronunciation due to nationality/regionalism. If you eliminate the possibility of rhyme affected by pronunciation changes and must decide the poet's intent, meaning can be a valuable clue. Examine the meaning of the line in the context of the stanza: the poet may be using the break from the established rhyme pattern for a specific *effect,* such as a shift in meaning, a contrast, or an attention-getting device.

Physical Form

The physical form of a poem—what it looks like on a page—can greatly affect its meaning and can even affect its "label" of "a poem."

Although the distinction between prose and poetry has already been addressed, the physical form of poetry cannot be discussed without examining the range of forms that exists between these two extremes.

Prose. Prose is written from margin to margin. Thoughts are written in complete sentences. Sentences are grouped into paragraphs. Paragraphs are arranged into subsections (under subheadings—particularly in nonfiction works). Subsections are joined to make chapters. Chapters are grouped under larger sections or parts. The sections or parts go together to form a book.

> **Book**
> > **Sections or parts**
> > > **Chapters**
> > > > **Subsections**
> > > > > **Paragraphs**
> > > > > > **Sentences**

Poetry. Poetry has a regular rhythm that can be measured and a rhyme scheme. A poem is written in lines that may—or may not—contain sentences or sentence fragments. Based on metrical patterns, rhyme schemes, and/or thought units, a poem is divided into stanzas. (Some poets refer to poem divisions that are regular and rhymed as stanzas, but when the subdivision is irregular and unrhymed, they may call it a **strophe.**) Generally, the rhyme scheme and metrical pattern of the initial stanza are repeated in subsequent stanzas. As previously mentioned, this is called **correspondence,** and greatly facilitates identifying, for example, the rhyme scheme in a poem in which one of the end-line words has changed in pronunciation. By looking at another stanza, you can easily determine where the word in question fits in the *established* rhyme scheme and metrical pattern.

> **Poem (Section—for example, book or canto)**
> > **Stanza (Strophe)**
> > > **Lines**
> > > > **Metrical feet**

A discussion of some of the various forms that you will find within and between these two extremes (prose and poetry) follows.

Prose Poetry. Is it prose or is it a poem? Viewed by some critics as "impossible—no such thing," the prose poem would seem to be an *oxymoron,* a contradiction in terms. Poetry written in paragraphs (with left and right margin justification), without the line breaks of regular verse, the prose poem relies on its compact intensity and repetition of rhyme and figurative elements. ("Belltones," page 4, is a previously cited example.)

Free Verse. Free verse is just that—free of a regular meter. Also called *open form* or *vers libre,* free verse is characterized by short, irregular lines, no rhyme pattern, and a dependence on the effective and more intense use of pauses, words selected not only for meaning but for how that meaning is intensified by their position in the poem. Notice the use of free verse in "Know Yourself" by Lillian E. Myers:

Know Yourself

There is a
truth
with us
and in us.
Is this the truth?

There is a
lie
with us,
but not in us.
Is this the truth?

Blank Verse. Blank verse is written in iambic pentameter, but with no rhyme pattern. It is the major verse form used by Shakespeare in his plays. In blank verse, divisions are referred to as *verse paragraphs* (although the verse paragraph can also be in free verse). Blank verse made its appearance in English literature first in drama and then in epics. More recently, it has been used frequently in A wide variety of long poems. For example, here is an excerpt from William Wordsworth's rather lengthy "Lines Composed a Few Miles Above Tintern Abbey on Revisiting the Banks of the Wye During a Tour, July 13, 1798."

Five years have passed; five summers, with the
    length
Of five long winters! and again I hear
These waters, rolling from their mountain-springs
With a soft inland murmur, Once again
Do I behold these steep and lofty cliffs,
That on a wild secluded scene impress
Thoughts of more deep seclusion; and connect
The landscape with the quiet of the sky.

Qualitative Verse. This verse has a measurable rhythm with an identifiable rhyme scheme. The poem is presented in a known stanza. The verse is accentual-syllabic: it depends on (1) how many syllables are in each line and (2) the accented and unaccented syllables forming patterns. (Do not confuse this with *quantitative verse,* which imitates Greek and Latin versification, depending on the duration of sound.)

A significant aspect of form in poetry is form of the stanza. Among the most common stanza forms are

> ▶ **Couplets**—two grouped lines that rhyme (called *distich* if they do not rhyme).
>
> ▶ **Heroic couplets**—Couplets written in iambic pentameter (very popular in English poetry during the 1800s and 1900s):

X / X / X / X / X /
Which gives the watchword to his hands full soon,
X / X / X / X / X /
To draw the cloud that hides the silver moon.

Stanza	No. of Lines	Meter	Rhyme Scheme
Ballad	4	lines 1 and 3 iambic tetrameter; lines 2 and 4 iambic pentameter	abcb
Elegiac	4	iambic pentameter	abab
Terza rima	3	iambic pentameter	aba, bcb, cdc, ded, . . .
Rime royal	7	iambic pentameter	ababbcc
Ottava rima	8	iambic pentameter	abababcc
Spenserian	9	lines 1–8 iambic pentameter; line 9 iambic hexameter (an Alexandrine)	ababbcbcc

Other terms referring to the number of lines in a stanza include the following:

tristich (triplet)	3 lines
quatrain	4 lines
quintain (quintet)	5 lines
sextain (sestet)	6 lines

Genre

The major genres of poetry are defined by patterns of rhythm, rhyme, physical form, and subject.

There are three major groups or divisions of poems, classifications that can be further subdivided into many different genres:

- ▶ Epic poetry (narrative mode)
- ▶ Dramatic poetry (dramatic mode)
- ▶ Lyric poetry (lyric mode)

Epic Poetry

An epic poem is a long poem written in the narrative mode. The characteristics of an epic poem include the following:

- ▶ Elevated style
- ▶ Adventurous plot
- ▶ Heroic figures
- ▶ A legendary main character
- ▶ An expansive setting
- ▶ Supernatural "machinery"
- ▶ The narrative as an "objective" account

Epic poetry usually follows a "formula" and utilizes a variety of epic conventions:

- ▶ A statement of the theme (called the *argument*) begins the epic.
- ▶ An *epic question* is posed to "invoke" a Muse.
- ▶ The story begins in the middle of the action (*medias res*) with explanations given later.
- ▶ The main characters give very long, very formal speeches.
- ▶ The names of warriors, ships, and so forth are listed.
- ▶ Throughout the narrative, the poet uses very complex, multilevel *epic similes* (extended comparisons).

Folk epics (traditional or primary epics) were handed down orally and often are of uncertain authorship. Literary epics are imitations of these. The importance of the epic to English poetry should not be underestimated. In the Renaissance, the epic was highly esteemed by critics and has influenced English writers over the years. To cite an example, Milton was influenced by Virgil's *The Aenid* when he wrote *Paradise Lost* in 1667.

The length and complexity of an epic, however, is quite imposing, hence the birth of the **mock epic** or *mock heroic* poem. Forms of high burlesque, these poems apply the conventional forms and styles of an epic to comparatively mundane, unimportant subjects. The grandiose treatment of insignificant subjects creates a comic disparity.

The influence of the epic poem on other narrative poem modes is arguable. Some narrative poems are rooted deeply in the epic traditions; others are not. Poems in the narrative mode range from folkloric poems to beast-fables in verse to "court epics" to verse novels (such as Elizabeth Barrett Browning's *Aurora Leigh*).

Dramatic Poetry

Some critics argue that the label "dramatic poetry" is somewhat ambiguous. Of course, the term refers to poems that are dominated in content, style, and structure by the dramatic form and/or by the many possible dramatic techniques, such as dialogue and blank verse. Other critics would include poetic drama (plays written in verse) under this large category that is held together by the special elements of the dramatic mode. What constitutes the dramatic mode?

▶ The work presents an abrupt change.
▶ The tone is influenced by the emotional involvement that arises from the interaction of the characters and the conflict of the situation.
▶ The plot line follows the rise and fall of the main character.

The dramatic mode of poetry (whether poems that are dramatic or poetic drama) can include the following:

▶ Dialogue written in verse (usually blank verse in the poetic drama)
▶ Monologues—long speeches uttered by one person

Unlike poems that contain dramatic elements, poetic drama is meant to be acted out. Works such as Shelley's *Prometheus Unbound* (written in 1820) and Milton's *Samson Agonistes* (written in 1671), however, are dramas that are *not* meant to be acted out. This genre is called the **closet drama.**

Lyric Poetry

In the lyric mode, the tone is reflective, at times even introspective, with the speaker discussing an experience or expounding upon an idea. Originally referring to songs sung to lyre music, now the term lyric refers to expressive, short nonnarrative poems; however, lyric also includes longer works such as some elegies. Lyric poetry includes a blend of elements:

- ▶ Melodious tone
- ▶ Spontaneously expressed emotion
- ▶ Unified structure (harmonious)
- ▶ Individualized
- ▶ Subjective

The broad range of poetic forms that fall under the label of lyric poetry is impressive. Although not all lyric poetry is intended to be sung, the intrinsic musical elements of lyric poetry that are rooted in its musical origins should be recognized (although not over-stated). Some of the subclasses of lyric poetry include the following:

A. Dramatic monologue. In a dramatic monologue, a persona (someone who is not the poet) unintentionally reveals his or her character by expressing a poem at a critical moment. There may or may not be a silent auditor—the person to whom the monologue is being addressed. In Robert Browning's "My Last Duchess" (see pages 136–137), the silent auditor is an agent for negotiating the Duke's next marriage arrangement.

Dramatic monologues, by definition, contain revelations of character—a case in which knowledge of form helps the reader to gain insight into another literary principle.

B. Elegy. Elegy is a lament over the death of someone (although elegy once referred to poems written in elegiac meter—lines that alternate hexameter and pentameter).

Read the first stanza of Thomas Gray's "Elegy Written in a Country Churchyard." Notice his use of the elegiac stanza (four lines of iambic pentameter with an **abab** rhyme scheme).

> **The curfew tolls the knell of parting day,**
> **The lowing herd wind slowly o'er the lea,**
> **The plowman homeward plods his weary way,**
> **And leaves the world to darkness and to me.**

Elegies include some love poems about death. Subtypes of elegy include the following:

▶ **Dirges**—short songs expressing grief over someone.
▶ **Pastoral elegies**—poems in which both the deceased and the mourner are presented as shepherds. These elegies often include mythology as part of the poetic structure.

C. Ode. An ode is a complex, serious, long lyric poem modeled after Pindar (the Greek poet) whose complex songs (originally used in dramatic poetry) were divided into numerous three-part units consisting of the strophe, antistrophe, and epode. The English ode has three forms:

▶ **Regular or Pindaric ode**—This form includes one stanza pattern for strophe and antistrophe and another stanza pattern for epode.
▶ **Irregular ode**—Each stanza has its own pattern. This form has been the most common ode form in English since it was first done in 1656 by Abraham Cowley.
▶ **Horatian (homostrophic) ode**—This form has one repeated stanza type that may vary within the established pattern. These odes are calmer—less passionate—than Pindaric odes.

Odes are very unified, with just one theme handled in an extremely dignified manner. The purpose of many odes is to eulogize someone or something, such as Alexander Pope's "Ode on Solitude." Notice the first and last stanzas:

> Happy the man, whose wish and care
> A few paternal acres bound,
> Content to breathe his native air,
> In his own ground.
> . . .
> Thus let me live, unseen, unknown,
> Thus unlamented let me die,
> Steal from the world, and not a stone
> Tell where I lie.

D. Sonnet. A sonnet is a fourteen-line iambic pentameter poem. There are three main types of sonnet:

1. The **Italian (Petrarchan) sonnet** consists of an octave (eight lines) or a set of two quatrains (four lines each) in an **abbaabba** rhyme scheme and asks a question or presents a statement that is answered or somehow addressed by the concluding

sestet (six lines) or set of two tercets (three lines each). Notice Wordsworth's use of the sonnet form in "Nuns Fret Not."

	X / X / X / X / X /	
line	Nuns fret not at their convent's narrow room;	a
	And hermits are contented with their cells;	b
	And students with their pensive citadels;	b
	Maids at the wheel, the weaver at his loom,	a
(5)	Sit blithe and happy; bees that soar for bloom,	a
	High as the highest Peak of Furness-fells,	b
	Will murmur by the hour in foxglove bells:	b
	In truth the prison, into which we doom	a
	Ourselves, no prison is: and hence for me,	c
(10)	In sundry moods, 'twas pastime to be bound	d
	Within the Sonnet's scanty plot of ground;	d
	Pleased if some Souls (for such there needs must be)	c
	Who have felt the weight of too much liberty,	c
	Should find brief solace there, as I have found.	d

First, in lines 1–9, Wordsworth tells the reader that some "imprison" themselves by choice (nuns, hermits, students); hence, if by choice, then they are not really in prison (lines 8–9). He concludes in lines 10–14 that the "prison" of the sonnet (the confines of structure required to write in this form) is actually a "solace" from "the weight of too much liberty"—poems lacking the tight structure of a sonnet.

2. The **English (Shakespearean) sonnet** consists of three quatrains (four lines each) and concludes with a couplet in an **abab cdcd efef gg** rhyme scheme. You can expect the final couplet either to summarize the theme variations in the first three quatrains or to be epigrammatic. Here is an example from Shakespeare.

	X / X / X / X / X /	
line	Why is my verse so barren of new pride,	a
	So far from variation or quick change?	b
	Why, with the time, do I not glance aside	a
	To newfound methods and to compounds strange?	b
(5)	Why write I still all one, ever the same,	c
	And keep invention in a noted weed,	d
	That every word doth almost tell my name,	c
	Showing their birth, and where they did proceed?	d
	O, know, sweet love, I always write of you,	e
(10)	And you and love are still my argument;	f
	So all my best is dressing old words new,	e

> Spending again what is already spent: **f**
>   For as the sun is daily new and old,   **g**
>   So is my love still telling what is told.   **g**

Lines 1–4 ask why the speaker does not try new methods of verse. (Notice the connotative implications of the first line—"Why is my verse so barren of *new pride*"—does he consider trying new forms of verse a means of pride?) Lines 5–8 ask why he still writes the same—to the extent that his work is easily identified as his. (Consider that these questions may be *rhetorical*; in other words, he may not expect a reply, but may be using the interrogative to emphasize his point. The rhetorical question will be discussed in more detail in a later section.) Lines 9–12 bring the reader to the subject of his writings: "you"—with the implication that there are only so many ways to describe his love. The concluding couplet is slightly aphoristic as he likens the sun, which is old yet seen new each day, to how he expresses his love.

3. The **Spenserian sonnet** consists of the quatrain being linked by a continuing rhyme scheme, namely **abab bcbc cdcd ee**.

Like as a Huntsman after Weary Chase

```
         X  / X   /   X  / X  / X    /
```
line	Like as a huntsman after weary chase,	a
	Seeing the game from him escaped away,	b
	Sits down to rest him in some shady place,	a
	With panting hounds beguiléd of their prey:	b
(5)	So, after long pursuit and vain assay,	b
	When I all weary had the chase forsook,	c
	The gentle deer returned the self-same way,	b
	Thinking to quench her thirst at the next brook:	c
	There she, beholding me with milder look,	c
(10)	Sought not to fly, but fearless still did bide;	d
	Till I in hand her yet half trembling took,	c
	And with her own good-will her firmly tied.	d
	Strange thing, meseemed, to see a beast so wild,	e
	So goodly won with her own will beguiled.	e

by Edmund Spenser

Once again, the concluding couplet summarizes the speaker's point. Also, be aware of the sonnet sequence (also called the sonnet cycle)—a device used by Shakespeare and Spenser. These cycles consist of a series of sonnets that are related by theme or some other means.

Overview

Here is a brief overview of the more common genres of poetry. Most are lyric; however, some include elements of the epic (narrative mode) and drama (dramatic mode).

Haiku

Haiku is a single-stanza, 3-line, (originally Japanese) lyric poem of 17 syllables. The subject is generally impressionistic of a scene in nature or a natural object:

Line 1 with 5 syllables
Line 2 with 7 syllables
Line 3 with 5 syllables

Haiku

Hear their sad refrain
To capture sense with a sound.
Doves before the rain.

by C. Myers-Shaffer

Poems Set to Music

1. **Hymns** Religious songs or hymns have appeared in both rhymed and unrhymed qualitative verse, as well as in prose.

2. **Songs** Lyric poems are meant to be sung. Songs are typically short and emotional on topics that range from love to hate, dancing to mourning, work to play. A familiar example is Ben Jonson's "Drink to Me Only with Thine Eyes."

Some works labeled as songs, however, cannot actually be sung, such as "The Love-Song of J. Alfred Prufrock" by T.S. Eliot. **Folk songs** are those of unknown authorship.

3. **Ballads** Narrative songs that may be sung or simply recited are ballads. The ballad tradition can be found worldwide.

Characteristics of the ballad:

▶ Theme: courage or love
▶ Little description or characterization
▶ Incremental repetition (repetition of words, lines, or phrases for effect)

Form of the ballad:

- ▶ The ballad stanza is usually iambic foot in four lines (quatrain) with an **abcb** rhyme scheme (sometimes based on approximate rhyme or on assonance and consonance). Lines 1 and 3 have four accented syllables; lines 2 and 4 have three accented syllables.
- ▶ A *refrain* (repetition of words, phrases, or lines at intervals) is used.
- ▶ Sometimes it has a concluding or summary stanza.
- ▶ Stock descriptive phrases are used.

Types of ballads:

a. **Popular ballad:** A narrative folk song
b. **Broadside ballad:** A song

- ▶ Topic: A current event, well-known person, or debated issue
- ▶ Tune: Well known
- ▶ Printed on one side of a sheet of paper

c. **Literary ballad:** An imitation of the popular ballad, but written by a "poet"

Because anonymous folk ballads are part of the oral tradition, the same ballad can surface from different regions, times, or peoples in different forms. The seventeenth-century "Barbara Allen" is such a folk song. One version is in ten stanzas. Here are the first three:

Barbara Allen

Stanza one: In Scarlet town, where I was born,
There was a fair maid dwellin',
Made every youth cry *Well-a-way!*
Her name was Barbara Allen.

Stanza two: All in the merry month of May,
When green buds they were swellin',
Young Jemmy Grove on his death-bed lay,
For love of Barbara Allen.

Stanza three: He sent his man in to her then,
To the town where she was dwellin';

"O haste and come to my master dear,
If your name be Barbara Allen."

Now compare the first three stanzas of this nine-stanza version:

Bonny Barbara Allan

Stanza one: It was in and about the Martinmas time,
             When the green leaves were a falling,
             That Sir John Graeme, in the West Country,
             Fell in love with Barbara Allan.

Stanza two: He sent his man down through the town,
             To the place where she was dwelling;
             "O haste and come to my master dear,
             Gin ye be Barbara Allan."

Stanza three: O hooly, hooly rose she up,
               To the place where he was lying,
               And when she drew the curtain by,
               "Young man, I think you're dying."

Changes due to the oral tradition also can be seen in "The Cowboy's Lament" when compared to "The Dying Cowboy" (nineteenth century). Compare the first stanzas of each.

The Cowboy's Lament

As I walked out in the streets of Laredo,
As I walked out in Laredo one day,
I spied a poor cowboy wrapped up in white linen,
Wrapped up in white linen as cold as the clay.

The Dying Cowboy

As I rode out by Tom Sherman's bar-room,
As I rode out so early one day,
'Twas there I espied a handsome young cowboy,
All dressed in white linen, all clothed for the grave.

For an example of the literary ballad, read these first four stanzas of Coleridge's *The Rime of the Ancient Mariner,* Part I.

It is an ancient Mariner
And he stoppeth one of three.
"By thy long gray beard and glittering eye,
Now wherefore stopp'st thou me?

The Bridegroom's doors are opened wide,
And I am next of kin;
The guests are met, the feast is set:
May'st hear the merry din."

He holds him with his skinny hand,
"There was a ship," quoth he.
"Hold off! unhand me, gray-beard loon!"
Eftsoons his hand dropt he.

He holds him with his glittering eye—.
The Wedding-Guest stood still,
And listens like a three years' child:
The Mariner hath his will.

4. **Chansons**   Chansons are simple poems meant to be sung.

5. **Epithalamium Poems**   Songs written to celebrate a marriage are called epithalamium poems.

6. **Madrigals**   Madrigals are love poems meant to be sung *a cappella* (without instrumental accompaniment) by five to six singers, their voices blending and weaving in and out of the melody.

Take, O! Take Those Lips Away

Take, O! take those lips away,
    That so sweetly were forsworn,
And those eyes, the break of day,
    Lights that do mislead the morn;
But my kisses bring again,
        Bring again,
Seals of love, but sealed in vain,
        Sealed in vain.

by William Shakespeare

7. **Rhapsody**   Once referring to epic poetry that is sung, now rhapsody refers to very emotional poems or any sequence of literary expressions that have been arbitrarily joined together.

8. **Serenades**   Serenades are evening songs.

9. **Aubades**   Early-morning songs, such as Shakespeare's "Hark, Hark, the Lark," are called aubades.

10. **Jingles**   The short, easy-to-sing songs used to sell products are known as jingles. Notable jingles on television include songs to sell toothpaste and hamburgers. Jingles can have negative connotations. Have you ever had a jingle in your mind that you could not stop repeating?

Light Verse

Light verse consists of poems intended to be humorous or witty. Types of light verse follow.

1. ***Vers de société***   These are characterized by:
   - ▶ Brief length
   - ▶ Playful mood
   - ▶ Social relationships as the subject
   - ▶ Sophisticated style
   - ▶ Terse tone
   - ▶ Brisk and generally rhymed rhythm

2. **Parody**   A parody is a comic or satiric imitation of a more serious work. It generally ridicules a work, an author, or a style. A parody can be fun to write, especially when the original poem has a very pronounced rhythm or mood. Edgar Allan Poe's "The Raven" has such a distinctive rhythm pattern that it works well in parody. Here is the first stanza of the original poem:

> **Once upon a midnight dreary, while I
>   pondered, weak and weary,
> Over many a quaint and curious volume of
>   forgotten lore,
> While I nodded, nearly napping, suddenly there
>   came a tapping,
> As of some one gently rapping, rapping at my
>   chamber door.
> "'Tis some visitor," I muttered, "tapping at my
>   chamber door—
>   Only this and nothing more."**

Here is a parody of the preceding stanza:

> **Once upon a schoolday dreary, while I studied,
>   weak and weary,**

> Over many a quaint and curious volume of
>   literature,
> Feeling grisly, grim and grumbling, suddenly there
>   came a rumbling,
> A gruesome gripping kind of rumbling, rumbling that
>   was premature.
> "'Tis my stomach," then I muttered, "rumbling
>   here so premature—
>   Candy bars will be the cure."

3. **Limerick**   A limerick is a poem of five anapestic lines with an **aabba** rhyme scheme. Lines 1, 2, and 5 are trimeter; lines 3 and 4 are dimeter. (Note: If the limerick consists of only four lines, the third line generally will have some internal rhyme.) The limerick is a form of nonsense verse.

```
X X   /  X  X    /   X X  /
I sat next/ to the Duch/ess at tea.                          a
  X   X  /   X X   /    X    X   /
It was just/ as I thought/ it would be:                     a
       X   /   X   X   / X X
       Her rumblings ab/dominal                             b
       X   /  X  X   /  X X
       Were simply phe/nomenal                             b
     X  / X  X      /    X   X   /
     And ev/eryone thought / it was me.                    a
```

This limerick illustrates the use of **substitution,** when the poet substitutes a different foot in place of the one established by the pattern already used. The pattern established in lines 1 and 2 of anapestic trimeter would allow you to assume that line 5 would also be anapestic trimeter. The first foot of line 5, however, is an iamb "substituted" for an anapest.

4. **Occasional Verse**   Occasional verse is generally written for specific occasions, such as coronations, birthdays, and deaths. For official occasions, the English poet laureate is expected to write the occasional poem. An often-cited occasional poem was written in 1681 by Andrew Marvell. The poem, "An Horatian Ode upon Cromwell's Return from Ireland," is based upon Cromwell's return to England in 1650, at which time he prepared to go to battle against the Scots.

5. **Epigrams**   Short poems that are characteristically witty with a twist in the thought at the end are called epigrams.

However, they can also be defined as simply clever sayings used for a variety of purposes, including to eulogize, to compliment, or to satirize. This anonymous Latin epigram sums up the point.

Three things must epigrams, like bees, have all,
A sting, and honey, and a body small.

6. **Epitaph**   Generally, an epitaph is a short poem (an epigram) intended for a tombstone (or as if for carving on a tombstone). The epitaph may be comic.

My Own Epitaph

Life is a jest; and all things show it.
I thought so once; but now I know it.

by John Gay

Some epitaphs are both lengthy and serious. William Blake, however, wrote an epitaph in which he compares his subject to an epigram:

Her Whole Life Is an Epigram

Her whole life is an epigram: smack, smooth &
   neatly penned,
Platted quite neat to catch applause, with a sliding
   noose at the end.

7. **Epigraph**   An epigraph or motto is the quotation or inscription on a statue, on a coin, before chapter headings, and on title pages of books.

8. **Clerihew**   The Clerihew is named after the writer of detective fiction (Edmund Clerihew Bentley). The subject of the Clerihew is the name of a person. The name appears on the first line of the quatrain. The rhyme scheme is **aabb** with no regular meter.

Sir Humphrey Davy
   Detested gravy
   He lived in the odium
   Of having discovered sodium.

9. **Nonsense Verse**   Nonsense verse is poetry characterized by

▶ Strong rhythm
▶ No logic
▶ Words that are coined, invented, or borrowed (without regard to appropriateness) from other languages

Visual Poems

The physical shape affects the meaning of a visual poem.

1. **Shaped Verse**   Shaped verse is also known as Renaissance emblem poetry.
The words are shaped to fit the meaning.

The Altar

A broken ALTAR, Lord, Thy servant rears,
Made of a HEART, and cemented with tears;
Whose parts are as Thy hand did frame;
No workman's tool hath touched the same.
A HEART alone
Is such a stone
As nothing but
Thy power doth cut.
Wherefore each part
Of my hard HEART
Meets in this frame,
To praise Thy name:
That, if I chance to hold my peace,
These stones to praise Thee may not cease.
O, let Thy blessed SACRIFICE be mine,
And sanctify this ALTAR to be Thine.

by George Herbert

2. **Concrete Poetry**   Concrete poetry or pattern poems are highly graphic, modern poems that are also graphic art.

A
l
p h a
b
et
Soup

A Bowl Can Do Each Friend Good
Hot In January—Knowing Life's
Mean, Nasty—Only Please
Quick—Run Straight To
Universal Values With
Xtra Yummy Zoups
(–oops–)

by Lillian E. Myers

3. **Acrostic Poems** In acrostic poems, the first letter of each line when read down joins to spell a word.

Acrostic

L	Little maidens, when you look
O	On this little storybook,
R	Reading with attentive eye
I	Its enticing history,
N	Never think that hours of play
A	Are your only HOLIDAY,
A	And that in a HOUSE of joy
L	Lessons serve but to annoy:
I	If in any HOUSE you find
C	Children of a gentle mind,
E	Each the others pleasing ever—
E	Each the others vexing never—
D	Daily work and pastime daily
I	In their order taking gaily—
T	Then be very sure that they
H	Have a life of HOLIDAY.

by Lewis Carroll
Christmas 1861

Riddles. Riddles are poems presented as mental puzzles meant to be solved. What is Lillian E. Myers describing in "That Sound"?

That Sound

What fun camping out—
    Wild animals all about.
Then it gets dark
    In the National park.

And after all are fed,
    You're tired and ready for bed.
The tents are all in a row
    And into bed you all go.

You hear that sound
    And out of bed you bound.
It's still quite early—
    Only about four-thirty.

That sound came from who-o-o
    Just in time to scare you.
A quivering sound that's eerie:
    The dark makes you leery.

The others hear it, too—
    That same sound that scared you.
Please try to identify
    That strange and scary cry.

by Lillian E. Myers

Satire

Some poems embody a satiric outlook. For example, formal verse satire, sometimes didactic in tone, satirizes some vice. Look for **Horatian** satire (gentle ridicule) in the poetry of W. H. Auden. **Juvenalian** satire is very formal, very cutting, but **Menippean** satire uses plot, dialogue, and a mixture of prose and verse.

Jonathan Swift, well known for his ability to satirize, penned "A Satirical Elegy" in 1722. This was written "On the Death of a Late Famous General"—John Churchill. Churchill was a member of royalty (Duke of Marlborough) and an English military hero whose character was eventually called into question. The first two stanzas follow.

A Satirical Elegy

On the Death of a Late Famous General

His Grace? impossible? what dead?
Of old age too, and in his bed?
And could that Mighty Warrior fall?
And so inglorious, after all!
Well, since he's gone, no matter how,
The last loud trump must wake him now;
And, trust me, as the noise grows stronger,
He'd wish to sleep a little longer.
    And could he be indeed so old
As by the newspapers we're told?
Threescore, I think, is pretty high;
'Twas time in conscience he should die.
This world he cumbered long enough;
He burnt his candle to the snuff;
And that's the reason, some folks think,
He left behind so great a *stink*.

Invective Poems

Invective poems are personal attacks or *lampoons* (satires against individuals).

Panegyric Poems

Panegyric poems praise someone or something, especially public figures and institutions.

Epideictic Poetry

Epideictic poems are special occasion poems.

- ▶ **Encomiums** are poems (often in the form of odes) that eulogize.
- ▶ **Epithalamiums** are poems (that can be songs) that celebrate a wedding.

Complaint

A complaint is a lyric poem (usually a monologue) in which the poet complains about the state of the world, his individual situation, or his mistress.

A Complaint by Night

Alas! so all things now do hold their peace,
Heaven and earth disturbed in no thing.
The beasts, the air, the birds their song do cease;
The nightès chare the stars about doth bring;
Calm is the sea; the waves work less and less,
So am not I, whom love, alas! doth wring,
Bringing before my face the great increase
Of my desires, whereat I weep and sing,
In joy and woe, as in a doubtful ease:
For my sweet thoughts sometime do pleasure bring;
But by and by, the cause of my disease
Gives me a pang, that inwardly doth sting,
When that I think what grief it is again,
To live and lack the thing should rid my pain.

by Henry Howard, Earl of Surrey

Confessional Poems

Confessional poems are a contemporary form of poetry that deals with very private matters.

Palinode

A palinode is a poem or song that retracts a previous work, often-times retracting an ode.

Metaphysical Poetry

Metaphysical or philosophical poetry was written in the seventeenth century as a revolt against Elizabethan love poetry. It is characterized by:

▶ The *metaphysical conceit*
▶ Psychological analysis
▶ Subjects: love and religion
▶ Use of the shocking
▶ Simple diction
▶ Form: an argument
▶ Style: rough

Death, Be Not Proud

Death, be not proud, though some have callèd
thee
Mighty and dreadful, for thou art not so,
For those whom thou think'st thou dost overthrow
Die not, poor Death, nor yet canst thou kill me.
From rest and sleep, which but thy picture be,
Much pleasure, then from thee much more must
flow;
And soonest our best men with thee do go—
Rest of their bones and souls' delivery!
Thou'rt slave to fate, chance, kings and desperate
men,
And dost with poison, war, and sickness dwell,
And poppy or charms can make us sleep as well,
And better than thy stroke; why swell'st thou then?
One short sleep past, we wake eternally,
And death shall be no more: Death, thou shalt die!

by John Donne

A type of metaphysical poetry is the *meditative poem,* written with Renaissance poetic techniques about religious topics for religious ceremonies.

Verse Epistles

Poems written as letters from the poet to (usually) a friend are called verse epistles.

Didactic Poetry

Didactic poems are poems meant to instruct.

Georgic Poems

Georgic poems are both didactic and descriptive. They teach about rural life, science, art, or some skill for the purpose of praising rural life. These poems are in contrast to the **pastoral poem**, which tries to fictionalize country life. Georgics that detail a specific place are *topographical.*

Stanza

The following stanza forms come from France.

▶ *Rondeau:* A poem of fifteen lines in three stanzas. Lines 9 and 15 begin a refrain. It has the rhyme scheme **aabba aabc aabbcc** with eight-syllable lines.

Alternate forms of rondeau have twelve lines (**abba abc abbac**) and the *rondeau redouble* (*six quatrains* of **abab** rhyme scheme, lines 1–4 from the last lines of quatrains 2, 3, 4, and 5).

▶ *Villanelle:* A poem of nineteen lines in which lines 6, 12, and 18 repeat line 1 and lines 9, 15, and 19 repeat line 3. It has the rhyme scheme aba' aba aba' aba aba' abaa'. "The Runaways" by Lillian E. Myers illustrates the rhyme scheme of a villanelle.

The Runaways

line		
	In the glory of that day,	a
	Do you remember how you planned	b
	When you decided to run away?	a
	You dreamed you'd stay	a
(5)	In love forever, your life to command	b
	In the glory of that day.	a
	You stopped worrying about yesterday.	a
	You were making your stand,	b
	When you decided to run away.	a
(10)	As you were going down the highway,	a
	Dreaming of sun-warmed sand	b
	In the glory of that day,	a
	You never gave a thought of how you'd pay	a
	The price that life would soon demand	b
(15)	When you decided to run away.	a
	You only knew that you should pray,	a
	When you put on that wedding band	b
	In the glory of that day	a
	When you decided to run away.	a

▶ *Triolet:* A poem of eight lines in which lines 7 and 8 repeat lines 1 and 2. Line 4 repeats line 1. It has the rhyme scheme **ab aa abab.**

Triolet

line	Easy is the triolet,	a
	If you really learn to make it!	b
	Once a neat refrain you get,	a
	Easy is the triolet.	a
(5)	As you see!—I pay my debt	a
	With another rhyme. Deuce take it,	b
	Easy is the triolet,	a
	If you really learn to make it!	b

by W. E. Henley

Form in Drama

Drama—a play—is a literary composition or story that is intended to be acted out by actors or players (usually) on a stage. Drama was present in ancient Greek Dionysian religious ceremony, but modern drama is more closely a product of Western European medieval drama, a new form that was developed from Christian Church ritual in the ninth century.

Dramatic Structure

Dramatic structure, of course, refers to *plot*. To confine a discussion of dramatic structure to just the narrative line of the play, however, is perhaps an oversimplification of the subject. Several other elements work together to form and at the same time counter one another to influence the structure of a play. For example, most plays are intended to be performed in a theater, in a movie, or on television, and each of these milieu has an inherent impact upon dramatic structure.

Even the physical format is significant:

Play
  Acts (the major divisions of a play)
    Scenes and/or episodes

Just as in prose narrative, the plot of a drama centers around conflict: person versus person, person versus group, person versus environment, person versus nature, or person versus self. Each event is arranged within the dramatic structure to move along the story line of the plot—the action—and to have some impact upon the audience.

The structure of a typical stage play might develop as follows.

1. *Exposition, introduction, or status quo*   During the opening of the play, you meet the main characters and establish the setting. Sometimes the story begins in the conflict (*in medias res*); sometimes you only get clues to the conflict to come. The opening scene does, however, develop a sense of credibility by "filling you in" on the circumstances that motivate the actors. Also, the introduction sets the tone. In the movie *E.T.,* the exposition introduces you to a mother and her children in an average American-home setting and endears the viewer to a gentle, supernatural, slightly comical alien who just wants to "phone home."

2. *Conflict or exciting forces*   The **conflict** is the point at which you recognize a threat to something and/or someone you have come to care about in the introduction or to something or someone that you are, in the course of the story, coming to care about. Obstacles are placed in the way of the *protagonist* (the main character). These obstacles may arise from another person, a group, nature, the environment, or psychological conflicts that are generated within the protagonist. Called the **exciting force,** it sets into motion the rising action in the play. Being able to identify the exciting force in the structure of a drama is very important because it gives the characters motivation for their words and deeds and the audience motivation to care.

What are some common exciting forces used in plays? (This list is not exhaustive of the possibilities but rather only illustrative of some of what has been done.)

▶ In plots in which the conflict is person versus person or group, the exciting forces might be competition (rivalry), pursuit (a chase or stalking), rebellion, revenge, love, hate, betrayal, war, or persecution.
▶ In plots in which the conflict is person versus environment or nature, the exciting forces might be a catastrophe, grief over death or loss, survival, or rescue.
▶ In plots in which the conflict is person versus self, the exciting forces might be self-sacrifice, greed, ambition, love, hate, or rebellion.

In a story, you can identify conflict from two perspectives: (1) in general terms, such as "The exciting force is rebellion," and (2) in specific terms, such as "Joe is rebelling against conforming to the values of his friends." For example, in the film *E.T.*, the exciting force is a chase. More specifically, government agents discover the possible existence of an alien and the chase begins as they try to capture E.T.

3. ***Rising action or complication***   As soon as the exciting force has set the action in motion, the struggle builds dramatic tension toward a confrontation. This stage in the dramatic structure consists of a series of emotional highs and lows, with each high gaining intensity. This conflict becomes more complicated. How? In escaping a sinking ship, for example, the hero goes through a series of progressively more dangerous "near misses" and "close calls," being rescued each time. Or the hero is in a love triangle and gets caught in a series of events involving suspicion, conspiracy, and deception. In the movie *E.T.*, the alien is hunted by government authorities and "barely" escapes as the pursuers close in on the children and the alien they are hiding.

4. ***Climax, crisis, or turning point***   Then it happens, the inevitable moment of confrontation. This is the point of *climax*, the turning point in the plot at which there is a reversal from rising action to falling action. The word *climax* actually has more than one usage in literary analysis. Climax is a synonym for crisis when you are determining the structure of a story or a drama, but climax can also refer to the point of highest intensity for the reader or audience—a point that might come before or after the crisis. In the case of *E.T.*, the emotional climax or point of highest intensity might be when the alien "dies." The structural climax (crisis or turning point), however, might be when the alien revives because it is at this point his "fortunes" have reversed. Although more near misses ensue, you know that somehow he will make it.

5. ***Falling action***   Briefer than rising action, the falling action may still have some suspenseful moments but, for the most part, gives the reader or audience a sense of completion, with the various unsettled issues at work within the plot reaching some state of resolution. In *E.T.*, there is one last race to the space ship and a moment for farewells to be said.

6. ***Resolution or dénouement***   The hero has won or lost; issues are resolved; order is restored. The alien goes home.

Structural Factors

How the structure is handled depends on many factors, including: (1) the length of the play and the intended audience, (2) the use of dramatic elements, (3) the settings, and (4) the genre of the play.

Length and Audience

In a typical three-act play, both the exposition and the introduction of the conflict may occur in Act I. The conflict may continue into Act II, with rising action leading to the point of crisis (the turning point) happening just before the curtain closes on the second act. Act III, then, is left to the falling action and the resolution.

The structure of a five-act tragedy cannot be better explained than by Gustav Freytag's (1863) *Technik des Dramas:*

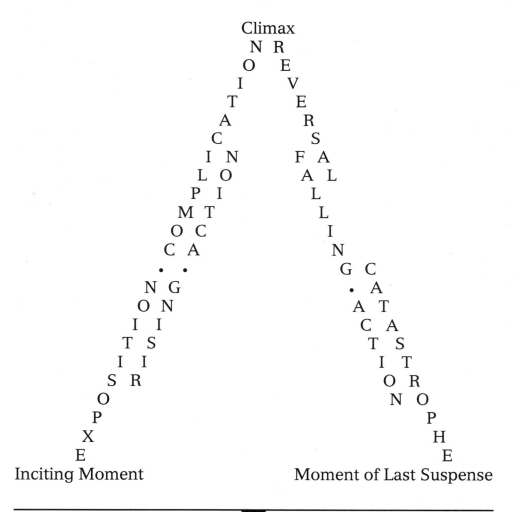

The intended audience—or rather the medium used to convey the enactment of the drama to the audience—is very important to structure. Stop and think about the structural challenges facing the writer of drama for television. At a stage performance, the audience arrives with the expectation of sitting and watching a performance straight through—with perhaps a few brief intermissions at most. Most big-screen movie theaters have no intermission (or maybe one popcorn break). During a two-hour television movie, however, there is a two- to three-minute intermission approximately every fifteen minutes and a longer break for commercials on the hour and sometimes on the half hour. Viewers see these breaks as opportunities to talk, to get a snack, to "channel surf." But for the writer, these intermissions are better described as *interruptions* in the dramatic structure. These breaks interrupt the continuity of the play and, as a result, pose a risk of losing the viewers. The result? A simplification of plot and an intensification of structure. The writer must "hook" the viewer into coming back to the story despite distractions like commercials and the refrigerator, particularly on the hour (and to a lesser degree the half hour) when the viewer anticipates slightly longer commercial breaks.

With these elements in mind, the structure of a television movie or program might look like the following. The numbers of segments, lengths and frequencies of commercials, and plot structure given here are generalizations intended to demonstrate how such elements influence one another and must be coordinated. Actual programming structures vary greatly from network to network, based upon such widely ranging factors as subject, target audience, and time-slot in which the program is to be broadcast. A program structure might be timed as follows:

Segment one
13 minutes: Exposition, introduction of conflict and exciting force
(3-minute commercial break)
Segment two
11 minutes: Rising action; end with a crisis that hints at a larger crisis ahead
(3-minute commercial break)
Segment three
11 minutes: Resolution of previous crisis; hint at upcoming larger crisis; end with rising action crisis
(2-minute commercial break)

Segment four
> 10 minutes: Intensify previous crisis; more hints at larger crisis; end with major cliff-hanger before on-the-hour break
>
> (5-minute commercial on the hour)

Segment five
> 13 minutes: Immediate gratification of cliffhanger; revelation of magnitude of larger crisis; end with emotional rising action crisis as plan to solve problem is revealed
>
> (2-minute commercial)

Segment six
> 12 minutes: Rising action crisis continues; intensity of larger crisis continues to increase; characters start implementing plan; abrupt jolt when plan fails
>
> (3-minute commercial)

Segment seven
> 12 minutes: Begin with new surge of crisis after plan fails; rising action crisis continues; end with turning point (crisis solved)
>
> (3-minute commercial)

Segment eight
> 13 minutes: Characters discuss implications of crisis and solution on future; minor crisis resolved; end of story

Dramatic Elements

A playwright's understanding of structure is not complete without a sense of awareness of the many techniques and devices—dramatic elements—available to create various effects. Here are just a few:

▶ **Foreshadowing** Hints at the future that can build anticipation and tension in the audience. In the movie *Back to the Future,* foreshadowing is very cleverly used in a psychologically reversed way as events in the present "foreshadow" events in the past.

▶ **Flashbacks** Descriptions or enactments of past events for the purpose of clarifying the situation, usually as it relates to the conflict.

▶ **Intrigue**   A scheme designed by one of the characters, the success of which depends on another character's innocence or ignorance of the situation. The usual result is a complication in the plot.

▶ **In medias res**   The first scene opening in the middle of the action.

▶ **Suspense**   Establishing caring on the part of the viewers for one or more of the characters, then presenting events that create a sense of uncertainty concerning what will happen to them.

▶ **Double plots**   Use of a *subplot* or second plot line weaving in and out of the main plot, especially evident in Elizabethan drama.

▶ **Surprise**   After the audience has a sense of expectation, events happen that are not expected.

▶ **Reversal**   When the main character either fails or succeeds, also called *peripety*.

▶ **Discovery**   When the main character finally realizes the reality of the situation.

▶ **Deus ex machina**   Once referring to the Greek practice of physically lowering a "god" to the stage at the end of the play to solve all the problems, today it refers to a contrived element in the plot used to resolve a problem.

▶ **Monologue**   When an actor delivers a speech in the presence of other characters who listen, but do not speak.

▶ **Three unities**   Although not adhered to by many playwrights, French and Italian critics of the sixteenth and seventeenth centuries believed that a play needs three unities to achieve *verisimilitude* (believability):

Unity of action (first suggested by Aristotle)
Unity of place (a single location)
Unity of time (the play portraying no longer than a twenty-four-hour period)

▶ **Dramatic conventions**   The elements of a play that the audience is willing to accept as real for the sake of the story: actors representing the characters of the story, the stage set representing a real location in time and space, suspended time or jumps forward or backward in time, Italians in Italy speaking English, and other such conventions.

▶ **The aside** When an actor speaks directly to the audience, however, the rest of the actors on stage supposedly cannot hear him or her. Assumed to be truthful, the *aside* was used in Renaissance drama to let the audience know the actor's inner feelings and in the nineteenth century to interject elements of comedy or melodrama.

▶ **Soliloquy** A speech delivered by an actor when he or she is alone, expressing thoughts.

▶ **Complications** Causing conflict by introducing new characters, information, or events.

▶ **Scenes** Portions of an act, sometimes triggered by the clearing of the stage for the next "scene." Some types of scenes include *relief scenes* (widely used in English drama) that allow the audience to relax briefly in the tension of the drama or to add a sense of poignant sadness and *balcony scenes*. (Remember *Romeo and Juliet?*)

▶ **Music** A mainstay of the musical drama, early tragedies had both dancing and choral singing. Also, background music is used extensively in television, movies, and on the stage to set the mood and tone. Music can help psychologically to establish the setting: the theme from *Bonanza* for a western, a minuet for a period play, native drums for Africa, an Italian opera for Italy, and Irish reel for Ireland, and Cajun music for New Orleans.

Setting

The setting of a story refers to the time and place of the story and to the socioeconomic background of the characters. In drama, *setting* also refers to the means necessary to translate the story to the audience.

In the theater, this translation depends greatly upon illusion—using lights, costumes, props, and so forth to allow the viewers to suspend reality for a brief time and to accept the story as real.

There are three different types of stages that vary with location, but the following diagrams will give you an idea of the basic principles of each.

Arena Stage. The arena stage places the play on an "island" in a sea of viewers. With the physical possibilities of setting greatly reduced, plays produced on an arena stage depend on a few props, costumes, the words of the play, and the delivery by the actors.

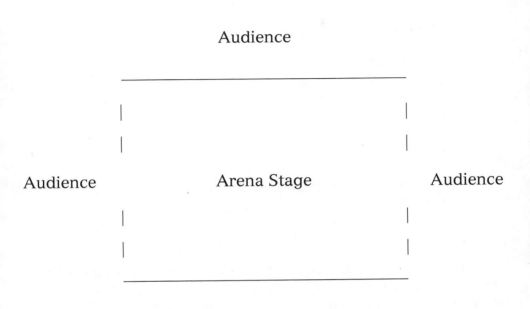

Also called the "theater-in-the-round," the arena stage is the popular choice for the circus and boxing matches. Historically, the arena was used for some of the earliest harvest-festival dramas and medieval rounds.

Thrust Stage. The thrust stage (also called the open stage or platform stage) projects into the audience, reducing the use of the wings and fly galleries, although they may or may not be there. These stages enable very economical productions. The "runway" upon which winners of beauty pageants, such as Miss America, Miss U.S.A., and Miss Universe, traditionally take their "victory walks" is a type of thrust stage.

Versions of the open stage appeared historically in China, Italy, Japan, and the playhouses of Elizabethan England.

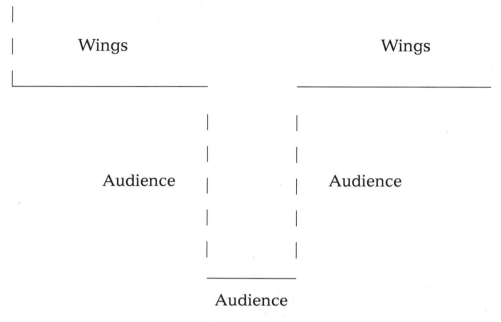

Audience

Thrust stage

Proscenium Stage.   In the proscenium-arch stage (also called the picture-frame stage), the auditorium is separated from the stage by a wall. The view from the audience renders a picture-frame effect.

{   {   {   o_____o   }   }   }

}   }   }   {   {   {

{   {   {   }   }   }

}   }   }   {   {   {

This type of stage can be found in many of the older American public school auditoriums and in the "legitimate" theater. Its obvious advantages include providing the means for elaborate settings and greater "illusion."

With the twentieth century, however, came a new opportunity—and challenge—for dramatists: *motion pictures.* Whether

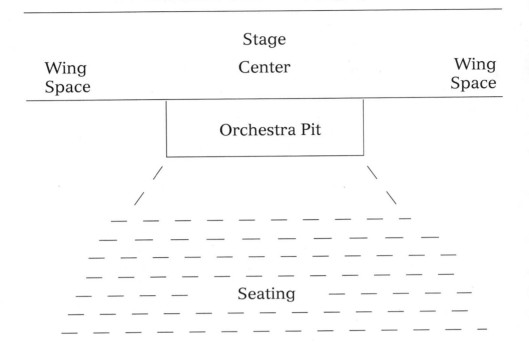

An aerial view of the proscenium stage

intended for movie theaters or television, motion pictures and advancing technology are inseparably linked. Even in the first silent films, the tremendous potential of this medium was clearly evident.

Unlike in a stage production, the filmmaker has the advantages of being able to use exterior scenes, *real* props (such as elephant herds), and computer graphics (such as those used in such movies as *E.T., Jurassic Park,* and *Star Wars*). Movies can be filmed on location, and if an actor forgets a line, the scene can be retaken.

Perhaps one of the major disadvantages to filmmaking is the lack of intimacy with the audience that is a natural part of a live theater performance. Not possible is the give-and-take rapport among the actor, the audience, and indirectly the writer. Not possible are the changes to what did not "work" in last night's performance before tonight's production. The greater distance between writer and audience translates into structural changes: the writer must "hook" the audience in some other way—perhaps by intensity of dialogue, by the use of "kept me on the edge of my seat" action, by captivating graphics, or by restructuring the plot.

Genre

One cannot look at the genre of drama played out on English and American stages without first looking at the history of drama in England—more specifically the Elizabethan popular theater.

The Early Church in England, in celebrating Christmas and Easter, developed special music in which choir groups would musically "respond" to one another. Sometimes a soloist would "answer" the choral group, or vice versa. This back-and-forth musical conversation eventually suggested to the Early Church the concept of dialogue. Soon costumes and settings were added and people began to "act out" their roles in dramas.

In a world without television, radio, or computer video games, such performances provided grand entertainment. Crowds grew in number, spilling out into the churchyards. Eventually, the secular communities became involved, starting festivals at which dramatic episodes were enacted in cycles of plays. The subjects for these "mystery" or "miracle" plays were still based on events in the Bible, and production fell into the hands of various trade guilds.

Secular involvement began to be reflected in these productions—at first with minor changes, like adding comic or tragic scenes that are not in the Bible, but eventually they became completely secular works. The first formal tragedy written and enacted in England was *Gorboduc,* written by Thomas Sackville and Thomas Norton, in 1561. It carried out the "tragedy of blood" tradition of Seneca, a first-century stoic philosopher. From this basis, then, evolved the drama of England and eventually the United States.

Drama can take two different fundamental forms under which many other genres fall: *tragedy* and *comedy.*

Tragedy

In a tragedy, the protagonist (the hero or heroine) is overcome in the conflict and meets a tragic end. The tone is serious and builds in the audience a fatalistic sense of the inevitability of the outcome and, as a result, is sometimes frightening. Yet the inescapable aspects of the catastrophe serve as a *catharsis* that somehow inexplicably purges the viewer of pity and fear. The significance, then, is not that the protagonist meets with an inevitable catastrophe, but rather the degree to which he or she deals with the conflict and the tragedy with dignity, courage, and honor.

What are the basic ingredients of a tragedy?

▶ Mode: narrative
▶ Protagonist: a *tragic hero,* honorable, high character, a person of conscience
▶ Catastrophe: the tragic conclusion of the conflict—usually death of the hero or heroine
▶ Catharsis: the purging of feelings of pity and fear through the vehicle of the play
▶ Spectacles: grand displays used to grab the attention of the audience
▶ Reversal: the point when the protagonist's situation changes from good to bad
▶ *Hamartia:* the protagonist's fatal error or the mistake made (for whatever reason) that leads to his or her downfall (e.g., *hubris*—too much self-confidence that results in mistakenly not heeding a warning)
▶ Recognition: simultaneous with the reversal, the protagonist recognizes the truth of the situation

Also, tragedy elicits pity and fear from the audience, and the protagonist begins in a state of happiness and falls into a state of unhappiness or death.

Classical tragedies are those written *by, about,* or *in the style and form of* the ancient Greeks and Romans.

Romantic tragedies are those that are not classical and include many of the tragedies written in Elizabethan England.

Revenge tragedies are characterized by:

▶ Senecan technique
▶ Plot line: father revenges son at direction of son's ghost or son revenges father at direction of father's ghost
▶ Sensationalized murders (the most extreme is called "tragedy of blood")

Domestic tragedies are those in which the main characters are everyday people who undergo disasters common to many. These are also called *bourgeois tragedies.*

Comedy

If the protagonist of a tragedy meets with a tragic end, one would like to simplify matters by defining comedy as a play in which the protagonist meets with a happy end. Life, however, is not so simple, and neither is dramatic comedy. Here are a few of the characteristics common to many forms of dramatic comedy.

- ▶ Purpose: to amuse the viewer
- ▶ Problems facing the protagonist: interesting to viewer, but not threatening
- ▶ Subject: generally a somewhat realistic view of people's lives, including the disparities between what they should be and what they are
- ▶ Emotional involvement of audience: a balance between two elements:

  1. A superficial involvement based on relevance to their own lives and on familiarity and

  2. Detachment arising from less involvement with the fate of the protagonist (as contrasted to the high levels of emotional involvement of the audience with the fate of the tragic protagonist)

- ▶ Intellectual laughter
- ▶ Style: friendlier as contrasted to the exalted style of tragic drama
- ▶ Includes a sustained plot
- ▶ Uses *humor*: laughter invoked by a good-natured look at the inconsistencies in human nature and of life
- ▶ Uses *wit* (in noncomedic forms referring to wisdom, but in comedy referring to the bright, intelligent use of words to invoke laughter)

The degree to which humor is used, the form it takes, and the manner of presentation are fundamental to **high comedy**, a "serious" form that intends the laughter to be at the characters—at their ridiculous conduct or attitudes—laughter that is intellectual, but not mocking. In contrast, **low comedy** is just plain fun with jesting and clownish behavior. Plays can be predominately high or low comedy, or elements of either (or both) can be incorporated into more serious forms. Compare the elements of low comedy used in the slapstick television plays of *I Love Lucy* to the high comedic elements used in *Cheers* in which the viewer laughs not just at the silly but also at the incongruous actions and attitudes of a group of people who interact with one another in lives that revolve around a bar. When Lucille Ball's plan backfires and the scene leaves her with a cream pie in the face, the viewer laughs with abandon at the silliness of her situation. When viewers laugh at jokes that reveal Norm as a "fixture" at the

Cheers bar, however, they laugh with a different sense of humor—a somewhat serious, thoughtful laughter about a man whose beer and social interaction at a bar has taken precedence over his wife, job, and home.

An example of how both high and low comedy can be used is the television sitcom *Family Matters*. Steven Urkel's character depends upon extensive use of low comedy, for instance, when he causes the entire Winslow family to fall into a heap in the middle of the living room floor and asks, "Did I do that?" Elements of high comedy are also used throughout as the comedy and laughter revolves around family issues (Should Eddie go to college?) and moral issues (Should Carl tell his wife the truth about his job promotion test results?). The use of high comedy makes the viewer think.

Comedy can take many forms. Of course, examples of each can be found in any age, yet some forms were more prevalent in certain literary periods.

Literary Age	*Comic Form*
Sixteenth century (particularly Elizabethan England)	Romantic comedy
Seventeenth century	Realistic comedy
Eighteenth century	Comedy of manners
	Sentimental
Nineteenth century	Burlesque
	Operetta

The following discussion looks at each of these comic forms.

Romantic Comedy

The plot in a romantic comedy revolves around a love story with a happy ending. Shakespeare's *As You Like It* is a notable example. A peculiar characteristic of the romantic comedy is that the heroine often will pretend (for whatever reason) that she is a man. An interesting reversal on the convention is the trend in the modern romantic comedy to have the hero mask as a woman, as in *Tootsie* and *Mrs. Doubtfire*.

Realistic Comedy

A reaction that began late in the sixteenth century against romantic comedy, realistic comedy is based on real life, usually in London, and is characterized by a cynical tone and extensive use of satire. An example is Ben Jonson's *The Alchemist*. Jonson also joined George Chapman to introduce a new form of realistic comedy called the *Comedy of Humours*. These plays focus on the humour or predominant character trait of the protagonist: melancholic, sanguine, choleric, and phlegmatic. (See the chart on pages 190–191.)

Comedy of Manners

The comedy of manners is a realistic form practiced during the Restoration (late seventeenth century) and then later for two revivals late in the eighteenth century and again late in the nineteenth century. The name indicates the subject: the contrived, self-conscious manners of society. The characters tend to be stereotypes, with heavy use of satire, clever dialogue, and forbidden, illicit love. The comedy of manners is also called *restoration comedy*.

Sentimental Comedy

Reacting to the immorality extant in the comedies of manners, this form came to be called "reformed comedy" that aimed to restore virtue to the comic stage. The result was a form steeped in sentimentality, with "perfect" heroes and contrived plots that destroyed the dramatic reality of the plays. *The Conscious Lovers* by Richard Steele is an example.

Burlesque

At the center of burlesque is difference—the difference between the style of the work and its subject, in other words, an elevated style for a base subject or a base style for an elevated subject. In drama, this form of comedy has many devices available, including song and dance routines and bawdy humor. An often cited example of burlesque in drama is *The Beggar's Opera* by John Gay.

Operetta

Operetta is also called the comic opera. These colorful musical productions, such as those of *Gilbert and Sullivan,* blend dialogue with singing in plots that are often romantic.

Other Forms of Comedy

Other forms of dramatic comedy include:

- ▶ **Comedy of Intrigue** (also called the *comedy of situation*) in which the twists and turns of the plot supersede the characters involved in the situations.
- ▶ **Farce-Comedies** in which farce (low comedy when the humor is based on the silliness of the situation) is central to the play. The characters generally are exaggerated stereotypes who get into unbelievable situations that often result in "slapstick" comedy. *Charlie's Aunt* by Brandon Thomas (1892) is a farce, and such sitcoms as *Three's Company* employ elements of farce comedy.
- ▶ **Court Comedies,** written for royal command performances, in which a clever style and light tone work together with a plot somewhat devoid of action and with elements of mythology and contrasting characterization.
- ▶ **Comedia dell'Arte** in which stock characters (historically played by Italian actors) were given a scenario or main idea of the plot and improvised the dialogue. Although Italian in origin, these improvisations greatly influenced Elizabethan dramatic comedy.
- ▶ **Satiric Comedy** in which satire is used to make ridiculous the root causes of social problems, particularly dysfunctional political policies, social customs, and contemporary thinking.

Tragicomedy

Both comic and tragic forms can properly include elements of the other, sometimes to the point that they are called **tragicomedy.** This form was used in Elizabethan and Jacobean England and is characterized by inclusion of both characters from the higher classes usually found in tragedy and characters from the lower classes found in comedy.

Also, there is the threat of inevitable tragedy but a plot line that ends with a victorious protagonist (often after some melodramatic turn of events). The tragicomedy as a dramatic form is attributed to Beaumont and Fletcher in the first decade of the seventeenth century. Killigrew's *The Prisoner* and Shakespeare's *The Winter's Tale* are both tragicomedies.

Other forms of drama can be classified as either tragedy or comedy. One example is the **chronicle play.** Based on sixteenth-century chronicles (historical records), these Elizabethan dramas were characterized by enactments of battles, funerals, and other historical events. Some incorporate the elements of the romantic comedy;

others are clearly tragedies. Yet a third group of chronicle plays, called the **history play**, is neither comic nor tragic. Perhaps the most famous examples of chronicle plays are based on *Chronicles of England, Scotland, and Ireland,* first published in 1578 by Raphael Holinshed and then revised in 1587. These revised chronicles became a major historical source for thirteen of Shakespeare's plays.

ENGLISH HISTORY AS SEEN IN SHAKESPEARE'S DRAMAS

Play	Covers	Play Written in
King John	1199–1216	ca. 1591
King Richard II	1398–1400	1595
King Henry IV, Part I	1402–1403	1597
King Henry IV, Part II	1403–1413	1598
King Henry V	1413–1422	1599
King Henry VI, Part I	1422–1453	ca. 1590
King Henry VI, Part II	1445–1455	ca. 1591
King Henry VI, Part III	1455–1471	ca. 1592
King Richard III	1471–1485	ca. 1593
King Henry VIII	1520–1544	1613

Also, based in part on Holinshed's *Chronicles* are Shakespeare's *King Lear, Cymbeline,* and *Macbeth.* According to Holinshed, Lear "was admitted ruler over the Britons in the year of the world 3105, at what time Joas reigned in Judah" and Cymbeline "was of the Britons made king after the decease of his father in the year of the world 3944, after the building of Rome 728, and before the birth of our Saviour 33."

Another form that can be tragedy or tragicomedy is the Restoration **heroic drama**. These attention-getting productions with settings in exotic places, such as Morocco, feature a hero torn between love and duty. Heroic dramas can include a sinister, evil male antagonist (a villain) who may be the father of the heroine and an equally evil female antagonist (a villainess) who tries to win the protagonist's affections. The dialogue is often in heroic couplets and overflowing with hyperbole.

The **interlude** (a type of play written in the fifteenth and sixteenth centuries) is part of the transition that drama underwent in form as it moved from the Church to the secular world and is significant to the development of realism in drama. These short, witty plays sometimes were simply a dialogue between two players. In Tudor England, they were performed at special banquets. Later *masques*—expensive spectacles or dramatic exhibitions in which the characters wore masks—were the court entertainment for Elizabeth I, James I, and Charles I. Ben Jonson eventually developed the *antimasque,* a comparatively uncivilized version in which low comedy and the grotesque were employed to contrast the elegance of the masque.

A form that is most often a comedy, the **melodrama** can also be an element in a tragedy. Melodrama means "a play with music" and was used in a period of English history when, during the nineteenth century, plays were allowed to be performed only in Patent Theaters (a monopoly) due to the Licensing Act, but musicals could be performed anywhere. By adding music and song, these dramas could be legally performed. Romantic and extreme in emotion, an argument could be made that the very early silent movies, characterized by the beautiful girl being tied to a railroad track by the evil villain who wants her land (greed) and her hand (in marriage) as a pianist performs live music to heighten the mood, are a form of melodrama.

Pantomime is drama acted out without words. These mixtures of drama and dance were popular in England in the 1700s but were especially enjoyed in Elizabethan drama as single episodes used for dramatic effect in spoken drama. This use is called the *dumb show*. The pantomime as a form survived into the twentieth century through silent films and such comedic actors as Charlie Chaplin and Red Skelton. Also, aspiring actors can be seen *miming for money* on street corners in major international cities.

Form Groups

In concluding this discussion of form, some attention needs to be given to the trends, movements, themes, and conventions (they are known by many different labels) that group certain works from prose, poetry, and drama together. Some examples include:

▶ **Pastoral Literature**   A life apart from the urban mainstream; rural setting; country people.
  Pastoral poems are poems about shepherds and rural life. Many were written between 1550 and 1750.
  Pastoral elegies are poems that use pastoral imagery to mourn a death.

Pastoral drama (also called pastoral plays) are plays that use shepherds and the conventions of pastoral poems. **Pastoral romance** uses shepherds and pastoral conventions in a long prose narrative (for example, *Rosalynde* by Thomas Lodge).

▶ **Literature of the Absurd**   Poems, prose, and plays that emphasize an existential sense of isolation, using such devices as black humor (morbid and grotesque humor) to show the writer's view of the absurdity of life.

▶ **Escape Literature**   Poems, prose, and plays with the main purpose to allow the reader to escape real life.

▶ **Genteel Tradition**   American poems, prose, and plays that stress conventional correctness.

▶ **History Literature**   Poems, prose, and plays based on history (prose forms can include historical fiction and historical novels).

▶ **Local Color Writing**   Predominately American poems, prose, and drama based on regionalisms, such as dialect, dress, geographical setting.

Questions to Apply the Literary Principles

Ask these questions to help you identify and understand form.

1. What organizing principles did the writer use?

2. How is the selection sequenced or ordered?

3. Is there any faulty reasoning present?

   ▶ If so, is it by the writer, the speaker, or a character?
   ▶ Is the faulty reasoning intentional or unintentional?
   ▶ Is it intended to mislead the reader or to reveal character?
   ▶ How does it affect the meaning?

4. If the selection is a narrative, how would you summarize the plot?

5. Into what genre(s) does the selection fit? Why?

6. If the selection is a poem, is there a significant rhyme scheme? Are there any variations in the rhyme scheme? Does this affect the meaning, tone, and so forth?

7. In a poem, what is the metrical scan? Are there any variations

in the rhythm? Does the rhythm affect the meaning, tone, and so forth?

8. What is the structure of the poem?

9. If the selection is a play, what is the plot development? What is the exciting force? What is the turning point?

Additional Points to Remember

▶ Be alert to the validity of the reasoning of a writer. Some things that are written are not valid, some things that are written are not true. You need to be able to distinguish:

1. valid arguments (logical conclusions based on true premises) from logical fallacies (errors in reasoning due to false premises or illogical consequences),

2. whether the invalidity of the faulty thinking is intentional or unintentional, and

3. whether the valid or invalid argument is the voice of the speaker or the voice of the writer and whether they agree.

Voice will be discussed in a later section, but at this point can you identify some of the more common logical fallacies you may encounter in literary selections? Whether they be persuasive speeches, powerful short stories, or expressive poems, logical fallacies are sometimes hidden (intentionally or unintentionally) within literary works. These fallacies might serve the purpose of the writer or they may reveal faulty thinking on his or her part. The presence of logical reasoning is form contributing to, shaping, and developing meaning. Logical fallacies are flaws (or misuses of organizing principles) in form that affect meaning.

Herbert Spencer (1820–1903)

In a discussion which took place at a reception at G. H. Lewes's, somebody asserted that everyone had written a tragedy. Lewes agreed with the statement, saying, 'Yes, everyone—even Herbert Spencer.'— 'Ah,' interposed Huxley, 'I know what the catastrophe would be—an induction killed by a fact.

A Validity Checklist

When reading a selection, look for

▶ **Consistency of thought**
▶ **Fairness**
▶ **Ambiguous thinking,** such as

1. Statements that have more than one meaning. (For example, "Several beautiful paintings are being hung in the lobby. Yours will be hung in the back office.") Regional dialects can sometimes be the source of these miscommunications.

2. Misuse of personification. (For example, "The company will have to take better care of its employees for me to work there." People within companies make policies to take care of people.)

3. Statements that are inappropriate in their context. (For example, a heavy-set lady is shopping and the clerk says, "That dress does *wonders* for your shape!") Note that when such statements are made intentionally, they can create a form of verbal irony.

4. Changing meanings of words. (Alice: He certainly is calm and collected about raising money for his rent. Jayne: He's collected, alright, from Moris, and Jules, and from me!)

5. Assumptions that if something is true of the whole, then it is also true of the parts, or that something true of the parts can be generalized to the whole. (For example, "*The Pizza Dilly* is a great pizza place, so we will get the pizza we ordered delivered on time." Even "great" places can have an occasional late delivery. Also consider, "The pizza has extra of my favorite cheese, so it will be delicious." What if the crust is burned?)

▶ **Misrepresentations of the facts** (distortions), such as

1. Assuming a premise is true without proof

2. Taking words out of context

3. Exaggerating a statement out of context

4. Diverting attention from the real issue by introducing a false issue

5. Calling names or attacking the credibility of a person

6. Making generalizations based on assumptions or on too little evidence

7. Asking a "loaded question" that just by answering implies guilt ("Have you stopped stealing from your neighbor?")

8. Establishing double standards through using connotatively charged words (Why is one person called "thrifty" or "frugal," but another is called "cheap" or "tight" with money, when both exhibit the same spending habits?)

9. Comparing dissimilar things as though they are similar

10. Omitting facts or ignoring alternatives

11. Presenting coincidence as a cause-and-effect relationship

12. Attempting to influence the reader through a sense of pity, ignorance, fear, expertise, or some other emotion, all based on false or misleading information

13. Stereotyping

14. Oversimplifying

Remember:

▶ Sometimes faulty reasoning is for the purpose of misleading the reader.
▶ Sometimes these errors in reasoning, however, are made by people within a story or by a speaker other than the writer—thus revealing character.

▶ Some writers use elements of one genre as literary devices within another. For example, autobiography is a nonfiction account of a person's own life, but in the novel *Moll Flanders,* Defoe uses autobiography as a literary device. Some fiction novels are actually autobiographical. Also, the diary has been used as a literary device in fiction.

▶ Watch for literary works that lie in a gray area between fiction and nonfiction. For example, historical fiction or historical novel is *fiction* that has historical people, places, and events interwoven. Also, watch for fictional biography, autobiographical fiction, *Roman à Clef* (a novel about real people but written as though it were fiction—such as Hemingway's *The Sun Also Rises*), and the nonfiction novel (Truman Capote's *In Cold Blood* or Karen Blixen's, a.k.a. Isak Dinesen's, *Out of Africa*).

▶ When reading a selection, be sure to establish clearly the main plot of a narrative. For example, in a framework story, there is a story within another story. An example might be a group of girls camping out and telling ghost stories around the camp fire. Each ghost story is a narrative "framed" by the narrative of the girls telling the stories.

The significance of the frame to the intent and effect of the work can vary. It might be used as a reason to tell the ghost stories or perhaps one main ghost story told by the eldest girl. Or it may become the main plot of the selection if the girls go on to have experiences beyond just telling stories—for example, an attack by a bear, an encounter with Africanized ("killer") bees, or a visit by an uninvited guest, such as a skunk. Some famous frame-tales can be found in the writings of Joseph Conrad. (Also, Mark Twain's "Jim Baker's Blue Jay Yarn.")

Another structural device used by fiction writers is the subplot. A subplot is a less important plot working within the structure of the main plot. Some work with the main plot, and others are to some degree independent of it. Also, be aware that some writers may have multiple subplots working throughout the main plot.

▶ Watch for use of the term **argument** in a multiple sense. Argumentation is commonly known as one of the four modes of writing (exposition, narration, description, and argumentation). Argumentation aims to convince the reader, and when the argument is flawed (either by inaccuracy in fact or form), the error is called a **fallacy**. *Argument* also refers to using either authority or syllogisms and analogies to prove whether a proposition is true or false. But Shakespeare and Milton used the word *argument* to refer to the theme of a literary work.

▶ Use these questions to differentiate **realism, farce**, and **fantasy.**

Form	Can it happen?	Does it ever happen?
Realism	yes	yes
Farce	yes	no
Fantasy	no	no

▶ When you see **triple rhyme** in a poem, often the tone will be satirical and/or humorous rather than serious.

▶ Poems with **sprung rhythm** are a special challenge to scanning. Sprung rhythm allows only single-stressed syllables (monosyllabic), the trochee, the dactyl, and the first *paeon* (one stressed syllable followed by three unstressed syllables) because the rhythm is based only on the number of stressed syllables per line and not on the number of unstressed syllables. The advantages? It produces a rhythm very close to natural speech rhythms. The disadvantages? Sprung rhythm in *very* difficult to scan. For example, you might want to research the poems of Gerard Manley Hopkins, the poet who coined the term *sprung rhythm*. Be sure to look at the rhythm of "Pied Beauty" by Hopkins:

Pied Beauty

Glory be to God for dappled things—
  For skies of couple-color as a brinded cow;
    For rose-moles all in stipple upon trout that
    swim;
Fresh-firecoal chestnut-falls; finches' wings;
  Landscape plotted and pieced—fold, fallow, and
  plow;
    And all trades, their gear and tackle and trim.
All things counter, original, spare, strange;
  Whatever is fickle, freckled (who knows how?)
    With swift, slow; sweet, sour; adazzle, dim;
  He fathers-forth whose beauty is past change:
              Praise him.

by Gerard Manley Hopkins

▶ Be especially alert in identifying "I" in a lyric poem. The speaker—even in a poem written in the first person—may not be the poet, but rather be an invented character.

▶ Remember that the focus in a *dramatic monologue* is on the speaker's unintentional revealment of his or her character. If the poem is a *dramatic lyric,* however, the focus is on the speaker's argument rather than his or her temperament. An example of the dramatic monologue is Browning's "My Last Duchess." A dramatic lyric is John Donne's "The Flea."

▶ When you see the word *folk,* this is a clue that the literary work, usually a (folk-) ballad, drama, epic, lore, song, or tale, is (1) of unknown authorship and (2) the product of the oral tradition.

▶ Do not be confused by the term *folklore.* **Folklore** was not used as a literary term until the nineteenth century, and it refers to many different genres that include a people's traditions. These traditions, of course, are filled with both customs and beliefs, traditions and rituals. As a result, they have given rise to innumerable formula plots, conventions, motifs, and literary traditions.

Folklore includes (to name a few):

popular ballads	riddles
cowboy songs	nursery rhymes
stories	legends

▶ Do not confuse the **ballad** (a narrative song) with the **ballade**—a French verse form that was used to a limited extent by Chaucer; however, the form was never used extensively in English poetry.

▶ There is some controversy among critics concerning the roles of **parody** and **burlesque.** Some see parody as a variety of high burlesque, but other critics see parody as literary opposite to burlesque in that a parody mocks style by keeping the writing in the target style but selecting a "silly" subject. Burlesque, on the other hand, lowers the style. Parody is, then, a form of travesty (ridicule of a subject by a mismatch of style with topic). Once travesty is so defined, burlesque is cited as the travesty of a literary form; parody is the travesty of a specific work.

▶ Although many use *plot* and *story* interchangeably, there is a difference between the two. A **story** is the narration of events according to their *sequence in time*. A **plot,** on the other hand, is a narration of events with emphasis on causal relationships.

▶ In drama, pivotal plot elements occur at certain points. The exposition most often is in the beginning—the first scene of the first act. Also, you may be able to pinpoint the conflict and the exciting force during the first act. If the crisis or turning point happens at the end of the next to the last act (as is sometimes but not always the case), then the falling action and resolution will play out in the final act. The acts previous to the turning point will consist of rising action with a series of complications. These complications or points of dramatic impact will often be placed just at the end of each act because structurally this heightens their effectiveness in keeping the plot moving and in holding the audience's attention. Consequently, read the last one or two pages of script at the closing of each act carefully. These portions of dialogue may contain important revelations of character, theme, and uses of the other literary elements.

CHAPTER

Principle Three:
Listen for Voice and Tone

George Meredith (1828–1909)

Robert Louis Stevenson numbers *The Egoist* among the books which have most powerfully influenced him, and owns to having read it seven or eight times. 'Meredith read me some chapters', he says, 'before it was published, and at last I could stand it no longer. I interrupted him, and said, "Now, Meredith, own up—you have drawn Sir Willoughby Patterne from me!" Meredith laughed, and said, "No, no, my dear fellow, I've taken him from all of us, but principally from myself."'

Voice

Narrative voice, in its most narrow sense, is who is telling the story. But narrative voice in action is far more than just the "narrator," and if you take away the restrictions implicit in the word *narrative,* you will find the fascinating world of voice, a place of illusion where the speaker may not be quite who or what he or she seems.

Voice in Prose

Before discussing the impact of differentiating the speaker from the writer, and the significance of the speaker's attitude, look at the foundation of narrative voice: point of view and how point of view can relate to the characterization of the narrator.

Point of View

Also called the *focus* of a narrative, point of view refers not only to who is telling the story (in other words, the narrator), but also to how the narrator relates to the story in terms of the action of the plot and how much he or she knows about what is going on both in the story and in the minds of the characters in the story.

Pretend that the "world" of a story is represented by this illustration:

[   ]

[The world of the   ]   The world outside

[narrative   ]   the narrative

[   ]

The place, time, characters, and events of the story all exist within the world of the narrative. The world outside the narrative is where the readers exist. The narrator, then, stands between the readers and the story; and his or her aim is to tell a story, to describe the characters and events as they move around within the confines of the world of the narrative while the reader watches and listens.

How does the narrator do this? There are several ways. The narrator might tell the story from a **third person limited** (also called limited omniscient, centered, or central consciousness) point of view. This type of story is written using third person pronouns (*he, she, they, him, her, them*) and is evidenced by such narrative constructions as "He said this or that" or "She walked to the fireplace." The third person narrator is telling the story from out-side the world of the characters. The narrator describes what goes on in that narrative world. Also, the narrator is able to tell readers the thoughts, opinions, motives, and inner feelings of *one* of the characters in the story, someone who often is the main char-acter or protagonist of the story. Suppose the major characters are Pam, Bob, and Sue, with Sue being the main character. The fol-lowing illustration places Sue at the focus point in the narrative world:

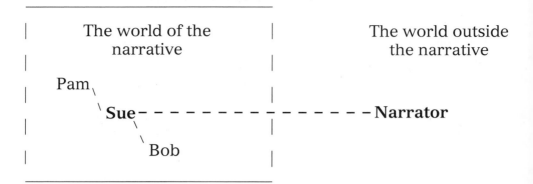

The world of the narrative | The world outside the narrative

Pam

Sue - - - - - - - - - - - - - - - - - Narrator

Bob

The narrator, who is not a character in the story, tells readers what Bob and Pam do and say (generally as these elements relate to Sue), but more importantly he or she tells *about* Sue—her consciousness—to the point that readers form some sense that they can "understand" her or perhaps even relate to her. You learn (through the narrator sharing Sue's thoughts, opinions, and feelings with readers) how she is dealing with the relationships and events that affect her and how she perceives the world around her. You see the other characters through her eyes.

Now examine the following selection. As you read, try to identify the main character and how the narrator treats her differently from the other characters.

> The dig site was almost two kilometers uphill from the camp, and the heat of the climb left all but the most athletic wishing the terrain had allowed them to set up camp closer.
>
> Salbro's tone left no doubt, though, that he would not tolerate any delays; and they were soon on their feet again and huddled like a football team around their coach. Only Rana stood slightly out of formation, her attention divided between Salbro's instructions and the mesmerizing mystery that was half buried in the pit just a few yards away. Guido, standing next to Rana, took advantage of the opportunity and swung his red bandana to wipe the sweat from his forehead. The abrupt motion caused Salbro to look in their direction just as Rana's gaze had left their leader's face to rest upon the pit.
>
> "Ms. Matten," Salbro's voice assumed the edge he used when irritated, "would you care to review for us the instructions that I have just given?"

Of course she couldn't. Salbro knew she couldn't. She looked in his eyes for some hint of compassion, but didn't find any. Then she caught Guido's triumphant look as he shifted his body slightly ahead of her, once again gaining Salbro's attention with perfect timing.

"Mr. Joyce, would you review the instructions for Ms. Matten since it seems that she has obviously weightier matters on her mind?"

Rana had no doubts about Guido's intentions concerning her and her place on the team, but each time his animosity surfaced, she still experienced a moment of "but what in the world did I ever do to him"-type confusion. She watched his face as he droned on about procedures for using brushes to remove the loose matrix from the fossil and the established stabilizing methods for the more fragile portions.

A few minutes later as they stood looking down into the dig site, Rana began to reconsider her impatience with Salbro over careful instructions. There before her were the remains of Pterosauria *Quetzalcoatlus,* the giant flying reptile of the Upper Cretaceous period. Even looking from above, she could see places where the bones of its almost forty-foot wingspan were either missing or still buried. Yet she could also see why Salbro was so excited with this rare find. The fossilized skeleton, with its wings stretched out and head intact, was a prize of unbelievable proportions.

Standing at the edge of the pit, Rana leaned forward, trying to adjust her eyes to the glaring sunlight that washed over stone, dirt, and skeleton to make a monochromatic sea of tan. Then the stone under her left foot broke loose, landing her in a heap of dust and dirt just inches away from the fossilized head.

She looked up to see Salbro's face, at first pale but now flushing to a bright red. There was no doubt in her mind that this time her position on the team was in serious jeopardy. But what she didn't expect was the intensity of her own anger when she spotted Guido's smug face looking down at her.

(Selection written by author)

The narrator tells the reader:

► What Rana, Salbro, and Guido do and (to a certain extent) say.
► What Rana thinks and feels.
► What Salbro thinks *as perceived by Rana* ("Salbro knew she couldn't. She looked in his eyes for some hint of compassion, but didn't find any.")
► What Guido thinks *as perceived by Rana* (". . . she caught Guido's triumphant look . . . .")

The technique of the narrator in literary narrative revealing the main character's thoughts was affected in the late nineteenth century by psychologist William James. Based on the earlier thinking of Alexander Bain, he put forth the concept of **stream of consciousness,** the flow of thoughts that people experience, thoughts that range from the unintelligible to the very rational and well-articulated. By the turn of the century, works began to include long passages in which the main characters engage in lengthy passages of introspection. Stream-of-consciousness techniques have been used well into the twentieth century. One such technique is the *interior monologue* in which the main character's thoughts are reported as they occur—often in vague terms with sometimes (but not always) illogical order and a lack of grammatical clarity.

Both James Joyce and William Faulkner used stream-of-consciousness techniques in their writings. Here is a sample from Faulkner's short story, "Barn Burning."

> They were running a middle buster now, his brother holding the plow straight while he handled the reins, and walking beside the straining mule, the rich black soil shearing cool and damp against his bare ankles, he thought *Maybe this is the end of it. Maybe even that twenty bushels that seems hard to have to pay for just a rug will be a cheap price for him to stop forever and always from being what he used to be;* thinking, dreaming now, so that his brother had to speak sharply to him to mind the mule:
> *Maybe he even won't collect the twenty bushels. Maybe it will all add up and balance and vanish— corn, rug, fire; the terror and grief, the being pulled two ways like between two teams of horses—gone, done with for ever and ever.*

Another third person point of view is the **third person unlimited** (also called omniscient) point of view, in which the narrator knows everything about everyone in every situation and feels free to reveal this information at will to the reader.

The world of the narrative	The world outside the narrative
Bob– – – – – – – – – – – – – – – –＼	
Sue – – – – – – – – – – – – – – Narrator	
Pam– – – – – – – – – – – –／	

You no longer need to rely upon Sue's observations; the narrator can directly reveal the thoughts, motives, and actions of Pam and Bob.

Another popular stance of the narrator is called **first person point of view.**

The world of the narrative	The world outside the narrative
Bob– – – – –＼ (Bill)	
Sue – – – Narrator	
Pam– – – – –／	

The first person narrator might be the main character, one of the minor characters, or simply an observer. Written in the first person "I," the readers can easily identify with the person telling the story and eventually become a part of the narrative. But when the narrator is also one of the characters, readers are *limited* in their view of the narrative world (in others words, the "world" of the characters in the story) to one as seen by an active participant in that world. This view, however, is one that generally has a heightened sense of both realism and sometimes (but not always) credibility.

Characterization of the Narrator

Regardless of the point of view used, the narrator can be *characterized* in several other ways. Sometimes the narrator is **self-conscious,** one who deliberately allows the reader to know that the work is a fictional account or goes so far as to point out the elements of narration at work. Read as an example this first paragraph of *The Posthumous Papers of the Pickwick Club* by Charles Dickens:

> . . . the earlier history of the public career of the immortal Pickwick would appear to be involved, is derived from the perusal of the following entry in the Transactions of the Pickwick Club, which the editor of these papers feels the highest pleasure in laying before his readers, . . .

The narrator points to himself as "the editor of these papers"—in the third person addressing "his readers."

Also, note in the first paragraph of *Oliver Twist,* how the narrator refers to the writing process:

> Among other public buildings in a certain town, which for many reasons it will be prudent to refrain from mentioning, and to which I will assign no fictitious name, there is one anciently common to most towns, great or small: to wit, a workhouse; and in this workhouse was born: on a day and date which I need not trouble myself to repeat, inasmuch as it can be of no possible consequence to the reader, in this stage of the business at all events: the item of mortality whose name is prefixed to the head of this chapter.

These paragraphs are found near the end of *Oliver Twist,* in which the narrator talks of "this tale" and describes his writing of the conclusion:

The fortunes of those who have figured in this tale are nearly closed. The little that remains to their historian to relate, is told in few and simple words.

... ...

And now, the hand that traces these words, falters, as it approaches the conclusion of its task: and would weave, for a little longer space, the thread of these adventures.

What is the effect of a self-conscious narrator on the reader? Because the narrator sometimes "lets us in" on the structural and more intimate aspects of telling the story (such as confessing that "the hand that traces these words, falters"), the reader is very likely to develop a bond with the narrator, an association that oftentimes increases a sense of confidence in the narrator's credibility as a witness of the events of the story. Readers tend to take for granted that the accounts, opinions, observations, and conclusions of the narrator are accurate and true.

Although readers may have a tendency to believe that the narrator is *always* credible and correct in his or her opinions, this assumption may not always be the case. Sometimes the narrator has an erroneous understanding of the situation. Take, as an example, works in which the narrator is the main character and you must rely upon his or her perspective. In such cases, the main character, through whose eyes you see the world of the story, may have a distorted view of things—is perhaps naive, too self-confident, mentally unstable, or even immature. Such a narrator is *characterized* as **unreliable** or **fallible.** An example is Huck Finn in the *Adventures of Huckleberry Finn.* Henry James makes extended use of the unreliable narrator, especially in some of his short stories and in *The Turn of the Screw.*

In addition, a narrator can be *characterized* as either **intrusive** or as **unintrusive** (objective, impersonal). As the name implies, the intrusive narrator gives opinions concerning the words and deeds, the personalities and motives, and the events and circumstances at work in the story. Sometimes these comments will even take the form of an essay that engages in "editorializing," and his or her comments are generally regarded as truthful or reliable.

Notice how the narrator interjects his opinions in this excerpt from *Oliver Twist:*

Although I am not disposed to maintain that the being born in a workhouse, is in itself the most fortunate and enviable circumstance that can possibly befall a human being, I do mean to say that in this particular instance, it was the best thing for Oliver Twist that could by possibility have occurred. The fact is, that there was considerable difficulty in inducing Oliver to take upon himself the office of respiration,—a troublesome practice, but one which custom has rendered necessary to our easy existence; and for some time he lay gasping on a little flock mattress, rather unequally poised between this world and the next: the balance being decidedly in favour of the latter. Now, if, during this brief period, Oliver has been surrounded by careful grandmothers, anxious aunts, experienced nurses, and doctors of profound wisdom, he would most inevitably and indubitably have been killed in no time. There being nobody by, however, but a pauper old woman, who was rendered rather misty by an unwonted allowance of beer; and a parish surgeon who did such matters by contract; Oliver and Nature fought out the point between them. The result was, that, after a few struggles, Oliver breathed, sneezed, and proceeded to advertise to the inmates of the workhouse the fact of a new burden having been imposed upon the parish, by setting up as loud a cry as could reasonably have been expected from a male infant who had not been possessed of that very useful appendage, a voice, for a much longer space of time than three minutes and a quarter.

The unintrusive narrator is quite the opposite of the intrusive; he or she reports without personal comment the words and deeds of the characters in the context of the events of the story. Is there such a thing as a totally unintrusive narrator? Possibly not. The connotative values of word choices alone reflect a certain degree of personal opinion; however, when the narrator refrains from direct statements of opinion and at least attempts the straightforward telling of the story, you can (perhaps with reservation) *characterize* him or her as unintrusive. Look to some of Ernest Hemingway's short stories for examples of the unintrusive narrator.

Until this point, you have examined briefly the *characterization* of the narrator or speaker including:

▶ From what point of view (first person or third person) the story is being told

▶ To what degree the narrator knows the minds of the characters (third person limited or third person unlimited narrator)

▶ To what extent the narrator is self-conscious, pointing out his or her role in telling the story

▶ To what degree the narrator is seen as a credible witness (ranging from the usually very credible self-conscious narrator to the not credible unreliable narrator)

▶ To what degree the narrator gives his or her opinions (intrusive or unintrusive narrators)

The role of the author or writer of the story, however, also needs to be considered.

The Speaker or the Author—Whose Voice?

Narrative writers must, in addition to determining from what point of view the story is to be told, decide what method(s) they will use to present the various parts of the narrative (presentation of the setting, the action, and the dialogue). Two of the more common means writers employ are the *panoramic method* and the *scenic method.*

Panoramic Method

In the panoramic method, the writer summarizes conversations and events by using exposition. Here is an isolated excerpt from George Eliot's (a.k.a. Mary Anne Evans's) *Middlemarch:*

> These peculiarities of Dorothea's character caused Mr. Brooke to be all the more blamed in neighbouring families for not securing some middleaged lady as guide and companion to his nieces. But he himself dreaded so much the sort of superior woman likely to be available for such a position, that he allowed himself to be dissuaded by Dorothea's objections, and was in this case brave enough to defy the world—that is to say, Mrs. Cadwallader the Rector's wife, and the small group of gentry with whom he visited in the north-east corner of Loamshire. So Miss Brooke presided in her uncle's household, and did not at all dislike her new authority, with the homage that belonged to it.

Some elements of the panoramic method used in the preceding paragraph include:

▶ The writer tells the reader that Mr. Brooke is criticized by his neighbor, rather than allowing the reader to "listen in on" the neighbors actually discussing the issue.

▶ The reader is told that Dorothea objected to a guide and influenced Mr. Brooke, but their conversation is not included.

▶ The reader learns that Mr. Brooke defied the Rector's wife; however, the reader does not see the encounter or hear their words.

▶ The writer tells the reader that Miss Brooke likes her position ("Miss Brooke . . . did not at all dislike her new authority . . ."—a use of language called *litotes*, when understatement results from negative affirmation—"did not dislike" means that she "did like") but does not convey to the reader any scenes (actions and direct dialogue) to demonstrate the point.

Rather than reporting the actual words and actions of Dorothea, Mr. Brooke, the neighbors, and the Rector's wife, the writer summarizes the conversations and events for the reader.

Scenic Method

In contrast is the **scenic method**. In its pure form, the **self-effacing author** is one whose existence is totally unrealized by the reader because the story is told objectively, using the *scenic method*. The effect of the scenic method is very dramatic as the author (writer) typically describes the setting and perhaps presents an insightful look into the inner mind of the main character and then launches directly into action and dialogue (like scenes in a play) to tell the story. The scenic method is employed in *The Portrait of a Lady* by Henry James (an often-cited example) and is used in various forms by writers yet today, such as Payne Harrison's *Thunder of Erebus*.

This conversation between two sisters has scenic elements at work in the following excerpt taken from *Middlemarch* by George Eliot:

> **. . . It was no great collection, but a few of the ornaments were really of remarkable beauty, the finest that was obvious at first being a necklace of**

purple amethysts set in exquisite gold-work, and a pearl cross with five brilliants in it. Dorothea immediately took up the necklace and fastened it round her sister's neck, where it fitted almost as closely as a bracelet; but the circle suited the Henrietta-Maria style of Celia's head and neck, and she could see that it did, in the pier-glass opposite.

'There, Celia! you can wear that with your Indian muslin. But this cross you must wear with your dark dresses.'

Celia was trying not to smile with pleasure. 'O Dodo, you must keep the cross yourself.'

'No, no, dear, no,' said Dorothea, putting up her hand with careless deprecation.

'Yes, indeed you must; it would suit you—in your black dress, now,' said Celia, insistingly. 'You *might* wear that.'

'Not for the world, not for the world. A cross is the last thing I would wear as a trinket.' Dorothea shuddered slightly.

'Then you will think it wicked in me to wear it,' said Celia, uneasily.

'No, dear, no,' said Dorothea, stroking her sister's cheek. 'Souls have complexions too: what will suit one will not suit another.'

'But you might like to keep it for mamma's sake.'

'No, I have other things of mamma's—her sandalwood box, which I am so fond of—plenty of things. In fact, they, are all yours, dear. We need discuss them no longer. There—take away your property.'

Celia felt a little hurt. There was a strong assumption of superiority in this Puritanic toleration, hardly less trying to the blond flesh of an unenthusiastic sister than a Puritanic persecution.

'But how can I wear ornaments if you, who are the elder sister, will never wear them?'

'Nay, Celia, that is too much to ask, that I should wear trinkets to keep you in countenance. If I were to put on such a necklace as that, I should feel as if I had been pirouetting. The world would go round with me, and I should not know how to walk.'

The dialogue and action are self-explanatory. In the scenic method, the writer "fades" into the background as the dynamic dialogue and action move the story from scene to scene, allowing the reader to be swept along by the story and to forget the author's existence.

Had the author wanted to write the previous dialogue in the panoramic method, he might have written: "After a minor quarrel with Celia, Dorothea refused to wear her mother's cross necklace."

Many times literary narrative, especially lengthy novels, will use both methods (scenic and panoramic), depending upon the effect desired by the writer and by the confines dictated by the plot. For instance, when action is a significant element, when a rapid exchange of conversation will intensify the story, elements of the scenic method are vital. What if, however, the story is spanning three generations of a family as they migrate from Europe to America, living through significant historical events, personal triumphs, and tragedies? Can every important event and meaningful coversation be reported like scenes in a play? Obviously, works of such magnitude sometimes *require* the author to summarize events and conversations, to use the panoramic method.

Establishing that the author (writer) can elect to use scenic and/or panoramic methods to present a narrative is an important first step to understanding some of the essential structural decisions that face a writer. Another very important decision that a writer must make is to decide on a narrator or speaker. (Some literary critics use the terms *narrator* and *speaker* interchangeably, but others prefer to reserve *speaker* to refer to the one speaking in a nonnarrative work.)

Some readers mistakenly assume that the author (writer) and the narrator (speaker) are the same. This is not always the case. Sometimes the author and narrator are the same, but at other times they are two distinctly different voices. When the narrative is in the first person, with a character being the one telling the story as the narrator or speaker, identifying the voice of the writer as different from that of the narrator can be very difficult.

The story world can be used to illustrate on a very basic level and to build, step by step, a basis for this distinction. Suppose the story is a first person narrative actually being told by the person who is living the events. This autobiographical story is told live as the events happen—as a news reporter does at the scene of an ongoing news story. The present tense adds a tone of excitement. The story might include elements of stream-of-consciousness writing, also. Here is Elaine's account of being trapped in a burning building:

> **I hope this microphone is still working and I'm still on the air** . . .

I am looking at the locked door. I can almost see how hot it must be! If I try to touch it, I'll get burned. The fire is raging on the other side. Jayne is screaming for someone to unlock the door. Smoke is choking me—my eyes are smarting with thick black fumes that blanket my head. I hear Roel calling my name. . . .

(illustration written by author)

"I" (Elaine) is the narrator, the main character, and (because this is an autobiographical story), the author.

The world of the narrative	The world outside the story
Elaine the **narrator, character, and author** Jayne Roel	

Now look at the difference a simple change in verb tense can make. Once again suppose this is a real-life event that happens to Elaine; however, rather than telling the story as it happens, she waits until the fire trucks leave and writes her story for broadcast much later—perhaps the next day:

I tried the microphone, but it wouldn't work. I looked at the locked door. I could almost see how hot it must have been. If I had tried to touch it, I would have gotten burned. The fire was raging on the other side. Jayne was screaming for someone to unlock the door. Smoke was choking me—my eyes smarted with the thick fumes that blanketed my head. I heard Roel calling my name.

The main character is still Elaine, but what about the narrator and author? In the first account, the narrator and author are Elaine *as she lived the experience.* In the second account, the author is Elaine *after the experience,* taking the role of a narrator telling about herself as a character at a previous time.

A story can be told by a participant from his or her perspective while it is happening; however, as soon as time elapses, the story can be retold only as an account in which the participant has a dual role: first as the person who was in the story and second as the narrator who is now outside of the world (the time and place) in which the events occurred. Where should Elaine appear on the illustration in her role as narrator? Who is telling the story?

The world of the narrative	The world outside the story
Elaine the character Jayne	Elaine the author and narrator (remembering the events)
Roel	

Now that a distinction has been established between the character and the author/narrator in a first person account, the illustration can be taken one step further. Suppose that Sally Smith, as an author, wrote the account of the events of the fire, placing Elaine Brown as a major character in the story. Elaine Brown is the main character narrating the story (written in the first person); however, Sally Smith is the author:

The world of the narrative	The world outside the story
Jayne Elaine Brown the character and narrator Roel	Sally Smith the author

Because the story is in first person, you might easily assume that the character/narrator's words, thoughts, and actions ("I thought this or I did that . . .") are also the words, thoughts, and actions of the author or writer of the story. Because Sally Smith (author) is writing the words and actions of Elaine Brown (character), those words and actions (whether in past or present tense) are those of a character in the story, however, and may or may not reflect Sally Smith's opinions, even though they are written in the first person. The narrator and the author are two different voices. This forms the basis for distinguishing *between the narrator (speaker) and the writer.* Unlike television talk shows, however, in which the program ends with an announcement that "The views expressed by the guests on this program are not necessarily those of this station or its management," distinguishing in a first person narrative the voice of the author from that of the character who narrates the story can only be accomplished through examining context and the particulars of the account.

Sometimes the speaker and the author can arguably be viewed as the same voice. For example, in Charles Dickens' *David Copperfield* (a story that Dickens based on some of his own life experiences and in which he expresses many of his own personal views), Dickens has written in the first person:

> **Whether I shall turn out to be the hero of my own life, or whether that station will be held by anybody else, these pages must show. To begin my life with the beginning of my life, I record that I was born (as I have been informed and believe) on a Friday, at twelve o'clock at night. It was remarked that the clock began to strike, and I began to cry, simultaneously.**

So in this story Dickens is the author, David is the main character, and David is the speaker who tells the story using the first person pronoun "I" as if he is the author. David is Dickens's **persona**; in other words, he is a character who narrates the story for the author. As Dickens's persona, David the narrator and Dickens the author have the same voice.

In other situations the speaker and author do not share the same voice. Read carefully the following excerpt from "A Modest Proposal," written in 1729 by Jonathan Swift at a time when landowners were turning deaf ears to the suffering of homeless Irish who were victims of a three-year drought.

> **It is a melancholy object to those who walk through this great town or travel in the country,**

when they see the streets, the roads, and cabin doors, crowded with beggars of the female sex, followed by three, four, or six children, all in rags and importuning every passenger for an alms. . . .

I think it is agreed by all parties that this prodigious number of children . . . is in the present deplorable state of the kingdom a very great additional grievance; and therefore whoever could find out a fair, cheap, and easy method of making these children sound, useful members of the commonwealth would deserve so well of the public as to have his statue set up for a preserver of the nation.

. . .

As to my own part, having turned my thoughts for many years upon this important subject, . . . it is exactly at one year that I propose to provide for them in such a manner as instead of being a charge upon their parents or the parish, . . . they shall on the contrary contribute to the feeding, and partly to the clothing, of many thousands.

. . .

I am assured by our merchants that a boy or a girl before twelve years old is no salable commodity; and even when they come to this age they will not yield above three pounds, or three pound and half a crown at most on the Exchange; which cannot turn to account either to the parents or the kingdom, the charge of nutriment and rags having been at least four times that value.

I shall now therefore humbly propose my own thoughts, which I hope will not be liable to the least objection.

I have been assured by a very knowing American of my acquaintance in London, that a young healthy child well nursed is at a year old a most delicious, nourishing, and wholesome food, whether stewed, roasted, baked, or boiled; and I make no doubt that it will equally serve in a fricassee or a ragout . . . .

Swift is the author; "I" is the speaker. Does this speaker, however, represent Swift's true opinions? Obviously not. Note the shocking nature of the speaker's proposal, particularly when he exposes his "plan" for turning children into a food source in the last paragraph of the excerpt, a totally alien concept to any civilized people. The writer might have directly said, "you are allowing these children to starve and to be treated like animals," but would such direct words have had the attention-getting effect and the same shame-producing impact that his proposal elicits? In the case of "A Modest Proposal," the author and the speaker do not share the same voice.

This illustration is an example of the **naive narrator,** a character who narrates in the first person as if he or she is the author, but whose opinions, actions, or thoughts are so naive or so obtuse (as in this case) that they ironically make the point of the author. If the naive narrator is a child whose simplicity of thought could conceivably end in tragedy, however, the result might be pathos rather than irony.

As you can see, then, even in a first person narrative, there is the voice of the speaker and the voice of the author. In other words, the first person speaker/narrator can be a *persona* of the writer/author, a persona who *may or may not* project the experiences or views of the author. Sometimes the difference is easy to recognize, as when the story is the first person account of a ten-year-old girl's experiences training a horse on a New Mexico ranch, and the story is written by a middle-aged male literature professor living in central New York. But sometimes the difference is not so easily distinguished.

The difference between the voice of the speaker and the voice of the author is no less important to address in the third person narrative than in the first person account. Because the story is told in the third person ("he said," "she said"), the "sense" of the author and the speaker might easily become blurred into one voice, especially when the narrator is omniscient. Wayne C. Booth's concept of the **implied author**—that author who is an imaginary, idealized person whose existence is sensed by the reader from the work as a whole—as opposed to the real author—who is not as "ideal" as the implied author—is important to keep in mind at this point. In a third person narrative, the potential exists for there to be three "different" voices: (1) the main character's thoughts and actions, (2) the opinions and perspectives of the narrator who is telling the story, and (3) the personal opinion and structural concerns of the author.

To summarize, there are three different voices at work in a narrative: the writer/author, the speaker/narrator, and the character. For example, in the narrative voice structure in the *Sherlock Holmes* mysteries of Sir Authur Conan Doyle, you will find:

Doyle—the author/writer
Dr. Watson—the speaker/narrator, a character in the story
and *persona* for Doyle
Holmes—the main character

The world of the narrative	The world outside the story
Watson character narrator	
Holmes main character	Sir Authur Doyle Author

When reading a passage from one of these mysteries, a relevant question might be (if, for example, the passage is Watson speaking), is this the voice of Dr. Watson, the persona for Doyle (the writer) speaking? (When the author creates a fictional character who writes the story or book, the device is called the **putative author.** Diedrick Knickerbocker is Washington Irving's putative author in *History of New York*.)

The Attitude of the Speaker

In examining such questions about narrative voice, one additional step must be taken—a step beyond just identifying whose voice is speaking—to determine what that voice is trying to say: *the attitude of the speaker*. Voice in this respect is an element in both narrative voice and in nonnarrative works. The difference in *the attitude of the speaker* (the voice of the speaker) and the attitude of the writer (the writer's voice) results in irony in Swift's essay, "The Modest Proposal" (an example of voice affecting a work to create an ironic tone). The main character or the speaker does not always voice the opinions of the author.

If the speaker is also the main character, then determining his or her voice *(the attitude of the speaker)* is important to character revelation.

Voice in Poetry

Another area in which determining the voice and *the attitude of the speaker* is important is in poetry, particularly in the lyric poem. Voice in narrative poetry has many of the same considerations as in its narrative prose form; however, voice in lyric poetry has some significant differences. As proposed by T.S. Eliot, voice in poetry encompasses three different perspectives: (1) the silent contemplations of the poet, (2) the meaning conveyed from the poet to the reader/hearer, and (3) the role of the persona that the poet uses in the poem.

As mentioned in the discussion of form, lyric poems are non-narrative works that express the speaker's feelings, state of mind, thoughts, and other expressions and are written generally in the first person. The usage of the first person "I" in the lyric poem does not necessarily mean that the poet is the speaker (just as the first person narrator of a story is not always the author). Although some argument can be made that the author's life cannot help but be reflected in the words of the lyric speaker, the temptation to overstate the case should be resisted in favor of recognizing the lyric speaker as part of the poem as a whole as the speaker addresses the situation to produce an effect.

The Dramatic Monologue

Perhaps this role of speaker can best be illustrated by looking closely at a type of lyric poem called the **dramatic monologue.** The characteristics of the dramatic monologue are

▶ A persona (called the lyric speaker and *not* referring to the poet) who expresses the lyric at some dramatic moment or in a situation
▶ A one-sided conversation in which the clues in the lyric reveal that this poem is part of a conversation addressed to someone, but only the lyric of the (persona) speaker can be heard—the others are *silent* auditors
▶ Revelation of the lyric speaker's character (usually unintentional) through what he or she says

This revelation of the lyric speaker's character demonstrates the significance of looking at voice from the perspective of the *speaker's attitude* to the meaning of a dramatic monologue. Bear in mind that very often the lyric speaker is a famous person—someone with whose life or circumstances the contemporary readers or hearers of the poem would have been expected to be familiar.

Read this often-referenced dramatic monologue by Robert Browning called "My Last Duchess." The lyric speaker is *not* Browning, but rather a sixth-century Italian duke named Alfonso II. He was married to a fourteen-year-old girl who died when she was just seventeen. Her death has been described as "suspicious"; however, Duke Alfonso went on to negotiate an arrangement to marry a member of Austrian royalty. He used an agent for these negotiations; that agent is the silent auditor to whom this lyric poem is addressed:

My Last Duchess
by
Robert Browning

line That's my last Duchess painted on the wall,
   Looking as if she were alive. I call
   That piece a wonder, now: Frà Pandolf's hands
   Worked busily a day, and there she stands.
(5) Will't please you sit and look at her? I said
   "Frà Pandolf" by design, for never read
   Strangers like you that pictured countenance,
   The depth and passion of its earnest glance,
   But to myself they turned (since none puts by
(10) The curtain I have drawn for you, but I)
   And seemed as they would ask me, if they durst,
   How such a glance came there; so, not the first
   Are you to turn and ask thus. Sir, 'twas not
   Her husband's presence only, called that spot
(15) Of joy into the Duchess' cheek: perhaps
   Frà Pandolf chanced to say "Her mantle laps
   Over my lady's wrist too much," or "Paint
   Must never hope to reproduce the faint
   Half-flush that dies along her throat": such stuff
(20) Was courtesy, she thought, and cause enough
   For calling up that spot of joy. She had
   A heart—how shall I say?—too soon made glad,
   Too easily impressed, she liked whate'er
   She looked on, and her looks went everywhere.
(25) Sir, 'twas all one! My favor at her breast,
   The dropping of the daylight in the West,
   The bough of cherries some officious fool
   Broke in the orchard for her, the white mule
   She rode with round the terrace—all and each

(30)   Would draw from her alike the approving speech,
Or blush, at least. She thanked men,—good! but
   thanked
Somehow—I know not how—as if she ranked
My gift of a nine-hundred-years-old name
With anybody's gift. Who'd stoop to blame
(35)   This sort of trifling? Even had you skill
In speech—which I have not—to make your will
Quite clear to such an one, and say, "Just this
Or that in you disgust me; here you miss,
Or there exceed the mark"—and if she let
(40)   Herself be lessoned so, nor plainly set
Her wits to yours, forsooth, and made excuse,
—E'en then would be some stooping; and I choose
Never to stoop. Oh sir, she smiled, no doubt,
Whene'er I passed her; but who passed without
(45)   Much the same smile? This grew; I gave commands
Then all smiles stopped together. There she stands
As if alive. Will't please you rise? We'll meet
The company below, then I repeat,
The Count your master's known munificence
(50)   Is ample warrant that no just pretense
Of mine for dowry will be disallowed;
Though his fair daughter's self, as I avowed
At starting, is my object. Nay, we'll go
Together down, sir. Notice Neptune, though,
(55)   Taming a sea-horse, thought a rarity,
Which Claus of Innsbruck cast in bronze for me!

Now, examine the poem to answer the following questions.

1. Can you distinguish between the speaker and the writer? The form (a dramatic monologue) dictates this distinction: the poet (Browning) has used a persona, a lyric speaker in the person of the Duke.

2. What in the poem reveals the speaker's attitude? Some lines are obvious; however, look for the more subtle hints at his character, for example, notice how easily he glides from the painting of his late wife to discussing another work of art—the bronze statue (lines 54–56).

3. Are there any clues to what Browning's attitude toward the Duke might be? Be sure to look for clues arising from the choice of words he had the Duke speak or from the elements of character Browning (the poet) chose to have this lyric speaker reveal.

4. Finally, what role does the silent auditor serve here? Notice lines 1, 5–7, 12–13, 35–41 (Is "you" referring specifically to the silent auditor—the marriage agent to whom he is speaking?), and 51–52.

As you examine poems for elements of voice, do not overlook some of the more obvious mechanical devices that can indicate the role of the speaker, such as use of quotation marks and of dialogue between two or more people. "Lord Randal," an anonymous work written sometime in the fifteenth century, illustrates a dialogue of two individual voices, neither of which is the poet speaking directly to the reader. Here is the first stanza:

"O where hae ye been, Lord Randal, my son?
O where hae ye been, my handsome young man?"
"I hae been to the wild wood; mother, make my bed
    soon,
For I'm weary wi hunting, and fain wald lie down."

In "Lord Randal" the *direct address* used in context identifies the two speakers as a mother and her son.

Now read this anonymous ballad, "The Three Ravens." The unabridged dictionary reveals that "derrie" has no specific meaning, but is just a word sometimes used in the refrains of ballads and that a "leman" is a lover. After reading the poem, identify the speakers and establish their attitudes as well as the possible attitudes of the poet.

The Three Ravens

line   There were three ravens sat on a tree,
        Downe a downe, hay downe, hay downe.
    There were three ravens sat on a tree,
        With a downe.
(5)   There were three ravens sat on a tree,
    They were as blacke as they might be.
        With a downe derrie, derrie, derrie, downe,
        downe.

    The one of them said to his mate,
    "Where shall we our breakfast take?"

(10)   "Downe in yonder greene field,
    There lies a knight slain under his shield.

"His hounds they lie downe at his feete,
So well they can their master keepe.

"His haukes they flie so eagerly,
(15)   There's no fowle dare him come nie."

Downe there comes a fallow doe,
As great with yong as she might goe.

She lift up his bloudy hed,
And kist his wounds that were so red.
(20)   She got him up upon her backe,
And carried him to earthen lake.

She buried him before the prime,
She was dead herselfe ere even-song time.

God send every gentlemen,
(25)   Such haukes, such hounds, and such a leman.

Concerning the preceding poem, answer the following questions.

1. Who are the speakers?
A narrator speaks in lines 1–8 and 16–25, and two ravens engage in dialogue in lines 9–15.

2. What are the attitudes of the speakers?
   The ravens: How do they view the slain knight? As a potential meal (lines 9–11). What is their attitude toward the hounds and hawks? As preventing them from approaching the dead knight (line 15). Also, however, note line 13—does the speaking raven possibly admire the hounds? Why is the poem called "The Three Ravens" and three ravens sit in the tree in line 1, but only two ravens speak? What is the role of the third raven?
   The narrator: How does the narrator view the ravens? He or she relates their situation and dialogue in a straightforward manner. What is his or her attitude toward the knight? The slain knight is almost ignored. The speaker does not reveal how the knight died nor describe the knight's character (as in "brave" or other such descriptive words). What attitude toward the "fallow doe" is revealed? Her noble actions are detailed (lines 16–23) and admired (lines 24–25). Toward the hawks and hounds? They, too, are admired.

3. What is the attitude of the poet?
   Here are some clues:

▶ A "fallow doe" represents the knight's lover. Why does the poet select this imagery?

▶ Ravens are prevented from feeding on a slain knight by his hound and hawks. What does this say about the character of the knight and the poet's seeming lack of direct portrayal of him?

In the poem, notice that the attitude of the "fallow doe" toward the slain knight is emphasized for its loyalty. By the last line, she is grouped with his hawks and hounds who were so loyal in protecting his body even after death.

In the context of the poem as a whole, what is ironic about the fact that the "fallow doe" is "great with yong" (note spelling—line 17) and dies (line 23)?

One final element of voice as it applies to poetry needs to be mentioned—voice as it relates to style. Some refer to this element of voice as the poet's "trademark"—those elements that combine to make the work of a particular poet identifiable. An example would be the "everyday man-next-door" perspective used by Robert Frost.

Voice in Drama

There are divergent views concerning the role of narrative voice in drama. On the one hand, there are those who see voice strictly as a determination of the relationship of the person who is telling the story to what is going on in the story. As such, narrative prose and poetry have speakers or narrators—mediators of the action who convey the story to the readers. Drama, however, lacks a narrator in the same sense as prose and poetry because in a drama, you see events and conversations being acted out without intervention. In this view, narrative voice is not an element of drama. How can you determine the characterization of the speaker and the attitude of the speaker if there is no speaker?

The opposing view would contend that there is a speaker even in drama—more difficult to perceive perhaps, but nonetheless a factor in the dramatic structure. How can you determine the speaker in a drama? Trying to establish the point of view is fruitless: the point of view refers to who is telling the story (first or third person). In a drama, the characters act out their own stories; therefore, the narrative is not "narrated" and, as a result, is not first person or third person. There generally is a main character; however, you do not see the world of the play through his or her eyes except for the few clues you may gather from the main character's words.

In order to determine the attitude of the speaker or narrative voice in a play, some look to the dramatist's use of dramatic conventions, especially the use of the chorus, the choral-character, the prologue, and the epilogue.

The Chorus

The **chorus** originally was composed of singers (and dancers) but eventually underwent a progression of forms until it came to be editorial-type comments, foreshadowing, and points for plot development recited between acts by a single actor in Elizabethan drama. The chorus sometimes contains clues to the attitude of the speaker. (Remember, however, that the speaker in a drama must be viewed in a totally different perspective from the point-of-view perspective in narrative prose, narrative poetry, and even to a certain extent lyric poetry, in which there is clearly a speaker who is telling the story or expressing the lyric.) Just as other dramatic conventions are used to substitute for reality (methods used by the dramatist to make the play seem "real" or devices used that the audience is expected to accept as substitutions for reality), the chorus is used to provide those elements that are lost in the absence of a true narrative speaker. As such, the chorus can provide a sense of the speaker's perspective, the narrative voice, the attitude of the speaker.

Here is the chorus from the Prologue before Act I, Scene I of *Romeo and Juliet.*

ACT I PROLOGUE
   [*Enter*] **CHORUS**
      CHORUS.
line   Two households, both alike in dignity,
       In fair Verona, where we lay our scene,
       From ancient grudge break to new mutiny,
       Where civil blood makes civil hands unclean.
  (5)   From forth the fatal loins of these two foes
       A pair of star-crost lovers take their life;
       Whose misadventured piteous overthrows
       Doth with their death bury their parents' strife.
       The fearful passage of their death-mark'd love,

(10)   And the continuance of their parents' rage,
         Which, but their children's end, naught could
             remove,
         Is now the two hours' traffic of our stage;
         The which if you with patient ears attend,
         What here shall miss, our toil shall strive to
             mend.   [*Exit*]

Notice the role of the chorus:

▶ It sets the scene (line 2).
▶ It foreshadows the ending (line 7).
▶ It tells the length of the play (line 12).
▶ It gives the cause of the tragedy (lines 1, 3).
▶ It promises more detail (lines 13–14).
▶ It editorializes through use of connotatively charged words ("grudge," "mutiny," "unclean," and "piteous").
▶ It directly addresses the tragedy of the story (lines 10–11).

What might the attitude of the speaker, the narrative voice, be in this play? Also, note that the chorus is written in traditional sonnet form.

The Choral-Character

A more recent development of the chorus convention is the use of the **choral-character.** The choral-character is actually a character in the play who takes over the role of the chorus, providing the audience with insight into the action, motivations, consequences, and indirectly into the speaker's voice.

The Prologue

The **prologue** was used commonly in Restoration and eighteenth-century drama. A character would directly address the audience before the first scene, giving the listeners information significant to their understanding of the plot. Sometimes the prologue would be written not by the authors but by noted literary friends.

The Epilogue

The **epilogue** is given by a character at the end of the play. Often the epilogue will, in a sense, "court" the audience by expressing wishes for good will. Although epilogues did not survive to any extent in the twentieth century, they were used extensively in the seventeenth and eighteenth centuries. Here is the epilogue spoken by the King in Shakespeare's *All's Well That Ends Well:*

EPILOGUE

Spoken by the King.

> The king's a beggar, now the play is done:
> All is well ended, if this suit be won,
> That you express content; which we will pay,
> With strife to please you, day exceeding day:
> Ours be your patience then, and yours our parts;
> Your gentle hands lend us, and take our hearts.

How would you summarize the *attitude of the speaker* toward the audience? Toward the plot of the play?

In summary, finding the narrative voice in a literary work involves identifying:

▶ The speaker or speakers
▶ The point of view of the speakers
▶ The role of the author
▶ The speaker's attitude

A discussion of narrative voice, especially as it is used in the characterization of the speaker, would not be complete, however, without also addressing grammatical voice.

Most writers are familiar with active voice and passive voice. When the subject does the action in a sentence or in the condition named by the verb, the voice of the verb is active (I threw a ball). When the subject receives the action, the voice of the verb is passive (The ball was thrown by me). Passive voice constructions are made with the past participle and a form of the verb *to be:* was thrown. Much of the writing done in English is in the active voice and the occasional shift to passive voice can be very effective, particularly when emphasis is to be placed on the object, as in "The difficult test was passed by the student" (emphasis is on the test) or when the actors (of the action) are not known, as in "Many books have been written this year" (Who wrote the books?).

Largely an element of a writer's style, overuse of the passive voice can affect the tone of a narrative and, as a result, might influence the reader's perception of the narrative voice and particularly the speaker's attitude. Compare these two versions of the same paragraph.

Version One

The ball was hit by Jim, but it was immediately caught by the outfielder. Roars were heard from the crowd. Tears streaming down his face were awkwardly wiped away by Jim's gloved hand. The truth was finally realized by him: the championship game was lost.

Version Two

Jim hit the ball, but the outfielder caught it immediately. The crowd roared. Jim's gloved hand awkwardly wiped away the tears streaming down his face. He finally realized the truth: the championship game was lost.

In a narrative, the use of active voice helps to intensify the action (a function of tone) and hold the reader's attention. Overuse of the passive voice misdirects attention away from Jim—the main subject of the sample narrative. But controlled use of passive voice can be useful: the shift from active to passive in the last sentence effectively serves to catch the reader's attention that something is different (in this case a significant point is being made). In narrative writing, as this example illustrates, use of active and passive voice has significant implications on the reader's perceptions of tone and meaning.

Questions to Apply the Literary Principles Concerning Voice

Ask these questions to help you identify and understand voice.

1. From what point of view is this story being told?

2. Who is the main character?

3. Who is the speaker?

4. Are the speaker and the author the same person?

5. What is the attitude of the author?

6. If the attitudes of the author and speaker differ, what is the effect?

7. Are there any stream-of-consciousness techniques present? If so, what is the effect?

8. Is the narrator intrusive or unintrusive?

9. Is the narrative written in the scenic method with a self-effacing author or in the panoramic method?

10. Is the point of view (if applicable) limited or unlimited third person?

11. Is the narrator credible? Naive?

12. Does the persona project the views of the author?

13. Does the narrative voice affect the tone?

14. If the selection is a lyric poem, who is the speaker? What is the speaker's attitude?

15. Is the poem a dramatic monologue? Why or why not?

16. If a play, are there any dramatic conventions present that might project a narrative voice?

Additional Points to Remember About Voice

▶ *Never* assume that the speaker and the author are the same person—even when the work is written in the first person.
▶ There are many descriptive adjectives relating to attitudes. Character traits (see page 175) are the foundations for such labels. For example, a speaker's attitude might be

assertive	dictatorial
boisterous	dilatory
bravado	insolent
callous	irascible
censorious	irrational
churlish	optimistic
complaisant	pacifiable
condescending	petulant
derisive	sanctimonious
derogatory	sanguinary

▶ Watch for shifts in points of view in a selection. A change from the third person to first person pronouns (from "he" or "they" to "I" or "we"), for example, is important to meaning and can affect the identification of the speaker and the speaker's attitude.

▶ What is the identity of *the narrator* in this excerpt from the *Pickwick Papers* (Charles Dickens)?

> "Straight and swift, I ran, and no one dared to stop me. I heard the noise of feet behind, and redoubled my speed . . . . When I woke I found myself here—here in this gay cell where the sunlight seldom comes, and the moon steals in, in rays which only serve to show the dark shadows about me, and that silent figure in its old corner. When I lie awake, I can sometimes hear strange shrieks and cries from distant parts of this large place. What they are, I know not; . . ."
>
> At the end of the manuscript, was written, in another hand, this note:—
>
> [The unhappy man whose ravings are recorded above, was a melancholy instance of the baneful results of energies misdirected in early life, and excesses prolonged until their consequences could never be repaired. . . . It is only matter of wonder to those who were acquainted with the vices of his early career, that his passions, when no longer controlled by reason, did not lead him to the commission of still more frightful deeds.]

In this selection, part of a manuscript is written in the first person, followed by a commentary (the "note") written in the third person by someone else in reference to the writer of the manuscript. Be aware, however, that there is yet a third voice. Although this limited excerpt reveals very little about his or her attitude, who is the voice that says, "At the end of the manuscript, was written, in another hand, this note:"?

Tone

Tone refers, in its most narrow sense, to the attitude of the literary speaker toward his or her listener. When identifying the tone or trying to describe the tone (of voice) used, generally such descriptors as happy, sad, ironic, abstruse, sincere, playful, straightforward, formal, informal, serious, condescending, and many more descriptive words are used. Usually the tone is described as, for example, "He has a somber tone of voice." In other words, tone answers the question: How does the literary speaker "sound" to the listener? As the phrase "tone of voice" implies, *sound* in this context does include an auditory impression; however, because most literary expressions (other than those in the oral traditions, speeches, drama, and poems meant to be read aloud) are intended to be read silently, *sound* also refers to the impression that is conveyed. Hence the question can be restructured to read: What impression is the literary speaker conveying to the reader? How does the literary speaker seem to the reader?

A subtle implication here is that the tone (of voice) somehow will reveal information about the speaker's opinion of the intelligence and sensitivity of the reader or listener. For example, an adult might use a condescending tone of voice with a child. Even an apology can be turned into further hostility through the tone (of voice) used. "I beg your pardon" can be sincere words of regret, or they can be sarcastically spoken. In listening to a speaker, you can distinguish his or her tone (of voice) through the verbal inflections used and facial expressions. How can you tell what tone a speaker is using in a written selection? Sometimes the writer will use graphic means to convey tone, such as italicizing words to show the speaker's verbal inflections. Also, the writer may use description to portray the attitude of the character in the written work. As in other aspects of analysis, context is very important to determining a character's/speaker's tone (of voice). Just as a person in an argument might say, "Did you hear the tone she used with me?"—the tone of voice in a literary selection is an element of communication with the reader (or with another character in the story). Tone (of voice) also implies that there is an auditor.

When considering the narrative voice, the reader needs to establish who is speaking and how that speaker might be characterized (recognizing the difference between the speaker and the writer and identifying the attitude of the speaker). The concept of tone is an almost inseparable element of voice, one that includes the speaker's attitude and extends to encompass the entire work.

Tone, atmosphere, mood, feeling—there is a great disagreement among literary scholars about how interchangeably these terms can be used. At one extreme are writers who consider these elements as synonyms; at the other extreme are those who would differentiate their shades of meaning. If the voice refers to who is speaking and the speaker's or writer's attitude in terms of what is being said, then perhaps tone might be defined as the speaker's or writer's attitude in terms of how he or she sounds saying it, contributing to atmosphere, mood, and feeling.

Defined as such, tone works on several different levels. There is a tone found in:

▶ Dialogue between characters as they interact (their tone of voice)
▶ Specific words, phrases, and sentences used at specific points as an expression of the writer's, narrator's, or speaker's tone of voice
▶ Each individual character's attitude
▶ The tone of the work as a whole

What elements contribute to make the tone of a work?

The Speaker

The speaker has an attitude toward the subject. *How* he or she expresses that attitude projects a tone. If the speaker's attitude is, for example, condemning of those who hunt for sport, his or her tone when describing a hunting scene might influence the readers to regard the act as grisly or morbid. The narrative voice is condemning; the tone is morbid. In contrast, if the speaker's attitude is admiring of hunters, his or her tone when describing a hunting scene might make the act appear adventurous or necessary (for food or protection). The narrative voice is admiring; the tone is exciting.

The Author

The author also has an attitude toward the subject. How the author expresses that attitude, however, depends upon the relationship of the speaker to the writer. If the speaker is the author's persona expressing his or her own views, the tone is more likely that expressed by the speaker. When the speaker speaks and acts *in contrast to* the views of the author, this discrepancy or difference in voice creates an ironic tone. Swift's "A Modest Proposal" is an example. (See pages 131–132.)

The Theme or Subject

Some themes or subjects carry with them intrinsic elements of tone; for instance, death usually has an unhappy tone, and birth generally has a happy tone. You should not assume, however, that a work about death is always in a negative tone: the tone is a product of many elements that work together, including the author's intent. The speaker's approach and the author's use of literary principles can turn a work about death into a celebration of life or, as in Henry Vaughan's poem, "Peace," written in the mid-1600s, an anticipation of peace.

> My soul, there is a country
>> Far beyond the stars,
> Where stands a wingèd sentry
>> All skilful in the wars;
> There above noise, and danger
>> Sweet peace sits crowned
>> with smiles,
> And one born in a manger
>> Commands the beauteous files;
> He is thy gracious friend,
>> And (O, my Soul, awake!)
> Did in pure love descend
>> To die here for thy sake.
> If thou canst get but thither,
>> There grows the flower of peace,
> The rose that cannot wither,
>> Thy fortress, and thy ease;
> Leave then thy foolish ranges,
>> For none can thee secure,
> But one, who never changes,
>> Thy God, thy life, thy cure.

The Characters

The characters in a work (what they say and do) and how they are *characterized* (what is said about them) can significantly influence the tone of a work. The individual temperaments of the characters—how they act and react, what they say, and how they say it—are all important elements of tone. Here is an excerpt of dialogue from *The Old Curiosity Shop* by Charles Dickens.

> "I can't see anything but the curtain of the bed,"
> said Brass, applying his eye to the keyhole of the door.
> "Is he a strong man, Mr. Richard (Dick Swiveller)?"

"Very," answered Dick.

"It would be an extremely unpleasant circumstance if he was to bounce out suddenly," said Brass. "Hallo there! Hallo, hallo!"

While Mr. Brass, with his eye curiously twisted into the keyhole, uttered these sounds as a means of attracting the lodger's attention, and while Miss Brass plied the hand-bell, Mr. Swiveller put his stool close against the wall by the side of the door, and mounting on the top and standing bolt upright, began a violent battery with the ruler upon the upper panels of the door.

Suddenly the door was unlocked on the inside and flung violently open. Miss Sally dived into her own bedroom; Mr. Brass, who was not remarkable for personal courage, ran into the next street, and finding that nobody followed him, armed with a poker or other offensive weapon, put his hands in his pockets, walked very slowly all at once, and whistled.

. . .

"Have you been making that horrible noise?" said the single gentleman.

"I have been helping, sir," returned Dick, keeping his eye upon him.

"How dare you then," said the lodger. "Eh?"

To this, Dick made no other reply than by inquiring whether the lodger held it to be consistent with the conduct and character of a gentleman to go to sleep for six-and-twenty hours at a stretch, and whether the peace of an amiable and virtuous family was to weigh as nothing in the balance.

"Is my peace nothing?" said the single gentleman.

"Yes, sir, indeed," returned Dick, yielding, "but an equal quantity of slumber was never got out of one bed and bedstead, and if you're going to sleep in that way, you must pay for a double-bedded room."

"Come here, you impudent rascal," was the lodger's answer as he reentered his room.

"Can you drink anything?" was his next inquiry.

Mr. Swiveller replied that he had very recently been assuaging the pangs of thirst, but that he was still open to "a modest quencher," if the materials were at hand. Without another word spoken on either side, the lodger took from his great trunk a kind of temple, shining as of polished silver, and placed it carefully on the table.

Greatly interested in his proceedings, Mr. Swiveller observed him closely. Into one little chamber of this temple he dropped an egg, into another some coffee, into a third a compact piece of raw steak from a neat tin case, into a fourth he poured some water. Then, with the aid of a phosphorus box and some matches, he procured a light and applied it to a spirit lamp which had a place of its own below the temple; then he shut down the lids of all the little chambers, then he opened them; and then, by some wonderful and unseen agency, the steak was done, the egg was boiled, the coffee was accurately prepared, and his breakfast was ready.

"Hot water—" said the lodger, handing it to Mr. Swiveller with as much coolness as if he had a kitchen fire before him, "—extraordinary rum—sugar—and a travelling glass. Mix for yourself. And make haste."

. . .

"The man of the house is a lawyer, is he not?" said the lodger.

Dick nodded. The rum was amazing.

"The woman of the house—what's she?"

"A dragon," said Dick.

"I want to do as I like, young man," he added after a short silence; "to go to bed when I like, get up when I like, come in when I like, go out when I like—to be asked no questions and be surrounded by no spies. In this last respect, servants are the devil. There's only one here?"

"And a very little one," said Dick.

"Let them know my humour," said the single gentleman, rising. "If they disturb me, they lose a good tenant. Good day."

"I beg your pardon," said Dick, halting in his passage to the door, which the lodger prepared to open. "—But the name," said Dick, "in case of letters or parcels—"

"I never have any," returned the lodger.

"Or in case anybody should call."

"Nobody ever calls on me."

"If any mistake should arise from not having the name, don't say it was my fault, sir," added Dick, still lingering.

"I'll blame nobody," said the lodger, with such irascibility that in a moment Dick found himself upon the staircase, and the locked door between them.

Notice how the conversation between Dick Swiveller and the nameless lodger contributes to tone: The lodger refers to Dick as an "impudent rascal," seems antisocial ("Is my peace nothing?" "I never have any [letters or parcels]" "Nobody ever calls on me."), and wants his own way ("I want to do as I like, young man"), yet he invites Dick to have a rum with him. Dick, on the other hand, blends a lack of intimidation and a wide-eyed amazement at the lodger's "temple." Combined with the comical scene of Dick, Brass, and Miss Sally trying to awaken the lodger, the interaction of the characters serves to make the tone both amusing and entertaining. Also, the actions and instructions of the nameless lodger add a slightly mysterious tone to the episode.

The Use of Language and Meanings of the Language in Context

How words are used in a selection, the connotations, the figurative language, all contribute directly to setting the tone. For example, look at how the meanings of the language in context set the tone in the excerpt from *The Old Curiosity Shop* (discussed in the previous section).

The narrator implies that Dick Swiveller views the lodger's mysterious cooking instrument as "a kind of temple, shining as of polished silver." The description is connotative of a special place dedicated to a lofty or great purpose. The image is continued by the cooking process being described as done "by some wonderful and unseen agency" and by the rum being described as "amazing." Based on the diction and context of the excerpt, what is the narrator's attitude (the narrative voice) toward Dick Swiveller? He views Dick as a distinctive buffoon-type character who provides comic relief to the plot and at the same time acts as an interactive vehicle to reveal the circumstances and character of the lodger. The narrative voice might be described as pragmatic and discerning. What is the narrator's tone? In other words, in what manner does he convey this attitude? In an amused tone? A humorous tone? Perhaps a comical tone?

Dick refers to the woman of the house as a "dragon." How does this figurative use of language further reveal Dick's character and attitude toward the woman in question? How would you describe the manner in which he conveys this attitude (his tone)?

The Sound of the Language

The rhythm and rhyme also affect the tone of a work, just as they affect the tone of music. This element of language has been referred to as its *tone color* and has been compared to the timbre in music. Just as certain musical selections can make people want to dance and others can give listeners the "blues," the rhythm and rhyme in literary selections (even in prose) can bring to the reader or listener certain tones.

The Setting

Setting in a literary selection refers to the following elements:

▶ **Geographical location**   This includes area or region, the general locale, descriptions of architecture, flora and fauna, floor plans, furniture arrangements, weather conditions, and so forth.

▶ **Time** This may refer to a historical period, a time of day, a season of the year, a projection into the future, a period of life (such as the time of "mid-life crisis"), or even a nonexistent time (used extensively in the science fiction genre).

▶ **Socio-economic conditions**   These are revealed, generally, on two different levels. First, there are those conditions and circumstances that relate directly to the characters. These include their occupations, family lives, life-styles, and social interactions. Second, there is the larger society that surrounds and affects the microcosm of the characters. This larger societal structure includes its predominate mores and the general social and work environments.

Although setting is generally associated with narrative writing, some aspects of setting, particularly those of socio-economic conditions, can affect the tone even in nonnarrative works. As an example, some works that describe local social customs, employing elements of local color writing and regionalism (nineteenth-century American narrative movements), definitely have a tone based on setting, despite their lack of a traditional narrative story line.

Some literary scholars refer to the elements of setting (particularly those elements of setting that can be pictured or seen "in the mind's eye" in lyric poetry) that are present in any literary work as the *opsis* of the work. But whether in a narrative or nonnarrative form, one of the significant influences of setting on tone is the emotional impact of the setting—emotions elicited from either the character or the reader in response to the setting. The effects on tone of some settings are dramatic and easy to identify: the romantic tone of a deserted island, the frightening tone of a lonely graveyard on a stormy night, the harsh tone of an inner city ghetto, the warm tone of a family gathering on Christmas Eve. Some, however, are more subtle, changing, or perhaps even unexpected, as when the romantic island becomes a place of fear and hardship when food and water supplies dwindle or when the harsh tone of the inner city ghetto changes to a warm, caring tone as residents join together to overcome their adversities.

The complexity of what constitutes tone should, at this point, be obvious. As previously mentioned, *tone, atmosphere, mood,* and *feeling,* although used synonymously by some, reflect shades of meaning for others.

Mood can refer to an emotional state, especially as projected by the characters in the work: "Joyce is in a foul mood" or "Eric is in a happy mood." Moods, of course, can change (as can many of the other elements of tone) within the work. As the attitude of the author toward the subject is revealed, his or her mood might be seen as self-righteous, defiant, proud, noble, or even reactionary, to name a few. When the author's voice is different from that of the main character or the speaker, the *mood* might differ from the tone (of voice) used by the author. For example, the mood of the speaker in "A Modest Proposal" (pages 131–132) could be described as helpful, conciliatory, and serious, but the tone of the author (Swift) is satiric, whose mood (quite possibly) was angry and indignant when he put pen to paper.

On the other hand, **feeling** has been defined as an intellectual state: the attitude of the author toward his subject on an intellectual rather than on an emotional basis. Conversationally, this might be approached with the question, "What is your *feeling* on the subject?" to which the respondent would express his or her views.

The setting, the tone (of voice) of the author and speaker, the emotional moods of the author, the speaker, and/or the characters, and the feelings of the author blend together to give the work its **atmosphere**—that prevailing and pervasive ambience that gives the reader the basis for expectation.

Atmosphere is often described using such terms as *mysterious, romantic, gloomy, horrifying, intellectual,* and other expressions depicting these types of effects. When movie critics label a motion picture as a "feel-good movie," they are referring to its atmosphere.

Because tone is partly the result of attitude, an investigation of its role in a literary work is not complete without a look at its role in the author's *style*. Style is a significant element in both narrative voice and tone (of voice):

▶ Narrative voice—the writer's or speaker's attitude
▶ Tone (of voice)—how the writer or speaker sounds (intellectually and emotionally) expressing that attitude to the auditor (listener)
▶ Style—how the writer uses the literary elements to express his or her attitude

Although a writer may try to emulate another author's style, like snowflakes, no two writers' styles are exactly alike. The labels readers place on a particular writer's style can be based on a wide range of factors.

For example, you might associate the style of a writer with his or her purpose (a scientific style, a journalistic style, a didactic style). Sometimes a writer consistently works in the same genre and one comes to describe his or her style based on that genre (a romantic style or a swashbuckler style). If a writer tries to emulate the work of a particular literary period, school, or favorite writer, you might label the style accordingly (a Shakespearean style, New Formalism style). Also, readers tend to label the style of a writer based on an overall impression of the "sense" they get of elements that are generally consistent throughout that particular author's work. You might label his or her writing style as imaginative (or unimaginative), exciting (or dull), sensitive (or insensitive). Once a writer has established a recognizable style, readers might measure each of his or her new works to see how it measures against their perception of his or her style. Readers can then talk about whether the new work is consistent with or is a departure from the writer's "style."

Literary scholars, however, take a more analytical approach to style, which will be discussed as tone is examined in prose, poetry, and drama.

Tone in Prose

As previously discussed, tone is *how* the writer or speaker sounds to the auditor in expressing his or her attitude (narrative voice).

The tone can reveal the speaker's opinion of the listener or reader. This is a significant factor in the writer's style (the way in which the writer uses literary elements to express his or her attitude).

Traditionally, literary scholars labeled style in terms of levels:

High or Grand Style

|

Middle or Mean Style

|

Low or Base (Plain) Style

The level of style used was dictated by the genre, the context or circumstances, and the social rank of the speaker.

Northrup Frye has pioneered an important variation on this view of style by categorizing the style before the level is determined:

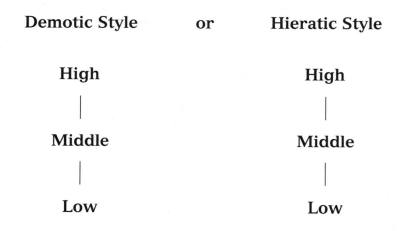

Demotic Style	**or**	**Hieratic Style**
High		**High**
|		|
Middle		**Middle**
|		|
Low		**Low**

In this view of style, the work is first determined to be either demotic, meaning that it uses the syntax and mechanics of ordinary speech, or hieratic, meaning that it uses more formal literary constructions. Once assigned a category, the level of the writing style is then determined within the category. In such a view, the significance of the speaker's or writer's tone in prose is self-evident.

What follows are several prose selections. The first is an excerpt from a speech delivered by President John F. Kennedy on July 25, 1961, in a broadcast to the American people. The second selection is the introduction to Sir Walter Scott's *Ivanhoe*. The final passage is a paragraph of *The Scarlet Letter* by Nathaniel Hawthorne.

After each selection is presented, its tone and how the tone and style are interrelated will be discussed. As you read each selection and think about the accompanying discussions concerning tone and style, an interesting aspect of the subject to think about is the extent of the writer's intent. Did the writer consciously and deliberately use the elements of style discussed to affect the tone, or were these effects the result of subconscious elements, such as passion for the subject, or the result of basic understanding of the writing process as it relates to producing certain effects in the minds and emotions of the hearers or readers? Perhaps this question cannot be answered, but the degree to which the writer consciously or unconsciously uses style to produce certain effects certainly merits discussion.

The Berlin Crisis
by
John F. Kennedy

Seven weeks ago tonight I returned from Europe to report on my meeting with Premier Khrushchev and the others. His grim warnings about the future of the world, his aide-mémoire on Berlin, his subsequent speeches and threats which he and his agents have launched, and the increase in the Soviet military budget that he has announced have all prompted a series of decisions by the administration and a series of consultations with the members of the NATO organization. In Berlin, as you recall, he intends to bring to an end, through a stroke of the pen, first our legal rights to be in West Berlin and secondly our ability to make good on our commitment to the two million free people of that city. That we cannot permit. . . .

West Berlin is 110 miles within the area which the Soviets now dominate—which is immediately controlled by the so-called East German regime. . . . We are there as a result of our victory over Nazi Germany—and our basic rights to be there deriving from that victory include both our presence in West

Berlin and the enjoyment of access across East Germany. These rights have been repeatedly confirmed and recognized in special agreements with the Soviet Union. Berlin is not a part of East Germany but a separate territory under the control of the allied powers. Thus our rights there are clear and deep-rooted. But in addition to those rights is our commitment to sustain—and defend, if need be—the opportunity for more than two million people to determine their own future and choose their own way of life.

Thus, our presence in West Berlin, and our access thereto, cannot be ended by any act of the Soviet government. The NATO shield was long ago extended to cover West Berlin—and we have given our word that an attack in that city will be regarded as an attack upon us all.

For West Berlin—lying exposed 110 miles inside East Germany, surrounded by Soviet troops and close to Soviet supply lines—has many roles. It is more than a showcase of liberty, a symbol, an island of freedom in a Communist sea. It is even more than a link with the Free World, a beacon of hope behind the Iron Curtain, an escape hatch for refugees.

West Berlin is all of that. But above all it has now become—as never before—the great testing place of Western courage and will, a focal point where our solemn commitments stretching back over the years since 1945 and Soviet ambitions now meet in basic confrontation.

It would be a mistake for others to look upon Berlin, because of its location, as a tempting target. The United States is there; the United Kingdom and France are there; the pledge of NATO is there—and the people of Berlin are there. It is as secure, in that sense, as the rest of us—for we cannot separate its safety from our own. . . .

We do not want to fight, but we have fought before. And others in earlier times have made the same dangerous mistake of assuming that the West was too selfish and too soft and too divided to resist invasions of freedom in other lands. Those who threaten to unleash the forces of war on a dispute over West Berlin should recall the words of the ancient philosopher: "A man who causes fear cannot be free from fear." . . .

So long as the Communists insist that they are preparing to end by themselves unilaterally our rights in West Berlin and our commitments to its people, we must be prepared to defend those rights and those commitments. We will at all times be ready to talk, if talk will help. But we must also be ready to resist with force, if force is used upon us. Either alone would fail. Together, they can serve the cause of freedom and peace. . . .

Thus, in the days and months ahead, I shall not hesitate to ask the Congress for additional measures or exercise any of the executive powers that I possess to meet this threat to peace. Everything essential to the security of freedom must be done; and if that should require more men, or more taxes, or more controls, or other new powers, I shall not hesitate to ask them. The measures proposed today will be constantly studied and altered as necessary. But while we will not let panic shape our policy, neither will we permit timidity to direct our program.

First, look at how the subject affects the tone of this speech. Soviet Premier Nikita Khrushchev was making threats concerning free world rights in West Berlin. The threats were of the nature that the situation might have led to a major military confrontation. The subject? The threat of war. *The resulting tone?* Serious, urgent, grave.

Next, look at the speaker's attitude toward the subject and his attitude toward his listeners to see how the tone is affected. He describes Krushchev's rhetoric at their meeting as "grim warnings," indicating that he views the Premier's position as threatening. He says that Khrushchev would end legal rights in West Berlin "through the stroke of the pen"—connotative of an overbearing (perhaps even capricious?) attitude on the part of the Premier. He points out America's right and need to be a presence in West Berlin. His attitude toward the subject? America is justified in resisting the threats made against West Berlin. *The resulting tone?* Confident, resolved.

The President has essentially three groups of listeners to this speech: the world community (who are poised, listening to see what America and the American President will do), Communist powers (particularly Premier Khrushchev), and the American people. To the world community he points out that he recognizes West Berlin as "the great testing place of Western courage and will"—a matter of "commitments"; however, he also forms psychological alliance with much of the free world. To the Communists and

Khrushchev he sends the message: "We have fought before." To the American people he gives assurances ("We will at all times be ready to talk, if talk will help"); he prepares Americans for the possibility of war ("But we must also be ready to resist with force, if force is used upon us") and for the sacrifices that might be ahead ("more men . . . more taxes . . . more controls . . .").

His attitude toward his listeners? He views the world community as both spectators and (particularly NATO, the United Kingdom, and France) allies, the Communist regime as a threat, and the American people as needing to know where they stand. *The resulting tone?* Responsible (to the world community), brave, unflinching (to the Communist aggressors), forthright (to the American people).

Because he is speaking to three different audiences—three groups of listeners—he uses elements of style to facilitate his message, to communicate three distinct messages to three different groups without ever addressing his remarks directly to any one of them. President Kennedy uses several stylistic devices to accomplish this: two will be examined here.

Notice in the first paragraph the sentence "His grim warnings . . . have all prompted a series of decisions . . . ." The syntax of this sentence cannot be closed until almost the end of the sentence. Use of this style in the first paragraph establishes a formal tone in which he introduces the gravity of his topic to all three audiences simultaneously. In the second paragraph, however, he changes (particularly in the first and second sentences) to a more loosely joined construction that could have a period before the end of the sentence and still be complete in terms of syntax. The more relaxed style helps to shift the focus as he explains to the world community in a more conversational tone why America is justified in its position in West Berlin. Although he does not use extreme forms of syntax, such as the periodic sentences of Boswell in the late eighteenth century and the nonperiodic sentences in the style of Addison, his subtle use of syntax helps to change the tone.

Also, most of the speech is written in a hypotactic style, a use of subordinate phrases, clauses, and conjunctions that establish relationships (often cause and effect). At precise times, however, he quite effectively changes to a more paratactic style (no subordination or conjunctions—other than perhaps *and*—are used between sentences) that very subtly changes the tone. For example, notice the effect of his use of the hypotactic style *and* paratactic style in this paragraph:

It would be a mistake for others to look upon
Berlin, because of its location, as a tempting target.
The United States is there; the United Kingdom and
France are there; the pledge of NATO is there—and
the people of Berlin are there. [parataxis] It is as
secure, in that sense, as the rest of us—for we cannot
separate its safety from our own . . . . [hypotaxis]

The speaker (President Kennedy) in this speech uses subtle
changes in his use of stylistic elements to alter his tone to convey
the message to the intended audiences more effectively.

Ivanhoe
by
Sir Walter Scott

In that pleasant district of merry England which
is watered by the river Don, there extended in
ancient times a large forest, covering the greater
part of the beautiful hills and valleys which lie
between Sheffield and the pleasant town of
Doncaster. The remains of this extensive wood are
still to be seen at the noble seats of Wentworth, of
Wharncliffe Park, and around Rotherham. Here
haunted of yore the fabulous Dragon of Wantley;
here were fought many of the most desperate battles
during the Civil Wars of the Roses; and here also
flourished in ancient times those bands of gallant
outlaws whose deeds have been rendered so popular in English song.

Such being our chief scene, the date of our story
refers to a period towards the end of the reign of
Richard I, when his return from his long captivity
had become an event rather wished than hoped for
by his despairing subjects, who were in the mean-
time subjected to every species of subordinate
oppression. The nobles, whose power had become
exorbitant during the reign of Stephen, and whom
the prudence of Henry the Second had scarce
reduced into some degree of subjection to the
crown, had now resumed their ancient license in its
utmost extent; despising the feeble interference of
the English Council of State, fortifying their castles,
increasing the number of their dependants, reducing all around them to a state of vassalage, ...

The situation of the inferior gentry, or franklins,
as they were called, who, by the law and spirit of the

English constitution, were entitled to hold themselves independent of feudal tyranny, became now unusually precarious. If, as was most generally the case, they placed themselves under the protection of any of the petty kings in their vicinity, accepted of feudal offices in his household, or bound themselves, by mutual treaties of alliance and protection, to support him in his enterprises, they might indeed purchase temporary repose; but it must be with the sacrifice of that independence which was so dear to every English bosom, and at the certain hazard of being involved as a party in whatever rash expedition the ambition of their protector might lead him to undertake. . . .

A circumstance which greatly tended to enhance the tyranny of the nobility and the sufferings of the inferior classes arose from the consequences of the Conquest by Duke William of Normandy. Four generations had not sufficed to blend the hostile blood of the Normans and Anglo-Saxons, or to unite, by common language and mutual interests, two hostile races, one of which still felt the elation of triumph, while the other groaned under all the consequences of defeat. The power had been completely placed in the hands of the Norman nobility by the event of the battle of Hastings, and it had been used, as our histories assure us, with no moderate hand. The whole race of Saxon princes and nobles had been extirpated or disinherited, ... At court, and in the castles of the great nobles, where the pomp and state of a court was emulated, Norman-French was the only language employed; in courts of law, the pleadings and judgments were delivered in the same tongue. In short, French was the language of honour, of chivalry, and even of justice, while the far more manly and expressive Anglo-Saxon was abandoned to the use of rustics and hinds, who knew no other. Still, however, the necessary intercourse between the lords of the soil, and those oppressed inferior beings by whom that soil was cultivated, occasioned the gradual formation of a dialect, compounded betwixt the French and the Anglo-Saxon, in which they could render themselves mutually intelligible to each other; and from this necessity arose by degrees the structure of our present English language, in which the speech of the victors and the vanquished have been so happily blended together; and which has since been so richly improved by importations from the classical languages, and from those spoken by the southern nations of Europe.

This state of things I have thought it necessary to premise for the information of the general reader, who might be apt to forget that, although no great historical events, such as war or insurrection, mark the existence of the Anglo-Saxon as a separate people subsequent to the reign of William the Second, yet the great national distinctions betwixt them and their conquerors, the recollection of what they had formerly been, and to what they were now reduced, continued, down to the reign of Edward the Third, to keep open the wounds which the Conquest had inflicted, and to maintain a line of separation betwixt the descendants of the victor Normans and the vanquished Saxons.

In this first person narrative excerpt, what is the speaker's subject? He is setting the scene for the story. The scene is England "toward the end of the reign of Richard I" when nobles had "exorbitant" power over the people. Such social conditions create a tone that is serious. What is the speaker's tone of voice regarding the subject? He does not refrain from connotative word choices that *editorialize*—revealing his opinion of the conditions in England at the time: outlaws described as "gallant," "despairing subjects," "oppression," "despising the feeble interference of the English Council of State," "reducing all around them to a state of vassalage" (the position of a vassal being subservient to the feudal lord). The resulting tone? A condemnatory tone toward the nobles. (Also, the speaker refers to the position of the independence of franklins, the inferior gentry, as "now unusually precarious"—giving the reader a sense of anticipation of trouble ahead.) This condemnatory tone is extended to include the speaker's opinion of the Norman-French in racial terms. In this regard, the speaker describes, in a rather patriotic tone, the Anglo-Saxon tongue as "more manly and expressive," as compared to Norman-French.

How do characters influence the tone in this selection? At this point—the introduction of the narrative—no characters (other than the first person narrator) have been introduced. The narrator has, however, invested significant effort in establishing the tone of the setting in its historical context. This situation gives the reader reason to *anticipate* that the focus of the narrative is on, not exclusively the characters, but also on how the events of the time and place (as they are historically significant) affect the lives of the characters and how, in turn, the lives of the characters may (or may fail to) affect historical events and outcomes. The narrator even directly states that he "thought it necessary" to inform readers of the historical context of the "line of separation" between the Normans and Saxons.

In examining the style of the narrative, you will find that the writer uses very little figurative language, but relies heavily upon connotative word choices, particularly in the contrast of the tone established in the first paragraph (the tone projected by the description of a beautiful place of fabulous events) with the following paragraphs (the tone projected by introduction of a blight imposed upon that beautiful place by hated conquerors).

Now read the following excerpt from *The Scarlet Letter* by Nathaniel Hawthorne:

> The Grass Plot before the jail, in Prison Lane, on a certain summer morning, not less than two centuries ago, was occupied by a pretty large number of the inhabitants of Boston; all with their eyes intently fastened on the iron-clamped oaken door. Amongst any other population, or at a later period in the history of New England, the grim rigidity that petrified the bearded physiognomies of these good people would have augured some awful business in hand. It could have betokened nothing short of the anticipated execution of some noted culprit, on whom the sentence of a legal tribunal had but confirmed the verdict of public sentiment. But, in that early severity of the Puritan character, an inference of this kind could not so indubitably be drawn. It might be that a sluggish bond-servant, or an undutiful child, whom his parents had given over to the civil authority, was to be corrected at the whipping-post. It might be, that an Antinomian, a Quaker, or other heterodox religionist, was to be scourged out of the town, ... It might be, too, that a witch, like old Mistress Hibbins, the bitter-tempered widow of the magistrate, was to die upon the gallows. In either case, there was very much the same solemnity of demeanour on the part of the spectators; as befitted a people amongst whom religion and law were almost identical, and in whose character both were so thoroughly interfused, that the mildest and the

severest acts of public discipline were alike made venerable and awful. Meagre, indeed, and cold, was the sympathy that a transgressor might look for, from such bystanders at the scaffold. On the other hand, a penalty which, in our days, would infer a degree of mocking infamy and ridicule, might then be invested with almost as stern a dignity as the punishment of death itself.

How does Hawthorne project the tone in this dramatic scene? First, he uses structure (comparison and contrast) to reveal the character of the people and, consequently, to project a tone. Another people would be anticipating "execution of some noted culprit." In contrast, these people would be drawn to the jail for a glimpse of the punishment for much lesser crimes. The list of things they deem worthy of such punishment defines the values and character of this group of people.

"Their eyes intently fastened on the iron-clamped oaken door" causes the reader to picture a silent, grim mob staring to see the criminal's fate. The list of crimes and the consequences that might have been the cause of the peoples' interest in the jail makes the reader picture horrific scenes of whippings, scourgings, and hangings. Use of such descriptive words as "Meagre, indeed, and cold, was the sympathy" and "the grim rigidity that petrified the bearded physiognomies" makes the reader picture stony faces inflicting pain in an unyielding manner. What is Hawthorne's style in this excerpt? He makes the reader picture the scene using a blend of structural and connotative devices including character revelation. The result is a distinctive tone or atmosphere.

Tone in Poetry

Many of the same elements at work to establish the tone in prose are also significant in its development in poetry: subject, the speaker's perspective, characters, the use of language, and the setting. Although it can be effectively used to influence the tone in prose, the one element that has significant impact on the tone of a poem is the sound of the language (rhythm and rhyme).

One needs to look no further than the limerick to probe the effect of rhythm and rhyme on tone. Meaning is at the root of a limerick's humorous impact (its funny tone), but the impact of the rhythm and rhyme scheme on its tone cannot be denied.

There Was A Young
Fellow Named Hall

There was a young fellow named Hall,
Who fell in the spring in the fall;
    'Twould have been a sad thing
    If he'd died in the spring,
But he didn't—he died in the fall.

                        Anon.

Also look to nursery rhymes for tones set by rhythm and rhyme. These musical rhythms and easy-to-complete rhymes create a wide range of tones (ranging from comforting to scary) that captivate children's attention.

I Had A Little Nut Tree

I had a little nut tree,
    Nothing would it bear
But a silver nutmeg
    And a golden pear;
The King of Spain's daughter
    Came to visit me,
And all for the sake
    Of my little nut tree.

                        Anon.

Now compare the amusing and lighthearted tone projected in the nursery rhyme "I Had a Little Nut Tree" with that of the following nursery rhyme:

There Was a Man

There was a man of double deed
Sowed his garden full of seed.
When the seed began to grow,
'Twas like a garden full of snow;
When the snow began to melt,
'Twas like a ship without a belt;
When the ship began to sail,
'Twas like a bird without a tail;
When the bird began to fly,
'Twas like an eagle in the sky;
When the sky began to roar,
'Twas like a lion at the door;

When the door began to crack,
'Twas like a stick across my back;
When my back began to smart,
'Twas like a penknife in my heart;
When my heart began to bleed,
'Twas death and death and death indeed.

Anon.

The speaker in "There Was a Man" projects the tone of a victim, but in "As I Went over the Water" the speaker has in today's slang what might be called an attitude.

As I went over the water,
    The water went over me.
I saw two little blackbirds
    Sitting on a tree;
One called me a rascal,
    And one called me a thief,
I took up my little black stick
    And knocked out all their teeth.

Anon.

Tone in poetry cannot be examined without addressing the verbal and musical aspects of poetry, whether the poem is sung or read aloud—its tone color (called timbre in music).

In songs, ballads, and other forms of poetry set to music, the tone is influenced greatly by the arrangement of the music itself. Examples include the emotional impact of rhythm and blues, the playful tone of an English children's ballad like "The Fox Went Out on a Chilly Night," the agitated tone in some rap music, the humorous tone in Country and Western's "Tennessee Bird Walk," the hauntingly sad tone of Patsy Cline singing "I Fall to Pieces," the serious tone of a tragic opera, the inspiring tone of a gospel song, and the reverent tone of a hymn like "Amazing Grace."

Poems not intended to be sung, however, can also rely on verbal and musical elements to project a tone. Rhythm and rhyme have been discussed at length in a previous section; the significance of rhythm ("the beat" of a poem) to establishing the tone of a poem can easily be seen. Rhyme, too, has obvious tonal qualities. You do need to recognize, though, that there is more to the sound of a poem as it relates to the tone it projects than just rhythm and rhyme. Tone in a poem is also a product of *sound effects*. Here are a few of the more commonly found sound effects.

Onomatopoeia

Although onomatopoeia does refer to words that imitate sounds—*buzz, roar, sweep, hiss, rattle*—its significance to tone is far more than this simple definition conveys. It also includes what some scholars refer to as *sound-symbolism* (although recent trends in literary analysis prefer the expression *icon* over *symbol* when referring to this aspect of written representation of sound). Regardless, onomatopoeia refers to words, lines, and passages whose sound, size, movement, and overall effect denote the sense or meaning. The sounds work together to carry the meaning. Consider Tennyson's *The Princess* ("Come Down, O Maid"—1847):

> . . . **The moan of doves in immemorial elms,**
> **And murmuring of innumerable bees.**

Notice how, in this first stanza of a poem written by Robert Burns in the late eighteenth century, the sounds work together to carry meaning and establish the tone.

Afton Water

> **Flow gently, sweet Afton, among thy green braes,**
> **Flow gently, I'll sing thee a song in thy praise;**
> **My Mary's asleep by thy murmuring stream,**
> **Flow gently, sweet Afton, disturb not her dream.**

by Robert Burns

The sounds here seem to have a "feel" about them that relates to the meaning and results in a tone.

Phonic Echo Devices

There are three major devices in which sound is repeated or "echoed."

Alliteration

In alliteration, the initial consonant or consonant cluster sounds in stressed syllables are repeated (generally in successive or closely associated stressed syllables).

> **Lo, *how* I *hold* mine arms abroad,**
> **Thee *to* receive ready . . .**

In its more extreme form, alliteration becomes the "tongue-twister"—those consonant-packed lines that you attempt to repeat "real fast" without "tripping" on your tongue: "Peter Piper picked a peck of pickled peppers" and "She sells sea-shells by the sea-shore." For a variety of reasons many people are attracted to alliteration, and examples can be found in many forms in addition to poetry.

Alliteration is used by the broadcast media as an attention-getting device, by advertisers to help a slogan stay in the consumer's mind, and by writers in general to lighten for the reader material that might otherwise be dry or boring. For example, a newspaper might use "The Top Ten Terrific Tomatoes to Try This Time for Your Texas Territory" to head a variety and region chart for growing tomatoes in Texas. A jingle for a new car wash named "Curly Carl's" that is in competition with "Sudsy Sam" might be

> Curly Carl can keep your car,
> Scrubbed, sparkling like a star.
> No scuffs, no scum, no scrapes, no scratches,
> So Sudsy Sam still can't match us.

Once again, the sounds have a "feel" that relates to the meaning and results in a tone.

Assonance

In assonance, the same (or similar) vowel sounds are repeated in nearby words (usually in stressed syllables). Unlike rhyme, which has similarity of both vowel and final consonant sounds (for example, *book* and *took*), assonance repeats only the vowel sounds and ends with different consonant sounds. Notice the use of elements of rhyme, alliteration (w), and assonance in this anonymous ballad:

> ### Helen of Kirconnell
>
> I wish I were where Helen lies,
> Night and day on me she cries;
> O that I were where Helen lies
> On fair Kirconnell lea:

"I" and "night" both contain the long *i* sound. This assonance is emphasized in the rhyme of "lies" with "cries." You also may find assonance a popular substitution for end rhyme, especially in the ballad form:

His hounds they lie downe at his feete,
So well they can their master keepe.

Consonance

Final consonant sounds of stressed syllables are repeated while the preceding vowels are different. Consonance is often used in conjunction with alliteration (as in *reader* and *rider*); however, initial alliteration is not always a factor (as in *learn* and *torn*). The aural appeal can be heard in George Wither's use of consonance in the last stanza of "Shall I Wasting in Despair" in which *d, r, v, l,* and *t* are repeated:

Great, or good, or kind, or fair,
I will ne'er the more despair,
If she love me, this believe,
I will die, ere she shall grieve.
If she slight me when I woo,
I can scorn, and let her go.
    For, if she be not for me,
    What care I for whom she be?

(Note also that the basis for "eye rhyme" often is consonance: *gone, stone.*)

Cacophony and Dissonance

These two sound effects can be examined in terms of comparison and contrast. Both terms refer to harshness of sounds that produce an unpleasant or unsettling tone. A sound has dissonance when it is harsh, inharmonious, or discordant with the sounds and rhythm that surround it. A sound has cacophony when it is simply harsh in and of itself, regardless of the sounds and rhythms that surround it. Cacophony is often an accident; dissonance (discordance with surrounding sounds and rhythms), on the other hand, can be very deliberate.

Note the conscious use of dissonance in "Broken-Down Car."

A budget bruised, bent blistered broken relic
    needin' fixin'.
Dented dimpled dinges from fender benders galore—
    grief over grime and time.

Courage: There goes cash on four tires.
Frame and bumpers lookin' good—not me
    still under hood.

Clank . . . grind . . . bang . . . grime grating against
   metal and skin.
Squirting oil and squirming torso—pain.

Start and stop motor again—not a gain.
   Sorry mess
Headin' for the Junk-heap next, I guess.

by C. Myers-Shaffer

Cacophony, harsh sounds (words) that are unpleasant in and
of themselves, can result from many things, such as too many
unvoiced plosives in a poem. Some poets feel that overuse of *s* or
sh sounds have a cacophonic effect and consequently try to avoid
them.

Euphony

Euphony refers to sounds that are pleasing and easy to pronounce,
producing a pleasant tone. Sounds exhibiting euphony (the opposite of cacophony) generally contain more vowel sounds (thought
to have more "sonority" or resonance than consonants and to
cause more vibration or "voicing" sounds when used) and lean
toward the liquids, nasals, and semivowels (*l, m, n, r, v, w*), with the
voiced consonants being heard as "softer" (*b, d, g, v, z*) and the
unvoiced consonants as "harsher" (*p, t, k, f, s*). Poetry exhibiting
euphony tends also to avoid difficult-to-pronounce sound combinations and to stress sound patterns that include repetitions. (See
poem on page 251.)

   In determining the *euphony* of a selection (its sense of a pleasing tone), do not overlook the part meaning sometimes contributes
to that sense of pleasantness. One poem that many consider "pleasant" to the tongue and ear is "The Raven," although the tone is
very disquieting. (See pages 283–287.)

Tone in Drama

As with poetry, drama shares with prose (particularly with the narrative form) many elements that help to set the tone, such as setting, use of language, and character revelation. But drama has one
unique feature that can definitely affect the tone, both of the individual elements of the play and of the play as a whole: drama is
meant to be acted on a stage by players. As a result, the playwright

can include stage directions instructing the actors concerning facial expressions, gestures, and tone of voice to use for delivery of the lines of dialogue. Even if the viewer misses the meaning of the words, he or she can still gain a sense of their tone by hearing the way they are *actually spoken*. Add to this that the viewer does not need to imagine the setting; the stage can be set up to replicate (to varying degrees) the setting so that he or she can actually see the place (or at the very least suggestions of the place). The result? A sense of tone based on the audience's physical, intellectual, and emotional senses.

Questions to Apply the Literary Principles Concerning Tone

Ask the following questions to help you identify and understand tone.

1. Who is the speaker?

2. What is the tone (of voice) of the speaker in the entire work?

3. Can the tone (of voice) of the author be identified? If so, does it differ from the tone (of voice) of the speaker?

4. With what tone (of voice) does each of the characters address one another?

5. How does the use of language and/or meaning of the language in context contribute to the tone?

6. Do the rhythm, rhyme, and other sound effects contribute to the tone in this work?

7. How does the setting contribute to the tone in this work? What, if applicable, is the work's atmosphere?

8. How does the writer's style contribute to the tone of this work?

Additional Points to Remember About Tone

▶ Become familiar with descriptive adjectives that relate to tone of voice (both of a speaker's tone and the tone of a work). A list of such words might include the following:

adulatory	coquettish	infatuated	polemic
amatory	defamatory	inhospitable	querulous
amorous	depreciatory	insidious	remorseful
appreciative	dyspeptic	irritable	sadistic
antagonistic	egotistical	magnanimous	sardonic
belligerent	embittered	malicious	scandalous
cajoling	enamored	menacing	scurrilous
choleric	flirtatious	minatory	surly
contentious	forbearant	morose	tranquil
compassionate	indulgent	ominous	unctuous

▶ Notice that many of the words that describe the tone of a work or the tone of voice a speaker uses also describe the style and/or the level of diction used. For example, *concise* can refer to the tone, the style, the syntax, and the diction, with each usage looking at the words of the selection from a slightly different perspective.

▶ A written work can project a tone on at least five different levels, including the tone of:

1. The speaker

2. The author

3. The work

4. Each individual character

5. A specific word, phrase, sentence, or portion of the work

Principle Four: Identify Character and Characterization

Gift of a Poor Blind Girl

A poor blind girl in England brought to a clergyman thirty shillings for the missionary cause. He objected, "You are a poor blind girl, and cannot afford to give so much."

"I am indeed blind," said she, "but can afford to give thirty shillings better perhaps than you suppose." "How so?" "I am, sir, by trade a basket-maker, and can work as well in the dark as in the light. Now, I am sure, in the last winter it must have cost those girls who have eyes more than thirty shillings for candles to work by, which I have saved; and therefore hope you will take the amount for the missionaries."

Anecdotes. 239. *Fables of Aesop, and Others: Translated into English with Instructive Applications by Samuel Croxall, D.D., 1722*

A **character** is a person (or a being given the characteristics of a person) who appears in, acts and/or speaks in, narrates, or is referred to in a literary work. **Characterization** is the methods or combinations of methods used to portray that person or being.

Distinguishing Traits

The basis for characterization is the revelation of the character's *identifying traits,* the mental and ethical (including moral) traits (qualities or characteristics) of the individual. The identification of character traits (their definitions, the involvement of implied moral judgment, and identification of what is their source and what elements work together to shape a person's "character") is the subject of debate among cultural psychologists and others who research the subject.

Some view character as a product of heredity; others see it as a product of environment. Which is the predominant factor in character development is arguable and interesting to keep in mind when reading literary works in which the author, through various literary means, reveals his or her bias on the subject in the course of presenting characters in the work. How readers and writers view character traits (as good or bad, as desirable or undesirable) is oftentimes a result of their home environment and of the culture that surrounds them. In England and the United States, traditionally, character and traits of character are defined in terms that are inherent in the Judeo-Christian tradition.

How do you define character traits? A person's temperament, disposition, and distinctive personal and social traits can be viewed as a function of his or her (1) attitudes, (2) emotional states, (3) response mechanisms, and (4) intrinsic values. All these elements combine to make an individual's personality. Within each of these areas is a continuum of traits that range (based on cultural and family traditions as well as personal perceptions) between two extremes. Although this treatment of the subject is by no means exhaustive, here are a few considerations to be made regarding each area.

Attitudes

A character's attitudes in terms of character are his or her mental positions or feelings with regard to self, other people, objects, or a subject. A person's attitude can be described as good or bad (as in "My son has such a bad attitude"), productive or unproductive, responsive or unresponsive, and the lists goes on. Evidently, there are many degrees of productivity and responsiveness; however, people frequently tend to make generalizations that polarize our perceptions of a person's attitude to either the positive or the negative.

How can an attitude be described? Some possibilities are shown here.

Positive Attitudes	Negative Attitudes
productive	unproductive
responsive	unresponsive
good	bad
kind	unkind
soft	firm
helpful	helpless
lenient	strict
inspired	uninspired
godly	irreverent
constructive	destructive
forgiving	unforgiving
happy	sad

The discussion of attitudes as they relate to character also includes those attitudes that are not individual in nature. A group of people (such as a family or community), a nation, or a literary work can have a prevailing attitude. Sometimes this is referred to as the climate—the political climate might be referred to as liberal or conservative; the intellectual climate might be referred to as decaying; the moral climate, as strict; the climate of opinion, as "going against" a particular stance; and the climate of the stock market, as bullish. A prevailing attitude or climate can also sometimes be identified in a literary work. Of course, the groups of characters within the work itself may also project a "climate" in and of itself—a prevailing attitude. When this prevailing attitude is seen consistently throughout the works of a particular writer, you might attribute this as part of his or her style. Sometimes the literary climate will produce groups of writers who share a prevailing attitude in their works, thus giving birth to a movement or tradition. An example might be the "tradition of black humor" that includes works by Kurt Vonnegut, Thomas Pynchon, and playwright Harold Pinter—works that in comically dealing with grotesque, horrid situations project attitudes (and as a result, tones) that are angry and bitter.

Emotions

The emotions of a character are his or her intense feelings. These emotions may include states of excitement, emotional attachment or dissociation, stability or instability, emotional insulation, emotionalism, and degrees of emotional appeal.

Some clues to a character's emotional state include references to the following traits:

▶ His or her sentiments, impressions, experiences, or a "deep sense" concerning something that reflect the character's emotional feelings

▶ Degrees of stimulation and exhilaration that reflect his or her state of excitement

▶ A character's (negative or positive) transference of feelings, identification with others (individuals or groups), and introjection or projection that reflect his or her state of attachment; as well as references to schizophrenia, multiple personalities, split personalities, double or dual personalities, personality disorganization, disconnection, and personality disintegration that relate to the character's state of dissociation

▶ His or her feelings of inferiority, inadequacy, moral deficiency, emotional immaturity, lability, or pathological mendacity that reflect the character's lack of stability—a state of instability

▶ Signs of escapism (flight and withdrawal), isolation, defense mechanisms, fantasy (dreamlike thinking), sublimation, rationalization, and negativism that reflect a character's state of emotional insulation

▶ Anxiety, hysteria, melancholia, depression, preoccupation, apathy, lethargy, stupor, euphoria, indifference, detachment, or elation that reflect his or her state of emotionalism

▶ The character's nature in terms of his or her demonstrativeness, sensationalism, or sense of the dramatic (melodrama) that influence the perception for the reader (or self-perception) of that character's degree of emotional appeal

Of course, certain attention must be paid to psychologically based inferences and direct characterizations that reflect a character's defects in the areas of personality (including pathological personality types, such as maladjusted, inferior, perverse, antisocial, sociopathic, psychotic, alcoholic, and masochistic) and social adjustment (assaultive reactions and antisocialism, among others). To appreciate fully and to identify adequately the emotional state(s) of a literary character sometimes requires some familiarity with symptoms of neuroses (such as traumatic anxiety, obsessive-compulsive, occupational, fright, and phobic); psychosomatic disorders (such as bulimia); disturbances in emotions (such as anxiety or hysteria), thoughts (such as delusions or mental blocks), and psychomotor disorders (such as convulsions or twitching); and mental states (such as amnesia, somnambulism, and trances).

Fundamental, however, to the examination of a character's emotions is the degree to which the individual exhibits feelings or lack of feelings. Also, of great importance to distinguishing character traits is identifying the role of hope and hopelessness in that character's perspective of life.

Sometimes a character has emotions that are reflected in almost all he or she says, does, or thinks. But these emotions, as with attitudes, can polarize to the positive or to the negative. Generally, the following emotions are regarded as positive because they are rooted in feelings:

affection	warmheartedness	vehemence
passion	sentiment	gusto
sensitivity	fervor	zeal
sympathy	ardor	responsiveness
tenderness	cordiality	demonstrativeness

In some circumstances, positives can be excessive:

mawkishness	insipidity
sentimentality	melodrama
"mush"	emotionalism
"wearing one's heart on one's sleeve"	

At the other extreme are those emotions connotatively regarded as negative because of their lack of feeling:

nonfeeling	untouchability	obduracy
emotionlessness	unresponsiveness	imperviousness
heartlessness	unimpressionableness	apathy
frigidity	callousness	listlessness
coldheartedness	hardness	lethargy
coldbloodedness	hardheartedness	indifference

The degree to which these emotions (the emotions that stem from feelings or from the lack of feelings) can be viewed as positive or negative, however, depends greatly on context.

The role of hope and of its opposite, hopelessness, on character development and revelation should not be underestimated. Hope is a powerful motivating force as seen in last-minute plays that win the championship game or in acts of heroism that save lives or win wars. Being in a state of hopelessness can be equally powerful, as seen in suicides, unfulfilled dreams, and lives that have lost meaning.

Words connotative of a character's sense of hope:

expectation	reliance	assurance
trust	assumption	dreams
confidence	optimism	faith

Are all hopes justified? Is the character deluding himself or herself?

bubble	fool's paradise	pipe dream

Words connotative of hopelessness:

impossibility	disappointment	cynical
despair	defeated	gloominess
desperation	pessimistic	irrevocability
despondent	irretrievable	incorrigible
forlorn	incurable	disconsolate

Sometimes understanding the role of hope in a character's life is very important to understanding his or her role in the work.

Another term you may encounter when examining a character's emotional state is *disposition*. "Emotional state" is connotative of that person's feelings at a *particular time*—his or her emotional state may be happy today, unhappy tomorrow. In contrast, a character's disposition is connotative of his or her feelings as well as *natural attitudes toward life* that are somewhat consistent throughout his or her life. Although George, for example, might be unhappy today, he generally has a happy disposition, outlook on life, or temperament.

Response Mechanisms

How does the character respond physically and emotionally to life? Character traits that are revealed by the character's response to the world about him or her can, as with attitudes and emotions, be discussed by examining the extremes.

▶ To what degree does the character exhibit signs of stress when put under pressure? These character traits include, for example, agitation, perturbation, trepidation, fury, frenzy, excitation, exhilaration, or explosion. In contrast, the character might react with dispassion, even-temperness, impassiveness, nonchalance, composure, serenity, self-confidence, offhandedness, placidity, or staidness.

▶ How nervous does the character become? A nervous character has agitation or trepidation or is unnerved, unstrung, demoralized, or shaken. In the opposite case, the character is steady, calm, unflinching, steel-nerved, or relaxed.

▶ Is the character patient or impatient? Tolerant or intolerant? Resigned or anxious?

Other character traits that are revealed by a character's response mechanisms include:

honest (dishonest)
fight (flight)
brave (coward)
courageous (fearful)
wise (foolish)
faithful (unfaithful)
rash (cautious)
pleasant (unpleasant)
witty (dull)
humorous (boring)
pitying (pitiless)
pleasant (unpleasant)
regretful (glad)

rejoicing (lamenting)
happy (sad)
cheerful (solemn)
contented (discontented)
social (unsocial)
hospitable (inhospitable)
companionable (secluded)
courteous (discourteous)
forgiving (unforgiving,
     revengeful, retaliatory)
giving (taking, envious,
     jealous, resentful)

Intrinsic Values

Character traits can also arise from examining the character's intrinsic values: those traits that result from the value judgments made in the heart of the person—what is really important (or not important) to him or her. At their core are fundamental concepts: home, family, country, religion, fellow-man, self, and other value-type concepts.

How the reader perceives the character traits that are part of the character's intrinsic values is largely a product of the attitudes, emotions, and response mechanisms he or she has exhibited in word and deed within the work. These perceptions can lead to generalizations about the person, based on his or her attitudes, emotions, and response mechanisms exhibited; and these generalizations then become judgments of "what kind of person he or she is." Are generalizations, based on character traits, always accurate statements of that person's intrinsic values? The appropriateness of such conclusions is debatable.

Based on the character traits revealed by a character's attitudes, emotions, and response mechanisms in a literary selection, the reader may conclude that he or she is trustworthy, criminal, proud, humble, fastidious, honorable, shallow. In other words, the reader may view a character as a devil or a saint. If the reader generalizes the exhibited traits of character to mean that the person is honorable or moral or shallow, the reader then tends to assume that this person will most likely exhibit the characteristics of "honor" or of "morality" or of "shallowness" in most situations because these characteristics arise from the person's intrinsic value system.

Methods of Characterization

Samuel Johnson

Mrs. Digby told me that when she lived in London with her sister Mrs. Brooke, they were, every now and then, honoured by the visits of Dr. Samuel Johnson. He called on them one day, soon after the publication of his immortal dictionary. The two ladies paid him due compliments on the occasion. Among other topics of praise, they very much commended the omission of all naughty words. 'What! my dears! then you have been looking for them?' said the moralist. The ladies, confused at being caught, dropped the subject of the dictionary.

Roles

As previously discussed, a character is a person (or a being given the characteristics of a person) who appears in, acts and/or speaks in, narrates, or is referred to in a literary work. Oftentimes the characters in a work can be identified by the role they play in relation to the story.

Hero   The leading male character who exhibits superior qualities

Heroine   The leading female character who exhibits superior qualities

Superhero(ine)   A larger-than-life hero(ine), usually super-natural

Villain(ess)   A character who is often characterized as evil and is in opposition to the hero(ine)

Antihero(ine)   A hero(ine) who is more ordinary than the traditional hero(ine)

Protagonist   The hero(ine)

Antagonist   The villain(ess)

These seven terms are commonly used when talking about the chief characters in a literary work. Also, a character might be described using one of the following terms.

Flat   A flat character is only two-dimensional and can be described without the kind of details one needs to see him or her as an individual. These roles are often played by "extras" in movie and television productions, although sometimes named stars will assume these roles as "cameo" spots.

Round   In extreme contrast to the flat character, the round character is three-dimensional, complex, as lifelike as the literary medium allows. Unlike the flat character, the round character is complex and changes or grows in the course of the story. Naturally, shades of "flatness" or "roundness" abound along the continuum between these two extremes, with the plot and the intent of the writer largely dictating the degree to which a character is developed. Generally, the main characters are round.

Stock   A stock character is a conventional stereotypical character that is expected to appear in certain literary forms, such as the "Prince Charming" in fairy tales. A stock character is frequently used in literary traditions, but does not necessarily represent a particular class or group.

Type   A type character embodies or exhibits the characteristics of a particular class or group of people. A type character may be very individualized and unpredictable in personality and action and still represent the class or group to which he or she belongs. Television situation-comedies, as well as more serious shows, abound with type characters: Dr. Quinn in *Dr. Quinn, Medicine Woman* is a type who represents the professional women who were forerunners of the twentieth-century women's movements; Corky on *Murphy Brown* is a type who represents women who were reared following the stereotypical models of women's roles (such as being a beauty contest queen) but who are attempting success in less traditional, more professional roles; the children in *Seventh Heaven* are types of children who are attempting to adjust to life in a larger-than-average family.

Stereotype   Unlike the type character, the stereotype is predictable, one who is repeated without variation and who lacks originality: the "tough" woman who (behind her crusty exterior) is soft-hearted; the leading man who is "tall, dark, and handsome"; the "absent-minded" professor. The stock character is a stereotype that arises from certain literary conventions, but stereotypes may also be the product of political and social trends and national mores.

Look for a moment at the nation's perception of a hero. A hero is traditionally portrayed as someone who is honorable and brave. Writers of certain literary forms have for many years characterized high-ranking military and political leaders (princes, kings, knights, generals, soldiers, and presidents) as men of honor and respect, willing to sacrifice self for country. They became heroes who were given stereotypical characteristics: tall, handsome, brave, strong, and brilliant military strategists and ingenious survivalists whether in jungles or deserts. Even those who were not-so-handsome or not-so-tall would still, under fire, exhibit the stereotypical characteristics of a hero. Such stereotypes depend upon a perception of military and political leaders as true heroes worthy of the honor and respect they receive.

Now that you have an overview of character traits, and a few of the basic labels by which characters are identified, examine the *techniques* that a writer can use to present a character and to reveal his or her character traits and/or the *ethos* or character (emotions) of either the writer or speaker.

Disclosure of Character

Characterization (character development in a story) can be accomplished through many different methods or techniques including (1) stereotyping, (2) exposition, (3) the character's actions, (4) the character's words, (5) the character's thoughts, (6) the words of others, and (7) the use of setting.

Stereotyping

Stereotyping as a method of characterization involves identifying a character with a group about which you have certain cultural assumptions (stereotypes). If a character is, as an illustration, a West Texas cowboy who is visiting Boston for the first time, the reader might make certain assumptions concerning his dress, speech, and character traits that are based on stereotypical conceptions of what a West Texas cowboy is like and of how he would manage in Boston. Obviously, this method of characterization can work for or counter to the purpose of the writer.

Exposition

Sometimes the author or speaker will describe the character. These explanatory messages from the author or speaker might include descriptions of the person's background, motivating forces, personality traits, relationships, and physical characteristics. Generally, a reader tends to accept these characterizations as truthful and accurate until proven to be otherwise by the character's own words, revealed thoughts, and actions.

An example of characterization through exposition can be seen in these few lines from the early nineteenth-century American short story "Rip Van Winkle" by Washington Irving:

> . . . I have observed that he was a simple, good-natured man; he was, moreover, a kind neighbor, and an obedient, hen-pecked husband. . . .
>
> Certain it is, that he was a great favorite among all the good wives of the village, . . .
>
> . . . He would never refuse to assist a neighbor even in the roughest toil, and was a foremost man at all country frolics for husking Indian corn, or building stone fences; the women of the village, too, used to employ him to run their errands, and to do such little odd jobs as their less obliging husbands would not do for them. In a word, Rip was ready to attend to anybody's business but his own; but as to doing family duty, and keeping his farm in order, he found it impossible.

At about the same time Irving was writing in America, Jane Austen (a writer of the Romantic Period) was in England writing this characterization in her Novel of Manners, *Persuasion*:

Vanity was the beginning and the end of Sir Walter Elliot's character; vanity of person and of situation. He had been remarkably handsome in his youth; and, at fifty-four, was still a very fine man. Few women could think more of their personal appearance than he did; nor could the valet of any new made lord be more delighted with the place he held in society. He considered the blessing of beauty as inferior only to the blessing of a baronetcy; and the Sir Walter Elliot, who united these gifts, was the constant object of his warmest respect and devotion.

Character's Actions

What does the character do at times of crisis? How does he or she react to conflict? To everyday situations? To extraordinary situations? A significant element to consider when examining characterization by actions of a character is the tendency toward being judgmental of the character based on what the reader thinks he or she would do in like circumstances. The value of such moral and ethical judgments in better understanding the character is yet another area of debate. Such excursions into the area of "If I were in this situation I would . . ." can, however, provide interesting grounds for plot analysis and self-examination.

Before making a value judgment based on a generalization concerning his or her character (such as "He is destructive" or "She is too lenient"), examine the person's actions to try to identify what individual character traits are revealed by those actions (such as "He exhibited anger and frustration when he destroyed the statue" or "She exhibited kindness, but also seemed intimidated when she did not punish her daughter for taking the car without permission"). Hasty generalizations that do not take into account context, cause-and-effect relationships, and individual personality traits that blend together within an action can lead to faulty conclusions concerning the character.

You can, however, learn a great deal about a character from the way in which he or she reacts in different circumstances and situations. In this excerpt from Jane Austen's *Persuasion*, what elements of Mary's character are revealed by the way that she treats Anne? What do Mary's actions reveal about her personality?

Something occurred, however, to give her a different duty. Mary, often a little unwell, and always thinking a great deal of her own complaints, and always in the habit of claiming Anne when any thing was the matter, was indisposed; and foreseeing that she should not have a day's health all the autumn, entreated, or rather required her, for it was hardly entreaty, to come to Uppercross Cottage, and bear her company as long as she should want her, instead of going to Bath.

Character's Words

You also can deduce a great deal about a character's personality from his or her own words. As with the other elements of characterization, do not overlook the significance of context and motivation when examining a character's words. You need to address such questions as:

▶ To whom is he or she speaking?
▶ Are his or her words true reflections of how the character feels or thinks?
▶ Is there any indication that he or she is putting forth a false character?
▶ What motivation might the character have for deception?

In addition, look for unintentional revelation of character. Sometimes a character will reveal significant hidden aspects of his or her personality from words spoken in an unguarded moment or during a heated argument.

Here is a conversation that takes place in *Persuasion*. What do Mary and Lady Russell unintentionally reveal about themselves in this exchange? Remember that this revealment is not unintentional on the part of the writer.

> 'Oh! he talks of you,' cried Charles, 'in such terms,'—Mary interrupted him 'I declare, Charles, I never heard him mention Anne twice all the time I was there. I declare, Anne, he never talks of you at all.'
>
> 'No,' admitted Charles, 'I do not know that he ever does, in a general way—but however, it is a very clear thing that he admires you exceedingly.— His head is full of some books that he is reading upon your recommendation, and he wants to talk to you about them; . . . I overheard him telling Henrietta all about it—and then "Miss Elliot" was spoken of in the highest terms! . . .'

'And I am sure,' cried Mary warmly, 'it was very little to his credit, if he did. Miss Harville only died last June. Such a heart is very little worth having; is it, Lady Russell? I am sure you will agree with me.'

'I must see Captain Benwick before I decide,' said Lady Russell, smiling.

'And that you are very likely to do very soon, I can tell you, ma'am,' said Charles. 'Though he had not nerves for coming away with us and setting off again afterwards to pay a formal visit here, he will make his way over to Kellynch one day by himself, you may depend on it. . . . So, I give you notice, Lady Russell.'

'Any acquaintance of Anne's will always be welcome to me,' was Lady Russell's kind answer.

'Oh! as to being Anne's acquaintance,' said Mary, 'I think he is rather my acquaintance, for I have been seeing him every day this last fortnight.'

'Well, as your joint acquaintance, then, I shall be very happy to see Captain Benwick.'

What roles does Charles play in this passage? How would you describe his character?

Character's Thoughts

A character's own thoughts (through such devices as interior monologue and stream of consciousness) can be a rich source for insight into motivation and character; however, be alert for elements of self-delusion on the part of the character. Also, be aware of the role that *perception* plays in thought. A character's perception includes:

▶ Awareness of the environment through his or her physical senses
▶ Realizations of events, activities, and conversations
▶ Insight into the deeper meanings of the words and events that occur
▶ Comprehension of the significance of these words and events

A character's thoughts can be penetrating, discerning, and discriminating; or they can be shallow, undiscerning, and indiscriminating.

In the context of the situation, is the person sagacious and shrewd? Sensible? Sensitive? Knowing? Discriminative? Or is his or her thinking shallow? Insincere? Insensitive? Indiscriminative?

Again, examine an excerpt from *Persuasion*. What does Anne reveal about herself with her thoughts?

> . . . He [Captain Benwick] had been engaged to Captain Harville's sister, and was now mourning her loss. They had been a year or two waiting for fortune and promotion. Fortune came, his prize-money as lieutenant being great,—promotion, too, came at *last*; but Fanny Harville did not live to know it. She had died the preceding summer, while he was at sea. Captain Wentworth believed it impossible for man to be more attached to woman than poor Benwick had been to Fanny Harville, or to be more deeply afflicted under the dreadful change. . . .
>
> 'And yet,' said Anne to herself, as they now moved forward to meet the party, 'he has not, perhaps, a more sorrowing heart than I have. I cannot believe his prospects so blighted for ever. He is younger than I am; younger in feeling, if not in fact; younger as a man. He will rally again, and be happy with another.'

Words of Others

A lot can be learned about a character by "listening in" on what other characters have to say about him or her.

In this excerpt, the reader learns something of the character of Captain Wentworth (in *Persuasion*):

> 'No,' said Anne, 'that I can easily believe to be impossible, but in time perhaps—we know what time does in every case of affliction, and you must remember, Captain Harville, that your friend [Captain Benwick] may yet be called a young mourner—Only last summer, I understand.'
>
> 'Ay, true enough,' (with a deep sigh) 'only June.'
>
> 'And not known to him, perhaps, so soon.'
>
> 'Not till the first week in August, when he came home from the Cape,—just made into the Grappler. I was at Plymouth, dreading to hear of him; he sent in letters, but the Grappler was under orders for Portsmouth. There the news must follow him, but who was to tell it? not I. I would as soon have been run up to the yard-arm. Nobody could do it, but that good fellow, (pointing to Captain Wentworth). The Laconia had come into Plymouth the week before; no danger of her being sent to sea again. He stood his chance for the rest—wrote up for leave of absence, but

without waiting the return, travelled night and day till he got to Portsmouth, rowed off to the Grappler that instant, and never left the poor fellow for a week; that's what he did, and nobody else could have saved poor James. You may think, Miss Elliot, whether he is dear to us!'

Use caution, however, in accepting the words of other characters. Be sure to examine their motives (and the possibility of differences in their perceptions) for how their personal interest might affect their words concerning the character in question, especially when the character who is speaking holds a different opinion or a different value system than that of the person about whom he or she is speaking. The hidden agenda of the speaker, the possibility of misrepresentation of the person who is the subject of the conversation, can only be discerned by context.

Here Anne (of *Persuasion*) overhears Wentworth and Louisa talking about Louisa's sister, Henrietta:

. . . Louisa's voice was the first distinguished. She seemed to be in the middle of some eager speech. What Anne first heard was, 'And so, I made her go. I could not bear that she should be frightened from the visit by such nonsense. . . . When I have made up my mind, I have made it. And Henrietta seemed entirely to have made up hers to call at Winthrop today—and yet, she was as near giving it up, out of nonsensical complaisance!'

'She would have turned back then, but for you?'

'She would indeed, I am almost ashamed to say it.'

'Happy for her, to have such a mind as yours at hand! . . . Your sister is an amiable creature; but *yours* is the character of decision and firmness, I see. If you value her conduct or happiness, infuse as much of your own spirit into her, as you can.'

This revealing passage gives insight into not necessarily Henrietta's personality, but rather into Captain Wentworth's and Louisa's *perception* of Henrietta's personality. As a result, the reader also learns a great deal about these two characters as well—concerning their beliefs and value systems. Another interesting note: Wentworth, in his conversation with Louisa, speaks directly to *her* concerning her personality ("but yours is the character of decision and firmness"). Not uncommon are conversations in which a character will compliment or criticize the character of the other speaker. Again, be sensitive to the roles of perception and motive.

Use of Setting

The effects of the stereotypes associated with characters from certain regional settings (environments) has already been briefly touched upon in the discussion of disclosure of character through *stereotypes*. The setting can, to varying degrees, be a factor in predicting character. Setting can also contribute to the elements that stimulate change in characters and be, as a result, significant to the story line. Even in those stories in which the characters do not change, as such, the setting can act as an agent of revelation of character.

An example might be a story set in a remote area of the Rocky Mountains. A group of people are on a back-to-nature excursion. Encounters with hardships that are a natural possibility in such a setting (a flash flood, a member falling and becoming injured, an attack by wild animals, running out of food, or becoming lost) can bring out in the characters' personalities tendencies toward bravery or cowardice, stamina or weakness, selflessness or selfishness, and other traits.

In real life, people are constantly affected by their environment—the settings around them. Likewise, the setting can affect characters in literature.

As you see, characterization can be accomplished by telling or by showing, through dialogue, action, examinations of motivating forces, and many other means. Character can be revealed through direct mention of the character trait, or it can be inferred indirectly through behavior.

The Four Humours

The concept of humours is based on early theories of physiology: there are (according to old theories of cosmology) four elements in the universe. The humours need to be in balance because if any one humour predominates, it can lead to sickness and disease and can affect personality.

The following chart summarizes these theories.

Element	Characteristic	Humour	Personality[*]
earth	cold, dry	black bile	melancholic —depressed, gloomy, gluttonous, sentimental

air	hot, moist	blood	*sanguine—*cheerful, hopeful, amorous
fire	hot, dry	yellow bile	*choleric—*angry, vengeful, impatient
water	cold, moist	phlegm	*phlegmatic—*stoic, apathetic, impassive, dull, cowardly

*A person was said to be of a sanguine personality, for example, if that humour was predominant. A well-balanced person has all four humours in balance.

The four elements and the four humours are significant to the Comedy of Humours and to many other forms of prose, poetry, and drama throughout English and (to a certain extent) American literature as a device used by writers to identify the personalities of characters.

Jane Austen, for example, refers to his "sanguine temper" in this description of Captain Wentworth in *Persuasion:*

Captain Wentworth had no fortune. He had been lucky in his profession, but spending freely, what had come freely, had realized nothing. But, he was confident that he should soon be rich;—full of life and ardour, he knew that he should soon have a ship, and soon be on a station that would lead to every thing he wanted. He had always been lucky; he knew he should be so still.—Such confidence, powerful in its own warmth, and bewitching in the wit which often expressed it, must have been enough for Anne; but Lady Russell saw it differently.—His *sanguine temper, and fearlessness of mind, operated very differently on her. She saw in it but an aggravation of the evil. It only added a dangerous character to himself. He was brilliant, he was headstrong.—Lady Russell had little taste for wit; and of any thing approaching to imprudence a horror. She deprecated the connection in every light.

The Effects of Characters on the Readers

Up to this point, the focus has been on the *techniques* of character-ization over substance, viewing characters as a "part" of a story and viewing characterization as a means to an end without really addressing characters and characterization as they blend into the literary work to create a unified whole.

As pointed out by novelist Kit Reed in *Mastering Fiction Writing* (Writer's Digest Books, 1991), writers sometimes "become" the characters in their stories, just as actors may become the char-acters that they are portraying. This is a very interesting and useful perspective for the reader of literature as well as for the writer. The reader also brings his or her own experience to the work and, to varying degrees, becomes the characters. Generally, the reader does form some type of relationship with the characters. In many respects, the degree of involvement you have with the characters and the extent of whatever esthetic distance may be between char-acter and reader quite often rests in the hands of the writer. For example, the writer may use the literary elements and characteriza-tions in such a way as to make the reader actually experience a sense of participation in the story—to become, through **empathy,** that character. Sometimes empathy is accomplished through vivid descriptions of experiences that are common to both the reader and the character. For instance, the reader can empathize with the Beadsman in the first stanza of John Keats's *The Eve of St. Agnes* because the reader can vicariously "feel" the cold as it is described:

> St. Agnes' Eve—Ah, bitter chill it was!
> The owl, for all his feathers, was a-cold;
> The hare limped trembling through the frozen grass,
> And silent was the flock in woolly fold:
> Numb were the Beadsman's fingers, while he told
> His rosary, and while his frosted breath,
> Like pious incense from a censer old,
> Seemed taking flight for heaven, without a death,
> Past the sweet Virgin's picture, while his prayer he
> saith.

The reader's *sympathy* in this context includes a sense of emo-tional agreement (empathy). In "Lord Randal," the anonymous fifteenth-century ballad, the reader can certainly feel pity and grieve both for the poisoned child and for his mother; however, the reader generally does not identify with them or "feel" what they are feeling, although the emotion of the last stanza is very moving:

"O I fear ye are poisond, Lord Randal, my son!
O   I fear ye are poisond, my handsome young
man!"
    "O yes! I am poisond; mother, make my bed
soon,
For I'm sick at the heart, and I fain wald lie
down."

(Note: "Make my bed soon" is an expression said to refer to making a coffin—a bed for the sleep of death with *bed* also referring to the grave.)

Of course, the character can also elicit feelings of **antipathy** from the reader—aversion, dislike, distrust, disassociation, and, as a result, distance from the reader.

Another element in this question of involvement of the reader with the character is **pathos**. Modern slang would probably call many scenes of pathos real "tear jerkers," but pathos does occur when a passage (or scene) "captures the heart" of the reader or audience with intense feelings of sorrow and pity, as when Little Nell dies in *The Old Curiosity Shop* by Charles Dickens:

> By little and little, the old man had drawn back towards the inner chamber, while these words were spoken. He pointed there, as he replied, with trembling lips.
> "You plot among you to wean my heart from her. You never will do that—never while I, have life. I have no relative or friend but her—I never had—I never will have. She is all in all to me. It is too late to part us now."
> Waving them off with his hand, and calling softly to her as he went, he stole into the room. They who were left behind drew close together, and after a few whispered words followed him. They moved so gently, that their footsteps made no noise; but there were sobs from among the group, and sounds of grief and mourning.
> For she was dead. There, upon her little bed, she lay at rest. The solemn stillness was no marvel now.
> Her couch was dressed with here and there some winter berries and green leaves, gathered in a spot she had been used to favour. "When I die, put near me something that has loved the light, and had the sky above it always." Those were her words.

> **The old man held one languid arm in his, and**
> **had the small hand tight folded to his breast, for**
> **warmth. It was the hand she had stretched out to**
> **him with her last smile—the hand that had led him**
> **on through all their wanderings. Ever and anon he**
> **pressed it to his lips; then hugged it to his breast**
> **again, murmuring that it was warmer now; and as**
> **he said it he looked, in agony, to those who stood**
> **around, as if imploring them to help her.**
> **But she was dead, and past all help, or need of it.**

Pathos, fundamentally, is a response from the heart of the individual, yet pathos or the lack of pathos is also often a reflection of society and the norms and cultures of the age. Dickens and the readers of his day lived in a world without television, action-news reports, and big-screen movie theaters. As a result, stage productions, concerts, and reading were major outlets for the feelings and interests of the people. The readers of *The Old Curiosity Shop* during the period when it was first written reacted strongly to Little Nell's death. According to one historian, a reader wrote in his diary that he had never read such painful words; and another reader threw his copy of the book out of a train window in his grief. Writers of the time record that American readers were also deeply affected; a crowd of concerned people gathered at a New York pier to shout questions at the passengers on an arriving ship concerning Little Nell's fate. These reactions show that they had become personally involved with the character Little Nell as if she were a real person. Compare their reactions to the death of Little Nell to reactions to the weekly television movies based on real-life tragedies. Have people been conditioned as a society to perceive events differently? Like the original readers of Little Nell's death, society sometimes fuses fiction and reality, but has that erasing of the line that divides fiction from reality produced different effects in peoples' perceptions today as compared to the past?

Finally, involvement of the reader with a character is also greatly influenced by the degree of probability that exists surrounding the words, thoughts, deeds, and circumstances of the character. For the reader to become involved, to care about the story and the character, these elements all must have a degree of probability. They must be convincing. The importance of probability is nowhere more greatly seen than in the area of character development.

Character Development

A character quite often is not static, but rather a changing dual element that involves both you (as the reader) and the character in the work. The element of change is at the root of character development:

▶ Character development involves the writer's exposition of various character traits and the revelation of these traits to the reader as the work progresses. In other words, you get to know a character as the story unfolds.

▶ Character development also involves the concept of the person in the literary work *being* a developing character. Certain aspects of a character may change or evolve as a result of events in the narrative. Whether a person can change personality, disposition, or other like elements of character is questionable (hence directly affects the credibility of the characterization of the character unless masterfully done), but changes of attitude, emotional states, and some response mechanisms are common and necessary to making a character seem real to the reader. Such changes can be the critical turning point of the story.

Character development, as already mentioned, must be *credible*—rooted in probability. Although credibility can be established—or destroyed—in many ways, there are a few areas that are considered pivotal to the credibility of the entire work.

Did the Character Have Sufficient Motivation to Change?

For the reader to be convinced that a character really has changed, he or she must also be convinced that there is some reason to change: directly stated, character change often is seen as a cause-and-effect relationship. To see the effect (the change) without seeing the cause or without being convinced that what is being presented as the cause is sufficient motivation (reason) for the change, weakens the credibility of the work.

Was There Sufficient Time (in Terms of Story Time) for the Character Change to Be Realistic and Probable?

People can suddenly change, but unless the reader or audience is thoroughly convinced of the motivation, such abrupt changes leave the audience with an uneasy sense of incredulity. Of course, a writer is faced with the problem of translating real time (two hours for a movie, three to four hours to read an average novel, for example) into story time, which may involve days, weeks, years, or generations. There are some techniques available to the writer to give the reader a sense of protracted time, such as weaving subplots in and out of the main story or changing points of view; however, regardless of the methods used, the reader needs to be convinced that the character who has changed or who is changing has a realistic amount of time in which to make these changes.

Sometimes this is expressed as a "gradual awakening or dawning of the truth" of a situation, especially when a change in attitude is the result of learning a before-hidden truth (a truth that was either accidentally or deliberately concealed from the character or was consciously or subconsciously avoided by a character who "refuses to see the truth").

Has the Reader Been Given Adequate Information About the Character to Make the Change Seem Believable?

A story, because of the physical confines of the medium, is a "slice of life." Even in stories that follow a character from birth to death, only certain amounts of the details of that life can be presented. Consequently, "filling in" the reader on the parts not chronicled in detail is important to establishing the credibility of a character change.

One method to do this is the use of **flashback,** such as dream sequences, recollections by a character, and other means in which past events are detailed. (Sometimes the flashback can be almost the entire story, for example, the story might begin with the main character awaiting sentencing after a jury trial. He sits "remembering" the events that lead to that point and then concludes with the judge's pronouncement of sentence.) Another means a writer can use to achieve credibility for change is the effective use of **foreshadowing,** a means of preparing the reader or audience for upcoming events. Foreshadowing devices include the clues in a mystery or a prevailing atmosphere, among others.

JAMES BRUCE (1730–1794)

Bruce's book [*Travels to Discover the Source of the Nile, 5 volumes, 1790*] is both dull and dear. We join in clubs of five, each pays a guinea, draw lots who shall have it first, and the last to keep it for his patience.

Bruce's overbearing manner has raised enmity and prejudices; and he did wrong in retailing the most wonderful parts of his book in companies. A story may be credible when attended with circumstances, which seems false if detached.

I was present in a large company at dinner, when Bruce was talking away. Someone asked him what musical instruments were used in Abyssinia. Bruce hesitated, not being prepared for the question; and at last said, 'I think I saw one *lyre* there.' George Selwyn whispered . . . , 'Yes; and there is one less since he left the country.'

Character in Prose

A discussion of the role of character in prose must begin with at least a brief mention of the seventeenth- and eighteenth-century literary form called the character. The character is brief, very descriptive, and focuses on a person who embodies a particular virtue, vice, or character trait.

Also, the term *character* refers to places as well as to people, such as "That wonderful restaurant on the corner has a lot of character." By extension, an entire literary work (whether prose, poetry, or drama) might be said to have character; as such, identifying character is appropriate even in nonnarrative prose that does not include people as characters. Arguably, such references to character in a nonnarrative work can incorporate elements of tone, voice, and author's style, for example, "His essay is *characterized* by a somber tone that conflicts with the trivial nature of the subject and by a propensity toward the macabre."

When *character* refers to a person, the person's name, physical description, and personality traits generally come to mind. These distinguishing features help to set that person—that character—apart from others. To *characterize* any literary work, then, means to examine it to determine its distinguishing features.

Character in Poetry

In addition to the character revelation that is a part of narrative poetry, there is the concept of **ethos** that involves the reader's (or hearer's) impression of the moral character of the speaker. This is related to a reader's perception of persona or the speaker's voice, particularly in lyric poetry. Character, even in the case of an implied author, is significant to poetry as well as to prose.

What insight can you gain about the character of the speaker of these lines? (Take particular note of the last stanza.) How would you summarize his system of values?

Still to Be Neat

Still to be neat, still to be dressed,
As you were going to a feast;
Still to be powdered, still perfumed;
Lady, it is to be presumed,
Though art's hid causes are not found,
All is not sweet, all is not sound.
Give me a look, give me a face
That makes simplicity a grace;
Robes loosely flowing, hair as free;
Such sweet neglect more taketh me
Than all th' adulteries of art.
They strike mine eyes, but not my heart.

by Ben Jonson

Character in Drama

Although drama generally lacks the more direct communication between writer and reader that typifies works not intended to be acted out, there are ways in which the character of the characters in a play can be revealed.

Certain forms of drama carry with them characters whose personalities are expected to be exhibited in set ways. Such classic stock characters include the **alazon** who is a braggart, the **eiron** who is a self-deprecatory character, the **pharmakos** who is a victim of circumstances, the **bomolochos** who is a buffoon, and the **agroikos** who is either rustic or easily deceived.

Also characters can reveal their thoughts (and hence elements of their personality traits) through such devices as:

- ▶ A **confidant**, generally a friend, who "draws out" the person into talking about private matters
- ▶ A **foil**, a contrasting character, who through that very contrast causes the audience to see more clearly the personality of another character
- ▶ An **aside** in which a character directly addresses the audience
- ▶ A **soliloquy** in which a character, alone on stage, delivers a speech that reveals his or her thoughts

Of course action and dialogue are also of immeasurable importance in determining the personality of a character and in establishing whether he or she is **static** (unchanging) or **developing** (changing). Because you can actually see the character onstage, you have the advantage of being able to determine those personality traits that are evidenced by facial expression, tone of voice, body language, dress, and bearing or demeanor.

Here is a very small excerpt from Act II, Scene II of Shakespeare's *Julius Caesar*. Although the selection is brief, notice the insight into Caesar's personality you can gain.

Scene II.

The same. A hall in CAESAR'S *palace.*
Thunder and lightning, Enter JULIUS CAESAR, *in his nightgown.*

JULIUS CAESAR.

[This sets the atmosphere → and permits you to know it is a threatening situation for Caesar.]

Nor heaven nor earth have been at peace to-night: Thrice hath Calphurnia in her sleep cried out, 'Help, ho! they murder Caesar!'— Who's within?

Enter a SERVANT.

SERVANT.

My lord?

JULIUS CAESAR.

[Here you learn that ⟶ Caesar is superstitious —believing the priests can give him insight into his chances for success.]

Go bid the priests do present sacrifice, And bring me their opinions of success.

SERVANT.

I will, my lord.   [*Exit*]
Enter CALPHURNIA.

CALPHURNIA.

> What mean you, Caesar? think you to walk forth?
> You shall not stir out of your house to-day.

JULIUS CAESAR.

[Caesar faces trouble with confidence—unafraid.] ⟶

> Caesar shall forth: the things that threaten'd me
> Ne'er lookt but on my back; when they shall see
> The face of Caesar, they are vanished.

Questions to Apply the Literary Principles

Ask these questions to help you identify and understand character.

1. Who are the characters? (names, ages, occupations, and so forth)
2. What role does each play? (hero, villain, or other)
3. What attitudes do you see at work in each of the characters? Emotions? Response mechanisms? Intrinsic values?
4. Is the character stock? Type? Stereotype?
5. Is the character flat or round?
6. How is each character characterized?
7. What "humour" would you assign each character?
8. Is the character static or changing?
9. How would you characterize the work as a whole? What are its distinguishing features?

Additional Points to Remember

▶ Watch for **fictive** characters. A *fictive* character is a romanticized, idealized version of a real person. Fictive characters also may be "types," because they represent a group, a historical period, or some other element. The "noble savage" of such American writers as James Fenimore Cooper is an example of a fictive character who is an idealized representation of American Indians in the wilderness.

▶ Remember: a **dynamic** character is one who changes; a **static** character is one who does not change.

▶ Sometimes the true character of a character can only be determined from the work as a whole because the clues to character taken out of context might be the result of the circumstances. Here are three examples:

1. An isolated incident may show a character to be sweet, kind, and caring. Context might reveal that the character is being "two-faced" because he or she has a selfish hidden agenda and ulterior motives.

2. An isolated incident may show a character to have a distinctive voice with a forceful personality. Context might reveal that the character, perhaps even unconsciously, has elements of a dual personality. This condition is not necessarily indicative of a personality disorder. Many people will answer the telephone or attend a business meeting using a more formal style of language, tone of voice, and overall demeanor than the characteristics that they exhibit in the more casual atmosphere that surrounds close friends and family.

3. An isolated incident may show a character who has courage and resolve (in other words, strong motivation) for a change or an action. Context might reveal that the character had good intentions, but ultimately lacked sufficient resolve and motivation or that subsequent factors interfered with or lessened that drive for executing the change.

▶ Watch for **caricature** in characterization. In caricature, a character is not believable because one character trait dominates his or her personality to the extreme.

▶ Tension or conflict (in addition to action) can significantly affect the more complex characters in a story. The more subtle sides of personality or character are often revealed in response to tension.

▶ A way to get to know characters is to develop a character analysis. A character analysis consists of a list of prepared questions that, once completed, will give you a highly detailed description of the character. The questions might range from physical appearance to how the character feels about his or her profession to the character's romantic life.

Television and movie scriptwriters Jurgen Wolff and Kerry Cox, in *Successful Script Writing* (Writer's Digest Books, 1988), have developed a character analysis that, although intended for use by scriptwriters in planning their characters when writing scripts, is very useful for the reader in search of a better understanding of character.

▶ When determining character in a selection, be sure to establish the following information as a background:

The point of view used in the selection
The voice
The speaker's attitude

▶ Character can also refer to places and things, such as people may refer to a restaurant as having "a lot of character." Here is a occasion when the writer refers to the character of the ocean.

A Descent into the Maelstrom

. . . As the old man spoke, I became aware of a loud and gradually increasing sound, like the moaning of a vast herd of buffaloes upon an American prairie; and at the same moment I perceived that what seamen term the *chopping* character of the ocean beneath us, was rapidly changing into a current which set to the eastward. Even while I gazed, this current acquired a monstrous velocity. Each moment added to its speed—to its headlong impetuosity. . . .

by Edgar Allan Poe

Principle Five: Define the Language (Uses and Meanings)

The ordinary accounts of this vortex had by no means prepared me for what I saw. That of Jonas Ramus, which perhaps the most circumstantial of any, cannot impart the faintest conception either of the magnificence, of the horror of the scene—or of the wild bewildering sense of *the novel* which confounds the beholder. I am not sure from what point of view the writer in question surveyed it, nor at what time; but it could neither have been from the summit of Helseggen, nor during a storm. There are some passages of his description, nevertheless, which may be quoted for their details, although their effect is exceedingly feeble in conveying an impression of the spectacle.

from "A Descent into the Maelstrom" by
Edgar Allan Poe

How Language Is Used

You are traveling the American Midwest and open the newspaper to learn about the area. There are the grocery store ads; this week's featured item in the bakery—apple pie.

A crust, cooked apples, cinnamon.

You have not had fresh apple pie in a long time. You can see it in your mind's eye now: hot apple pie, rich pastry crust that flakes apart when your fork hits it. Steam rises from the slice and softly brushes your cheek as the slice is lifted from the rest of the pie—and it smells *so-o-o* good. You begin to breathe deeper. Aromas of hot cinnamon and vanilla and baked apples swirl around your head. Maybe add a thick slice of American cheese that melts down into the apples and sauce. No, better yet—a big scoop of rich vanilla ice cream that melts and makes a creamy, thick sauce all around the chunks of steamy apples, mixing with the cinnamon in great big swirls of flavor. Your mouth waters in anticipation of that first bite. After all, it's your duty to eat a slice of fresh-baked apple pie, because what represents America better than the flag, Mom, and apple pie?

Welcome to the world of **imagery.**

Roughly defined, imagery—the use of images—refers to the mental pictures you get as a result of words. An image can be **literal,** a standard meaning like the mental picture of apples and cinnamon baked in a pastry crust for an apple pie, or it can be **figurative,** like the American love of country associated with apple pie. Imagery can refer to visual pictures that come to mind or to sensual qualities (kinesthetic/motion, auditory/hearing, thermal/heat, tactile/touch, gustatory/taste, and olfactory/smell). Imagery can also refer to the abstract, the nonsensual qualities of love, hate, peace, fear, and other emotions.

An **image,** then, is the suggestion that certain words (certain uses of language) make to our minds, the mental representation. **Imagery** is a collection of images. Look at the collection of images used in the apple pie illustration. You see the pie (visual), smell the pie (olfactory), feel the steam (tactile), and taste the pie (gustatory). When one sense is described by terms usually associated with another sense, such a mixture of sensory images is called **synaesthesia:** "a red-hot candy." Imagery can also take on patterns as the images are used throughout a work, or can be seen as **image-clusters** (recurring groupings of images) that can actually affect the tone of a work.

To summarize, words create images in people's minds, some of which are literal and some of which are figurative.

Figurative Language

Figurative language is using the choice of words to bring to mind figurative imagery. What constitutes figurative language? As has been clearly established, definitions and the assignment of various literary concepts to specific categories is an area of controversy among literary scholars—and figurative language is no exception. You can, however, make some generalizations for the purpose of facilitating the study of figurative language.

Figurative language can be divided into three main categories.

Figures of Thought

Figures of thought are also called **tropes.** A trope is the meaning a word has *other than* its literal meaning. Trope refers to change or turn, in other words, using a word in other than its literal sense, such as in comparison. For example, when the romantic young lover compares his girlfriend's blue eyes to "cornflowers on a sunny day," the word *cornflower* is no longer restricted to a blue flower (the literal meaning). It now is a trope (a figure of thought) with another, figurative meaning.

Figures of Speech

Figures of speech are also called **rhetorical figures** or **schemes.** Rhetorical figures depart, not from the literal meaning of the words, but from the standard usage or order of the words (or some other departure other than in meaning), thus making a special effect. An example of such figures of speech is the rhetorical question. A question normally begs reply, but in the rhetorical question, no reply is expected; the question is being asked to emphasize the obvious, albeit unspoken answer.

Figures of Sound

Figures of sound include the sound effects discussed in the section on form. Examples are alliteration, assonance, and consonance.

Graphically, one view of figurative language might look like this:

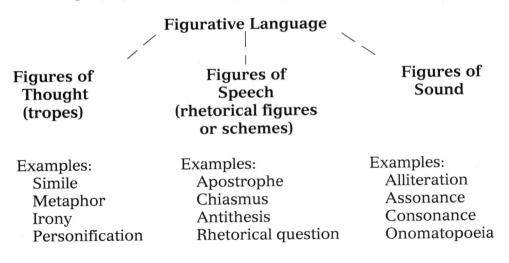

Figurative Language

Figures of Thought (tropes)	Figures of Speech (rhetorical figures or schemes)	Figures of Sound
Examples:	Examples:	Examples:
Simile	Apostrophe	Alliteration
Metaphor	Chiasmus	Assonance
Irony	Antithesis	Consonance
Personification	Rhetorical question	Onomatopoeia

There is a trend away from this view, however, largely due to the confusion generated by the tendency of many to refer to **figures of speech** as a more inclusive term under which tropes and rhetorical figures fall as major categories. Use the Index to find definitions and illustrations for the following terms.

Figurative Language

Figures of Speech   **Figures of Sound**

Tropes   **Rhetorical Figures**

Examples:	Examples:	Examples:
Simile	Apostrophe	Alliteration
Metaphor	Chiasmus	Assonance
Irony	Antithesis	Consonance
Personification	Rhetorical questions	Onomatopoeia

Although you need to be aware of the former triadic view of figurative language, the latter assignment of terms will be used in this discussion. Also, you should realize that placement of the various figures of speech under the category of trope or rhetorical figure does not meet with universal consensus among scholars. For example, one literary dictionary might place the **zeugma** (defined later in this section) under trope but another might identify it as a rhetorical figure. Regardless, **figures of speech** are of major significance both to understanding and appreciating a literary work, and you need to recognize their uses and their effects.

Figures of Speech

Here are some of the major **figures of speech.**

Figures of Speech Based on Analogy

Analogy, which has its origin in mathematics, involves explaining the unknown and unfamiliar by drawing comparisons to the known and familiar. In mathematics you figure

$$\frac{a}{b} = \frac{c}{d}$$

a (an analogue) is to *b* in the same relationship as *c* (another analogue) is to *d*; therefore, although *a* and *c* are not necessarily identical, they are similar because *a* has the same relationship to *b* that *c* has to *d*.

Analogies are drawn to explain, describe, argue, and justify; however, whatever the purpose in making the comparison, at the root of analogy are two distinct units of thought: the **vehicle** and the **tenor**. The **tenor** is the subject or idea you are trying to explain, and the **vehicle** is the means by which you explain it. If you try to describe a zebra by comparing it to a horse with stripes, the zebra is the tenor and horse is the vehicle. Likewise, if you wanted to explain some abstract concept, such as rage, you might compare it to a consuming fire: Tenor? Rage. Vehicle? Fire.

Simile

Simile is a comparison using *like* or *as*. This trope can be found in most forms of literature as people attempt to communicate by making direct, unveiled analogies. This is perhaps the result of a psychological need to try to understand the unknown by associating it with elements of the known. A person who has never tasted buffalo meat might ask someone who just ate a buffalo burger, "What does it taste *like*?" The answer, "It tastes *like* a very strong beef burger," is a simile.

Similes are characterized by their directness, as in the opening couplet of Henry Constable's sixteenth-century poem:

Hope, like the Hyena

**Hope, like the hyena, coming to be old,
Alters his shape, is turned into despair.**

The speaker compares hope that is delayed ("old") to a hyena that changes shape *like* hope changes into despair. What is the tenor? Hope. Its vehicle? The hyena.

Sometimes the simile is sustained for an entire stanza or even an entire poem. Here is the first stanza of Thomas Lodge's "Love in My Bosom." The vehicle is a bee. What is the tenor?

Love in My Bosom

**Love in my bosom like a bee
Doth suck his sweet;
Now with his wings he plays with me,**

Now with his feet.
Within mine eyes he makes his nest,
His bed amidst my tender breast;
My kisses are his daily feast,
And yet he robs me of my rest.
   Ah, wanton, will ye?

Novelists often use simile to describe characters, drawing on comparisons to reveal both personality and appearance. In *Jane Eyre,* Charlotte Brontë helps readers visualize Jane's mental state and body language with this description:

I had now swallowed my tea. I was mightily refreshed by the beverage; as much so as a giant with wine: it gave new tone to my unstrung nerves, and enabled me to address this penetrating young judge steadily.

Another common simile is to use comparison to illustrate degree or extent, such as "hard as a rock," "dry as a covered bridge," "slippery as an eel," and "trustworthy as a fox in a chicken coop." Charlotte's sister Emile Brontë uses such a comparison to describe Hindley Earnshaw in *Wuthering Heights:*

. . . But cheer up! He died true to his character, drunk as a lord—Poor lad; I'm sorry, too.

Metaphor

Metaphor, unlike the direct nature of the simile, is an **implied** comparison: rosy-red lips (tenor—lips; vehicle—a red rose). Recognition of the tenor-vehicle relationship is more subtle, yet sometimes it is clearly stated as in this third stanza from Thomas Nashe's sixteenth-century "Adieu, Farewell Earth's Bliss":

Beauty is but a flower
Which wrinkles will devour;
Brightness falls from the air,
Queens have died young and fair,
Dust hath closed Helen's eye.
I am sick, I must die.
   Lord, have mercy on us!

Beauty is the tenor. The vehicle? A flower.

In prose works, you can find metaphors woven in and ⸱ᵗ of the writing, adding descriptive elements that help readers picture scenes and understand characters. For example, Charlotte Brontë uses metaphor in this description of Jane Eyre:

> 'You have a very bad disposition,' said she,
> 'and one to this day I feel it impossible to understand:
> how for nine years you could be patient and quies-
> cent under any treatment, and in the tenth break out
> all fire and violence, I can never comprehend.'

Anne Brontë begins her novel *Agnes Grey* with an amusing metaphor:

> All true histories contain instruction; though,
> in some, the treasure may be hard to find, and when
> found, so trivial in quantity that the dry, shrivelled
> kernel scarcely compensates for the trouble of
> cracking the nut.

At other times the metaphor (like simile) can be a **controlling image.** A controlling image is a metaphor or some image that runs throughout a work. The controlling image in Shakespeare's "Sonnet 97" is a simile comparing the speaker's absence from his love to the winter season. It begins with

> How like a winter hath my absence been
> From thee, the pleasure of the fleeting year!
> What freezings have I felt, what dark days seen!
> What old December's bareness everywhere!

and ends with

> . . . the very birds are mute.
> Or, if they sing, 'tis with so dull a cheer,
> That leaves look pale, dreading the winter's near.

In Michael Drayton's "To Nothing Fitter," the controlling image is more complex, with metaphoric comparisons being made on several levels. The subject of the poem ("thee") is com-
pared to a rich son (lines 1–2) who inherits and squanders wealth (lines 3–7). The subject's wealth, however, is his "love, that is on the unworthy placed"—another metaphor. Now align lines 7–8 with the final two lines (13–14). What metaphor is at work here?

To Nothing Fitter

line   To nothing fitter can I thee compare
       Than to the son of some rich pennyfather,
       Who having now brought on his end with
         care,
       Leaves to his son all he had heaped together;
(5)   This new-rich novice, lavish of his chest,
       To one man gives, doth on another spend,
       Then here he riots, yet amongst the rest
       Haps to lend some to one true honest friend.
       Thy gifts thou in obscurity dost waste,
(10)   False friends thy kindness, born but to
         deceive thee,
       Thy love, that is on the unworthy placed,
       Time hath thy beauty, which with age will
         leave thee;
       Only that little which to me was lent
       I give thee back, when all the rest is spent.

Sometimes a tenor will have more than one vehicle: "His attitude was ice-cold, rock-hard, and knife-sharp." Anthony Munday uses over twenty vehicles in "I Serve a Mistress."

I serve a mistress whiter than the snow,
Straighter than cedar, brighter than the glass,
Finer in trip and swifter than the roe,
More pleasant than the field of flowering grass;
More gladsome to my withering joys that fade,
Than winter's sun or summer's cooling shade.

Sweeter than swelling grape of ripest wine,
Softer than feathers of the fairest swan,
Smoother than jet, more stately than the pine,
Fresher than poplar, smaller than my span,
Clearer than beauty's fiery pointed beam,
Or icy crust of crystal's frozen stream.

Yet is she curster than the bear by kind,
And harder-hearted than the agèd oak,
More glib than oil, more fickle than the wind,
Stiffer than steel, no sooner bent but broke.
Lo! thus my service is a lasting sore;
Yet will I serve, although I die therefore.

Mixed metaphors are the result of a blend of incongruous
¬ for the same tenor. Mixed metaphors can be effectively

used, but when poorly done, a mixed metaphor can produce undesirable effects: "She watched the eagle sail the sea of air currents with egg-beater movements and calypso rhythms." Comparing the air currents (the tenor) to the sea (the vehicle) is a common metaphor: however, this poor bird's flight (the tenor) is being compared to three very incongruous vehicles: a ship ("sail"), an egg-beater ("egg-beater movements"), and dance music ("calypso rhythms"). You may find mixed metaphors in prose narratives, such as "She sailed into the room and clawed through the books on the tables."

As is evident, to the extent that metaphoric language is developed, its complexity and subtlety of use varies greatly. The **epic simile** is a very formal simile in which the vehicle is developed so extensively that the reader loses sight of the original relationship between it and its tenor. The tone of the epic simile is ceremonial; the style copies that of Homer (hence, you may find sources that refer to the epic simile as the Homeric simile). John Milton includes the epic simile in *Paradise Lost*.

You also may encounter the term **conceit.** Originally referring simply to a concept, the idea of a conceit has undergone a change in status. A conceit is a very intricate parallel drawn between two otherwise *dissimilar* concepts or things. These poetic metaphors were found, during the 1700s and 1800s, to be too artificial and strained. Conceit is viewed with more neutrality today, with some contemporary poets making very effective use of it, particularly in American poetry. There are two types of conceit. The Petrarchan conceit (named after the Italian poet Petrarch) was a favorite of Renaissance English poets—especially in their love sonnets, either for imitation or for contempt. The comparisons in Petrarchan conceits are highly exaggerated, as in Chidiock Tichborne's "Elegy."

> My prime of youth is but a frost of cares,
>   My feast of joy is but a dish of pain,
> My crop of corn is but a field of tares,
>   And all my good is but vain hope of gain;
>   The day is past, and yet I saw no sun,
>   And now I live, and now my life is done.

In great contrast to the Elizabethan Petrarchan conceit are the metaphysical conceits that often were the controlling images used by the metaphysical poets of the seventeenth century. The vehicles for these conceits were taken from the complexities of life with witty, sometimes shocking comparisons. John Donne used the metaphysical conceit extensively, as in "The Flea" (1633). He begins with

> Mark but this flea, and mark in this
> How little that which thou deny'st me is;
> It sucked me first, and now sucks thee,
> And in this flea our two bloods mingled be; . . .

He continues to develop the conceit but does not directly state the shocking comparison until the second stanza:

> Oh stay, three lives in one flea spare,
> Where we almost, yea more than, married
> are.
> (note) → This flea is you and I, and this
> Our marriage bed, and marriage temple
> is; . . .

In some uses of metaphor, the tenor is not directly named but only implied. These sophisticated comparisons are called **implicit metaphors,** and you must rely upon context for meaning. In a work about a young woman's growing affection for a young man, a descriptive line might read "The bud drowned in the seas of distrust and envy." The *bud* is a vehicle for an implied tenor that can only be determined by the situation: undeveloped love. In contrast, the second metaphor at work here has directly stated tenors (distrust and envy) for its vehicle (seas).

Also, a metaphor can "die." **Dead metaphors** are those that are so commonplace people no longer perceive the fact that the vehicle and tenor do not match: "pig-headed attitude," "the skin of one's teeth," "the core of the subject," "to set your heart on . . .," "the apple of her eye," and "the long arm of the law."

When metaphors are extended into narrative form in which the actual story and its elements (actions, places, people, and things) represent elements outside the story, often with the characters and events representing ideas, the work is called an **allegory.** John Bunyan's *The Pilgrim's Progress* is an allegory in which the journey of "Christian" (a character in the story) from the City of Destruction to the Celestial City allegorizes the Christian doctrine of salvation.

Personification

Personification (also called **prosopopoeia,** if the figure being ̃ed speaks) inanimate objects or abstract ideas are given human characteristics. In the third stanza of "The Aged Lover Renounceth Love" (Lord Thomas Vaux's sixteenth-century work), age and "lusty life" are both personified:

> **For age with stealing steps**
>   **Hath clawed me with his crutch,**
> **And lusty life away she leaps**
>   **As there had been none such.**

Age is given the human characteristics of walking and hitting someone with a crutch. Lusty life (youth) is given the human characteristic of leaping.

In Robert Browning's "In the Doorway," a fig-tree is personified:

> **Our fig-tree, that leaned for the saltness, has furled**
>   **Her five fingers,**
> **Each leaf like a hand opened wide to the world**
>   **Where there lingers**
> **No glint of the gold, summer sent for her sake:**
> **How the vines writhe in rows, each impaled on its stake!**
> **My heart shrivels up, and my spirit shrinks curled.**

When you are working with personification (whether in poetry or in prose), do not stop with just identifying what is being personified and what human characteristics that object or concept is being given. Personification is figurative language that personalizes the work to the reader. By giving that object or abstract concept human qualities, it has something in common with *people*—an association that is bound to create in the reader some sort of reaction. That effect might be positive (as when death is personified as a comforting friend), negative (as when death is personified as a sinister character), ironic, or any number of other possible effects. The sea can be personified as a friend or an enemy, as brave or cowardly, as calm or angry.

How can you tell the effect of personification in a work? Generally, writers use personification for a purpose, and that purpose, in turn, is related to the effect. Very often the effect of the personification will be used to further the meaning. If the meaning of a work involves the tragedy of parting from a loved one, the writer might personify the sea upon which the person sails away as a sinister enemy. Also, the personification might be used to amplify the tone. For example, a frightening tone might be served by a sea personified as brooding and angry. Similarly, the speaker's voice is an element. Context, then, is pivotal to finding the effect of personification.

In Sir Phillip Sidney's sixteenth-century poem "Loving in Truth," he personifies Invention, Nature, and Study:

line Loving in truth, and fain in verse my love to show,
That she, dear she, might take some pleasure of my pain,
Pleasure might cause her read, reading might make her know,
Knowledge might pity win, and pity grace obtain,
(5) I sought fit words to paint the blackest face of woe,
Studying inventions fine, her wits to entertain,
Oft turning others' leaves, to see if thence would flow
Some fresh and fruitful showers upon my sunburnt brain.
But words came halting forth, wanting Invention's stay;
(10) Invention, Nature's child, fled step-dame Study's blows;
And others' feet still seemed but strangers in my way.
Thus great with child to speak, and helpless in my throes,
Biting my truant pen, beating myself for spite:
"Fool," said my Muse to me, "look in thy heart and write."

What is the *effect* of this personification? The first four lines set up the situation: The speaker wants to write a poem that will show the woman he loves how much he loves her. Lines 5–8 outline that he studied "inventions" and "others' leaves" (other poets' writings) for ideas, but his brain is "sunburnt"—what today might be called "writer's block" or "burnout." Lines 9–10 (the lines that contain the personification) reveal that although he wanted "Invention" (originality) that is "Nature's child" (unlearned, natural) ⸴ it "fled" from "step-dame Study's blows." Line 11 confirms ⸴ the style of others' works did not help him. He com‑ ⸴lf to a pregnant woman in line 12, his message wants so to be delivered; he is desperate by line 13. But line 14 makes his point: originality must come from within.

Within this context, what is the *effect* of personifying Invention and Nature? One possible effect is to make originality, as "Nature's Child" seem innocent (as a child), nonthreatening, and desirable. The personification of Study, on the other hand, heightens the perception that the speaker has lost his fresh approach (perhaps) to imitation of others' works (a "step-dame" relationship to Invention in contrast to Invention as "Nature's Child"—a natural relationship). The effect of the personification of Invention, Nature, and Study is to emphasize that writing a poem is a natural process from within rather than an artificial process.

Reification

Reification is a means of describing abstract ideas as if they were concrete things. Reification cuts through the forms of analogous relationships, sometimes using metaphor (for example, "Life is a flowing stream"), sometimes personifying the abstraction (as in, "Love wonders the lonely paths in my heart"). The effect, regardless of the type of analogy used, is to give readers a sense of tangible reality for otherwise difficult-to-explain ideas.

Allusion

Allusion is a reference in a literary work to some person, place, thing, or event outside the work, or to some other literary work. These references illustrate or emphasize through comparison or contrast, but when there is discrepancy between the subject and the allusion, the effect can be ironic. (See the discussion on page 234.)

Some literary scholars contend that allusions can be directly stated references or that they can be inferences. However, the current trend seems to be to confine allusions to the indirect references that cause the reader to call upon memory and its associated emotions, connotations, feelings, and tones.

There are several different kinds of allusion. **Topical allusions** are based on current events and serve a significant role in the stand-up comedy routines of such performers as David Letterman, Jay Leno, and other late-night television talk show hosts. **Personal allusions** are references to events, facts, and other information in the writer's own life. Obviously, the significance of many topical and personal allusions are lost to readers of later generations.

Allusions to historical events and personages, other works (the writers, the works themselves, or the styles of the works), **and documented information,** however, have a sense of timelessness, although realizing the full significance may require a broad base of knowledge on the part of the reader.

Allusions can be culturally based or they can be more universal in nature. Sometimes the title of a work holds an allusion that sets the tone, subject, or voice of its content. The title of John Ashbery's 1965 poem "Civilization and Its Discontents" is an allusion to Sigmund Freud's book of the same title that addresses instinct and civilization.

Some allusions are popular among writers and are used over the centuries. The Trojan War has remained a rich source of allusion for both prose and poetry for many generations. These two stanzas from Thomas Nashe's "Adieu, Farewell Earth's Bliss" (1592) are characteristic:

> **Beauty is but a flower**
> **Which wrinkles will devour;**
> **Brightness falls from the air,**
> **Queens have died young and fair,**
> (allusion) → **Dust hath closed Helen's eye.**
> **I am sick, I must die.**
> **Lord, have mercy on us!**
>
> **Strength stoops unto the grave,**
> (allusion) → **Worms feed on Hector brave,**
> **Swords may not fight with fate,**
> **Earth still holds ope her gate.**
> **Come! come! the bells do cry.**
> **I am sick, I must die.**
> **Lord, have mercy on us!**

The allusion to Helen as beautiful and Hector as brave has been used so extensively as to become traditional types of beauty and bravery.

Another source for allusion is Greek and Roman mythology. For example, Matthew Arnold's "Memorial Verses," for the day that William Wordsworth died (April 27, 1850) alludes to the Titans of Greek myth to emphasize the "Titanic" size (colossal, very large) ˆˆ strife described in this excerpt from the second stanza:

> **With shivering heart the strife we saw**
> **Of passion with eternal law;**

And yet with reverential awe
We watched the fount of fiery life
(allusion) → Which served for that Titanic strife.

Allusion can also be accomplished through writing in the same style, rhythm, or other elements of another work. Not to be confused with **parody** (as discussed on page 79) in which the composition imitates another work for the purpose of ridicule, allusion of this type calls to mind the other work, with (hopefully) the associated connotations, feelings, and effects desired by the writer. This is done occasionally in gospel music. For example, a modern gospel song might begin or include within its stanzas a few strains in the style of "Rock of Ages" or "Amazing Grace." Or the effect might be gained by quoting another work with a slight change in, for example, words or rhythm.

The works of ancient writers, the paintings of famous artists (such as Degas, El Greco, and Brueghel), the stoic philosophies of Seneca, wars, politics—these are just a sampling of the sources from which writers pull their allusions. Yet one source of literary allusion stands out, both because of its prevalence in terms of numbers of references in English and American literature and because of its influence as a prevailing belief system: the Bible.

Old English translations were available during the seventh century. Although there were many English versions in between, the first *printed* English Bibles were not available until the sixteenth century with William Tyndale's English translation of the New Testament in 1525–1526.

In 1611, England's King James the First sponsored an English translation from the Greek "New Testament" and Hebrew "Old Testament." The King James Version, also called the Authorized Version, is the most popular English Bible and a best-seller yet today.

The significance of the King James Version as a work of great literature has been acknowledged by writers and critics throughout the generations. The Bible's themes and language (part prose, part verse) are exceptional, and as stated in *Words with Power* (published in 1990 by Harcourt Brace Jovanovich) by famed literary critic and Professor Northrop Frye of the University of Toronto, "few would deny that some of the greatest poetry the world has ever seen is included in it [the Bible]."

Literary study went through a period in which, although recognition of the literary merits of the Bible as a work of literature was acknowledged, the study and recognition of biblical influences on the literary heritage of England and America were neglected and perhaps to a certain extent even rejected. Viewed as a great work of literature, the King James Bible can be read or ignored; viewed as a major influence on English literature of the last four centuries, it must be addressed. From this perspective, then, the recent trend among some literary scholars is to include at last this formerly neglected area of literary study.

Professor Frye makes this very strong statement in *The Great Code* (published in 1982, 1981 by Harcourt Brace Jovanovich): "I soon realized that a student of English literature who does not know the Bible does not understand a good deal of what is going on in what he reads: the most conscientious student will be continually misconstruing the implications, even the meaning." Although not all writers did use or are using the Bible as a source for allusions, a significant number of important works of English and American literature indisputably include biblical references and allusions that range from occasional biblical references to literature in which the very structures of the works themselves rely upon the readers' knowledge of the Bible for understanding the writers' meanings.

Based on Judeo-Christian traditions, the English-speaking culture assimilated many of the principles, values, and teachings of the Bible. As a result, both religious and secular writings oftentimes reflect these influences. Some biblical phrases and concepts often used include:

- ▶ The apple of my eye
- ▶ A Judas
- ▶ A prophet has no honor in his own country
- ▶ The salt of the earth
- ▶ Hiding your light under a bushel
- ▶ Man does not live by bread alone
- ▶ Turning water into wine
- ▶ Walking on water
- ▶ Casting the first stone
- ▶ My brother's keeper
- ▶ A house divided cannot stand
- ▶ Standing against a Goliath
- ▶ Forty years in the wilderness
- ▶ Being thrown to the lions
- ▶ Being thrown into the fiery furnace

- Trying to pass a camel through the eye of a needle
- The patience of Job
- Wisdom of Solomon
- A coat of many colors

This list could go on and on. After years of usage in secular writing, readers today and even some of the speakers and writers incorporating these ideas into their writing may not recognize that these phrases and concepts are found in the Bible.

One significant factor that separates the Bible from other works that have become the basis for or influential factors on other literary works (such as the influence of Holinshed's *Chronicles* on Shakespeare, as discussed in a previous section, page 106) is the pervasiveness of the Bible's influence. This is a book that affected to varying degrees a people's belief system and, as a result, influenced history with a major impact on that people's literature. That these beliefs would be incorporated into their literature on many different levels was inevitable.

Professor William Harmon and the late C. Hugh Holman of the University of North Carolina at Chapel Hill give readers further insight into the subject on pages 49–52 of *A Handbook to Literature,* Sixth Edition (1990, Macmillan Publishing Company) in which they address the Bible both as a work of literature and as an influence on writers spanning many generations, citing several noted twentieth-century American novelists.

Some of the biblical analogies are direct references, as in Edwin Morgan's "Message Clear" (1968) based on "The Gospel according to John" 11:25 (Chapter 11, verse 25) and in Lord Byron's "The Destruction of Sennacherib," a poem based on the account in II Kings, Chapters 18 and 19 of the destruction of King Sennacherib of Assyria by God when the king attacked Jerusalem. Others, though, include not only allusionary references, but also reflect a Bible-based belief system. What allusions to scripture do you see in this poem?

Leave Me, O Love

line   Leave me, O Love, which reachest but to dust,
And thou, my mind, aspire to higher things;
Grow rich in that which never taketh rust:
Whatever fades but fading pleasure brings.
(5)   Draw in thy beams, and humble all thy might
To that sweet yoke where lasting freedoms be;

> Which breaks the clouds and opens forth the
>   light
> That doth both shine and give us sight to see.
>   O take fast hold; let that light be thy guide
> (10)   In this small course which birth draws out to
>   death,
> And think how evil becometh him to slide,
> Who seeketh heav'n, and comes of heav'nly
>   breath.
>   Then farewell, world, thy uttermost I see;
>   Eternal Love, maintain thy life in me.

by Sir Philip Sidney

Examining one by one the allusions at work in this poem, the reader finds:

Line 1   Love (personified, hence carnal) "reachest but to dust" alludes to Genesis 3:19.

Line 2   The mind aspiring to higher things alludes to Colossians 3:2.

Lines 3 and 4   Treasures in Heaven do not rust—an allusion to Matthew 6:19–20.

Line 5   A call to the humbling of might alludes to Luke 14:11 and I Peter 5:5.

Line 6   The yoke is an allusion to Matthew 11:28–30.

Lines 7and 8   These allusions are to the return of Jesus (Luke 21:27–28), the light of God (Ephesians 5:14, 2 Timothy 1:10, I John 1:5), and John 1:4.

Line 9   Taking "fast hold" alludes to Hebrews 4:14 and the light as guide alludes to Psalm 48:14 and Luke 1:79.

Line 10   This line alludes to the brevity of carnal life (Psalm 103:15–16).

Line 11   This line alludes to John 3:20.

Line 12   "Heavenly breath" is an allusion to Genesis 2:7 and John 20:22.

Lines 13 and 14   These lines allude to Matthew 28:20 and I John 5:4, with Eternal Love being an allusion to I John 4:16 and Romans 8:38–39 and with "thy life in me" alluding to John 3:16, 14:23, and 15:10 and I John 2:24–25 and 5:11–12.

The meaning in this poem appears to be the speaker's expounding upon Romans 6:23, and as you can see, the meaning of the poem is lost without an understanding of the speaker's scriptural allusions. Many times the scriptural allusions will be interspersed in a work. Even then, however, a familiarity with the Bible can be pivotal to understanding the references used.

Prose writers, too, within the Judeo-Christian tradition of England and America rely heavily on the King James Bible as a source for literary allusion. Most Americans are familiar with Patrick Henry's most famous speech in which he challenged "Give me liberty, or give me death!" Notice his extensive use of biblical allusion in these excerpts from the speech.

Liberty or Death
by
Patrick Henry

An allusion to:

Mr. President, it is natural to man to indulge in the illusions of hope. We are apt to shut our eyes against a painful truth and listen to the song of that siren, till she transforms us into beasts. Is this the part of wise men, engaged in a great and arduous struggle for liberty? Are we disposed to be of the number of those, who, having eyes, see not, and having ears, hear not, the things which so nearly concern their temporal salvation? For my part, whatever anguish of spirit it may cost, I am willing to know the whole truth, to know the worst and to provide for it.

Mark 8:18 →

I have but one lamp by which my feet are guided, and that is the lamp of experience. I know of no way of judging of the future but by the past. And judging by the past, I wish to know what there has been in the conduct of the British ministry for the last ten years to justify those hopes with which gentlemen have been pleased to solace themselves and the House? Is it that insidious smile with which our petition has been lately received? Trust it not, sir; it will prove a snare to your feet.

Luke 22:47–48 → Suffer not yourselves to be betrayed with a kiss. Ask yourselves how this gracious reception of our petition comports with these warlike preparations which cover our waters and darken our land. Are fleets and armies necessary to a work of love and reconciliation? Have we shown ourselves so unwilling to be reconciled that force must be called in to win back our love? Let us not deceive ourselves, sir. These are the implements of war and subjugation, the last arguments to which kings resort. . . . If we wish to be free—if we mean to preserve inviolate those inestimable privileges for which we have been so long contending—if we mean not basely to abandon the noble struggle in which we have been so long engaged, and which we have pledged ourselves never to abandon until the glorious object of our contest shall be obtained, we must fight! I

Psalm 46:7–11 → repeat it, sir, we must fight! An appeal to arms and to the God of Hosts is all that is left us!

• •

Jeremiah 6:14, It is in vain, sir, to extenuate the
and 8:11→ matter. Gentlemen may cry, peace, peace!—but there is no peace. The war is actually begun! The next gale that sweeps from the north will bring to our ears the clash of resounding arms! Our brethren are already in the field! Why stand we here idle? What is it that gentlemen wish? What would they have? Is life so dear, or peace so sweet, as to be purchased at the price of chains and slavery? Forbid it, Almighty God! I know not what course others may take, but as for me *Give me liberty, or give me death!*

Regardless of the reader's personal beliefs, the value of a familiarity with this great and lasting work—the Authorized, King James Version of the Bible—to the serious reader of English and American literature needs to be considered.

Nomenclature

Nomenclature refers to the names people, places, things, and ideas are called. Among the Anglo-Saxon peasants of early England, people were addressed by their first names; however, English family names (surnames) came into use during the fourteenth century.

At first these surnames indicated heritage, with "son of" used as an affix to the father's name: son of Jacob became Jacob*son,* son of Erik became Erik*son,* and the trend continued with such names as John*son,* and Richard*son.* Then people became known by the name of where they lived (Hill, Rivers, Austin, London), by occupation (Weaver, Harper, Thatcher)—or, as in Scotland, identified by the occupation of their fathers: McPherson, meaning son of (Mc) the parson (Pherson).

Evidently, in their search for means of identification, the English named themselves based on practical associations. This sense of the practical is carried into the literary figures of speech that deal with what to call—how to identify—things, places, and most especially people. Some of these figures of speech reflect popular usage; others are more literary-based.

The **kenning** originated as an Old Germanic descriptive or figurative phrase used in Old English in such works as *Beowolf.* The phrase serves as a synonym in place of the simple or ordinary name, such as "the foamy-necked" or "the sea-farer" *for ship.* Generally, a kenning is **periphrasis,** meaning that it is an indirect, sometimes wordy, way of stating something. An example of periphrasis would be to refer to a pen as "a procurer of gains and debts, and love requited." Also, such statements as "I would if I could but I can't so I won't" or "I am most desirous to make your acquaintance" are periphrasic.

A kenning will often include **metonymy**—when a closely associated name of an object is used in place of a word, such as referring to a king as "the ring-giver" or "the crown," or to his position of authority as "the throne." In the United States, people often refer to the executive branch of the federal government or to the President as "the White House." James Shirley uses metonymy in this seventeenth-century poem "The Glories of Our Blood and State":

> **The glories of our blood and state**
>   **Are shadows, not substantial things;**
> **There is no armour against fate;**
>   **Death lays his icy hand on kings:**

metonymy →   **Sceptre and crown**
             Must tumble down,

> **And in the dust be equal made**
> **With the poor crooked**
> **scythe and spade.**   ← metonymy

"Sceptre and crown" is a metonymy for the king, and "scythe and spade" is a metonymy for the working man.

You also may encounter **synecdoche,** a trope in which the name of a part represents the whole or the name of the whole represents the part. Workers may be referred to as "hands." A country's "ears and eyes" are its spies. A "roof over your head" is a home, and a musical producer might refer to the lead singer as "the voice."

Antonomasia is a figure of speech used extensively in politics. In antonomasia, a proper name is used to represent an idea, such as "Watergate" refers to an entire network of events during the 1970s. Sometimes the antonomasia is a person's name, as when Western movie enthusiasts say "There aren't any John Waynes in movies anymore"—John Wayne representing (a type of) the rugged, "all-male" Western hero who exhibits certain expected characteristics. Occasionally, the antonomasia will come in the form of an **epithet** (a periphrasic descriptive adjective, noun, or noun phrase describing a particular characteristic of a person or thing). An epithet might be to describe a puzzle as a "brain-twister," a home as a "sanctuary from the storm," or an admired leader as a "shining beacon of light." An epithet is often used as a substitution for a proper name, for example when, in referring to Elvis Presley, tabloid headlines read "The King of Rock 'n Roll Spotted in White House Tour Group." Note that the epithet is not restricted to just the negative name calling normally associated with the term.

A **symbol** (in contrast to metaphor that serves to illustrate) is a type of image that first makes one think of some objective thing. A symbol also brings to mind another level of meaning, a level of meaning that oftentimes embodies abstract concepts, that in turn elicit from the reader a range of emotions.

In these lines from "The Canonization," John Donne uses two traditional symbols: the eagle to represent strength and the dove to represent purity.

> **Call us what you will, we are made such by love.**
> **Call her one, me another fly,**
> **We're tapers too, and at our own cost die;**
> → **And we in us find th'eagle and the dove.**

Generally, symbols depend for their associated meanings upon the context of the literary work in which they are used.

UNIVERSAL SYMBOLS

Symbol	Meaning, Level one	Meaning, Level two	Possible Emotions*
National flag	Cloth with pattern	Represents country	Pride, patriotism
Sea	Large body of water	Represents countless people	Fear of invasion, pity on the masses
Red rose	Flower	Represents love	Sentimentalism, special person
Purple	Color	Represents royalty	Respect, honor
Wedding ring	Gold band worn on left hand	Represents a state of being married	Fidelity, loyalty
Long-horned steer	Steer with long, curved horns	Represents football team at a Texas school	School loyalty and rivalry
Yellow*	Color	Represents cowardice and fear also	Shame, dishonor
		Slow down and	Caution
		Homecoming, reunion (ribbons)	Support, honor and happiness

*Notice that the same symbol can have both negative or positive connotations depending on usage or context.

Figures of Speech Based on Rhetoric

In its broadest sense, rhetoric relates directly to the use of language for the purpose of persuading the readers or hearers. Consequently, rhetoric must deal in some way with effective:

▶ Proof and information
▶ Arrangement of the information

▶ Presentation of the information in terms of syntax, diction, and mechanics

Rhetoric traditionally has three main categories or types:

Deliberative rhetoric is aimed at moving the hearers or readers to some action either pro or con about some public policy.

Forensic rhetoric is aimed at proving someone's guilt or innocence. From television crime shows, you may recognize forensic medicine as medical evidence at crime scenes that can be used to prove or disprove in a court of law a suspect's involvement in a crime—his or her guilt or innocence.

Epideictic rhetoric is aimed at displaying rhetorical skills at some special occasion by praising (or perhaps condemning) a person or group.

Of course, all the literary principles can contribute to the effectiveness of a rhetorical work. Likewise, most figures of speech can be used to further the purpose—to persuade the readers or listeners. There are some figures of speech, however, that are generally considered rhetorical in nature.

Rhetorical Questions

Rhetorical questions are those asked, not for the purpose of eliciting an expressed answer, but rather for their rhetorical effect: an emphasis of the speaker's point. When, as a point in case, a man stops another on the street, asking for the correct time and the second man holds up his wrist to show that he does not have a watch and says "How should I know?" no answer is expected, but the point could be: "You are being unreasonable in expecting me to know what time it is." (Determination of intent, of course, in a case such as this, would depend a great deal on the facial expressions and tone of voice used by the man when he says "How should I know?"—did he smile and shrug, indicating he, too, was at a loss about the time; or did he growl the words with a snarl on his face, indicating a hostile "don't bother me" attitude?)

The "Give me liberty, or give me death!" speech of Patrick Henry uses the rhetorical question extensively. Sir Thomas Wyatt bases title and poem on a rhetorical question as seen in the first stanza in "And Wilt Thou Leave Me Thus?"

> **And wilt thou leave me thus?**
> **Say nay, say nay, for shame!**
> **To save thee from the blame**
> **Of all my grief and grame.**

And wilt thou leave me thus?
Say nay! say nay!

Amplification

Amplification is a device used by teachers extensively and is used throughout this reference guide. In amplification, a word, concept, point, or idea is defined or explained; then the initial definition or explanation is followed by another, more detailed explanation. Amplification is rhetorically effective for several reasons:

▶ The restatement emphasizes the importance of the idea.
▶ The restatement clarifies the idea, thus enabling the reader or listener to understand it better.
▶ The restatement facilitates the reader's or listener's retention of the idea.

The additional details in the restatement can include more facts, an illustration, another figure of speech, a change in diction or level of language, and other devices.

In this excerpt from James Madison's June 6, 1788, speech, Madison (who favored a federal constitution) is arguing against a speech made the previous day by Patrick Henry in which Henry spoke against ratification.

line   I must confess I have not been able to find his
usual consistency in the gentleman's argument on
this occasion. He informs us that the people of the
country are at perfect repose; that is, every man
(5)   enjoys the fruits of his labor peaceably and securely,
and that everything is in perfect tranquility and
safety. I wish sincerely that this were true. If this be
their happy situation, why has every state acknowledged the contrary? Why were deputies from all the
(10)   states sent to the general convention? Why have
complaints of national and individual distresses
been echoed and reechoed throughout the conti-
nent? Why has our general government been so
shamefully disgraced and our Constitution violated?
(15)   Wherefore have laws been made to authorize a
change, and wherefore are we now assembled here?

Madison points out that Henry "informs us that the people of the country are at perfect repose." He **amplifies** "perfect repose" in lines 4–6. He gives an example using figurative language ("fruits of his labor") and amplifies with a generalization. Interestingly, Madison then uses a series of rhetorical questions that attack the amplification Madison supplied to Henry's assertion that the country is "at perfect repose."

(Another rhetorical device Madison employs is a form of repetition called **palilogy**: notice the effect when he keeps repeating "Why . . . ? Why . . .?" in lines 8–13.)

Aposiopesis

You are in a supermarket. A child is screaming, and you can hear the parent's exasperated, high-pitched, slightly threatening tone, "If you don't stop it, I'll . . . ." Or you hear children playing, and one squirts water on the other. The victim starts chasing the attacker and cries, "Wait'll I catch you . . . I'm gonna . . . ." This is aposiopesis. It is a very deliberate trailing off of the speaker's voice, an incomplete sentence, stopping midway in a sentence.

In rhetorical writing, what purpose does aposiopesis serve? One purpose is to allow the hearers to supply their own words—a technique that can emphasize the point. Also, it allows a speaker to convey meaning, to express a message without actually putting it into words that can be later quoted—or misquoted—a very advantageous situation in some circumstances. James Fenimore Cooper uses aposiopesis in *The Pilot*:

> "I contend not against your misguided reason," said Colonel Howard, rising with cool respect. "A young lady who ventures to compare rebels with gallant gentlemen engaged in their duty to their prince, cannot escape the imputation of possessing a misguided reason. No man—I speak not of women, who cannot be supposed so well versed in human nature—but no man who has reached the time of life that entitles him to be called by that name, can consort with these disorganizers, who would destroy everything that is sacred—these levellers who would pull down the great to exalt the little—these Jacobins, who—who—"
>
> "Nay, sir, if you are at a loss for opprobrious epithets," said Katherine, with provoking coolness, "call on Mr. Christopher Dillon for assistance; he waits your pleasure at the door."

Another aspect significant to rhetorical writing is delivery, particularly of speeches. An important aspect of a speech is establishing the rapport with the hearers. There are ways in which a speaker can use delivery (the way in which the speech is given) to claim the attention of the audience. One way is to plan moments of silence or deliberate pauses, causing the hearers to continue the unspoken thought. Of course readers cannot know how speeches were delivered prior to modern recording devices, having only written copies, for example, of the Gettysburg Address; however, you can become sensitive to the point at which a speaker may have paused during his or her verbal discourse. Developing such awareness can help you identify key points in the speaker's argument.

Clarence Darrow, in 1924, was opposed to capital punishment. The situation of the following excerpt was an appeal to the court on behalf of two teenagers who had been convicted of killing another teenager:

> **I do not know how much salvage there is in these two boys. I hate to say it in their presence, but what is there to look forward to? I do not know but what Your Honor would be merciful if you tied a rope around their necks and let them die; merciful to them, but not merciful to civilization, and not merciful to those who would be left behind. To spend the balance of their days in prison is mighty little to look forward to, if anything. Is it anything? They may have the hope that as the years roll around they might be released. I do not know. I do not know.**

What would be the effect if he paused each time he said "I do not know"? (Why do you think he kept repeating "I do not know"?)

Paraposiopesis

Paraposiopesis is when the interruption is an actual expression of emotion. In addition, sometimes the speaker mentions his or her inability to express his or her emotion at the point at which the sentence is broken off (for example, "I don't know what to say . . ."). This usage is called **aporia,** a rhetorical device described in the *Webster's New Twentieth Century Dictionary* (Unabridged). It is also cited by *The New Princeton Encyclopedia of Poetry and Poetics* (1993) as a figure that becomes **adymaton,** an expression of impossibility (for example, "When elephants fly, I'll . . .").

Notice how the speaker in "My Last Duchess" searches for words when he says: "A heart—how shall I say?—too soon made glad." (See page 136.) Also, Sinclair Lewis's main characters react emotionally in "Virga Vay & Allan Cedar":

> "Oh, sweet, be careful! It *might* explode!"
> "Yes, it—" Then he shouted. "Listen at us! As if we cared if we got blown up now!"

Graphically, (sometimes but not always) aposiopesis is shown with ellipsis (...), or with an em dash (—) or double dash (-- or - -). Not all uses of ellipsis and dashes, however, are indicative of aposiopesis; rather they depend on meaning and context.

Apophasis

Apophasis occurs when the speaker makes a point by pretending to deny it. For instance, "If I did not know you are an honest person, I would think you took that money," or "I would have to conclude your participation in this plan was with knowledge and premeditation, were it not for our long years of friendship and trust."

Anachronism

Anachronism refers to violations of time and space in which an event or person is placed in the wrong time. When these violations appear in movies and television, the viewers include them in a broad category of cinematic error called "bloopers." Examples of anachronistic-type bloopers are when the soldiers defend the fort against an Indian attack in 1855 by setting up a Gatling gun (not invented until 1861) or when Geronimo (not born until 1829) attacks a fort in 1820. Such anachronisms can be found in prose, poetry, and drama. For instance, what is the anachronism in this excerpt from Shakespeare's *Julius Caesar?*

MARCUS BRUTUS. Alas, good Cassius, do not think of him:
If he love Caesar, all tha he can do
Is to himself,—take thought, and die for Caesar:
And that were much he should; for he is given
To sports, to wildness, and much company.

TREBONIUS. There is no fear in him; let him not die;
For he will live, and laugh at this here-after.

[*Clock strikes.*]

MARCUS BRUTUS. Peace! count the clock.

CASSIUS.   The clock hath stricken three.

TREBONIUS.   'Tis time to part.

A clock that can strike the hour? In Caesar's Rome?

Here are a few lines of John Keats's "On First Looking into Chapman's Homer." Can you find the anachronism?

> Yet did I never breathe its pure serene
> Till I heard Chapman speak out loud and bold:
> Then felt I like some watcher of the skies
> When a new planet swims into his ken;
> Or like stout Cortez when, with eagle eyes
> He stared at the Pacific—and all his men
> Looked at each other with a wild surmise—
> Silent, upon a peak in Darien.

Hint: Who discovered the Pacific Ocean?

Do not mistakenly assume that all anachronisms are accidental errors; some are quite purposeful with "poetic license"—a rhetorical means that can have desired effects, such as Mark Twain's extended use of anachronism in *A Connecticut Yankee in King Arthur's Court* for an ironic effect.

Litotes

Litotes is a favorite of Anglo-Saxon writing. In litotes, a sense of understatement is achieved through negative affirmation (the negative of the opposite), which actually confirms or increases the importance of what is being discussed.

Litotes	Meaning
not bad	good
not fat	thin
not least	great
not unbecoming	appropriate
not the smartest	stupid

Of course, much of the rhetorical effect of litotes depends upon its use in context.

Hyperbole and Meiosis

Hyperbole (overstatement or exaggeration) and **meiosis** (understatement) are tropes that can be used for a wide variety of both serious and comic effects.

Hyperbole can be especially comic. Texans, as a case in point, are noted for their use of hyperbole, exaggeration, in a state where "the men are braver, the sky is bluer, the steaks are bigger, and the women are prettier than anywhere else in the world." Some stand-up comedians who perform before live audiences make extensive use of hyperbole. An example is the comedian who begins his routine by bragging about how hot he makes his chili, to which the audience shouts "How hot is it?" Comedian: "It's *so* hot it'll melt your spoon!"

Sometimes hyperbole is sincere, as when a lover wants to emphasize the extent of his or her love, or ironic. Read this first stanza of Andrew Marvell's "To His Coy Mistress":

To His Coy Mistress

→   Had we but world enough, and time,
This coyness, Lady, were no crime.
We would sit down, and think which way
To walk, and pass our long love's day.
Thou by the Indian Ganges' side
Should'st rubies find: I by the tide
Of Humber would complain. I would
→   Love you ten years before the Flood:
And you should if you please refuse
→   Till the conversion of the Jews.
My vegetable love should grow
→   Vaster than empires, and more slow.
→   And hundred years should go to praise
Thine eyes, and on thy forehead gaze.
→   Two hundred to adore each breast:
→   But thirty thousand to the rest.
An age at least to every part,
And the last age should show your heart.
For, Lady, you deserve this state;
Nor would I love at lower rate.

by Andrew Marvell

Its opposite, **meiosis** or understatement, treats a serious subject as though it is much less important than it is. Often meiosis projects a derogatory manner (unlike litotes that, through negation, frequently elevates the importance of its subject); however, context may dictate any number of effects, such as irony. The effect of the understatement in the last stanza of Thackeray's "Sorrows of Werther" is based on the incongruity of Charlotte's reaction to a man's death over her.

Sorrows of Werther

Werther had a love for Charlotte
    Such as words could never utter;
Would you know how first he met her?
    She was cutting bread and butter.

Charlotte was a married lady,
    And a moral man was Werther,
And, for all the wealth of Indies,
    Would do nothing for to hurt her.

So he sighed and pined and ogled,
    And his passion boiled and bubbled,
Till he blew his silly brains out,
    and no more was by it troubled.

Charlotte, having seen his body
    Borne before her on a shutter,
Like a well-conducted person,
    Went on cutting bread and butter.

by William Makepeace Thackeray

Paradox

Paradox, an important element in metaphysical poetry and in epi-grammatic writing, is a statement that seems to contradict itself, yet is actually true. You can hear paradox in conversations in everyday life: a couple may look at a pug-faced dog in a store window and exclaim "He's so ugly he's cute!"

The second stanza of Chidiock Tichborne's sixteenth-century "Elegy" is built upon paradoxical relationships:

My tale was heard and yet it was not told,
    My fruit is fallen and yet my leaves are green,
My youth is spent and yet I am not old,
    I saw the world and yet I was not seen;
      My thread is cut and yet it is not spun,
      And now I live, and now my life is done.

An **oxymoron** occurs when words, terms, or expressions appear to be self-contradicting: bittersweet, a dry martini, sweet-and-sour, love-hate relationships, passive resistance, jumbo shrimp, or a kind ogre.

Sometimes you will find passages in which the speaker makes extensive use of oxymorons, as Romeo's speech in *Romeo and Juliet* (Act I, Scene I) in which he speaks in such terms as "loving-hate" and "cold fires." More often, though, the oxymoron will be used with more restraint, primarily for the contradictory effect that produces such feelings as an emphasized sense of confusion, frustration, or determination (to name a few). Context, once again, is a prime determinant of the effect. Also, be alert for the "play on words" that so many times is within the oxymoron. The fourth stanza of Sir Thomas Wyatt's "Marvel No More" ends with an oxymoronic play on words ("Doth cause my mourning cheer"), as does Shakespeare's "Sonnet 40" in line 13 ("Lascivious grace, in whom all ill well shows").

Irony

Irony is a concept that involves opposites. The many types of irony form two distinct categories: **situational** or **dramatic irony,** in which the result following a sequence of events is the opposite of what is expected, and **verbal irony,** in which the speaker uses words that express the opposite of what is actually meant.

First, examine a few of the many forms situational irony can take. Ironic situations are a mainstay of popular comedy. The acting comedy of Lucille Ball, for example, relied heavily on situational irony as a source of humor. Often Lucy, who wanted to be part of her husband's nightclub act, would devise a plan to be part of the show. Rather than achieving her expected results, however, her plans usually ended with Lucy being locked in a closet, hanging from a balcony, or recovering from some other embarrassing situation.

Occasionally, a situation is ironic when someone who intends harm against another becomes the victim of his or her own plan, for instance, when a prankster is splashing paint on a neighbor's car, but an unexpected wind causes the paint to blow back on the prankster's own parked car, ruining the finish. Sometimes, if the person's motives are unjustified and he or she becomes the victim of an ironic situation, the person is said to have gotten what he or she "deserves."

Situational irony can be sad or even poignant, as when parents secure weapons to protect their children from danger, only to have a child injured or killed by one of those same weapons. On very subtle levels, situations can be intrinsically ironic, such as when the undeserving, cowardly, or lazy are rewarded and the deserving, brave, or industrious are punished.

Sometimes irony results from making false assumptions, and the very presence of an ironic outcome might lead you to examine the validity of the assumptions you have made.

Verbal irony occurs when the speaker says the opposite of what he or she means. How can you tell that verbal irony is at work in a statement? One clue is through the speaker's "ironic" tone of voice and through facial expression. The effect of the irony is a product of the speaker's intent.

For instance, a married couple plan to meet another couple at a restaurant for dinner. The wife arrives first, as usual for this couple. The other couple arrives and ask about her overdue husband. "He'll be here in a moment, I'm sure," she says with a laugh and wink, "Steve is *never* late!" Obviously from her tone, body language, and emphasis on *never,* Steve generally *is* late (a knowledge that, by implication, is shared by the other couple); however, his wife is not distressed but rather views this as a comical part of Steve's personality. What if her attitude is different—perhaps critical because Steve's habitual tardiness had caused the couple serious social, business, and family problems? "He'll be here in a moment, I'm *sure,*" she says through clenched teeth, her gaze rolling toward the ceiling in disdain. "*Steve* is *never* late!" The tone is hostile; the intent is critical. When the intent of the irony is to criticize by use of praise, the form is called **sarcasm.** The sarcastic tone of Robert Browning's "Soliloquy of the Spanish Cloister" is an oft-cited example, as is Swift's "Modest Proposal." (See page 131.)

Verbal irony, although sometimes described as "tongue in cheek," is not always sarcastic in tone or intent. The irony may be the result of **understatement,** also called **meiosis** ("I think we have a little water in the basement"—when the basement contains a three-foot deep flood), in which the irony intensifies the meaning of what is said; the result of **overstatement,** also known as **hyperbole** ("This pimple outshines a neon sign!"), in which the irony lessens the importance of the meaning of what is said; or the result of **contradiction in context** (such as describing a cruel, uncaring person in terms that are endearing).

Very often verbal irony is subtle and difficult to recognize. In Andrew Marvell's "To His Coy Mistress," the speaker begins with:

> Had we but world enough, and time,
> This coyness, Lady, were no crime,
> We would sit down, and think which way
> To walk, and pass our long love's day.

He concludes the poem, however, by saying:

> Thus, though we cannot make our sun
> Stand still, yet we will make him run.

What is ironic about the speaker's words? Upon what is this irony based? These words are ironic because they are based upon contradiction in context: at first the speaker bemoans how short the time—there is not enough time for her to be coy (an implication from the statement that "Had we but world enough, and time, . . . "). But he concludes that because they cannot stop the sun (a symbol for time), their love will make time go faster (the sun run)—an irony in the speaker's argument.

The relationship of verbal irony to meaning is, at this point, self-evident, as demonstrated by a master of verbal irony, Alexander Pope. Here is his "Epigram from the French." What verbal irony is at work here?

Epigram from the French

> Sir, I admit your gen'ral rule
> That every poet is a fool.
> But you yourself may serve to show it,
> That every fool is not a poet.

by Alexander Pope

Perhaps the speaker's auditor has stated that all poets are fools—a generalization that would include the speaker. Does the speaker really agree ("admit your gen'ral rule")? The final couplet confirms that he is speaking ironically, as he indulges in a generalization that the auditor (probably not a poet) is proof that not all fools are poets.

Figures of Speech Based on Syntax

Although diction refers to word choice (vocabulary), syntax refers to how the words are arranged into patterns. A few of the more common figures of speech that depend on syntax are summarized in the following chart.

FIGURES OF SPEECH BASED ON SYNTAX

Figure of Speech	Characteristic Syntactical Structure	Examples
Antithesis	Balance of contrasting terms; parallelism	O, change thy thought, that I may change my mind:
Apostrophe	Direct address to an auditor (called **invocation** if to a muse)	My pen, take pain a little space To follow that which doth me chase
Hyperbaton	Transposition or rearrangement of normal sentence order	Which when she entered, although the younger except, none could attain, fixed the smile for the rest. . . .
Hypallage	An epithet or qualifier placed next to less proximate of a group of nouns	"the Gypsy's wondering curse" for "the wondering Gypsy's curse"
Sleight of "and"	Tropes that use coordinating conjunctions; for example, the Zeugma	
	a. Same grammatical relation, but different idiomatic use	a. He will pay Jane her due and her rent.
	b. Two different verbs	b. He bussed the table in the restaurant and the children to school.
	c. Subject-verb agreement problem	c. You or she is going to have to leave.

What effects can you expect from the use of figures of speech based on syntax? Figures such as antithesis and apostrophe can, depending on context, project a formal tone or render the work more or less emotional. Hyperbatons and hypallages can add a sense of confusion, particularly when the speaker is portraying a state of mental anxiety, as an example. Sleights of "and" can be witty, provocative, or disruptive, again based on context. Of course, this is only a partial list of the many effects syntax-based figures can have in a work.

Another interesting and somewhat complex figure of speech is the **chiasmus.** Taking its name from the Greek letter *Chi* (χ), the chiasmus is achieved when the second part resembles a reverse image of the first part. For example,

▶ a chiastic phrase: sun-warmed winter fun
▶ a chiastic sentence: Children are happy; happiness is child-like.
▶ a chiastic syntactic structure:
Her door flew open,   but closed stayed her mind.
(Subject-verb-adverb, conjunction adverb-verb-subject)

Diction

Diction refers to the enunciation or exact articulation of words and also refers to word choice. Diction, in terms of its significance to understanding literature, can be discussed from several perspectives, including diction as a use of language, poetic diction, and diction as it relates to contextual meanings (particularly as diction and syntax interact to produce a writer's style).

Diction—the writer's word choice—can be based on many different sources, levels, and purposes. Sources for words can range from Germanic to Latinate, archaic to modern, eclectic "borrowed expressions" (such as a Gallicism, which is a borrowing from French) to those of Anglo-Saxon origin, and so forth. The levels can range from formal to informal, technical to non-technical, standard to nonstandard. The purpose could be for literal communication, figurative meaning, expression of opinion, teaching, contemplation, or spurring to action.

As a use of language, *diction* (word choice) plays an obvious role, particularly in **imagery** and **figures of speech.** Sometimes the change of a single word can make or destroy the tone or the meaning of a selection; hence, a writer's diction is generally aimed at producing a desired effect, an effect that may go beyond the literal meaning of the word choice.

To some degree, diction can be viewed as isolated word choices. For example, a **malapropism** is the use of a word that is inappropriate for the context, but that resembles a word that is appropriate. The effect, of course, of using the incorrect word can be amusing (as when Norm Crosby fills his routine with malapropisms for the purpose of making the audience laugh); or it can be embarrassing when the error in word choice is unintentional. When the malapropism is used in the dialogue of a character, the effect depends upon the situation of the story: the malapropism might serve to enlighten the reader and/or the other people engaged in the dialogue concerning the character's educational level, as an example. Richard Brinsley Sheridan's Mrs. Malaprop in *The Rivals* (1775) is the character whose constant misuse of words, such as "a progeny of learning," gave rise to the expression "malapropism." In the case of Mrs. Malaprop, she was trying to display mastery of a large vocabulary.

Can you spot any malapropisms in this excerpt from *Romeo and Juliet,* Act II, Scene III? What is the effect?

NURSE.   If you be he, sir, I desire some confidence with you.

BENVOLIO. She will indite him to some supper.

MERCUTIO. A bawd, a bawd, a bawd! so-ho!

The first malapropism is the nurse's use of *confidence* where she most likely means *conference*. The effect this malapropism has on Benvolio is to cause him to mock her by deliberately using a malapropism: "indite" for "invite."

Diction also deals with the sounds of the words, their pronunciation/enunciation. Some words have changed in pronunciation. **Metathesis** is a change in which sounds within a word change position. This change might affect the spelling, such as in Old English, *bird* was spelled and pronounced *bridd*. At other times, however, the metathesis is not accorded the validity of a spelling change, but rather is a product of a regional or ethnic dialect. When this is the case, the writer might indicate the dialect by writing the word as it is phonetically pronounced by the character in dialogue. For instance, a character might pronounce *predict* as *perdict* or *pretty* as *perty*. The effect of phonetically "spelling out" a character's use of metathesis is to give the reader more insight into that character as an individual.

Related to metathesis is the **spoonerism,** named after Dr. W. A. Spooner (New College, Oxford). In a spoonerism, the speaker accidentally exchanges the initial consonants of two or more words: "a dork way" for a "work day," a "sunken drop" for a "drunken sop," or "libeled rafter" for "ribald laughter." Unlike metathesis, however, the spoonerism has a more limited effect in dialogue, except in the case of very specialized characterization.

Four terms relate to omitting letters in words. **Apocope** is omitting final letter(s) or syllable(s) of a word, as in *thro'*. **Aphaeresis** is omitting unstressed syllable(s) at the beginning of a word, as in *'til*. **Syncope** is omitting a letter or syllable from the middle of a word, as in *e'en* for *even,* for the purpose of meter, to avoid the reduplication of a letter when a suffix is added, or as a natural result of a word passing from Latin to English or of shortening a word. **Elision** is omitting part of a word, frequently when two or more words are run together, as in *th'world* for *the world.* Some other examples include *call'st, th'other, 'tis,* and *'twill.*

Puns are word choices that are referred to as a "play on words"—two words have the same sound but very different meaning. The use of these words often elicits a smirky smile and guttural groan on the part of the hearers. For a very long time puns were held in low esteem, but in current discussion they enjoy a higher status. Although frequently used for comic effect, puns can be used quite seriously, particularly as used in literature written prior to the eighteenth century. Famous writers of puns include John Donne, Shakespeare, Bennett Cerf, Ezra Pound, and T.S. Eliot.

Puns rely, of course, on context for their witty overtones because the context gives significance to *both* meanings. A married couple are driving down a country road on a beautiful spring day. They are engaged in a lively discussion in which the husband, who is driving, is describing at length some "picky" details that he feels are wrong with the plan his wife just proposed for their upcoming vacation. Just as he makes what he feels is a most convincing argument ("You get off from work thirty minutes earlier than I do, so I should get to select where we go on vacation"), they approach two small rabbits playing in the middle of the road. One rabbit streaks to the right while the other bunny races to the left. "Darling," she smiles sweetly, "you are *splitting hares!* "

An often-quoted pun appears in *Romeo and Juliet,* Act III, Scene I when Mercutio is wounded:

ROMEO.   **Courage, man; the hurt cannot be much.**

MERCUTIO. **No, 'tis not so deep as a well, nor so wide as a church-door; but 'tis enough, 'twill serve: ask for me to-morrow, and shall find me a grave man.**

What is the pun at work here? "Grave" can refer to either a "serious" man (as, indeed, his wound is a serious situation) and to a man in his grave. Do you see any other figures of speech here?

Here is the last stanza of John Donne's "A Hymn to God the Father." What puns can you find?

> **I have a sin of fear, that when I have spun**
> **My last thread, I shall perish on the shore;**
> **But swear by Thy self, that at my death Thy Son**
> **Shall shine as he shines now, and heretofore;**
> **And, having done that, Thou hast done;**
> **I fear no more.**

A very obvious pun is "Son" and *sun.* (Keep in mind that the pun as a literary device can be *very* serious.) There is another pun at work in the final stanza (and throughout the entire poem). Hint: Look again at the poet's name.

Diction also refers to the level of words used: vocabulary that is high, plain, or low. Many different descriptive systems have been developed to try to identify the different levels of diction writers and speakers use.

Diction Described by Dialect

Dialects are the speech patterns (including diction, grammatical constructions, and accents) of a defined geographical region or group.

Generally, this descriptive system identifies *Standard English* as the speech used by the mainstream professionals of the age in question. The "standard" often cited to exemplify twentieth-century Standard English is that of speech-trained television and radio journalists. *Nonstandard English,* then, could be said to be all language that does not conform to this standard.

Standard English can be Formal, General, or Informal in level with diction playing a significant role in the determination. For example, General English often includes the use of **vernacular,** the jargon of the person's profession or the diction that is specific to the region. Informal English is marked by colloquial expressions, slang, and clipped words that are sometimes drawn from nonstandard usage. Nonstandard English consists of colloquial expressions, slang, and clipped words plus diction that is characteristically considered "nonstandard," such as *ain't.* The grammatical constructions of Nonstandard English do not conform to the rules of Standard English, particularly in the use of pronouns and subject-verb agreement, or to the rules of standardized spelling. Keep in mind, however, that words and constructions considered Nonstandard today may well have been considered Standard (or vice versa) in a previous period. Since the pronoun *they* was once considered to be a singular pronoun, "If a person laughs, they must be happy" would have been considered a Standard usage. Even double negatives and "ain't" were once a part of Standard English.

Diction Described by Purpose

The purpose of language is communication. Consider the use of technical terms, so useful and appropriate for instructing or enlightening professionals in a given field, (terms that become an *-ese* as in *educationese* or *doctorese* to the untrained layperson). Oftentimes the reader or hearer will respond to technical language with the plea, "Can you put that in plain English?" As a result of advanced technology (home computers with ROM-drive and VCRs), technical writers (a very lucrative field in which professional writers write reports, instruction manuals, instructional charts, and articles) are being called upon to "translate" the technical world of science and technology into a language that can be understood by the nontechnical world.

The diction used in this book is technical to the extent that its purpose is to help prepare people to be more informed readers and writers. Naturally, most technical diction will be found in nonnarrative prose writing; however, it can also be found in some surprising packages. Take, as an example, this poem in which Samuel Taylor Coleridge gives "Metrical Feet: Lesson for a Boy" (1806). "Derwent" is his son.

Metrical Feet

Lesson for a Boy

Trōchĕe trĭps frŏm lōng tŏ shŏrt;
From long to long in solemn sort
Slōw Spōndēe stālks; strōng fŏot! yet ill able
Ēvĕr tŏ cōme ŭp wĭth Dāctўl trĭsўllăblĕ.
Iāmbĭcs mārch frŏm shŏrt tŏ lōng—
Wĭth ă lēap ănd ă bōund thĕ swĭft Ānăpĕsts thrōng;
One syllable long, with one short at each side,
Ămphrĭbrăchўs hāstes wĭth ă stātelў stride—
Fīrst ănd lāst bēĭng lōng, mĭddlĕ shŏrt, Ămphĭmācer
Strikes hĭs thūndĕrĭng hŏofs lĭke ă prōud hĭgh-brĕd
    Rācer.
If Derwent be innocent, steady, and wise,
And delight in the things of earth, water, and skies;
Tender warmth at his heart, with these meters to
    show it,
With sound sense in his brains, may make Derwent
    a poet—
May crown him with fame, and must win him the
    love
Of his father on earth and his Father above.
        My dear, dear child!
Could you stand upon Skiddaw, you would not from
    its whole ridge
See a man who so loves you as your fond S. T.
COLERIDGE.

by Samuel Taylor Coleridge

Diction Described by Tone

The diction of communication can give the work a formal or an
informal tone. Formal writing depends upon diction that is
higher level vocabulary; informal writing engages casual diction,
such as the **colloquial expressions, idiomatic diction** (based on
tradition rather than on logic, for instance, "call off," "get on," or
"set about"), and **slang** (vernacular language) of everyday
speech.

Before leaving diction, some words need to be said about a

relatively recent trend in literary "awareness": sexist versus non-sexist writing, especially in the area of social titles and descriptive labels.

Today, "Ms.," "chairperson," "business people," and other such nonsexist terms are in broad general use. As you read period literature, however, you will find social titles and descriptive labels that are gender based. You also will discover that some titles and labels underwent changes in both meaning and status over the years. As a result, you will miss important clues to understanding if you do not recognize the meaning of the title or label *as used in the period in which the work was written.* For example, when did *man* change from referring predominantly to *mankind* (both sexes included) to referring to an *adult male?* When Thomas Jefferson wrote "All men are created equal," what did *he mean?*

Space precludes an exhaustive look at how the perceptions of gender in terms of roles, status, and customs have changed over time and how these perceptions are reflected in literature (such as the personification of machines and nature as female, with hurricanes being named with male as well as female names being a relatively recent practice). Yet, there are a few terms that beg to be addressed here.

1. **Man, woman.** As the following chart shows, *man* originally meant human being (male or female) but came to mean male. A female might be referred to (in early English writings) as a *man.*

	Old English Writing	Eighteenth-Century Writing
Adult male	wer	man[*]
Adult male person	waepman	man
Humankind (male and female being inclusive)	man	man
Adult female person	wifman	woman
Adult female	wif	wife

[*]By the nineteenth century, *man* was used mostly as a synonym for *male,* especially in legal matters.

Man, then, continued to some degree to refer to humankind, but in popular practice gradually came to mean an adult male. The problem comes in reading period literature: when the writer refers to *man,* is he or she referring to just adult males or also to females?

In the literature of the last half of the twentieth century, some writers very slowly gained an awareness of "sexist language." As a result, readers taught during this period of greater sensitivity may tend to mirror this view when reading the writings of other periods: to assume that a seventeenth-century writer means humankind when referring to *man* could be a mistake. This may or may not be the case, particularly in issues of interpretation of the law.

2. **He, she.** Originally, *they* was used as a singular pronoun: "If a person comes, *they* should be shown in" or "Each person should speak *their* minds."Grammarians, however, objected to the lack of pronoun-antecedent agreement, hence the assignment of *he* to fill this syntactical role.

He (as used in the sixteenth century) did not refer to both sexes (as today speakers mean both men and women when they say: "When a person drives a car, *he* should obey the traffic laws"). This masculine usage may reflect the fact that the first English grammar books (written in the sixteenth and seventeenth centuries) were written by males for male readers (few females could read or write).

He (as used in the example sentence given in the previous paragraph to refer to both male and female in a general, more inclusive sense) was not introduced until the eighteenth century and was not extensively used until the nineteenth century, when an Act of Parliament decreed that females would be included in masculine-gender words. Misuses of this order, however, have occurred. Consequently, current nonsexist writing uses *both* pronouns: "When a person drives a car, he or she should obey the traffic laws."

3. **Mrs., Miss, Ms., Madam.** Today, a *mistress* (a noun) refers to the head of a household or to a woman having an affair with a man other than her own husband. Although *mistress* (used as a noun) did refer to a prostitute in the 1600s and 1700s, it also was a commonly

used social title used before the woman's name: *Mistress* (abbreviations *Mrs.* and *Miss*).

Mrs.—used to address a married or unmarried adult female

Miss—used to address female children

By the end of the 1700s, the social customs began to take the form that is seen today:

Mrs.—used to address a married female

Miss—used to address an unmarried female

In the 1800s, *Mrs.* came to be used before the husband's full name (as in Mrs. John Smith) to refer to the wife. Not until the mid-twentieth century was *Ms.* used to refer to a woman whether married or unmarried. *Madam* (ma'am) is a form of *polite* address to a woman and has also ironically been used as the title of a woman who has a house of prostitution.

4. **Master, Fellow, Esquire**. Historically, *master* was the masculine equivalent of *mistress*; however, recent attention is being paid to acknowledging that women, too, can show "mastery" in certain areas and hence can be addressed as *master*. Male children may be referred to as master; and in period literature, an owner of slaves is often referred to as *master*.

Fellow, an Old English word, originally was sex neutral, referring to a partner or co-worker. Although modern connotations associate the term as more masculine (possibly due to the form *fellowman*), *fellow* was used to refer to a male or female (including a wife).

An *esquire* (esq.) was a male attendant to an English knight or one of the English landed gentry (with *esquiress*— the female form—referring in rather limited use to a variety of positions, such as a mourner or a slave girl). Today, *esquire* might appear after the name of an attorney (in practice in the United States) whether male or female.

What conclusion can be reached concerning sexism and diction? Obviously, awareness of the issue has been the impetus to change; however, do not impose today's consciousness on yesterday's norms. If you are seeking to gain insight into the meaning of a work, try to view the diction used in the context of the period in which it was written.

Use of Language in Prose, Poetry, and Drama
Effects

Being able to name, define, and recognize in use the different types of figurative language is helpful, but being able to identify what *effect* the use of figurative language has within the literary work is crucial.

Epiphany

A discussion of *effects* should include at least brief mention of **epiphany**. Historically, epiphany first referred to the January sixth Church festival called by that name. Literally meaning "a manifestation," epiphany came to mean a revelation of God's presence in the world.

What has this to do with the *effects* of how language is used in a literary work? James Joyce borrowed the term in the mid-twentieth century to describe a sudden revelation of some commonplace object. Since that time the term has been used to describe the point at which the commonplace is revealed to be radiant. The term **epiphany** came to be used in the same way that the expression **"the moment"** was used in previous literary study. The role that the writer's use of language (the symbols, images, and other uses of language) plays in facilitating this revelation—**the moment** or the **epiphany**—is self-evident. Joyce's *Dubliners* is considered a collection of epiphanies, and William Wordsworth's "The Solitary Reaper" describes such a moment of revelation. Here is the final stanza of "The Solitary Reaper."

> Whate'er the theme, the maiden sang
> As if her song could have no ending;
> I saw her singing at her work,
> And o'er the sickle bending;—
> I listened, motionless and still;
> And, as I mounted up the hill,
> The music in my heart I bore,
> Long after it was heard no more.

Poetic Diction

Poetic diction refers to language that is normally associated with poetry—that has a "poetic effect." The trend in modern writing is to use the diction of everyday speech; however, English poets of various periods (such as the Romantics) sought a "language of poetry" with an effect that would transcend that of everyday speech.

The poetic diction in vogue varied with the period and the group involved. Eighteenth-century writers, as an example, favored periphrasis (substituting ornate descriptions for ordinary expressions), personifications, and archaisms. The effect? An artificial, stilted form.

Poetic diction can be the basis of some very interesting word studies. Take the word *fain* as an example. A word study reveals that *fain* as a verb is obsolete, as an adverb is used with *would* (She *would fain* have come with him tonight), but as an adjective has two uses, both of which are identified as "Archaic" and "Poetic." *Fain* as an adjective can mean pleased or it can mean making do, as expressed today. Usually *fain,* when it means accepting less than desired circumstances, is accompanied by the infinitive form of the verb.

Christina Rossetti uses *fain* in this latter sense in "A Bed of Forget-Me-Nots":

> **Is LOVE so prone to change and rot**
> **We are fain to rear Forget-me-not**
> **By measure in a garden-plot?—**

Dramatic Irony

Irony has already been discussed in some detail (page 234); however, the *effect* of dramatic irony merits some mention. In drama, irony takes a different form that, naturally, significantly influences the effect. Dramatic irony involves the audience having an awareness or knowledge of some information that is not known by the characters in the play. The effect is **tragic** (tragic irony) when the very words spoken by a character unwittingly foretell the coming disaster (unknown by the characters but known by the hearers).

Epiphany, poetic diction, dramatic irony—these are just a sampling of the many effects use of language can have in a work.

Questions to Apply the Literary Principles Concerning Use of Language

Ask the following questions to help you identify and understand how language is used.

1. Do you recognize any figures of speech based on analogy? (similes, metaphors, personification, allusions, and so forth)

2. Do you recognize any figures of speech based on rhetoric? (rhetorical questions, amplifications, and so forth)

3. Do you recognize any figures of speech based on syntax?

4. How would you describe the diction used?

5. What is the effect of each use of language?

Additional Points to Remember About Use of Language

▶ Love, time, and death are without doubt among the most widely personified concepts in literature. Yet, the range of effects the personification of these three topics can produce is almost as numerous as the poems in which they appear. Stereotypically, love is sometimes portrayed as Cupid in literature, particularly poetry; death is commonly portrayed as a skeleton; and time is many times personified as an old man with a scythe. As you identify figurative language, look for the different *effects* produced by the personification of love, time, and death.

▶ Spend some time with a variety of literary dictionaries, such as Holman and Harmon's *A Handbook to Literature,* Abram's *A Glossary of Literary Terms,* and *The New Princeton Encyclopedia of Poetry and Poetics.* No one book can exhaust the different perspectives of literary study. By cross-referencing several different sources, you will find examples illustrating the different figures of speech, literary movements, and many other areas. You may want to consult several sources for examples and explanations of those areas that are new to you. Also, you may find in your local library's computer the location of British and American anthologies (the Norton Anthologies are extremely popular). You may enjoy spending some time browsing through the appendixes, glossaries, and explanatory matter that are part of many of these literary collections. You should find a wealth of information, often with full-context illustrations.

▶ Do not confuse **personification,** in which human characteristics are given to inanimate objects or abstract ideas, with **anthropomorphism,** which is presenting a nonhuman (such as an animal or a mythical god) as a human. The rabbit who declares that he is "late" in *Alice in Wonderland* is an anthropomorphism; the rabbit described by the hunter as "a worthy opponent who planned his strategy well—laughing at my clumsiness and disdaining the sophistication of my weapons" is being personified.

▶ For some fun with figures of speech, look for collections of amusing ways to use language. For example, in the December 1994 issue of *Texas Monthly* magazine you will find "More Colorful Texas Sayings Than you Can Shake a Stick at: 622 wise and witty ways to talk Texan."

▶ Keep an *unabridged dictionary* within close reach when reading and writing. The slang of yesterday, for instance, may no longer carry the same meaning today; however, an unabridged dictionary can help you better understand the diction used today and in other periods of time.

▶ Do not assume that every word or phrase that has "multiple meanings" is an intentional attempt at figurative language. Sometimes such use is an **ambiguity,** the effect of which is confusion. Ambiguity can result from syntax problems, an unclear relationship between a pronoun and its antecedent, or a context that does not clarify the intended meanings of multiple-meaning words. When the *intended effect* is to project a tone or atmosphere that is confused, unclear, or ambiguous, such ambiguities are useful; but if the intended effect is otherwise, such ambiguities can destroy the integrity of the work. The term **ambiguity** refers to misuse of words with multiple meanings, and the term **plurisignation** refers to their effective use.

▶ You may encounter writers who use the word **type** (defined in this book as a character who represents a group) as a synonym for **symbol.**

▶ Cliches, figures of speech, and expressions that have been overused and have been labeled "trite" are often found in literature. There was a point in time, however, when a given figure of speech or expression would have been considered "fresh" and "new." At what point does a clever or useful figure of speech or expression cross the line to become trite or a cliche? Keep in mind the various groups that use words, such as literary writers (essayists, poets, and others), journalists, and radio personalities. A poet used a figure of speech two hundred years ago that was fresh, new, and clever—so clever that his contemporaries and the generations that followed took the expression from context and used it to the point that it is now considered trite. How does this affect perceptions of the poet's original use of the expression? Is his poem of lesser importance today? Do cliches have any place in contemporary writing? What do you anticipate will be the trite expressions of the future?

▶ Just as a mixed metaphor combines unlikely vehicles for the same tenor, a similar concept applies to the mixed figure in which unlikely figures of speech are blended together in use. It also might be called mixed imagery. "My new car is a lemon; she quits on me every chance she gets." (The mixed imagery here is simile and personification.)

▶ Do not confuse the **euphemism**, which is replacing of an offensive expression with an inoffensive one, with **euphony**, which is the pleasant sound found in some works.

This little poem may help you differentiate the two:

Is It Euphemism or Euphony?

Is it euphemism or euphony?
>The answer has evaded me.
Euphemism, they say, is to render
>A harsh word into one kind and tender.
We don't say "leg"; we say a "limb."
>Don't call him "skinny," instead say "trim."
But when a poem has euphony,
>It simply "sounds" pleasant to you and me.
Now all your doubts should flee when you see:
>Is it euphemism or euphony?

by Lillian E. Myers

Contextual Meanings

Read not to contradict and confute, nor to believe
and take for granted, nor to find talk and discourse,
but to weigh and consider. Some books are to be
tasted, others to be swallowed, and some few to be
chewed and digested: . . .

**Of Studies
by Francis Bacon (1561–1626)**

As with the other areas of linguistics (the study of language),
such as **phonology** (the study of speech sounds) and **morphology**
(the study of word formation), **semantics** (the study of meanings in
language) and **syntax** (the arrangement of words into patterns) are
complex areas of study.

Denotation

Simply stated, **denotation** is the basic or literal meanings of a
word. Note that this definition employs the plural meanings—
hence serves to emphasize what can be a major obstacle in the way
of an exact interpretation of what a word, phrase, or line means in
a literary selection.

Words often have multiple literal meanings and only through
careful exploration of the context in which they are used can you
learn the intended denotation (literal meaning). Problems can arise
when the reader or listener is unaware of the multiple meanings of
a word.

A word in isolation can have meaning, but *the meaning*
depends on context. Look at the multiple meanings of *air* that
appear in the *Merriam-Webster Dictionary:*

air n   **1: the gaseous mixture surrounding the earth
2: a light breeze 3: MELODY, TUNE
4: the outward appearance of a person or
thing: MANNER 5: an artificial manner 6:
COMPRESSED AIR (—sprayer) 7: AIRCRAFT
(—patrol) 8: AVIATION (—safety) 9: the medium
of transmission of radio waves; also: RADIO,
TELEVISION**

    1. We must measure the <u>air</u> pressure.
       ["the gaseous mixture surrounding the earth"]

2. The warm <u>air</u> of the ocean brushed her face.
["a light breeze"]

3. That song has a lovely <u>air</u> to it.
["MELODY, TUNE"]

4. He has a friendly <u>air</u>.
["the outward appearance of a person or thing: MANNER"]

5. He had a phony <u>air</u> about him.
["an artificial manner"]

6. He used an <u>air</u> sprayer to paint the car.
["COMPRESSED AIR (—sprayer)"]

7. She was a member of the <u>air</u> patrol.
["AIRCRAFT (—patrol)"]

8. The commission voted on <u>air</u> safety.
["AVIATION (—safety)"]

9. She was on the <u>air</u> last night.
["the medium of transmission of radio waves; also RADIO, TELEVISION"]

Obviously, one element of semantics is the *interplay* of dictionary meaning and context. Another element that is very significant to the denotation of words in context is "sloppy" or careless use of words (**diction**) that is so often witnessed in everyday speech.

Lack of precision in day-to-day conversations has resulted in confusion over words that are similar both in their individual meanings and in their shades of meaning. The words *assure*, *ensure*, and *insure* are examples. These three words tend to be used interchangeably, yet each has its own meaning:

Assure means to give a promise to a person—"Let me assure you that I'll be there on time."
Ensure means to make sure—"Your participation will ensure the success of the program."
Insure means to protect with insurance—"I must insure the house against flood damage."

Being able to differentiate such often-confused words is important to understanding denotative meaning. Even words that quite rightly might be grouped as synonyms can have shades of meaning that should not be disregarded. The noun *remnant* illustrates the point. *Remnant* usually means a small amount left or a piece of fabric left on a bolt. Synonyms for *remnant* include residue, portion left, rest. Consequently, in "The *remnant* of the solution was in the bottle," the words *residue, portion left,* or *rest* could quite appropriately be used in place of "remnant." In "The store clerk put the *remnant* of the fabric on sale," "remnant," of course, refers to the rest of the fabric. But would the shades of meaning—the denotations of *remnant*—allow a person, assuming that remnant has *rest* as a synonym, to say "I think I'll have a short *remnant* before dinner tonight"?

Denotation is a word's literal meanings, including its shades of meaning that depend upon context for identity.

Another element of denotation (the literal meanings of words) involves diction (the writer's or speaker's choice of words): the degree to which the words used are **specific** or **general,** and **concrete** or **abstract.**

> General words denote a group or class: *cat*
> Specific words denote members of a group or class: *Siamese, tabby*
> Concrete words denote people and things that are perceived by the five senses: *a warm coat*
> Abstract words denote concepts and ideas: *pride, responsibility*

Concrete words are easily defined; abstract words, however, often defy universally accepted definitions because they cannot be measured or described by our physical senses. The more specific and concrete the diction used, the easier it is to establish the meanings. Look at this series of five statements. Which statement contains the most easily defined underlined word?

1. "I like having <u>protection</u> around."

2. "I like having an <u>animal</u> around."

3. "I like having a <u>dog</u> around."

4. "I like having a <u>Great Dane</u> around."

5. "I like having my dog <u>Killer</u> around."

In the first statement, "protection" is very abstract and general. It might refer to a barbed-wire fence, bodyguards, bolted doors, a weapon, or any number of other means of protection. The second sentence is far more concrete (animals can be seen, felt), but it is still rather ambiguous, rather general. The third sentence begins to give a more specific, concrete picture—obviously this person likes having some type of dog around. What breed? Sentence four gives an even more concrete picture; however, the fifth sentence is both concrete and specific.

Levels of abstraction will vary in context, depending upon the writer's use of specific examples that tend to make the writing more concrete. Writers, in other words, can clarify abstract concepts through use of specific examples, but they can also increase the levels of abstraction by making generalizations.

Syntax

Diction is the choice of words used; **syntax** is their arrangement into patterns. Just as diction (vocabulary) has been grouped into different levels for ease in identification, certain grammatical patterns of words (syntax) have been identified and labeled.

Some sources use the word **grammar** as a synonym for **syntax**. Although such usage is common, **grammar** actually involves not just syntax (study and description of the grammatical arrangement of words into patterns) but also includes **morphology** (study and description of word formation) and **phonology** (study and description of the sounds of words). In its fullest sense, then, syntax is the arrangement of words and the grammatical relationships of the words and the groups of words in a sentence.

There are many different grammar systems, but each should in some way address the role of syntax to meaning. Consider, as an example, what is commonly called "traditional grammar." This grammar system is based on Latinate and literary models and was developed by eighteenth- and nineteenth-century grammarians. In traditional grammar, there are eight parts of speech with rules governing how they should and should not be used. This is a contrast to "structural grammar" of the mid-twentieth century that concentrates on patterns of syntax and sound as they actually are used (and not necessarily dictating how they *should* be used). Transformational-generative grammar emphasizes syntax by trying to examine and explain how the organization of sentences into such parts as phrases and words interact with those ideas that come to mind both to convey and to understand meaning. (If you are interested in transformational-generative grammar, look to some of the work done by Noam Chomsky.)

Regardless of what system of grammar you prefer, there are a few general comments that can be noted concerning syntax and the role it plays in determining contextual meanings.

Syntax (the arrangement of words into patterns in a sentence) also involves the **function** these words and groups of words serve within the sentence. Words and groups of words can serve in many different functions: **subject, verb, object, modifier, connective, complement, preposition,** and **absolute.**

In English, the most common sequence pattern is subject-verb-object. Other common sequence patterns include subject-verb-modifier/complement.

Very often, but not always, the **subject** will appear before the verb. Exceptions include such constructions as "There are three mice in the room" in which the subject, "mice," comes after the verb "are." **Verbs** can be transitive and be followed by an object, intransitive and not be followed by an object, or linking and used to connect a complement (an adjective or noun) to the subject. **Objects** can be direct receivers of action (He threw the ball) or indirect receivers of action (He threw me the ball). **Complements** follow linking verbs.

Modifiers describe or limit, with adjectives and adverbs usually appearing before the word(s) they modify, with phrase and clause modifiers usually coming after—although exceptions to the generalization abound. **Connectives** include *coordinating conjunctions* that connect words that are in similar functions (such as two subjects: "Jane *and* John went home"), *subordinating connectives* that connect a subordinate clause to a main clause ("I can't continue *unless* you stop eating"), and *transitional connectives* ("There will be a test on Monday. *As a result,* she will not assign any further homework.")

Prepositions both connect and show a relationship of the word that follows to another word, quite often one that precedes ("The ball rolled *under* the table."—"under" tells where the ball rolled). **Absolutes** are not grammatically related to anything; they just "feel right" and somehow help the sentence ("*No, I can't!*" or "*For crying out loud,* do you expect him to believe her?").

The functions of words and where they are placed in relation to the rest of the sentence significantly contribute to their relationship to one another and, as a result, to their meaning. The function and the syntax, then, provide the context for meaning.

Prose Rhythms

In addition, diction, syntax, and function can join together to project **prose rhythm.** By definition, prose lacks a sustained rhythm; however, prose writers can use elements of rhythm to capture, propel, or abruptly stop their readers at a given point. Prose rhythm involves more than the rhythmic beat you hear; it also includes a rhythmic progression of thought.

Prose rhythm is a valuable tool for both fiction and nonfiction writers and can provide an enjoyable experience for the reader. This concept can be illustrated by looking at the different types of sentences.

The Loose or Common Sentence

This is the most-used sentence structure in the English language. It generally is written in one of three basic forms, each of which can be expanded by coordinating similar structures into the sentence or by modifying parts of or the entire sentence with more information:

Subject	Transitive Verb	Object
The car	hit	a tree.

Subject	Intransitive Verb	
Susan	cried.	

Subject	Linking Verb	Complement
Roger	was	a student.
The dog	is	happy.
The book	is	there.

Effect: As the most common sentence structure used, there is a sense of met expectation (comfortable style due to familiarity). The writing tends to be "choppy" if most of the sentences contain little coordination or modification. Too much elaboration, however, results in a difficult, wordy style.

The Periodic Sentence

In contrast to the loose sentence in which the subject often appears early in the sentence, the subject and its verb come much later in the periodic sentence and serve as a climactic statement to a series of subordinate clauses or phrases. The rhetorical benefits of "building" to the main point can clearly be seen:

> **Reaching deep within herself for some type of consolation, some small reflection of the pride and dignity that had once been the fighting edge of her courage, some reassurance that all was not lost, the *destitute woman opened the courtroom door.***

Effect: The rhetorical buildup to the main point can be rhythmic and dramatic.

The Parallel Sentence

Parallel sentences consist of a series of phrases, main clauses, or subordinate clauses:

> **The mother was always *laughing at his jokes, crying over his heartbreaks, and justifying his faults.***

> **The children laughed; the dog yelped; the young girl cried.**

> **You should always remember *which key unlocks the chain, which chain binds the heart,* and *which heart breaks for you.***

Effect: The parallel sentence appeals to the reader's sense of logic in sequencing similar ideas or items and provides a sense of prose rhythm to the writing.

The Balanced Sentence

The balanced sentence is a type of parallel construction in which two major sentence elements that contrast with one another are balanced between a coordinating conjunction:

> **The river's ravishes stunned the older on-lookers, *but* the water's pull mesmerized the younger ones.**

> **Working on the project satisfied his sense of justice, *but* destroyed his sense of independence.**

Effect: The balanced sentence, as a type of parallel sentence, provides a sense of prose rhythm to the sentence but also provides emphasis or contrast—an element of logic.

The introductory paragraph of *A Tale of Two Cities* can be used to put this information into practical application. After reading the paragraph, identify what sentence structures are used and their effects on the meaning.

A Tale of Two Cities

It was the best of times, it was the worst of times, it was the age of wisdom, it was the age of foolishness, it was the epoch of belief, it was the epoch of incredulity, it was the season of Light, it was the season of Darkness, it was the spring of hope, it was the winter of despair, we had everything before us, we had nothing before us, we were all going direct to Heaven, we were all going direct the other way—in short, the period was so far like the present period, that some of its noisiest authorities insisted on its being received, for good or for evil, in the superlative degree of comparison only.

by Charles Dickens

The bulk of the paragraph consists of a series of main clauses that are structured as loose or common sentences using a very simple, plain, easy-to-understand level of diction. This structure provides a comfortable, nonthreatening beginning. So many short sentences would normally be "choppy"; however, they have been joined together **mechanically** with commas (representing "and") and have been joined together **structurally** with parallel sentence construction.

We had: It was: the best of times
everything before us   the worst of times
nothing before us   the age of wisdom
                                            the age of foolishness
                                            the epoch of belief
                                            the epoch of incredulity
We were: the season of Light
all going direct to Heaven   the season of Darkness
all going direct the other way   the spring of hope
                                            the winter of despair

This use results in a rhythm that literally pulls the reader along, far outweighing any staccato effect the short, loose sentences might have otherwise produced.

Next, examine the contents of the syntactical structure used in the excerpt. "It was" is the subject-verb for the first ten independent clauses. The subject-verb changes to "We had" and "We were" respectively in the final four independent clauses. What is the effect of this change? One possible effect is that the momentum builds with a series of paradoxical statements with "it"—a neutral, **third person** pronoun—as the subject. The change to "we"—a **first person** pronoun—is startling; it jars the reader from any "lull" the otherwise comfortable rhythm might have given him or her. Notice also how the paradoxes change from "time," "ages," "epochs," "seasons," "spring . . . winter," to "everything . . . nothing *before us*" and to the promise, "We were all going direct to Heaven" countered by the threat "We were all going direct the other way."

The syntactical structure makes the reader comfortable, appeals to his or her sense of logic through parallel sentence structure, and then gains attention first with a change in pronoun usage, followed by the abrupt break in syntax with the use of an absolute, "in short." What is the significance of the use of this absolute to the meaning of the paragraph? It divides the paragraph structurally into two parts: the first part is a series of paradoxical relationships of a period that at first seems impersonal, but eventually comes to be on a more personal level as it relates to the "we" of the story. The second part summarizes that these paradoxes of that period are "like the present period"—a meaning that personally involves the reader.

Sentence structure affects both prose and poetic rhythms.

What sentence structures does Shakespeare use in his "Sonnet 64" and how do they effect meaning?

Sonnet 64

line When I have seen by Time's fell hand defaced
The rich proud cost of outworn buried age;
When sometime lofty towers I see down razed,
And brass eternal slave to mortal rage;
(5) When I have seen the hungry ocean gain
Advantage on the kingdom of the shore,
And the firm soil win of the watery main,
Increasing store with loss, and loss with store;
When I have seen such interchange of state,
(10) Or state itself confounded to decay,
Ruin hath taught me thus to ruminate,
That Time will come and take my love away.

**This thought is as a death, which cannot choose
But weep to have that which it fears to lose.**

by William Shakespeare

The first sentence is lines 1–12. Notice the parallel constructions:

Line 1   "When I have seen . . ."
Line 3   "When sometime lofty towers I see . . ."
Line 5   "When I have seen . . ."
Line 9   "When I have seen . . ."

These are subordinate clauses—so where are the subject and the verb of the sentence? They do not appear until line 11: "Ruin hath taught." Lines 1–12 consist of a periodic sentence in which the speaker builds to his point. This heightens the impact of the meaning of the concluding couplet that is a loose sentence, in structural contrast to the preceding periodic sentence.

Another element of syntax that is helpful in determining meaning and can affect both prose and poetic rhythm is the **transitional marker**. Transitional markers are relationship words— words that somehow establish some type of meaning between the words that appear before the marker and those that follow. Naturally, these include that large group called the **conjunction.** Most readers are aware that *and* signals combining relationships or addition and *but* signals an exception. Although some transitional markers carry obvious meanings, others have more subtle shades of meaning that may be similar but that are not exactly the same:

Thus involves how, why, or to what extent something is done and suggests results.
Thence implies a forward progression from a specified point in space or time.
Also is a marker for additional information.
Moreover indicates an excess beyond that designated previously.
Nevertheless means despite the circumstances.
However marks relationships of manner, degree, or exception.

Structural Clues to Meaning

Some other clues to meaning that can be found within the structure of sentences are discussed next.

What Ideas Are "Important" As Opposed to What Ideas Are Not

Those ideas that the speaker considers important might be emphasized graphically with italics, underlining, capital letters, and graphic devices. Structurally, they might be placed in the main noun-verb structure of the sentence, with those ideas that are simply supportive to that main idea subordinated in subordinate clauses or modifying phrases.

Who or What Is Doing the Action

When the speaker uses active voice, the reader knows who or what is doing the action; when the speaker uses passive voice, the identity of who or what is doing the action is de-emphasized—and the reader may not hear the "actor's" identity at all. In the sentence "It was agreed upon that the party would be canceled," the speaker does not tell the reader who canceled the party. In "The party was canceled by Bob and Ted," you learn who canceled the party, but the passive voice de-emphasizes Bob's and Ted's role, placing greater emphasis on the subject: the party was canceled. In "Bob and Ted canceled the party," the emphasis is placed on Bob's and Ted's role in the action of the sentence.

When the Action Takes Place

Recognizing that the tense of a verb used (present, past, or future) affects meaning may seem like an obvious observation; however, the shades of meaning implicit in the different tenses, particularly the perfect tenses and the progressive forms, need to be addressed. Following is a brief review.

Simple tenses convey what is happening *now*, what happened *before now*, and what will happen *after now*.

Simple Present Tense:	I work.	I ride.
Simple Past Tense:	I worked.	I rode.
Simple Future Tense:	I will work.	I will ride.

The simple present tense also is used when a future event has a set time ("The sale *starts* next Tuesday"), the information is a general truth ("A yard *measures* thirty-six inches"), the action happens regularly ("She *meets* her mother every afternoon after school"), or the information is not dependent upon time ("The poet *speaks* of lace and satin in his latest work").

Perfect tenses are used when the action or state of being has already been completed or will be completed at a particular time.

Present Perfect Tense:	I have worked.
Past Perfect Tense:	I had worked.
Future Perfect Tense:	I will have worked.

The present perfect indicates that the action or state of being began in the past and its effects continue into the present. In past perfect, the action was completed prior to another action taking place. In future perfect, the action will be completed prior to a specific time. Perfect tense can also be expressed in the infinitive: to have worked.

Simple and perfect tenses can take the **progressive verb form** in which the action or state of being is ongoing:

Simple Present Progressive Verb Form:	I am walking.
Simple Past Progressive Verb Form:	I was walking.
Simple Future Progressive Verb Form:	I will be walking.
Present Perfect Progressive Verb Form:	I have been walking.
Past Perfect Progressive Verb Form:	I had been walking.
Future Perfect Progressive Verb Form:	I will have been walking.

Remember: The passive voice consists of past participle plus a form of *to be*.

Present Passive Voice:	Mail is sent by John. (present tense of *to be* with past participle)
Past Passive Voice:	Mail was sent by John. (past tense of *to be* with past participle)
Past Progressive Passive Voice:	Mail was being sent by John. (past progressive of *to be* with past participle)

Knowing *when* the action or state of being occurs or occurred is very significant to meaning in context.

How does the tense affect the meaning in this example?

> **Jayne was unaware that the keys were still in the lock, and she was equally unaware that the throbbing in her ears was being made by the intensity of her own heartbeat. Where were those keys? A chilling wind brushed her face as she glanced toward the entrance to the garage.**
>
> **"I will stay calm," she whispered, momentarily closing her eyes against painful, stinging tears. Her right index finger began to hurt, and she realized that she had been cutting it on the zipper-edge of the opening of her purse as she searched through it for her keys.**
>
> **by author**

The story's primary tense is simple past: "Jayne was . . . the keys were . . . she was . . . ." The throbbing in her ears; however, is past progressive passive (the throbbing . . . was being made by . . .). What are the effects of this tense? The sense of ongoing action of the progressive tense adds tension when presented in a context connotative of danger—"a chilling wind," the need to "stay calm," emotion intense enough that she does not realize that she is hurting herself. What do the passive aspects of this construction do to the meaning? They place the emphasis on the throbbing in her ears rather than on its cause (her heartbeat). Notice the shift in emphasis if the construction is changed to simple past: . . . she was equally unaware that the intensity of her own heartbeat caused the throbbing in her ears. What tense does she use when she whispers, "I will stay calm"? Its effect? Why is the tense of "she had been cutting it . . ." important to the meaning of the selection?

Connotation

Denotations are the literal meanings of words; **connotations** are their emotional meanings. Sometimes associations result from a person's own nonverbal experiences. Such associations can be very powerful. A particular song might be associated with a first love. Certain foods can bring to mind a person, an enjoyable vacation, or a particular place. Events in your life may be remembered when you hear a name, smell a fragrance, or experience a familiar feeling. Such associations can be positive or negative, but seldom without some type of emotional response.

Similarly, words can gain connotative meaning for a person through his or her personal experiences. These connotations might be negative or positive, sad or happy, discouraging or encouraging—reflecting any number of emotional responses. Connotative meanings also can be universal (shared by most people) or shared by some group (such as a nation, an organization, a race, a religion, a profession or trade).

As an example of connotative meanings, suppose that you develop a new type of vacuum cleaner that you believe surpasses any other on the market. You would possibly refer to it as your "invention." Invention is a rather neutral word (since inventions can be either useful or nonuseful)—with perhaps slightly positive connotations that anyone who "invents an invention must be an inventive inventor"—a "feel-good" association of ideas. Someone (who is perhaps jealous of your success?) might come to see your new vacuum cleaner and later refer to it in conversation as your new "contrivance." Although technically accurate (a contrivance is a mechanical device or appliance), contrivance also carries with it some negative connotations related to its other definition: a scheme. Such a word is suggestive of such questions as "Does this vacuum cleaner really work, or has this person just developed a scheme to make money?" Even the word *invention*, itself, which is neutral or somewhat positive in connotative value, can become negative in certain contexts, because another definition of invention involves something made up.

Words, then, can stir emotions and can cause a person to make certain associations. A writer can elicit emotions from his or her readers simply by selecting connotatively charged words. This translates into tremendous power—power to influence beyond the effects of denotation.

1. **For the public speaker,** connotation can help persuade the hearers to adopt certain views and to take desired action. Connotation can be a very effective rhetorical device.

2. **For the story writer,** connotation can help the readers identify with the character in the narrative. For example, when the "young man" in a story "doesn't want to go to his house," the language is

rather neutral. It may be a bit negative for some people who might associate the phrase "young man" with a boy who has been disobedient to adults and who consider the fact that he "doesn't want to go to his house" as implying an attitude problem. What if you say "the little boy is afraid to go home"? Now the connotative meaning is much more sympathetic, with "home" being connotative of safety and comfort, but this poor little fellow is "afraid" to go there!

What connotations about character do you gain from this brief narrative selection?

Alice reached for the new dress and hummed softly under her breath as she slipped it on. She was amused by the contrast of her pallid skin against the shocking red silk.

To illustrate connotation, examine two words: "hummed" and "amused." "Alice . . . hummed softly . . ." What connotations are associated with humming? For many people humming implies happiness and indicates a personality that is perhaps playful. Now look at the description of Alice in her new dress—hardly a description of classical beauty—"pallid" being connotative of the paleness that comes from either having been ill or indoors too much. Yet, this character is "amused" by the "contrast." What are the connotations concerning someone who is "amused" by her own less-than-perfect appearance?

One type of humming is a "drone" and a type of amusement is a "diversion." What if the sentence read "Alice . . . *droned* softly . . ., she was *diverted* by the contrast . . ."? How does this change of two words change the connotations about her character?

3. **For the nonnarrative prose writer,** connotation can be a problem to avoid when neutrality is essential. Writers *use* words to communicate, and sometimes connotation can actually hinder that communication. When the intended use is poetic, connotation is a useful element, but when the intended use is scientific, connotation can convey meanings that are contrary to the point or perhaps even false. When the prose

writer's aim is to instruct or inform concerning processes and facts, avoiding additional connotative meaning is essential.

4. **For the poet,** connotation can add another layer of meaning to the work as a whole. Examine the following portion of a poem ("Of the Birth and Bringing up of Desire") by Edmund De Vere, Earl of Oxford. What connotative meanings *beyond* denotation are conveyed by such expressions as "pride and pomp," "sugared joy," "sad sighs," and "sweet thoughts, which liked me best"?

> When wert thou born, Desire?
> > In *pride and pomp* of May.
> By whom, sweet boy, wert thou begot?
> > By Self Conceit, men say.
> Tell me, who was thy purse?
> > Fresh Youth, in *sugared joy*.
> What was thy meat and daily food?
> > *Sad sighs* and great annoy.
> What haddest thou to drink?
> > Unfeigned lovers' tears.
> What cradle wert thou rocked in?
> > In hope devoid of fears.
> What brought thee to thy sleep?
> > *Sweet thoughts, which liked me best.*

> [Emphasis added]

5. **For some advertisers,** connotation is a means to influence the public to buy. Local supermarket shelves are evidence of the affective overtones of connotative language used in product merchandising. Use of connotative language to manipulate people is widespread. Such use is one form of what William Lutz calls "doublespeak" in his book of the same name.

Public officials must exercise caution in using connotative word choices. This caution is reflected in such examples as police reports in which "suspects" of criminal activities are referred to as "actors." Special interests movements often use connotative language to put forth their agendas. In the last half of the twentieth century, during the women's movement as an example, housewives (women who work at home raising children and running a family) were sometimes referred to as "domestic engineers."

This brief overview of connotative language might be summarized with the following illustration:

Positive Connotation	Neutral	Negative Connotation
an antique	an old chair	junk

Implications

Implications and **inference** are two easily confused words that have related meanings. An implication is an involvement or indication that is made indirectly by association; an inference is a conclusion drawn from facts or premises. The speaker implies (hints at, suggests) some idea from which the hearer or reader infers (receives, draws) a conclusion.

Implications can come in many different forms. Some writers, as a case in point, make a distinction between **implicit statements** in which such information as who, what, where, when, why, and how is implied through context and **explicit statements** in which the writer, to put it in modern slang, "spells it all out." To tell someone that "sometimes water systems can become contaminated" is implicit; to tell someone that "the Health Department found unsafe levels of bacteria in the water system of the XYZ Restaurant and shut it down this morning" is more explicit.

Implications can be subtle or they can be easily seen. What implication does the speaker make in this sentence from a short story ("Liberty Hall") by Ring Lardner?

> **On the fourth awful day Ben gave out the news— news to him and to me as well as to our host and hostess—that he had lost a filling which he would not trust any but his own New York dentist to replace.**

What is the speaker implying when she says "news to him"? Could it be that he really had not lost a filling, but simply wanted an excuse to leave? In this case, finding the context of the short story in which this sentence appears is the only way to realize the true meaning and significance of this implication.

The implication made in this sentence from a short story ("An Outpost of Progress") by Joseph Conrad is less subtle:

He had charge of a small clay storehouse with a dried-grass roof, and pretended to keep a correct account of beads, cotton cloth, red kerchiefs, brass wire, and other trade goods it contained.

What are the implications in the statement that he "pretended to keep a correct account"? The obvious answer is that although he led others to believe the accounts were accurate, they were not; and he knew that they were not. This much can be learned from the implications of "pretended." Can you, from these implications, make an inference concerning *why* he did this? Perhaps he did not have the ability to keep accurate books and as a result tried to cover careless and perhaps unintended errors. Or did he deliberately mislead others to cover embezzlement or harm them financially? Once again, the context of the entire story is necessary to make such inferences.

Contextual Meanings in Prose, Poetry, and Drama

Isolated words and phrases depend upon context for both their level of meaning and for their implied meaning, as well as for any inferences that can be drawn from those implications. Prose sentences, too, can carry many different meanings, depending on their context. Here are some examples.

1. ***The facts and nothing but the facts*** Some prose writing is purported to be fact. There are two very important elements you should keep in mind when looking at the meaning in context of statements that are intended to be based on facts: First, **not all things asserted to be "facts" are true.** Second, **facts, in most cases, are verifiable—they can be proven as either true or false.** Of course, the first logical place to look for verification is the context in which the statement is given; however, very often you must look elsewhere at the records of others, accounts of witnesses, and so forth (outside the context) to determine the accuracy of the "facts."

2. ***"In my opinion . . ."*** Not all speakers and writers state clearly that they are expressing an opinion rather than a fact. Yet, you can differentiate between facts and opinions and as a result gain significant insight

into their meanings in context. A statement based on the writer's opinion—on his or her judgment—cannot be verified as true or as false. How can the reader know, then, what such a statement means and whether to trust or to believe the statement? Very often, this determination is based on the credibility of the speaker or writer and on the context or the circumstances in which the statement is made. Because the statement cannot be *verified* by context or by means outside the context, the reader must look at the speaker very closely: Is the speaker known to be reliable? What circumstances (events or concerns) surround the making of the statement? Might the speaker have a hidden agenda? Many more such questions can be asked about statements of opinion, the answers of which directly relate to and influence the meaning, because this evaluation of the position of the speaker, in a sense, provides the context.

Here is an illustration taken from a speech by Theodore Roosevelt in 1903 to the Leland Stanford Junior University in California. The topic is the preservation of forests.

California has for years, I am happy to say, taken a more sensible, a more intelligent interest in forest preservation than any other state. It early appointed a forest commission; later on some of the functions of that commission were replaced by the Sierra Club, a club which has done much on the Pacific coast to perpetuate the spirit of the explorer and the pioneer. Then I am happy to say a great business interest showed an intelligent and farsighted spirit which is of happy augury, for the Redwood Manufacturers of San Francisco were first among lumbermen's associations to give assistance to the cause of practical forestry. The study of the redwood which the action of this association made possible was the pioneer study in the cooperative work which is now being carried out between lumbermen all over the United States and the Federal Bureau of Forestry.

Based on context, what does President Roosevelt mean when he says "California has for years . . . taken a more sensible, a more intelligent interest in forest preservation than any other state"? The statement is obviously an opinion—for how can one verify "more sensible" or "more intelligent" in this context? But look at his use of *verifiable facts to support his opinion.* The reader or listener can go to other sources to ascertain the forest commission's appointment, its functions compared to those of the Sierra Club, the assistance of the Redwood Manufacturers of San Francisco, and the pioneer study that they made possible. So what does he mean, based on context, when he says that "California has . . . taken a more sensible, a more intelligent interest . . ."? He means that the government, service clubs, and lumbermen's associations of California led the way with concrete, verifiable actions toward forest preservation.

3. *"Well, what you really ought to do . . ."*
Normatives, directives—these terms both refer to statements that aim to influence people either directly or indirectly to conform to some standard or designated norm. Occasionally, these directives are straightforward, and the writer literally says that you *should* do this or that you *ought* to do that.

Very often directives and normatives are not so easily spotted because, after all, their purpose is to influence—a purpose at the root of propaganda. Society, of course, must have norms or standards by which its members can live; however, it is important to be able to recognize when people are being directed and to what norms they are being directed to conform. Only then can the reader or listener make a conscious and informed choice as to conduct as it relates to these norms.

In this concluding paragraph of the speech by Roosevelt on forest preservation, what norms are being set for these young university men? What directives does the speech give them?

Citizenship is the prime test in the welfare of the nation; but we need good laws; and above all we need good land laws throughout the West. We want to see the free farmer own his home. The best of the

public lands are already in private hands, and yet the rate of their disposal is steadily increasing. More than six million acres were patented during the first three months of the present year. It is time for us to see that our remaining public lands are saved for the home maker to the utmost limit of his possible use. I say this to you of this university because we have a right to expect that the best-trained, the best-educated men on the Pacific Slope, the Rocky Mountains and Great Plains states will take the lead in the preservation and right use of the forests, in securing the right use of the water, and in seeing to it that our land policy is not twisted from its original purpose, but is perpetuated by amendment, by change when such change is necessary in the line of that purpose, the purpose being to turn the public domain into farms each to be the property of the man who actually tills it and makes his home on it.

Notice the directives being set before them:

(1) "taking the lead in the preservation and right use of the forest," (2) "securing the right use of the waters," and (3) "seeing to it that our land policy is not twisted." Why? Because a norm has been set by the speaker in this speech: "We want to see the free farmer own his own home" and "we have a right to expect that the best-trained, the best-educated men on the Pacific Slope, the Rocky Mountains and Great Plains states will take the lead . . . ."

Poetic Syntax

Elements of poetic language are commonly found in prose. The use of metaphor, as an example, is found in this excerpt from a speech made by Booker T. Washington concerning slavery:

A ship lost at sea for many days suddenly sighted a friendly vessel. From the mast of the unfortunate vessel was seen a signal, "Water, water; we die of thirst!" The answer from the friendly vessel at once came back, "Cast down your bucket where you are." And a third and fourth signal for water was answered, "Cast down your bucket where you are." The captain of the distressed vessel, at last heeding the injunction, cast down his bucket, and it came up full of fresh, sparkling water from the mouth of the Amazon River. To those of my race who depend on bettering their condition in a foreign land or who underestimate the importance of cultivating friendly relations with the Southern white man, who is their next-door neighbor, I would say: "Cast down your bucket where you are"—cast it down in making friends in every manly way of the people of all races by whom we are surrounded.

Yet, there is a **poetic syntax** that by definition includes both the emotive language that speaks to the reader's emotions over and above the descriptive and expository neutrality of **referential** (also called **cognitive**) language and a use of syntax that focuses on its effect over its conformity to rules. Some literary scholars cite this freedom in the use of syntax as a major line drawn between prose and poetry. Regardless, the syntax of poetry is a product of form and a major contributor to meaning. How do poets use syntax? Space precludes an exhaustive list, but a few notable ways include:

▶ Use of words that are normally assigned one function in an unusual function in a syntactical structure. For example, *was* normally functions as a verb and *lifetime* as a noun. The poet might assign *was* to the role of subject, and use *lifetime* as a verb.

<u>Was</u> is a lifetime ago . . .
And she has <u>lifetimed</u> her existence away.

▶ Inversion of normal syntactical patterns, such as placing the modifier after rather than before the word it modifies:

This <u>Hermit good</u> lives in that wood
Which slopes down to the sea. [emphasis added]

Or placing the predicate modifier first in the sentence:

Silent is the house: all are laid asleep. [emphasis added]

What would be the normal syntactical pattern for this structure?

With olives ripe the sauces
Were flavored, without exception.

▶ Repetition of syntactical patterns:

My Mind to Me a Kingdom Is
(fifth stanza)

Some have too much, yet still do crave;
I little have, and seek no more.
They are but poor, though much they have,
And I am rich with little store.
<u>**They poor, I rich; they beg, I give;**</u>
<u>**Thy lack, I leave; they pine, I live.**</u>
[emphasis added]

by Sir Edward Dyer

There are many more ways poets can use syntactical patterns to achieve their purposes; however, context remains one of the most useful elements in determining meaning, particularly when the poetic syntax makes meaning more obscure.

Questions to Apply the Literary Principles Concerning Contextual Meanings

Ask these questions to help you identify and understand contextual meanings.

1. Do you understand the denotations of all the words employed in the work?

2. What "shades of meaning" are intended?

3. Do any of the words or phrases have multiple meanings? Does context support any of these alternate usages?

4. What is the level of abstraction (or concreteness) in the work? Degree of specificity?

5. Are there any unusual syntactical patterns used? What is the effect? Is there a prose or poetic rhythm?

6. What is the main clause (as opposed to those clauses that are subordinated)?

7. Who or what is doing the action (as applicable)?

8. When does the action take place (based on verb tense)?

9. Do any of the words, phrases, or lines carry with them connotative meanings in this context?

10. What implications are made in the context?

Additional Points to Remember About Contextual Meanings

▶ Just as connotations can be based on individual experiences, cultural groups, national identity, and so forth, they also can be directly affected by time. Connotation is a function of diction (word choice). As such, not only can denotations of words change over the years, but also the connotations can change.

The color red is an example. Today *red* denotatively refers to a color. Connotatively you might think of red as a symbol for blood, fire, communism, or a warning to stop. But in the last century red also was a symbol for immorality (as in the story *The Scarlet Letter*). If you were to read an account of a woman wearing a red dress, you would probably not take notice; however, such a dress would have very negative connotations for readers of the past, connotations that would reflect badly on the character wearing the offending color.

Conversely, being called a hussy today has negative connotations that did not exist back when a hussy simply referred to a housewife.

▶ The poetic syntax of poetry selections most generally can be understood in context; however, instances in which the poetic syntax unites with other uses of language (such as complex imagery or dissonance) can make the meaning obscure beyond identification. Some twentieth-century poems are deliberate interplays of syntax, symbolism, strange wordplays, and other such devices that produce a sense of obscurity. Although some historical use of obscurity was for the purpose of circumventing political censorship (such as the political commentaries "hidden" in the obscure language of some Renaissance English poets), very often such obscurity does not serve such a pragmatic function.

Some poems, like some abstract art, do not necessarily have "a meaning," but rather the meaning is a product of what the individual reader or hearer brings to the work. In such cases, the context is outside the poem. Other poems are so intimately a reflection of the poet's personal experiences that the full extent of the meaning cannot be determined without knowledge of the event, people, or circumstances that inspired the work—the context is the poet's life. For example, nineteenth-century poet Leigh Hunt wrote a poem called "Jenny Kissed Me":

> **Jenny kissed me when we met,**
> **Jumping from the chair she sat in;**
> **Time, you thief, who love to get**
> **Sweets into you list, put that in:**
>
> **Say I'm weary, say I'm sad,**
> **Say that health and wealth have missed me,**
> **Say I'm growing old, but add,**
> **Jenny kissed me.**

Here is the story behind this little poem: "Jenny" was Mrs. Jane Welsh Carlyle. Leigh Hunt, her friend, fell ill with influenza, a disease that in the early 1800s claimed many lives. Mrs. Carlyle, who was quite concerned about her friend, was so excited upon seeing Hunt recovered that she impulsively kissed him, inspiring him to write "Jenny Kissed Me."

PART II

Putting the Principles of Literature to Work

The Principle of
Perpetual Motion

The sad-faced crowd lining the streets of London whispered among themselves as they waited. "A hero he was—and so young!" Long, detailed accounts were rehearsed about his bravery in battle. "He wouldn't even take no water or help to save 'imself, but what that they should help the others first," an emotional voice recounted.

Soon the distant clatter of horses' hooves silenced the whispers, and the people watched in heartbroken disbelief as the funeral procession slowly passed by on its way to St. Paul's Cathedral. Suddenly, a cry first startled the mourners, then rallied them to form a chorus, "Farewell: Farewell! the worthiest knight that lived!"

Later that night, royalty and the socially privileged joined behind palace gates to grieve the loss of the godson of Philip II of Spain, the death of one of their own. They talked of his bravery and the untimely nature of his death, of course. In these halls, however, the sense of loss took a different direction. In addition to his gallantry as a courtier and valor as a Protestant knight, talk centered on his learning and wit, on his works as a poet, prose writer, and critic. Not yet thirty-two years old, Sir Philip Sidney was dead.

by author

Many literary scholars today recognize the tremendous historical contributions of Sidney to British literary traditions. He wrote the first English sonnet sequence (*Astrophil and Stella*), a work considered to be the precursor of the English novel (*Arcadia*), and the first important English work of Renaissance criticism (*Apologie for Poetrie* or *Defense of Poesie*). The works of this young adventurer and writer are impressive. Can his life and work, however, hold any significance for readers and writers today, nearly five-hundred years after his death?

If you want to become more perceptive in your reading skills or if you want to become a more effective writer, the answer is a definite "yes." As a successful reader and writer of his day, Sidney exemplifies putting the principles of communication into a form of perpetual motion. You, too, can put these principles to work for you.

For generations people have attempted to create a perpetual motion machine that would continue in self-sustained movement. Physically, such a machine violates laws of thermodynamics and, consequently, is considered impossible. Figuratively speaking, however, written communication (ideas related from writer to reader) provides opportunities to make a *type* of perpetual motion in skills and learning a reality.

Written communication consists of three basic components: reading skills on the part of the reader, writing skills on the part of the writer, and experience on multiple levels for both reader and writer. What enables a reader to be perceptive? Once basic reading skills are in place, the reader gains better insight into and under-standing of what is written and the message intended by the writer through integrating different levels of experience gained through previous reading, life, and actually using the tools of writing to communicate.

What enables a writer to be more effective? Once basic writing skills are in place, the writer learns to use language to communicate with more clarity and with greater insight also through integrating various levels of experience gained through previous writing, life, and reading what others have written.

The more and better a writer reads, the more effective is the writing produced; the more and better a reader writes, the more reading comprehension is gained. Once the motion is begun, the experience of the one is constantly providing energy for the other.

Sir Philip Sydney, in many respects, exemplifies this reader-writer synergy. A careful observer of the life around him, he added to his personal experiences extensive reading in many different areas and studied such varied subjects as music and astronomy. He studied foreign languages and translated writings about the

Christian religion. These experiences gave rise to a man who not only could write prose and poetry with distinction but could write in the role of critic *about* the prose and poetry that he read. He read poetry. He wrote poetry. He read about poetry (such as Stephen Gosson's *The Schoole of Abuse*). He wrote about poetry (*An Apology of Poetry*). And the cycle continued.

The following activities can help you, too, experience this reader-writer synergy and begin a form of perpetual motion in your life.

Recognizing the Principles of Literature in the Writings of Others

From the Reader's Perspective

There are many approaches you can employ to identify how writers use the principles of literature. You should begin, however, by becoming familiar with the basics. The five principles of literature described in Part I of this book work within all prose, poetry, and drama. *All* literary forms have meaning, form, voice and tone, character (characters and/or the distinguishing traits of the work itself that can be characterized), and language (uses and contextual meanings). Consequently, even if you prefer to read and write prose, understanding how the principles work in poetry and drama will help you gain perception and insight. The poet can learn from studying prose and drama just as the dramatist can learn from poetry and prose.

What follows is Edgar Allan Poe's "The Raven" in its entirety. Teachers, critics, and anthology editors for generations have pointed to "The Raven" as an American classic because of its distinctive use of rhythm, rhyme, and alliterative elements that contribute to its tone. Also, as a narrative poem, "The Raven" includes uses of the literary principles that apply to prose forms as well as poetry.

First, read the poem for enjoyment. Notice the use of internal rhyme: "dreary" and "weary"; "napping," "tapping," and "rapping"; "remember," "December," and "ember"; "morrow," "sorrow," and "borrow." In the third stanza, listen to the effects of "silken, sad, uncertain rustling." As you read, think about these questions: How do these elements work together to give the poem its atmosphere? How would you describe the atmosphere of "The Raven"?

The Raven

by
Edgar Allan Poe

stanza

1 Once upon a midnight dreary, while I pondered,
    weak and weary,
    Over many a quaint and curious volume of for-
    gotten lore,
While I nodded, nearly napping, suddenly there
    came a tapping,
    As of some one gently rapping, rapping at my
    chamber door.
"'Tis some visitor," I muttered, "tapping at my
    chamber door—
    Only this and nothing more."

2 Ah, distinctly I remember it was in the bleak
    December,
    And each separate dying ember wrought its
    ghost upon the floor.
Eagerly I wished the morrow; vainly I had sought
    to borrow
    From my books surcease of sorrow—sorrow for
    the lost Lenore,
For the rare and radiant maiden whom the angels
    name Lenore—
    Nameless *here* for evermore.

3 And the silken, sad, uncertain rustling of each
    purple curtain
    Thrilled me—filled me with fantastic terrors
    never felt before;
So that now, to still the beating of my heart, I
    stood repeating,
    "'Tis some visitor entreating entrance at my
    chamber door—
Some late visitor entreating entrance at my cham-
    ber door—
    This it is and nothing more."

4 Presently my soul grew stronger: hesitating then
    no longer,
    "Sir," said I, "or Madam, truly your forgiveness
    I implore;
But the fact is I was napping, and so gently you
    came rapping,

And so faintly you came tapping, tapping at my
   chamber door,
That I scarce was sure I heard you"—here I
   opened wide the door—
   Darkness there and nothing more.

5   Deep into that darkness peering, long I stood
      there, wondering, fearing,
      Doubting, dreaming dreams no mortal ever
      dared to dream before;
   But the silence was unbroken, and the stillness
      gave no token,
      And the only word there spoken was the whis-
      pered word "Lenore!"
   This I whispered, and an echo murmured back the
      word "Lenore!"
      Merely this and nothing more.

6   Back into the chamber turning, all my soul within
      me burning,
      Soon again I heard a tapping, somewhat louder
      than before.
   "Surely," said I, "surely that is something at my
      window lattice;
      Let me see, then, what thereat is, and this mys-
      tery explore—
   Let my heart be still a moment and this mystery
      explore—
      'Tis the wind and nothing more."

7   Open here I flung the shutter, when, with many a
      flirt and flutter,
      In there stepped a stately Raven of the saintly
      days of yore.
   Not the least obeisance made he, not a minute
      stopped or stayed he,
      But with mien of lord or lady perched above my
      chamber door—
   Perched upon a bust of Pallas just above my
      chamber door—
      Perched and sat, and nothing more.

8   Then, this ebony bird beguiling my sad fancy into
      smiling
      By the grave and stern decorum of the counte-
      nance it wore,
   "Though thy crest be shorn and shaven, thou," I
      said, "art sure no craven,

Ghastly, grim, and ancient Raven, wandering
from the nightly shore:
Tell me what thy lordly name is on the night's
Plutonian shore!"
Quoth the Raven, "Nevermore."

9   Much I marveled this ungainly fowl to hear discourse so plainly,
Though its answer little meaning, little rele-
vancy bore;
For we cannot help agreeing that no living human
being
Ever yet was blessed with seeing bird above his
chamber door—
Bird or beast upon the sculptured bust above his
chamber door—
With such name as "Nevermore."

10   But the Raven, sitting lonely on the placid bust,
spoke only
That one word, as if his soul in that one word
he did outpour.
Nothing further then he uttered, not a feather
then he fluttered;
Till I scarcely more than muttered, "Other
friends have flown before:
On the morrow he will leave me, as my hopes
have flown before."
Then the bird said, "Nevermore."

11   Startled at the stillness broken by reply so aptly
spoken,
"Doubtless," said I, "what it utters is its only
stock and store,
Caught from some unhappy master whom unmer-
ciful Disaster
Followed fast and followed faster till his songs
one burden bore,
Till the dirges of his hope that melancholy burden
bore
Of 'Never—nevermore.'"

12   But the Raven still beguiling my sad fancy into
smiling,
Straight I wheeled a cushioned seat in front of
bird and bust and door;
Then, upon the velvet sinking, I betook myself to
linking

Fancy unto fancy, thinking what this ominous
   bird of yore,
What this grim, ungainly, ghastly, gaunt, and ominous bird of yore
Meant in croaking "Nevermore."

13   This I sat engaged in guessing, but no syllable
      expressing
   To the fowl, whose fiery eyes now burned into
      my bosom's core;
   This and more I sat divining, with my head at
      ease reclining
   On the cushion's velvet lining that the lamplight
      gloated o'er,
   But whose velvet-violet lining with the lamplight
      gloating o'er,
   She shall press, ah, nevermore!

14   Then, methought, the air grew denser, perfumed
      from an unseen censer
   Swung by seraphim whose foot-falls tinkled on
      the tufted floor.
   "Wretch," I cried, "thy God hath lent thee—by
      these angels he hath sent thee
   Respite—respite and nepenthe from thy memo-
      ries of Lenore!
   Quaff, oh quaff this kind nepenthe, and forget this
      lost Lenore!"
   Quoth the Raven, "Nevermore."

15   "Prophet!" said I, "thing of evil! prophet still, if
      bird or devil!
   Whether Tempter sent, or whether tempest
      tossed thee here ashore,
   Desolate yet all undaunted, on this desert land
      enchanted—
   On this home by Horror haunted—tell me truly,
      I implore:
   Is there—is there balm in Gilead?—tell me—tell
      me, I implore!"
   Quoth the Raven, "Nevermore."

16   "Prophet!" said I, "thing of evil—prophet still, if
      bird or devil!
   By that Heaven that bends above us, by that
      God we both adore,
   Tell this soul with sorrow laden if, within the dis-
      tant Aidenn,

It shall clasp a sainted maiden whom the angels
    name Lenore:
Clasp a rare and radiant maiden whom the angels
    name Lenore!"
Quoth the Raven, "Nevermore."

17   "Be that word our sign of parting, bird or fiend!"
    I shrieked, upstarting:
  "Get thee back into the tempest and the Night's
    Plutonian shore!
Leave no black plume as a token of that lie thy
    soul hath spoken!
  Leave my loneliness unbroken! quit the bust
    above my door!
Take thy beak from out my heart, and take thy
    form from off my door!"
  Quoth the Raven, "Nevermore."

18   And the Raven, never flitting, still is sitting, *still* is
    sitting
  On the pallid bust of Pallas just above my cham-
    ber door;
And his eyes have all the seeming of a demon's
    that is dreaming,
  And the lamp-light o'er him streaming throws
    his shadow on the floor;
And my soul from out that shadow that lies float-
    ing on the floor
  Shall be lifted—nevermore!

Answer the questions that follow. Note: Do not slow yourself
down with the literary terms here. Identifying what the rhythm does
to the meaning of the poem, for example, is far more important at this
point than knowing what the rhythm is called. (See page 52.)

Answers will vary because they are based on the effects the
work has on you as an individual. The overall benefit, however, of
applying these types of questions to a work is to develop a better
understanding of how the principles of literature work together and
increase your reading perception. Although the following questions
refer to "The Raven," many of these questions can be asked about
other works.

Meaning   (For help in determining meaning, see page 25.)
▶ What is the purpose of the poem? (Select all that apply.)
   descriptive/expressive   narrative
   expository/informative   argumentative/persuasive

▶ Citing specific examples from the poem, why did you select these purpose(s)?
▶ What is the subject (in a word or phrase)?
▶ What is the theme in one sentence?
▶ Can you summarize the poem in one paragraph?

Form   (For help in determining form, see page 42.)
▶ What is the rhythm? Describe the rhythm in your own words. Also, if you want to identify the name of its foot and meter, see pages 53–61.

Voice and Tone   (For help in determining voice and tone, see page 116.) Ask yourself the following questions:
▶ Who is "I" in the poem?
▶ How would you describe the attitude of "I" toward Lenore?
▶ How does the attitude of "I" toward the raven change?
▶ What is the attitude of the author toward the speaker?
▶ What is the attitude of "I" toward the unknown visitor in stanza 4?
▶ What changes in tone are introduced in the twelfth stanza?
▶ How does the theme influence the tone?
▶ How does the setting influence the tone?
▶ What does the speaker's tone suggest concerning the raven?
▶ How would you describe the tone of the speaker in the second stanza? Eighth stanza? Fifteenth stanza? Last stanza?
▶ What is the tone of the entire poem?

Finally, look at the structural elements as they relate to tone and atmosphere.

▶ Examine the rhyme scheme. What is its effect on the atmosphere?
▶ Examine the rhythm. How does it affect the atmosphere?
▶ Alliteration and assonance refer to the repetition of consonant and vowel sounds, respectively. How does the use of alliteration and assonance affect the atmosphere of this work?
▶ Notice the use of italics in the second, thirteenth, and (especially) the last stanzas. What are the effects of each?
▶ Can you paraphrase this poem, stanza by stanza? Try developing the paraphrase into a short story.
▶ How does the plot affect the atmosphere?
▶ Notice the poignant impact of stanza 16. Also, look at the

use of the words "Quaff" and "nepenthe" in stanza 14. The significance of *word meaning* in this stanza is very important to understanding what is being conveyed to the reader. What is the author telling you? Does this information change the atmosphere and mood?

Character (For help in determining character and characterization, see page 174.) Ask yourself the following questions:
▶ Describe the speaker's attitude and emotional state.
▶ How does the speaker respond to his situation?
▶ In your opinion, what kind of person is the speaker?
▶ Do you see any stereotypes in the poem? If yes, can you describe them?
▶ What thoughts, statements *about* the speaker, statements *by* the speaker, and actions in the poem reveal the speaker's character?
▶ How would you characterize this poem? (For help in characterizing a work, see pages 197–198.)

Word Use and Context (For help in determining word use and context, see page 203.) Ask yourself the following questions:
▶ Do you see any of these commonly used figures of speech?

Simile	Metaphor
Allusion	Personification
Paradox	Hyperbole (overstatement)
Irony	Meiosis (understatement)

▶ Can you spot any poetic diction (see page 248) or poetic syntax (see page 272)?
▶ Do any of Poe's word choices have connotations that add to the poem's meaning?

Now that you have experienced identifying the use of the literary principles in "The Raven," you can use Part I of this book and the "Questions to Apply the Literary Principles" (pages 35, 108, 144, 172, 200, 249, 274) to examine other written works.

From the Writer's Perspective

Have you ever wondered what was in the mind of a writer when he or she wrote a particular work? How did the writer get the idea for the story? Are any of the characters based on real life? Did the writer figure out the entire plot first, or did he or she develop a character and use the plot as a vehicle to reveal the character's personality?

Are successful writers aware of the principles of literature as they write? In *Creating Characters with Charles Dickens* (The Pennsylvania State University Press, 1991), for example, Doris Alexander identifies people who surrounded Charles Dickens (friends, relatives, public figures) and explores through his personal writings how they became characters in his fictional works. She discusses how he conformed characters to the circumstances of the story and examines the writing process in his life.

Many people assume that Edgar Allan Poe's "The Raven" came from the writer's own experience. Is this poem a spontaneous emotional release of the poet's own anguish, or is it the result of the deliberate honing of a writer's skill? The answers to these questions might be found in Poe's essay, "The Philosophy of Composition," in which he claims to reveal the process he used as a writer when he wrote "The Raven." His self-analysis of the writing process is interesting and can help you shift your thinking from a reader's to the writer's perspective. Also, the following excerpts from his essay reveal a *surprisingly modern approach* to the writing craft. Here, then, are Poe's own words on how and why he wrote "The Raven."

The Philosophy of Composition

Charles Dickens, in a note now lying before me, alluding to an examination I once made of the mechanism of *Barnaby Rudge,* says—"By the way, are you aware that Godwin wrote his *Caleb Williams* backward? He first involved his hero in a web of difficulties, forming the second volume, and then, for the first, cast about him for some mode of accounting for what had been done."

. . . Nothing is more clear than that every plot, worth the name, must be elaborated to its *dénouement* before anything be attempted with the pen. It is only with the *dénouement* constantly in view that we can give a plot its indispensable air of consequence, or causation, by making the incidents, and especially the tone at all points, tend to the development of the intention.

There is a radical error, I think, in the usual mode of constructing a story. Either history affords a thesis—or one is suggested by an incident of the

day—or, at best, the author sets himself to work in the combination of striking events to form merely the basis of his narrative—designing, generally, to fill in with description, dialogue, or authorial comment, whatever crevices of fact, or action, may, from page to page, render themselves apparent.

I prefer commencing with the consideration of an *effect*. Keeping originality *always* in view—for he is false to himself who ventures to dispense with so obvious and so easily attainable a source of interest—I say to myself, in the first place, "Of the innumerable effects, or impressions, of which the heart, the intellect, or (more generally) the soul is susceptible, what one shall I, on the present occasion, select?" Having chosen a novel, first, and secondly a vivid effect, I consider whether it can be best wrought by incident or tone—whether by ordinary incidents and peculiar tone, or the converse, or by peculiarity both of incident and tone—afterward looking about me (or rather within) for such combinations of event, or tone, as shall best aid me in the construction of the effect.

Edgar Allan Poe (1809–1849) begins the essay by referring to a letter written to him by Charles Dickens concerning the structure of a work by William Godwin. The reference serves to remind readers that Poe was both a writer and a literary critic who had editorial experience and many published reviews to his credit (for the *Messenger*).

Poe establishes two interrelated, major points: In his opinion,

1. A writer must have a dénouement (also called resolution; refers to the final outcome of the plot) "constantly in view" as the work is written. This approach means dealing with the literary principle of form. (See pages 40 and 46–47.)

2. A work should begin with deciding upon an effect that acts upon "the heart, the intellect, or (more generally) the soul." Establishing an effect cuts across all the principles of literature because how tone (mentioned by Poe), character development, form, meanings, and language are used and developed can heighten (or destroy) a desired effect.

What did Poe look for in an effect? It should be *novel* (something new to the readers) and *vivid* (something that stands out with intensity).

Can you think of an original dénouement for a short story or narrative poem? What novel, but also vivid, effect on readers could be produced by a story leading up to your dénouement? Review the principles of literature. Can you think of any other ways to approach writing a short story or narrative poem? For example, some writers design the story around a character and, based on the character's personality profile, see how the plot develops as the character initiates events and reacts to changing circumstances. Poe's point? **Writers should establish an approach to writing and carefully decide where to begin.**

Poe continues:

> I have often thought how interesting a magazine paper might be written by any author who would—that is to say who could—detail, step by step, the processes by which any one of his compositions attained its ultimate point of completion. Why such a paper has never been given to the world, I am much at a loss to say—but, perhaps, the authorial vanity has had more to do with the omission than any one other cause. Most writers—poets in especial—prefer having it understood that they compose by a species of fine frenzy—an ecstatic intuition—and would positively shudder at letting the public take a peep behind the scenes, at the elaborate and vacillating crudities of thought—at the true purposes seized only at the last moment—at the innumerable glimpses of idea that arrived not at the maturity of full view—at the fully matured fancies discarded in despair as unmanageable—at the cautious selections and rejections—at the painful erasures and interpolations—in a word, at the wheels and pinions—the tackle for sceneshifting—the step-ladders and demon-traps—the cock's feathers, and red paint, and the black patches, which, in ninety-nine cases out of the hundred, constitute the properties of the literary *histrio*.
>
> I am aware, on the other hand, that the case is by no means common, in which an author is at all in condition to retrace the steps by which his conclusions have been attained. In general, suggestions, having arisen pell-mell, are pursued and forgotten in a similar manner.
>
> For my own part, I have neither sympathy with the repugnance alluded to, nor at any time the least difficulty in recalling to mind the progressive steps

of any of my compositions; and, since the interest of an analysis, or reconstruction, such as I have considered a *desideratum,* is quite independent of any real or fancied interest in the thing analyzed, it will not be regarded as a breach of decorum on my part to show the *modus operundi* by which some one of my own works was put together. I select *The Raven,* as most generally known. It is my design to render it manifest that no one point in its composition is referrible either to accident or intuition—that the work proceeded, step by step, to its completion with the precision and rigid consequence of a mathematical problem.

Robert Louis Stevenson once wrote that "There is nothing more disenchanting to man than to be shown the springs and mechanism of any art. All our arts and occupations lie wholly on the surface; it is on the surface that we perceive their beauty, fitness, and significance; and to pry below is to be appalled by their emptiness and shocked by the coarseness of the strings and pulleys."

Poe seems to think that (from a writer's perspective) to have readers learn about the "painful erasures" that go on during the writing process would shatter "authorial vanity." He then speculates that many writers cannot remember or clearly define the process they went through when writing a particular work (a problem that he claims not to have).

Can a writer reveal step by step how a work was written? Opinions vary; however, **attempting to understand the writing process is important for the reader as well as the writer.** Discovering the process behind writing may be "disenchanting," as Stevenson would say, but for the reader, learning about the options open and those closed to writers can mean greater insight into the meaning of the work.

The developing writer also can benefit from examining the works of others for clues to the writing processes they used, experimenting with those processes, and developing original alternatives.

Back to Poe's essay:

Let us dismiss, as irrelevant to the poem, *per se,* the circumstance—or say the necessity—which, in the first place, gave rise to the intention of composing a poem that should suit at once the popular and the critical taste.

We commence, then, with this intention.

The initial consideration was that of extent. If my literary work is too long to be read at one sitting, we must be content to dispense with the immensely important effect derivable from unity of impression—for, if two sittings be required, the affairs of the world interfere, and every thing like totality is at once destroyed. But since, *ceteris paribus,* no poet can afford to dispense with *any thing* that may advance his design, it but remains to be seen whether there is, in extent, any advantage to counterbalance the loss of unity which attends it. Here I say no, at once. What we term a long poem is, in fact, merely a succession of brief ones—that is to say, of brief poetical effects. It is needless to demonstrate that a poem is such, only inasmuch as it intensely excites, by elevating the soul; and all intense excitements are, though a physical necessity, brief. For this reason, at least one half of the *Paradise Lost* is essentially prose—a succession of poetical excitements interspersed, *inevitably,* with corresponding depressions—the whole being deprived, through the extremeness of its length, of the vastly important artistic element, totality, or unity, of effect.

It appears evident, then, that there is a distinct limit, as regards length, to all works of literary art—the limit of a single sitting—and that, although in certain classes of prose composition, such as *Robinson Crusoe* (demanding no unity) this limit may be advantageously overpassed, it can never properly be overpassed in a poem. Within this limit, the extent of a poem may be made to bear mathematical relation to its merit—in other words, to the excitement or elevation—again in other words, to the degree of the true poetical effect which it is capable of inducing; for it is clear that the brevity must be in direct ratio of the intensity of the intended effect:—this, with one proviso—that a certain degree of duration is absolutely requisite for the production of any effect at all.

Holding in view these considerations, as well as that degree of excitement which I deemed not above the popular, while not below the critical, taste, I reached at once what I conceived the proper *length* for my intended poem—a length of about one hundred lines. It is, in fact, a hundred and eight.

How long should a work be? Have you ever watched a very lengthy television miniseries with episodes spaced so far apart that you lost track of the characters and lost interest in the story? Poe recognizes that if a story is too long, "the affairs of the world interfere, and every thing like totality is at once destroyed."

Another keen observation made by Poe is that "all intense excitements are, . . . brief." In the language of his day, Poe seems to be describing what people today refer to as a reader's "short attention span." This concept (keep the story short and exciting) has been embraced by today's multimedia works, partly because of public demand. For some readers, the best complement a writer can receive is that his or her fictional work is a "quick read."

Clearly, in narrative poetry, Poe prefers a short length with intense effects. Poe also makes another important point for today's writers: some types of prose works (such as *Robinson Crusoe*) do not demand unity and can have longer lengths. In other words, length (whether the work is narrative or nonnarrative) is related to purpose. For example, reference and instructional works, intended to be used in sections for specific purposes, can vary in length. *Gone with the Wind* is a very long prose narrative but is considered by many to be a riveting classic.

The question remains: How long should a story be? Poe concludes that *the length should be in relationship to the degree of effect*. Does this mean that a work should end when the desired effect is achieved? Perhaps, however, Poe decides at this point to end "The Raven" at 100 lines, with a "degree of excitement . . . not above the popular, while not below the critical, taste." This comment reveals Poe's practical awareness of the need for his work to have commercial appeal. Kenny Rogers, in the popular song, "The Gambler," knows when to hold his cards and knows when to fold them. **The writer, likewise, must develop an intuitive sense of when to end a story.**

More from Poe's essay:

> **My next thought concerned the choice of an impression, or effect, to be conveyed; and here I may as well observe that, throughout the construction, I kept steadily in view the design of rendering the work *universally* appreciable. . . . Beauty is the sole legitimate province of the poem. . . . When, indeed, men speak of Beauty, they mean, precisely, not a quality, as is supposed, but an effect— . . .**

> Now I designate Beauty as the province of the poem,
> merely because it is an obvious rule of Art that
> effects should be made to spring from direct
> causes— . . . Now the object, Truth, or the satisfac-
> tion of the intellect, and the object Passion, or the
> excitement of the heart, are, although attainable, to
> a certain extent, in poetry, far more readily attain-
> able in prose. Truth, . . . and Passion . . . are
> absolutely antagonistic to that Beauty which, I main-
> tain, is the excitement, or pleasurable elevation, of
> the soul. . . .

Moving from considering the length, Poe next decides upon his desired effect or impression made by the poem upon the reader. He confesses that he wants the work to be *"universally appreciable."* He sees "Beauty" as an effect that excites and elevates the soul, "Truth" as "the satisfaction of the intellect," and "Passion" as "the excitement of the heart," with Truth and Passion antagonistic to Beauty.

Although sounding more suited to a philosophy class than to a discussion on how to write, Poe's ideas are based on a practical idea: **Do you want your story to communicate to the reader's intellect (truth), heart (passion), or soul (beauty)?**

Next, Poe discusses tone:

> Regarding, then, Beauty as my province, my next
> question referred to the tone of its highest manifes-
> tation—and all experience has shown that this tone
> is one of *sadness*. Beauty of whatever kind, in its
> supreme development, invariably excites the sensi-
> tive soul to tears. Melancholy is thus the most legiti-
> mate of all the poetical tones.

Poe bases his tone on his desired effect, deciding that the best tone to achieve Beauty (reaching the reader's soul) is sadness. Are there other tones that reach a reader's soul? In contrast, what tone could you use to reach a reader's intellect?

Poe's next consideration is to develop a "pivot":

> The length, the province, and the tone, being
> thus determined, I betook myself to ordinary induc-
> tion, with the view of obtaining some artistic
> piquancy which might serve me as a key-note in the
> construction of the poem—some pivot upon which

the whole structure might turn. In carefully thinking over all the usual artistic effects—or more properly *points,* in the theatrical sense—I did not fail to perceive immediately that no one had been so universally employed as that of the *refrain.* . . . The pleasure is deduced solely from the sense of identity—of repetition. I resolved to diversify, and so heighten, the effect, by adhering, in general, to the monotone of sound, while I continually varied that of thought: that is to say, I determined to produce continuously novel effects, by the variation of the *application* of the refrain—the refrain itself remaining, for the most part, unvaried.

These points being settled, I next bethought me of the nature of my refrain. Since its application was to be repeatedly varied, it was clear that the refrain itself must be brief, . . . In proportion to the brevity of the sentence, would, of course, be the facility of the variation. This led me at once to a single word as the best refrain.

Once again, Poe's opinions foreshadow a technique used in writing today: the "hook."

The hook is a device that will capture the reader's (or viewer's/listener's) attention. A hook might be the cliff-hanger just before the commercial break in a television drama, the hit-you-in-the-face action scene that begins a movie, the inviting anecdote that begins a magazine article, or the refrain (the repetitive words, phrases, or lines) that hooks the listener into the rhythm and meaning of a song. (See pages 34 and 75.)

Poe recognizes that the hook can be the "pivot upon which the whole structure might turn" and selects the *refrain* because of its popularity. He likes the repetition of a refrain, but also wants a novel effect. His solution is to select a single word for the refrain (keeping it brief), but he varies the thought each time the word is used.

Poe discusses how he selected the single word for the refrain:

The question now arose as to the *character* of the word. Having made up my mind to a refrain the division of the poem into stanzas way, of course, a corollary; the refrain forming the close of each stanza. That such a close, to have force must be sonorous and susceptible of protracted emphasis admitted no doubt; and these considerations inevitably led me to the long *o* as the most sonorous vowel, in connection with *r* as the most producible consonant.

The sound of the refrain being thus determined, it became necessary to select a word embodying this sound, and at the same time in the fullest possible keeping with that melancholy which I had predetermined as the tone of the poem. In such a search it would have been absolutely impossible to overlook the word "Nevermore." In fact, it was the very first which presented itself.

Next, Poe makes the connection between sound and meaning as they relate to tone. His qualifications for his one-word refrain: a word that contains the vowel *o*, the consonant *r*, and a meaning that produces a melancholy tone.

Solution: *nevermore.*

Poe continues:

The next *desideratum* was a pretext for the continuous use of the one word "Nevermore." In observing the difficulty which I at once found in inventing a sufficiently plausible reason for its continuous repetition, I did not fail to perceive that this difficulty arose solely from the pre-assumption that the word was to be so continuously or monotonously spoken by a *human* being—did not fail to perceive, in short, that the difficulty lay in the reconciliation of this monotony with the exercise of reason on the part of the creature repeating the word. Here, then, immediately arose the idea of a *non-reasoning* creature capable of speech; and, very naturally, a parrot, in the first instance, suggested itself, but was superseded forthwith by a Raven, as equally capable of speech, and infinitely more in keeping with the intended *tone.*

. . . I asked myself—"Of all melancholy topics, what, according to the *universal* understanding of mankind, is the most melancholy?" "Death"—was the obvious reply. "And when," I said, "is this most melancholy of topics most poetical?" From what I have already explained at some length, the answer, here also, is obvious—"When it most closely allies itself to *Beauty*." The death, then of a beautiful woman, is, unquestionably, the most poetical topic in the world—and equally is it beyond doubt that the lips best suited for such topic are those of a bereaved lover.

The tone (melancholy or sad) of Poe's intended poem **dictates his choice of a character** to repeat the refrain (a nonreasoning creature rather than a human; a raven rather than a parrot) **and of the topic** (death of a beautiful woman).

More from Poe's essay:

> I had now to combine the two ideas, of a lover lamenting his deceased mistress, and a Raven continuously repeating the word "Nevermore." I had to combine these, bearing in mind my design of varying, at every turn, the *application* of the word repeated; but the only intelligible mode of such combination is that of imagining the Raven employing the word in answer to the queries of the lover. . . . I saw that I could make . . . the first query to which the Raven should reply "Nevermore" . . . a commonplace one—the second less so—the third still less, and so on—until at length the lover, startled from his original *nonchalance* by the melancholy character of the word itself—by its frequent repetition—and by a consideration of the ominous reputation of the fowl that uttered it—is at length excited to superstition, and wildly propounds queries of a far different character—queries whose solution he has passionately at heart—propounds them half in superstition and half in that species of despair which delights in self-torture—propounds them not altogether because he believes in the prophetic or demoniac character of the bird (which, reason assures him, is merely repeating a lesson learned by rote) but because he experiences a phrenzied pleasure in so modeling his questions as to receive from the *expected* "Nevermore" the most delicious because the most intolerable of sorrow. Perceiving the opportunity thus afforded me—or, more strictly, thus forced upon me in the progress of the construction—I first established in mind the climax, or concluding query—that query to which "Nevermore" should be in the last place an answer—that in reply to which this word "Nevermore" should involve the utmost conceivable amount of sorrow and despair.

At this point, **Poe engages organizing principles.** (See the discussion of organizing principles on pages 38–40.) He decides to build the emotional effects of the poem in a climactic progression. He does this by manipulating elements of character development as the lover changes from an attitude of nonchalance to one of superstition. (See the discussion of character development on pages 183 and 195.)

Poe's essay continues:

> Here then the poem may be said to have its beginning—at the end, where all works of art should begin—. . . .
>
> I composed this stanza [number 15] at this point, first, that by establishing the climax, I might the better vary and graduate, as regards seriousness and importance, the preceding queries of the lover; and secondly, that I might definitely settle the rhythm, the meter, and the length and general arrangement of the stanza,—as well as graduate the stanzas which were to precede, so that none of them might surpass this in rhythmical effect. Had I been able, in the subsequent composition, to construct more vigorous stanzas, I should without scruple, have purposely enfeebled them, so as not to interfere with the climacteric effect.

Having established the climax (the raven answering "Nevermore" to a question that results in the most intense moment of the tone—sadness and despair), **Poe begins the actual writing of the poem by composing the final stanza.** This approach helps him establish parameters for his writing: the mechanics of the poem (the rhythm, meter, and stanza length) and the climactic high-point.

Poe continues with a discussion of orginality:

> And here I may as well say a few words of the versification. My first object (as usual) was originality. . . . Of course, I pretend to no originality in either the rhythm or meter of *The Raven* . . . each of these lines, taken individually, has been employed before; and what originality *The Raven* has, is in their *combination into stanza;* nothing even remotely approaching this combination has ever been attempted. The effect of this originality of combination is aided by other unusual, and some altogether novel effects arising from an extension of the application of the principles of rhyme and alliteration.

Originality is important for writers and, according to an article titled "Originality" in the *Writer's Encyclopedia* (Writer's Digest Books, 1996), a concept that is challenging to define, difficult to attain, but what many editors want.

In addition to legal definitions that involve origins of a work, originality involves (for the most part) finding unique and different ways to express old ideas. Poe, in his search for originality, looks to the principles of literature to achieve a fresh approach by taking well-used rhythms and meters and combining them in different ways.

Next, Poe decides upon a setting:

> The next point to be considered was the mode of bringing together the lover and the Raven—and the first branch of this consideration was the *locale*. For this the most natural suggestion might seem to be forest, or the fields—but it has always appeared to me that a close *circumscription of space* is absolutely necessary to the effect of insulated incident:—it has the force of a frame to a picture. . . .
>
> I determined, then, to place the lover in his chamber—in a chamber rendered sacred to him by memories of her who had frequented it. . . .
>
> The *locale* being thus determined, I had now to introduce the bird—and the thought of introducing him through the window, was inevitable. . . .
>
> I made the night tempestuous, first, to account for the Raven's seeking admission, and secondly, for the effect of contrast with the (physical) serenity within the chamber.
>
> I made the bird alight on the bust of Pallas, also for the effect of contrast between the marble and the plumage— . . . the bust of *Pallas* being chosen, first, as most in keeping with the scholarship of the lover, and secondly, for the sonorousness of the word, *Pallas*, itself.

In the narrative form, setting can affect almost every aspect of the story. The setting (the time and place) of a story involves the past, present, and future of the place and the people in it, their resulting opinions, culture, style and dress, speech accents, and mannerisms. How the setting is handled can, for example, influence character development, advance (or hinder) plot development, and establish (or diminish) the mood and tone.

Poe recognizes that his setting must enhance his desired effects. He decides that "a close *circumscription of space* is absolutely necessary to the effect of insulated incident:—it has the force of a frame to a picture." As a result, he places the lover in a chamber filled with memories. He then uses setting in contrasting relationships to propel the story and further enhance the effect. He places shutters on the windows for the bird to beat against, simulating someone tapping at the door. He "made the night tempestuous" to "contrast with the (physical) serenity within the chamber." He contrasts the bird's feathers to the marble bust upon which it rests.

More from Poe's essay:

> **About the middle of the poem [stanzas 7–9], also, I have availed myself of the force of contrast, with a view of deepening the ultimate impression. For example, an air of the fantastic—approaching as nearly to the ludicrous as was admissible—is given to the Raven's entrance. . . .**
>
> **The effect of the *dénouement* being thus provided for, I immediately drop the fantastic for a tone of the most profound seriousness—this tone commencing in the stanza [10] . . . , with the line,**
>
> **But the Raven, sitting lonely on that placid bust, spoke only, etc.**
>
> **From this epoch the lover no longer jests—no longer sees any thing even of the fantastic in the Raven's demeanor. He speaks of him as a "grim, ungainly, ghastly, gaunt, and ominous bird of yore," and feels the "fiery eyes" burning into his "bosom's core." This revolution of thought, or fancy, on the lover's part, is intended to induce a similar one on the part of the reader—to bring the mind into a proper frame for the *dénouement*—which is now brought about as rapidly and as *directly* as possible.**

Having established a building momentum of contrasts through the use of setting, Poe then applies the same technique of contrast to character development: the raven's entrance is "as nearly to the ludicrous as was admissible," then his description of the raven suddenly sounds "a tone of the most profound seriousness." Consequently, "the lover no longer jests." **Contrasts within a story can produce vivid effects and help plot and character development.**

Poe's essay concludes:

> With the *dénouement* proper—with the Raven's reply, "Nevermore," to the lover's final demand if he shall meet his mistress in another world—the poem, in its obvious phase, that of a simple narrative, may be said to have its completion. So far, every thing is within the limits of the unaccountable—of the real. . . .
>
> But in subjects so handled . . . there is always a certain hardness or nakedness, which repels the artistical eye. Two things are invariably required—first, some amount of complexity, or more properly, adaptation; and, secondly, some amount of suggestiveness—some undercurrent, however indefinite, of meaning . . . which imparts to a work of art so much of the *richness*. . . .
>
> Holding these opinions, I added the two concluding stanzas of the poem—their suggestiveness being thus made to pervade all the narrative which has preceded them. The undercurrent of meaning is rendered first apparent in the lines—
>
> > "Take thy beak from out *my heart,* and take thy
> > form from off my door!"
> > Quoth the Raven, "Nevermore!"
>
> It will be observed that the words, "from out my heart," involve the first metaphorical expression in the poem. They, with the answer, "Nevermore," dispose the mind to seek a moral in all that has been previously narrated. The reader begins now to regard the Raven as emblematical—but it is not until the very last line of the very last stanza, that the intention of making him emblematical of *Mournful* and *Never-ending Remembrance* is permitted distinctly to be seen: . . .
>
> > And my soul *from out that shadow* that lies
> > flowing on the floor
> > Shall be lifted—nevermore.

Poe ends his essay with a synopsis of the plot of "The Raven" to what would seem to be the natural point of dénouement or "natural termination" (stanza 16). However, he adds two more stanzas to the poem so that readers will seek and ultimately find a "moral" in the story. More than a surprise ending, Poe adds another layer of meaning that imparts what he calls "richness" to a work of art. More than a simple narrative, **he wants his poem to have lasting**

impact. Is this idea being used by writers today? Be sure to read the review of Susan Wilson's novel *Beauty* on page 384.

Poe's essay reveals some useful ideas for modern writers. A few include the following:

1. A memorable story has riveting cause-and-effect relationships.

2. Writers need a practical awareness of what gives a work commercial appeal (to readers and critics).

3. A written work should be aimed at the reader (suited to the audience) with a clearly defined target—the reader's intellect, heart, or soul.

4. Use of a hook will help hold the reader's attention.

5. An original approach is fundamental.

What other ideas can you add to this list?

How does Poe achieve the best length, riveting effects, a hook, an original approach, and at the same time suit his work to the intended audience in "The Raven"? He accomplishes all these goals by effectively using the principles of literature.

Recognizing the Principles of Literature in Your Own Writing

A young woman was about to write a check for some purchases. She looked up at the clerk, expecting him to tell her the total. Their eyes met. She smiled. He smiled. She looked quizzically at him. He continued to smile, obviously enjoying the moment. Time passed. Finally, she asked him what the total would be for her check; and he pointed to a small computer screen that was displaying the total just inches from her face. "Oh my," she laughed, a little embarrassed. "If it had been a snake, it would have bitten me!"

His eyes grew large and his face became sternly earnest. "No, no," he protested warmly. "We would never have anything dangerous in here that could harm *you.*"

by author

When two people are speaking to one another, as in the example just given, they can discern through audible tones of voice, facial expressions, and body language whether they understand one another. They can alter what they say based on these perceptions and interactive give-and-take verbal exchanges. In contrast, a writer may not know whether his or her readers understand what is being said. Also, a writer seldom has an opportunity to clarify his or her meaning.

When readers come to a written work, they bring with them a vast array of opinions, ideas, and experiences that influence their perceptions of what the writer means. A reader may not understand a writer's meaning because the concepts presented are outside his or her realm of experience. The reader may have deep-seated preconceptions about the subjects and, as a result, may "read" his or her own ideas into what is written, completely missing the points that are intended. Sometimes communication is lost because the reader strongly disagrees with some point and dismisses the work altogether. Usually, the writer has little control over these types of communication breakdowns.

On the other hand, there are ways in which the effectiveness of communication rests in the hands of the writer. Writers who do not understand how to use the principles of literature risk producing ineffective writing that does not communicate their message. For example, a very popular literary technique used by essay writers (especially for magazine articles) is to begin with an anecdote that illustrates the point and is woven throughout the essay or used to tie-in the ending. This usage of the anecdote can be very effective to communication *if there really is a relationship between the point being made and the story being told.* When a writer attempts to force a relationship that does not really exist, communication is hampered and may even be lost.

Being able to recognize forced relationships can help the reader be more perceptive and the writer improve his or her writing skills. For example, a writer might begin an essay on driving safety with an anecdote about a race car driver and then build the essay by drawing a series of conclusions for driving safety based on the experiences of the race car driver. The use of this literary technique may be valid, but effective only if there really is a relationship between what happens to a trained professional driver on the race track and what happens to the average motorist on the nation's highways.

From Reader to Writer

To help you learn how to recognize the principles of literature in your own writing, begin the reader/writer synergy by reading the following autobiographical essay by Lillian Myers, "An Encounter with Honey Bees." You will be asked a series of comprehension questions based on each of the fundamental literary principles. Then you will be asked to redirect your thinking to ways in which you can use these same principles in your own writing.

An Encounter with Honey Bees

The area where we live has received national attention because Africanized "killer" honey bees have been found here. A local man was stung severely after the sound of his lawn mower disturbed the bees. In another incident, a swarm of bees stung two dogs to death and trapped the dogs' owners in the bathroom of their home until emergency workers could come to rescue them from the angry bees.

Reading in the newspaper about these bee attacks causes me to remember when I, too, had a frightening and painful encounter with honey bees.

When my four brothers and I were children, our parents encouraged us to pursue personal projects. My brothers had acquired a skep of honey bees as one of our wonderful ventures. Honey bees are known as *social* bees and are considered very beneficial because they pollinate vegetable gardens, fruit trees, flowers, and many farm crops, such as clover. Some amateur beekeepers call their standard wooden hives *bee skeps,* although a "skep" is a special dome-shaped hive made of interwoven straw instead of wood. My brothers were busy with many things, and I found that I became fascinated with this new project. I was a teenager at the time, and this new interest delighted me. I was very happy that I had made friends with the bees.

One of my projects was bringing ferns and violets from the woods and planting them in the area beneath the front window of the house. The skep of bees had been conveniently located across the driveway beside my favorite flower bed. By the end of summer, I had removed several delicious combs of honey; and on an especially beautiful morning, I was about to remove another tempting honeycomb.

The beehive was a square box with a small hole at the lower front edge for the bees to gain entrance. The combs hung down into the box and were removed through the top. My beekeeping downfall was the result of the covering that prevented rain from entering the hive. This was a single sheet of roofing tin about one foot longer on each side than the size of the box. In the center on the top had been placed a large rock sufficient in weight to hold the tin in place. I had to remove the rock; the resulting sound was a shotlike blast that must have reverberated through the beehive with such a force that it startled the bees.

Before I could realize what had happened, the entire colony of bees attacked me. They settled right on my head, stinging fiercely. When a bee attacks, its muscles force a stinger into the flesh to pump poison into the victim. Barbs on the stinger hold it tightly in the flesh; the stinger is pulled from the bee's body and the bee soon dies. Of course, I began to scream.

My mother heard my screams and was shocked to see the seething balloon of bees my head had become. My life was saved when God gave her the presence of mind to know what to do in this critical moment. My mother had been watering flowers nearby and quickly doused my head with a bucket of water. She continued to throw water on me with as much force as possible to dislodge the bees and managed to pull me into the house. She received a number of stings herself and cried in sympathy as she picked the stingers out of my face, neck, ears, and head. She lost count in the seventies.

I remained in shock for hours, unable to lay my head on a pillow. My eyes, nose, ears, and mouth swelled into a grotesque mask. I looked and felt terrible even weeks later with a blotchy, itchy head, face, and neck and with two black eyes.

Having miraculously survived this ordeal and the following weeks of unbelievable agony, the fact that for a long time I was nervous when I heard a buzzing sound is understandable. For many years even the buzz of an ordinary housefly would make me ill and trembling with fear.

The last of the honey was never removed from that skep of bees. The entire bee hive was hauled away. Many professional beekeepers wear hoods and gloves and, if necessary, use smoke to control angry bees.

My experience demonstrates that when sufficiently frightened, even domesticated honey bees will attack. In fact, according to recent field guide publications, the stings of domesticated bees are just as poisonous as those of Africanized bees. Experts tell us, however, that Africanized bees are "wild" honey bees. They avoid humans when possible, but will aggressively defend their hive if they are disturbed.

Honey bees are essential; we need honey bees for our agricultural crops and honey production. My experience illustrates, however, that we also need to learn how to live in harmony with bees and that care should be taken not to startle or disturb bees, whether domesticated or wild.

Examine the Meaning of the Essay

The meaning of a work can involve its main idea or central theme, the writer's message, and the subject. Think about this question:

▶ How would you describe (1) the main idea, (2) the writer's message, and (3) the subject of this essay?

The subject is obviously a bee attack on a teenage girl. Context clues to the meaning of this selection are scattered throughout the essay; however, the main idea and message are summarized in the final paragraph where the reader learns that honey bees must be handled with care and a sensible approach is important.

Gain a writer's perspective of meaning. Make a list of five major events in your life. Looking at each event individually, what would be your purpose or intent in writing down an account (either as an essay or narrative poem) of what happened to you?

Examine the Form of the Essay

Form can involve the genre (poetry, prose, drama, as well as the types of poetry, prose, or drama), the cause-and-effect relationships in a work, and the organizational patterns used. Think about these questions:

▶ What purpose does the account of "killer bees" serve in the first paragraph?
▶ Do you see any progressions of thought in the essay?

Principles of form are a significant vehicle in this essay. The writer uses progressions of thought (such as from trust to fear), presents cause-and-effect relationships (such as the poison causing shock), and establishes structural relationships (such as introducing her own experience by recounting reported attacks of "killer" bees). In addition, she uses such structural elements as spatial relationships (notice that the skep was "conveniently located across the driveway beside my favorite flower bed"); and she also uses chronological sequence.

Gain a writer's perspective of form. Think of the most dangerous event of your life. How would you structure an autobiographical essay/article or poem describing that event? You might consider using (1) the organizational principles listed on pages 38–39, (2) progressions of thoughts or emotions (such as from joy to sorrow), (3) contrasts (of moods or other elements of the setting, feelings, interests, and so forth), and (4) comments, observations, and dialogue designed to elicit desired responses from characters in the essay or from the readers.

Examine the Narrative Voice and Tone of the Essay

Narrative voice and tone can involve who is telling the story (first or third person), the attitudes of the narrator or speaker, the attitudes of characters within the story, and the tone (of voice) used by the narrator, speaker, and characters within the story. Think about these questions:

▶ How would you describe the speaker's attitude toward bees by the final paragraph?

▶ What is the parents' attitude toward their children's activities?

▶ Can you identify what phrase in paragraph four makes the speaker's involvement with bees seem inevitable?

Of course, this selection is a first person narrative. The attitude of the speaker is pragmatic because, despite this frightening experience that might have made her hostile toward the bees that caused her such pain, she still recognizes that society needs bees in the food chain and the responsibility for safety rests with people learning how to live in harmony with them. Her parents, as revealed in paragraph three, "encouraged us to pursue personal projects," making their attitude supportive. The fern and violet bed places the speaker "conveniently located" near the bees, making involvement with them seem inevitable.

Gain a writer's perspective of voice and tone. Select one memorable event in your life that you could describe in a short essay or poem. Make a list of your attitudes toward the people, things, and circumstances involved in that event, as well as your overall attitude toward the event itself. Be sure to include any changes in attitude you may have experienced during or as a result of the event. Also, consider your attitudes toward the readers of your proposed essay or poem and toward the subject. Next, develop a list of ways that you might convey these attitudes without directly stating them. You can develop levels of tone by the ways you present the characters (actions and dialogue), events, and setting—tones that can reflect (or contrast) these attitudes.

Examine the Character(s) in the Essay and the Character of the Essay

Characters can include the people in a literary work, their personalities, and their traits. Also, an event or a work itself can be characterized by a description of its distinguishing traits. Think about these questions:

- ▶ How would you characterize the bees in the third paragraph?
- ▶ How would you characterize the bee attack?
- ▶ What are the speaker's priorities by the end of the essay?

Character and characterization can be examined from several different perspectives. For example, the speaker's character could be described as enthusiastic because she, along with her brothers, pursued independent projects; and she made friends with the bees. The way in which she characterizes the bees as productive companions in the third paragraph and their attack as an agonizing accident (the result of an unexpected loud noise that "startled the bees") makes the speaker seem very practical in her outlook. This idea is further supported by her prioritizing education over reactionary measures when she describes in the last paragraph the "need to learn how to live in harmony with bees."

Gain a writer's perspective of character (ization). How would you characterize yourself? Begin by selecting five adjectives that best describe your character/personality. Then arrange the five adjectives from most to least descriptive of your personality. Next, take each of these character-related adjectives and try to think of something that has happened in your life that would reveal this side of your character to an onlooker. For example, if you describe yourself as an outgoing person, you might think of the time that you approached new neighbors to welcome them to their new home. Perhaps you consider yourself romantic, proven by the love poetry you write or by your preference for strolls along a moonlit beach.

This technique can be used to develop fictional story characters: Make a list of adjectives describing your fictional character, then plan ways you can reveal these character traits to your readers. The character traits will provide the basis for that character's actions, reactions, and interactions within the framework of the story.

Examine the Language (Uses and Meanings) of the Essay

Perhaps the most commonly found figurative uses of language are

analogy	*personification*
simile	*allusion*
symbols	*hyperbole (overstatement)*
irony	*meiosis (understatement)*
metaphor	*paradox*

In addition to using figurative language, writers often rely upon not only denotative meanings but also connotative word choices that carry with them implied meanings as well as upon words that have multiple meanings. Think about these questions:

▶ Can you identify a literary device used in paragraph six?
▶ What connotations surround, "I remained in shock for hours" (paragraph seven)?
▶ How would you paraphrase "presence of mind" in the sixth paragraph?

In contrast to the descriptive simile ("the shot-like blast") in the fifth paragraph, "the seething balloon of bees" is an example of a metaphor that does not include "like" or "as" in the comparison. Connotative word choices throughout the essay help establish meaning. Referring in paragraph one to the famous "killer" bees symbolizes the bees' vicious nature and at the same time connotes the degree of extreme pain inflicted by the bees when they sting. "I remained in shock for hours," of course, is connotative of the forceful nature of the attack and the great surprise the writer must have experienced as a result of the incident, in addition to the extreme pain and effects of the poison. Being able to paraphrase (to reword the meaning) is very useful to understanding meaning: to have "presence of mind" clearly is to be quick thinking.

Gain a writer's perspective of how language is used and what it means. "Stubborn as a mule," "gentle as a dove," "acid-tongued," and "rock-solid" are comparisons used to describe people. Once again, select a special event in your life. What simile or metaphor can you think of that would best describe you in that situation? If you used that figurative language to describe yourself as a character in an essay or poem, what impression about you as a person do you think its use might give readers?

Also, think about this: A clear understanding of the writer's intended meanings of the words used is vital to effective communication. Therefore, unless the writer provides direct definitions (as in instructional writing), a writer is faced with two possibilities:

1. Select words that he or she is certain can be understood by the intended readers.

2. Provide contextual clues that will help the reader discover what unfamiliar words mean.

How do you know which choice to make? One approach is to determine your audience first. Then examine your subject. Sometimes the subject demands the use of words unfamiliar to the intended audience. Begin looking at ways you can use contextual clues to help your readers keep up with your meaning. You might give an example that illustrates the meaning of a word or you could compare or contrast it to something else. For example, you are writing a science fiction story in which several scientists, cut off from civilization, are searching for the proper materials to complete repairs to an important experimental instrument. To heighten the sense of frustration the characters are feeling, you decide to have them find some corundum. What is corundum? See if you can tell from the following context clues.

> **Palmer began to dig deeply into the alluvial sand with the toe of his heavy boot, prodding and scraping until finally he struck something hard. Very hard. Kneeling down, he searched until his fingers caught on the object buried just below the surface. He quickly began digging sand away to expose it.**
> **Attracted by the intensity of Palmer's digging, Seagram walked over just in time to see Palmer's flushed look as he uncovered his prize. "See," Palmer's voice was shaking from the heat and the excitement of his discovery. "I told you we would find a corundum deposit in this valley."**
> **"And I told you, Palmer, that using corundum is too risky." Seagram moved closer and lowered his voice so the others wouldn't hear. "It's hard—but not hard enough—and the crystal shape won't work. The *only* mineral that will work is a diamond."**

Another way you can clue your readers into the meaning of a word is to provide synonyms or state the meaning in a different way:

> **Palmer began to dig deeply into the alluvial sand with the toe of his heavy boot, prodding and scraping until a little cloud of dust began to billow gently**

upward toward his face. He was sure he could find
corundum in this valley, and if he could only find
enough of the super-hard mineral, he could possibly
make the repairs in time, regardless of the risk.
He was about to give up and try another spot when
he hit something hard.

corundum illustrations
written by author

Used effectively, providing context clues for your readers can actually help you develop the structure of your writing.

The Literary Principles in Your Own Writing

To examine how you actually use the literary principles in your own
writing, first select a work that, in your opinion or perhaps in the
opinions of others, is one of your best written efforts. It might be a
short story, a poem, an essay or magazine article, or any other form
of written work that you feel communicates your meaning and intent.

Next, examine how you used the principles of literature in
your writing and experiment with some alternatives.

You will notice that the ideas that follow, to a certain degree,
address both prose and poetry and the roles of the literary principles common to each. You might ask, "I write prose, not poetry.
Why should I work with poems?" Prose and poetry share certain
aspects of the literary principles. Prose writers can benefit from
poetic experience by gaining, for example, a sense of prose rhythm
(see page 257), intensity of meaning, and awareness of the speaker's
role that are so much a part of writing and appreciating poetry.

Concerning Meaning   (See page 25.) What did you intend
the meaning of this work to be?

Identify the subject and the theme; then, state your purpose in writing the work. Exactly what ideas do you want the
readers to gain?

Your purpose will determine the form, approach, vocabulary, tone, and almost every aspect of the work. An instructional
book could be structured to include a detailed table of contents
and index, key terms in boldface print, illustrations and examples of important concepts, and so forth. The style would be
informational with an instructional tone. In contrast, a book
written by a humorist about the rigors of suburban life would

not need an index or highlighted terms and would be written in a humorous style with a lighthearted tone.

Does your work actually convey your desired meaning to the readers? As a reality check, you might ask several people to read your work. Then ask each one the following two questions:

▶ What do you believe the purpose of this work is?
▶ What do you think I want you to know after reading this selection?

Now compare the readers' responses to your own statement of intended meaning. Did you communicate effectively the meaning that you desired? If not, what do you think caused the breakdown in communication and how can you revise your work to fulfill your purpose and intended meaning?

Concerning Form (See page 37.) Look at your use of organizational principles and how the work is structured. Also, try the following idea to gain experience and flexibility in working with different literary forms.

Experiment with developing your purpose and meaning using a different form than the one you used originally. For example, on page 170 is a poem entitled "Broken-Down Car." The purpose is to describe and the intent is for readers to gain an emotional sense of the discouragement that the speaker experienced as a result of trying to repair a broken-down car.

How could this same purpose and meaning be restructured into prose? At first glance, a writer might think in terms of an essay on how to repair an old car; but this approach would not fulfill the purpose (to describe) because it would clearly be to inform readers on a how-to basis. Also, such an essay might easily lose the intended emotional impact, thus altering the meaning.

One possible approach that would, however, hold to the integrity of purpose and meaning would be to write a narrative in which the speaker relates an experience he or she had in trying to keep an old car running, using a limited budget. Within this use of form, the opportunities for description would be plentiful (descriptions of unsuccessfully trying to get money from loan officers, family, and friends to complete repairs; descriptions of trying to do repairs on a trial-and-error basis due to inexperience). Also, the emotional intensity of the meaning could be heightened with descriptions of discouragement after multiple failures. The work could culminate with an emotionally charged scene in which the speaker watches the car being towed to the junk yard for scrap metal.

Using your own work, translate your purpose and meaning into a different form. For example, write a poem based on your essay or turn your short story into a dramatic scene.

Concerning Voice and Tone (See page 116.) Return to the original form of your work under discussion. If your work is a narrative, is the narrative in the first person ("I did this and that") or does the narrator describe events in the third person? What would happen to your story if you changed the point of view? Changing from first to third person would mean that your narrator would no longer be a character in the story. How could you handle the role in the story that the narrator once played? If the change is from a third person, unseen narrator to a first person point of view, you will need to create a place for the narrator within the story. Can you turn one of your existing characters into a first person narrator? Using a photocopy of your narrative, try experimenting with first and third person to see what happens to the intensity of the work.

If your prose work is nonnarrative, the question becomes "Who is speaking?" Is your essay, for example, written with you as the speaker or is your speaker really a persona? Once again, consider the point of view. Have you concealed yourself from your readers by using the third person, or do you want to speak directly to them? As with the narrative form, see what happens to your work if you change the point of view of the speaker.

If your work is a poem, what is the attitude of the speaker? (Keep in mind that the speaker and the author are not necessarily one and the same.) In "Broken-Down Car," the attitude of the speaker changed within the poem from frustrated to defeated. What changes would have to be made to this poem in order for the attitude of the speaker to be seen as optimistic rather than frustrated and defeated? First, the use of dissonance produces a harsh tone that supports a feeling of emotional frustration. These sounds would need to be replaced with elements of euphony (see pages 171 and 251). Of course, within the poem itself, the speaker would need to meet with some element of success or at least some reason to hope for success.

Examine the attitude of the speaker in your poem or prose work. What tone does that attitude produce? To gain experience in working with the principles of voice and tone, what changes would you need to make to change the attitude of your speaker (whether in poetry or prose)? For example, if your speaker is assertive, can you make him or her complaisant? Sensitive, if callous? Cheerful, if churlish? Defeated, if hopeful? Uncertain, if authoritative? If you could make these changes, how would you describe the new tone of the work?

Concerning Character   (See page 174.) If your work contains characters, select one and, using the discussion of attitudes, emotions, response mechanisms, and intrinsic values that you will find on pages 175–251, develop a character sketch or personality profile of that person. How did you reveal that character's personality within your work? Did you use stereotyping? The character's actions? Words? Thoughts? The words of others? The use of setting?

Does the character in your work change? What was the motivation for the change? Was there sufficient time for a change in character to seem realistic? Also, did you give the readers enough information to know the character well enough to believe such a change?

If your work does not contain a "character," examine to see whether adding an anecdotal incident involving a character would help make your point. Would using dialogue at any point in the work add dramatic impact? Essayists, for example, have been known to carry on a type of conversation with the readers, such as

> **I might ask you to carry my books, help me with my math homework, or give me a ride home on your bike. But would you consider, even for a moment, allowing me to invade your space with my music, my tastes in clothes, my likes and dislikes. I can see you shaking your head. What, you ask, is my point? My point is that. . . .**

> **by author**

Also, look at your work from a larger perspective. How would you *characterize* (describe the distinctive elements of) your story, poem, essay/article? Your answer might involve references to tone, voice, and style. Ask someone else to read your work and characterize it. Is it sentimental? Judgmental?

Would the work be characterized as apathetic? Cynical? How do you *want* readers to characterize your work?

Concerning Language (Uses and Meanings) (See page 203.) Read your work for uses of figurative language. What are the effects on the meaning and tone? For example, read this couplet from Thomas Nashe's "Adieu, Farewell Earth's Bliss":

Beauty is but a flower
Which wrinkles will devour;

Nashe metaphorically compares beauty to a flower. The effect is to emphasize that beauty is fragile and subject to the physical ravishes of age.

As you examine each of your uses of figurative language, ask yourself this question: *Is this use of language fresh and effective or is it trite and ineffective?*

Next, look at the verb tense used in your work. In a narrative, what tense is used can be very significant to the impact of the story. Using a photocopy of your narrative, if the story is written in the past tense, change it to present; if written in the present tense, change it to past. Allow some time to pass; then, read both versions. Which tense creates the impact or tone you desire for this narrative?

Finally, you can develop ways to use literary principles to create desired effects and communicate your meanings. For example, when you spot uses of the literary principles that you consider especially effective, make note of them and begin experimenting with different ways those principles can be incorporated into your writing.

Developing and Writing a Literary Analysis

Increasing numbers of workers are leaving office settings to do their work at home by computer and fax, losing the interactive verbal environment of face-to-face contact. As a result, just understanding the "surface" or denotative meanings of a written work, regardless of its form, is no longer sufficient. Perceptive reading, being able to "pick up on" connotative meanings, multiple layers of meaning, intended meanings, and intended effects of a written communication can give you an intuitive edge that allows you the opportunity to respond in the most appropriate and advantageous manner. Likewise, your writing (whether a short story or an office memo) needs to communicate exactly what you mean and produce the effects you intend.

Developing perceptive reading and effective writing skills is a gradual process. This chapter gives you an opportunity to gain experience in reading for details and looking for subtle distinctions in a variety of literary works. Also, you can use this section to learn how to identify and use the principles of literature in your own writing.

What Is a Literary Analysis?

Literary analysis is an examination of a work of literature to discover uses of the principles of literature and the effects those uses produce. As this definition implies, discovery is a major feature of literary analysis. Although some uses of the literary principles may be quite obvious, recognizing other uses and their effects may require close and perceptive reading. You can use Part I, the Instructional Reference Guide, in this book to give you terms, definitions, and illustrations to identify, think about, and discuss the literary principles.

Improving Your Reading Skills

The first step in perceptive reading is to understand what a work means on literal level. *A technique used by many perceptive readers is to paraphrase.* When you read material that seems difficult to understand, focus your comprehension skills and attention by paraphrasing or restating in your own words what the writer is saying.

The second step is to find some way to relate ideas and information to your own life, opinions, or interests. *Part of perceptive reading is adding your experiences and ideas to those of the writer.* Compare and contrast ideas, accept concepts, and determine ways to use them or challenge ideas and explore alternatives. This technique improves memory and develops interpretive skills that lead to new ways of thinking.

Another step of perceptive reading, developing a literary analysis, requires reading for more than literal meaning. Analyzing literature requires you to:

▶ Look for and identify organizational patterns
▶ Utilize elements of psychological analysis to determine character
▶ Think on multiple levels as you search for figurative meanings
▶ Incorporate multi-sensory skills as you determine rhyme and (both prose and poetic) rhythm patterns as they relate to meaning
▶ Learn how to structure your thinking so that you view the work both in its parts and as a whole (crucial to determining overall style and tone)

Such skills sound very complex; however, once the process of analyzing a work of literature begins, many people find that the excitement of discovery turns the experience into a type of adventure on several levels:

Analyzing a work of literature is like being on a treasure hunt. The five principles of literature, in a manner of speaking, provide you with a treasure map. The "treasure" that you are seeking is to understand what you read on more insightful levels. As in any treasure hunt, you can experience the thrill of discovery each time you find a gem of hidden meaning.

Analyzing a work of literature is like solving a mystery. Sometimes the treasure alludes you, and the treasure hunt becomes a mystery that needs to be solved. Perhaps you instinctively know that the tone of a work changes at some point. Why has this happened? You begin to look for clues. Was there a change in setting? Did a character undergo an attitude change? Were previously hidden motives revealed? Maybe the style of the writing underwent subtle, almost imperceptible changes, such as a change in the prose rhythm.

Analyzing a work of literature is like performing a medical examination. When doctors see a problem during a medical examination, they may try to determine the cause and find a cure. Similarly, as you examine (analyze) a written work, you may spot a problem with how one or more of the literary principles are used. Perhaps, as an illustration, a character in a story does not seem believable, so you begin to ask questions about how the character is presented in the context of the story: Does the character change in the story? Is the change believable? Could a person make such a change in the amount of time given? How does the character respond to what is going on in the story? After this examination, you might conclude, for example, that the character's reactions are stereotypical or verbal responses are hackneyed. As a result, he or she may lack dimension as a character and depth as a person.

You might determine ways the problem could have been overcome if the writer had been aware of it. As a result, you are strengthening your reader-writer synergy as you become more perceptive in your reading and discover new sensitivities as a writer.

Analyzing a work of literature is like turning a casual acquaintance into a friend. To some degree, reading a work of literature acqaints you with its general content and allows you to understand its meaning on a superficial level. Analyzing that same work of literature gives you a more personal, intimate view. This sense of familiarity can bring with it greater understanding and flexibility in your thinking. Analyzing the work gives you a sense of ownership because you have invested some of yourself in trying to identify as much of the expressions and meaning as you can.

There are many more analogies that can be drawn to illustrate the process of analyzing the literary principles in action. Each different metaphor or approach may reveal to you additional information about the work (whether your own writing or the writings of others) and greater insight into the literary principles. Such multidimensional thinking can further strengthen your reader-writer synergy.

Readers tend to bring something of themselves into what they read, projecting their own personalities into the reading experience, and each work will elicit a different response according to the individuals who read it. A literary analysis (like the book review that will be discussed in the next chapter) is based on the personal opinions of an individual reader. See page 365 ["What Are the Expectations of the Readers?"] and page 367 ["Gain Perspective"]. Although a reader might have great skill and experience in developing an analysis, the analysis still is an expression of that one person's opinions.

The principles of literature described in Part I of this book provide a system to analyze, discuss, and develop a written work. Keep in mind, however, that how the principles are expressed is the choice of the writer and the judgment of the effectiveness of that expression is the opinion of the reader.

Analytical reading can, among other things, help you increase yours skills in

▶ Solving problems
▶ Using contextual clues
▶ Recognizing relationships
▶ Viewing ideas from different perspectives
▶ Thinking multidimensionally

Once you learn to read analytically, these skills can transfer to anything you read, making you a more perceptive reader.

Improving Your Writing Skills

The same literary analysis skills that benefit your reading perception can also improve your writing skills.

First, you can develop an awareness of the many ways other writers have used the literary principles. This awareness can, in turn, give you greater flexibility of approaches and techniques to use in your own writing.

Second, problem-solving techniques developed in analyzing the works of others can be used to identify and troubleshoot problems in your writing, as well.

Third, learning how to use contextual clues to gain meaning in the writing of others can help you establish a connection with your readers when you write. Deliberately examining your writing to suit vocabulary to audience and providing your readers with context clues to help them understand your meaning can keep readers (your audience) focused in your mind throughout the writing process.

Fourth, flexible thinking from different perspectives will greatly enhance your reading perception and help you make writing decisions that are free to adapt to changing circumstances. You can gain the confidence you need to experiment until you accomplish just the right combination that works.

Fifth, identifying the interwoven nature of the five literary principles when they are used by other writers requires multidimensional thinking. The same is true when you write. For example, a *character's voice* projects a *tone* that must be true to the intended *meaning* using *language* that suits the *form*. In other words, you should not focus on one principle, disregarding or at the expense of even one of the others. A breakdown at any level compromises the work.

Part I (the Instructional Reference Guide) of this book is generally aimed at examining the literary principles from the reader's perspective. As a writer, you can use Part I to become sensitive to viewing your own writing as readers might.

In addition, to make practical application of the principles described in Part I, you might ask the question, "How can I use this idea in my writing?" For example, on pages 58–59 is a discussion of poetic rhythm, including caesura (a pause that affects the rhythm) and spondaic foot (two or more strong syllables). The role of these two elements of form for the poet is easy to see. Both caesura and spondaic foot are attention-getting devices. Can you think of any ways you can use these two devices in your prose writing?

Some ways include:

▶ A sudden shift from lengthy, complex sentences to a short, simple sentence (causing a pause for readers)

▶ A series of rhetorical questions followed by several single-word, strongly accented interjections. For example,

> **I ask you, do we want our children to continue playing in a park where the equipment is unsafe? Do we want to drive for miles over poorly paved roads? Do we want to reelect the persons responsible for these problems? I say, No! No! No!**
>
> **by author**

▶ A pause in thought, such as when the writer shifts abruptly from a light-hearted tone to a somber statement that makes a profound or thought-provoking point.

Can you add to this list?

As you read and analyze the works of others, look for new and different ways the writers have used the principles of literature and ask yourself the question, "How can I use this idea in my writing?"

The Literary Analysis Paper and Literary Essay

A literary analysis can be as formal as a complex written dissertation or as informal as a period of quiet reflection and study after reading a literary work.

The literary analysis paper generally is written as part of an assignment for a literature class and should adhere to the guidelines put forth by the instructor. In contrast, the literary essay might be written for submission to publications aimed at literary scholars or students of literature. This chapter can also be used to develop the background work necessary for writing such papers.

The literary essay contains the results of the systematic analysis of a written work of literature (whether prose, poetry, or drama). It can deal with all five of the principles of literature, focus on only one or two, or discuss some significant point working within one of the principles. Poe's "The Philosophy of Composition," discussed on pages 290–304, provides an example of a literary essay written in 1846 about "The Raven" by the poem's own author.

Depending upon the audience, sometimes a writer is called upon to interpret a work or include comments concerning what the work means to him or her as a reader. An even more editorial approach is to include your reactions to the work, such as what you like or dislike about it, how it makes you feel, and your personal opinions concerning its subject. Opinions vary from reader to reader. Consequently, this approach is *very* subjective and may not express a valid judgment of the real value of a literary work. For example, despite the fact that the tone of "The Raven" is considered by many to be the poem's strength, some readers may dislike the tone and as a result would judge the poem based on their feelings (subjectively) rather than on the true literary merit of the work.

The Effects of Understanding the Literary Principles

As you learn to think, read, and write with the literary principles in mind, you may discover that your opinions concerning some works will change. You might find, for example, that a work you once thought was well-written actually contains a problem with character development. (As a writer, of course, you would begin thinking of alternative ways the author could have handled the story to eliminate the problem.) On the other hand, you may decide that a work you previously judged as poorly written contains merit after all. For instance, in applying the literary principles to the work, you might realize that at first you did not have a clear understanding of the book's audience and purpose. The work may actually be well-suited to its *intended* audience and purpose, meaning that your original opinion was inaccurate or unfair. Recognizing the literary principles in reading works of others and in your own writing will give you a more mature and valid basis for your analysis of a literary work.

Sample Approaches

The form of your literary analysis depends on your purpose. If you are analyzing a work for your personal enjoyment and development, you probably will make marginal notes (assuming that you own the book) or jot down comments and observations in a notebook. An analysis for presentation or discussion in a reading club may require more detailed notes, perhaps an outline, and a more formal, organized approach. Of course, the literary analysis paper and the literary essay require a specific statement of purpose and systematic design.

Every analysis should begin with a quiet reading of the work for pleasure. As you read, you may want to paraphrase the meaning (put it in your own words) and contemplate what point(s) the writer is trying to make. After reading, you can turn to the "Questions to Apply the Literary Principles" in Chapters 3–7 and answer those questions that apply to the work.

On the following pages you will find five works of literature (essay, short story, sonnet, lyric poem, and a narrative poem) and some model approaches and guidelines you might use in reading analytically.

The selections are taken from works written before 1900 to give you an opportunity to read for details, look for subtle distinctions, and use context clues to understand meanings that may be unfamiliar to you. Developing this skill can help you understand what you read regardless of your familiarity with the subject or the culture of the writer (a helpful skill in a global society).

Examining an Essay

The Character of Ned Softly
by
Joseph Addison (1672–1719)

paragraph

(1)   *Idem inficeto est inficetior rure,*
Simul poemata attigit; negue idem unquam
Æque est beatus, ac poema cum scribit:
Tam gaudet in se, tamque se ipse miratur.
Nimirum idem omnes fallimur; negue est
*   quisquam*
Quem non in aliqua re videre Suffenum
Possis.   —Catullus, "de Suffeno," xx.14.

(2)   Suffenus has no more wit than a mere clown when he attempts to write verses; and yet he is never happier than when he is scribbling: so much does he admire himself and his compositions. And, indeed, this is the foible of every one of us; for there is no man living who is not a Suffenus in one thing or other.

(3)   I yesterday came hither about two hours before the company generally make their appearance, with a design to read over all the newspapers; but, upon my sitting down, I was accosted by Ned Softly, who saw me from a corner in the other end of the room, where I found he had been writing something. "Mr Bickerstaff," says he, "I observe by a late paper of yours, that you and I are just of a humor; for you must know, of all impertinences, there is nothing which I so much hate as news. I never read a gazette in my life; and never trouble my head about our armies, whether they win or lose, or in what part of the world they lie encamped." Without giving me time to reply, he drew a paper of verses out of his pocket, telling me, "that he had something which would entertain me more agreeably; and that he would desire my judgment upon every line, for that we had time enough before us until the company came in."

(4)   Ned Softly is a very pretty poet, and a great admirer of easy lines. Waller is his favorite: and as that admirable writer has the best and

worst verses of any among our great English poets, Ned Softly has got all the bad ones without book: which he repeats upon occasion, to show his reading, and garnish his conversation. Ned is indeed a true English reader, incapable of relishing the great and masterly strokes of this art; but wonderfully pleased with the little Gothic ornaments of epigrammatical conceits, turns, points, and quibbles, which are so frequent in the most admired of our English poets, and practised by those who want genius and strength to represent, after the manner of the ancients, simplicity in its natural beauty and perfection.

(5)   Finding myself unavoidably engaged in such a conversation, I was resolved to turn my pain into a pleasure, and to divert myself as well as I could with so very odd a fellow. "You must understand," says Ned, "that the sonnet I am going to read to you was written upon a lady, who showed me some verses of her own making, and is, perhaps, the best poet of our age. But you shall hear it." Upon which he began to read as follows:

TO MIRA, ON HER INCOMPARABLE POEMS.

I

(6)   "When dress'd in laurel wreaths you shine,
     And tune your soft melodious notes,
You seem a sister of the Nine,
     Or Phoebus' self in petticoats.

II

(7)   "I fancy, when your song you sing,
     (Your song you sing with so much art)
Your pen was pluck'd from Cupid's wing;
     For, ah! it wounds me like his dart."

(8)   "Why," says I, "this is a little nosegay of conceits, a very lump of salt: every verse has something in it that piques; and then the dart in the last line is certainly as pretty a sting in the tail of an epigram, for so I think you critics call it, as ever entered into the thought of a poet." "Dear Mr. Bickerstaff," says he, shaking me by the hand, "everybody knows you to be a judge of these things; and to tell you truly, I read over Roscommon's translation of

Horace's 'Art of Poetry' three several times before I sat down to write the sonnet which I have shown you. But you shall hear it again, and pray observe every line of it; for not one of them shall pass without your approbation—

"When dress'd in laurel wreaths you shine.

(9)   "That is," says he, "when you have your garland on; when you are writing verses." To which I replied, "I know your meaning; a metaphor!" "The same," said he and went on—

"And tune your soft melodious notes.

(10)   "Pray observe the gliding of that verse; there is scarce a consonant in it; I took care to make it run upon liquids. Give me your opinion of it." "Truly," said I, "I think it as good as the former." "I am very glad to hear you say so," says he, "but mind the next—

"You seem a sister of the Nine.

(11)   "That is," says he, "you seem a sister of the muses; for, if you look into ancient authors, you will find it was their opinion that there were nine of them." "I remember it very well," said I; "but pray proceed."

"Or Phoebus' self in petticoats.

(12)   "Phoebus," says he, "was the god of poetry. These little instances, Mr. Bickerstaff, show a gentleman's reading. Then, to take off from the air of learning, which Phoebus and the muses had given to this first stanza, you may observe, how it falls all of a sudden into the familiar, 'in petticoats'!"

(13)   "Let us now," says I, "enter upon the second stanza; I find the first line is still a continuation of the metaphor—

"I fancy, when your song you sing.

(14)   "It is very right," says he; "but pray observe the turn of words in those two lines. I was a

whole hour in adjusting of them, and have still a doubt upon me whether in the second line it should be, 'Your song you sing;' or, 'You sing your song.' You shall hear them both—

> "I fancy, when your song you sing,
> (Your song you sing with so much art);

Or, "I fancy, when your song your sing,
> (You sing your song with so much art)."

(15)   "Truly," said I, "the turn is so natural either way, that you have made me almost giddy with it." "Dear sir," said he, grasping me by the hand, "you have a great deal of patience; but pray what do you think of the next verse—

> "Your pen was pluck'd from Cupid's wing."

(16)   "Think!" says I, "I think you have made Cupid look like a little goose." "That was my meaning," says he, "I think the ridicule is well enough hit off. But we come now to the last, which sums up the whole matter—

> "For, ah! it wounds me like his dart.

(17)   "Pray how do you like that 'Ah!' doth it not make a pretty figure in that place? 'Ah!'—it looks as if I felt the dart, and cried out as being pricked with it—

> "For, ah! it wounds me like his dart.

(18)   "My friend, Dick Easy," continued he, "assured me he would rather have written that 'Ah!' than to have been the author of the 'Æneid.' He indeed objected, that I made Mira's pen like a quill in one of the lines, and like a dart in the other. But as to that—" "Oh! as to that," says I, "it is but supposing Cupid to be like a porcupine, and his quills and darts will be the same thing." He was going to embrace me for the hint; but half a dozen critics coming into the room, whose faces he did not like, he conveyed the sonnet into his pocket and whispered me in the ear, "he would show it me again as soon as his man had written it over fair."

Here are just a few points that you might consider in reading this essay.

Meaning

This is an entertaining essay that seems to aim at sharing with the reader an intellectually stimulating encounter between two men. Although the subject is poetry, the essay focuses on a poem written by Ned Softly and is concerned with an informal literary analysis of that poem.

Form

As the title of the selection suggests, the form of this essay is the **character,** traditionally defined as a short description of a type character who exemplifies some vice or virtue. In this case, Addison individualizes the character and combines it with a periodical essay form. The reader learns from introductory material (not reprinted here) that this essay appeared in *The Spectator.*

The essay is a narrative episode to the extent that the speaker is almost anecdotally relating his encounter and conversation with Ned Softly:

    I. Introduction (paragraph 3)
       A. Speaker is reading newspapers.
       B. Speaker is approached by Ned Softly.
    II. Body (paragraphs 4–17)
       A. Speaker and Ned read poem as a whole.
       B. Speaker and Ned make a line-by-line analysis of poem.
    III. Conclusion (paragraph 18)
       A. Speaker gives Ned a hint.
       B. Ned promises another encounter.

The structure of the lyric love poem is in two parts of four lines written in iambic pentameter with an **abab cdcd** rhyme scheme. Although identified by Ned as a "sonnet" (paragraph 5), this work contains only eight lines. The role of the quotation and introduction (paragraphs 1–2) will be addressed later.

Narrative Voice

Written in first person narrative, the speaker is a man of letters. Use of first person, the complementary words of Ned Softly, and the speaker's own words make him seem quite credible. The speaker's attitude toward Ned might be described as condescending: "a very pretty poet" (paragraph 4), "incapable" (paragraph 4), "pain" (paragraph 5), "so very odd a fellow" (paragraph 5). Although impossible to determine from an essay isolated from the historical context in which it was written, the reader might assume that when Ned Softly calls the speaker "Mr Bickerstaff," the speaker is a mask or persona of the author.

Tone and Character

The speaker's tone (of voice) seems formal to modern perceptions, as becomes a late seventeenth-century man of letters. Yet, his patient indulgence with Ned, someone he obviously considers his inferior as "a true English reader, incapable of relishing the great and masterly strokes of this art," seems very conversational in tone. The speaker's opinion of Ned is revealed and the tone of his responses to Ned's conversation is set when he says, "Finding myself unavoidably engaged in such a conversation, I resolved to turn my pain into a pleasure, and to divert myself as well as I could with so very odd a fellow." Because he cannot avoid the situation, he intends to use it for entertainment. This is also a revelation of character on the part of Bickerstaff. On one hand, he esteems himself perceptive enough to judge the learning of others; on the other hand, he has the capacity for what people today call "making lemons into lemonade"—turning unpleasant situations into pleasant ones through adopting a positive attitude. Bickerstaff refers to Ned as one among "you critics" in paragraph 8; he says that Ned has "made me almost giddy" with his use of words in paragraph 15; he says that Ned "made Cupid look like a little goose" in paragraph 16. What is the tone of these remarks?

The revelation of Ned's character and the tone of his remarks are far less subtle than those of Bickerstaff. The reader learns some insight into Ned's character through Bickerstaff's comments, notably:

▶ He likes "easy" lines.
▶ He likes Waller's poetry, but rather than the best verses, he has the "bad ones without book."
▶ He repeats poems "to show his reading."

The reader also learns about Ned's character through his own words:

▶ He identifies with Bickerstaff's personality ("you and I are just of a humor").
▶ He is not interested in current events or the national interests.
▶ He elicits Bickerstaff's attention concerning his verses "without giving me time to reply." (This can be viewed in several ways: some people might label this aspect of his character as overbearing or pushy. You also could cite such conduct as indicative of a self-centered personality, yet a case could be made that Ned is simply excited and overzealous concerning gaining Bickerstaff's approval.)
▶ He views the lady who is the object of his verse as an excellent poet ("perhaps, the best poet of our age"), indicating an appreciation for a work regardless of the sex of the poet.
▶ He looked to Horace's "Art of Poetry" to write his sonnet, indicating a "by the book" approach to an artistic endeavor.
▶ He is not satisfied with Bickerstaff's approval and complementary words about the poem as a whole, but "shows off" the poem line by line.
▶ He reveals that he deliberately wants to "show a gentleman's reading" in the verses; he wants people to know that he is well-read.
▶ He has "anguished" over each word of the poem (including diction and syntax): "I was a whole hour in adjusting of them [two lines]"—perhaps tendencies toward being a perfectionist.
▶ He is impressed by the opinions of others (such as Dick Easy).
▶ For some reason (one about which readers can only speculate), he does not want to share his poem with other critics "whose faces he did not like."
▶ He has secretarial help ("his man" in paragraph 18).
▶ He appreciates help from Bickerstaff ("He was going to embrace me for the hint").
▶ He assumes that Bickerstaff will want to see the "sonnet" again.
▶ He is secretive about the "sonnet."

Many of these insights into Ned's character help identify what tone he uses in talking to Bickerstaff.

Taking the previously discussed elements into account, Bickerstaff's character might be generalized as a man who is self-assured, respected, opinionated, and congenial. His character sets a tone of good-natured indulgence. Ned's character could be generalized as a man who is impressionable, enthusiastic, eager to impress others, and fastidious about details. His character adds a tone of intense exuberance to the sketch.

Having established a background discussion of the use of character and tone in this essay, you need to look once again at the form and voice. Look closely at the quote from *Catullus* and the commentary paragraph that follows it (paragraphs 1–2). Obviously Ned is characterized as a Suffenus-type, one who admires himself (as a man of learning) and admires his own compositions, despite his lack of original talent. The commentary contains another insightful point: "there is no man living who is not a Suffenus in one thing or other." Does this mean that even Bickerstaff has elements of Suffenus in his character?

In terms of form, the quotation and comment serve to introduce the character trait(s) that are the focus of the sketch, to foreshadow the "Character of Ned Softly," and to summarize the main point by means of a generalization about the character of man ("there is no man living who is not a Suffenus in one thing or other"). What is the effect of this use of form? A major effect is irony: Bickerstaff indirectly characterizes Ned as a Suffenus type, yet he, himself, must fall into the same "foible of every one of us . . . in one thing or another" that characterizes Suffenus and Ned.

In terms of voice, this introduction presents the reader with a challenge: who is speaking? If the speaker is Bickerstaff, the effect of the form is to reveal an ironic tongue-in-cheek *awareness* on his part. If, on the other hand, you are listening to the voice of the writer of this character sketch, the effect is even more profound because the writer is revealing his own view concerning Ned and Bickerstaff, as well as revealing the irony of Bickerstaff's *lack of awareness* of his own "foible."

Language (Uses and Meanings)

This selection is rich in figurative language. A *few* uses include:

► "trouble my head" (paragraph 3)—slang
   Effect: a conversational tone

- ▶ "nosegay of conceits" (paragraph 8)—metaphor
  Tenor: the poem, consisting of conceits (elaborate
  metaphors that were considered strained and artificial in
  the eighteenth and nineteenth centuries)
  Vehicle: nosegay (small collection of flowers)
- ▶ "lump of salt" (paragraph 8)—metaphor
  Tenor: the poem
  Vehicle: lump of salt

Can you identify the comparison(s), including the tenor(s) and vehicle(s) in this line?

". . . then the *dart* in the last line is certainly as pretty a sting in the tail of an epigram, . . . (paragraph 8)

- ▶ "a sister of the Nine" (paragraph 10)—literary allusion
  Effect: "an air of learning"
- ▶ "made Cupid look like a little goose" (paragraph 16)—
  simile
  Tenor: Cupid
  Vehicle: goose

One of the more obvious examples of the use of syntax in this selection is Ned's own discussion of word order when he debates between "(Your song you sing with so much art)" and "(You sing your song with so much art)." Can you identify the significance in syntactical terms of the one against the other?

In "You sing your song . . .," the function order is subject-verb-object, the most commonly used syntactical order that places emphasis on the subject (You). In contrast, "Your song you sing . . ." is in the object-subject-verb order. The result? Emphasis is placed on the song.

Read the following list and define the meaning of each as used in context:

- ▶ "you and I are just of a humor" (paragraph 3)
  Possible answers: A "humor" (often spelled *humour*)
  refers to the four humours or predominant features of a
  person's character and personality. (See chart on pages
  190–191.) Ned believes that he and Bickerstaff share the
  same opinions on the subject.
- ▶ "a very pretty poet" (paragraph 4)
  Possible answers: The context is especially important in

determining the use of the word *pretty* in this selection. Ned's character has been established as someone who is a Suffenus type, enthusiastic about writing poetry and greatly admiring his own work. In this context, "pretty" is an ironic word choice. "Pretty" means clever or artful—an opinion Ned holds of himself. The connotative definitions of "pretty," however, reinforce Bickerstaff's opinions concerning Ned: as a "pretty poet" his work sounds pleasant but does not have strength or intensity. Also, do the names of the characters in this work (Softly and Bickerstaff) have any significance to revelation of character?

▶ "easy lines" (paragraph 4)

Possible answers: What are "easy" lines from a "pretty poet"? Such a poet would like lines that are not difficult to understand or write.

▶ "Ned Softly has got all the bad ones without book" (paragraph 4)

Possible answers: The clue to "without book" is found in the comment "which he repeats upon occasion, to show his reading and garnish his conversation." In other words, Ned has memorized (can repeat without looking at a book) Waller's worst verses so that he appears learned.

How Can You Use These Ideas in Your Writing?

The analysis of the poem in the essay is rather technical, but the writer "frames" the analysis in a light-hearted, entertaining little story that is filled with character revelation and dialogue. Lesson: An article explaining a technical process or idea might be framed in a narrative that serves two purposes:

1. The frame can act as a hook to capture the reader's attention.

2. The structure of the narrative can divide the explanation of the technical process into parts. A character who is giving the technical explanation might be interrupted by someone entering the room. The explanation could be resumed after a brief social interaction or any number of other scenes. The narrative portions would then help to "pull" the readers along, despite the technical nature of the explanation.

Suppose, for example, you are writing an article on the care and feeding of rabbits. Audience: children between 8 and 12. Rather than listing steps and supplies, you might frame the procedures in a first person narrative in which a bunny escapes and must be rescued. The same topic aimed at adults (commercial production that would include health care procedures) could be framed in an anecdote or series of episodes written in a humorous tone.

Do you see any other ideas from the Ned Softly essay? You might, as an example, consider how the writer handles tone and the different ways he reveals character without directly describing personalities.

Examining a Short Story

The Imp of the Perverse
by
Edgar Allan Poe

(1)   In the consideration of the faculties and impulses—of the *prima mobilia* of the human soul, the phrenologists have failed to make room for a propensity which, although obviously existing as a radical, primitive, irreducible sentiment, has been equally overlooked by all the moralists who have preceded them. In the pure arrogance of the reason, we have all overlooked it. We have suffered its existence to escape our senses, solely through want of belief—of faith;—whether it be faith in Revelation, or faith in the Kabbala. The idea of it has never occurred to us, simply because of its supererogation. We saw no *need* of the impulse—for the propensity. We could not perceive its necessity. We could not understand, that is to say, we could not have understood, had the notion of this *primum mobile* ever obtruded itself;—we could not have understood in what manner it might be made to further the objects of humanity, either temporal or external. It cannot be denied that phrenology, and in great measure, all metaphysicianism, have been concocted *a priori*. The intellectual or logical man, rather than the understanding or observant man, set himself to imagine designs—to dictate purposes to God. Having thus fathomed to his satisfaction the intentions of Jehovah, out of these intentions he built his innumerable systems of mind. In the matter of phrenology, for example, we first determined, naturally enough, that it was the design of the Deity that man should eat. We then assigned to man an organ or alimentiveness, and this organ is the scourge with which the Deity

compels man, will-I nill-I, into eating. Secondly, having settled it to be God's will that man should continue his species, we discovered an organ of amativeness, forthwith. And so with combativeness, with ideality, with causality, with constructiveness,—so, in short, with every organ, whether representing a propensity, a moral sentiment, or a faculty of the pure intellect. And in these arrangements of the *principia* of human action, the Spurzheimites, whether right or wrong, in part, or upon the whole, have but followed, in principle, the footsteps of their predecessors; deducing and establishing every thing from the preconceived destiny of man, and upon the ground of the objects of his Creator.

(2)   It would have been wiser, it would have been safer to classify, (if classify we must,) upon the basis of what man usually or occasionally did, and was always occasionally doing, rather than upon the basis of what we took it for granted the Deity intended him to do. If we cannot comprehend God in his visible works, how then in his inconceivable thoughts, that call the works into being! If we cannot understand him in his objective creatures, how then in his substantive moods and phrases of creation?

(3)   Induction, *a posteriori,* would have brought phrenology to admit, as an innate and primitive principle of human action, a paradoxical something, which we may call *perverseness,* for want of a more characteristic term. In the sense I intend, it is, in fact a *mobile* without motive, a motive not *motivirt.* Through its promptings we act without comprehensible object; or, if this shall be understood as a contradiction in terms, we may so far modify the proposition as to say, that through its promptings we act, for the reason that we should *not.* In theory, no reason can be more unreasonable; but, in fact, there is none more strong. With certain minds, under certain conditions, it becomes absolutely irresistible. I am not more certain that I breathe, than that the assurance of the wrong or error of any action is often the one unconquerable *force* which impels us, and alone impels us to its prosecution. Nor will this overwhelming tendency to do wrong for the wrong's sake, admit of analysis, or resolution into ulterior elements. It is a radical, a primitive

impulse—elementary. It will be said, I am aware, that when we persist in acts because we feel we should *not* persist in them, our conduct is but a modification of that which ordinarily springs from the *combativeness* of phrenology. But a glance will show the fallacy of this idea. The phrenological combativeness has for its essence, the necessity of self-defence. It is our safeguard against injury. Its principle regards our well-being; and thus the desire to be well, is excited simultaneously with its development. It follows, that the desire to be well must be excited simulta-neously with any principle which shall be merely a modification of combativeness, but in the case of that something which I term *perverseness,* the desire to be well is not only not aroused, but a strongly antagonistical sentiment exists.

(4)   An appeal to one's own heart is, after all, the best reply to the sophistry just noticed. No one who trustingly consults and thoroughly questions his own soul will be disposed to deny the entire radicalness of the propensity in question. It is not more incomprehensible than distinctive. There lives no man who at some period, has not been tormented, for example, by an earnest desire to tantalize a listener by circumlocution. The speaker is aware that he displeases; he has every intention to please; he is usually curt, precise, and clear; the most laconic and luminous lan-guage is struggling for utterance upon his tongue; it is only with difficulty that he restrains himself from giving it flow; he dreads and depre-cates the anger of him whom he addresses; yet, the thought strikes him that by certain involu-tions and parentheses, this anger may be engen-dered. That single thought is enough. The impulse increases to a wish, the wish to a desire, the desire to an uncontrollable longing, and the longing, (to the deep regret and mortification of the speaker, and in defiance of all consequences,) is indulged.

(5)   We have a task before us which must be speedily performed. We know that it will be ruinous to make delay. The most important crisis of our life calls trumpet-tongued, for immediate energy and action. We glow, we are consumed with eagerness to commence the work, with the anticipation of whose glorious result our whole

souls are on fire. It must, it shall be undertaken to-day, and yet we put if off until to-morrow; and why? There is no answer, except that we feel *perverse*, using the word with no comprehension of the principle. To-morrow arrives, and with it a more impatient anxiety to do our duty, but with this very increase of anxiety arrives, also, a nameless, a positively fearful, because unfathomable craving for delay. This craving gathers strength as the moments fly. The last hour for action is at hand. We tremble with the violence of the conflict within us,—of the definite with the indefinite—of the substance with the shadow. But, if the contest have proceeded thus far, it is the shadow which prevails,—we struggle in vain. The clock strikes, and is the knell of our welfare. At the same time, it is the chanticleer-note to the ghost that has so long overawed us. It flies—it disappears—we are free. The old energy returns. We will labor *now*. Alas, it is *too late!*

(6)   We stand upon the brink of a precipice. We peer into the abyss—we grow sick and dizzy. Our first impulse is to shrink from the danger. Unaccountably we remain. By slow degrees our sickness, and dizziness, and horror, become merged in a cloud of unnameable feeling. By gradations, still more imperceptible, this cloud assumes shape, as did the vapor from the bottle out of which arose the genius in the Arabian Nights. But out of this *our* cloud upon the precipice's edge, there grows into palpability, a shape, far more terrible than any genius, or any demon of a tale, and yet it is but a thought, although a fearful one, and one which chills the very marrow of our bones with the fierceness of the delight of its horror. It is merely the idea of what would be our sensations during the sweeping precipitancy of a fall from such a height. And this fall—this rushing annihilation—for the very reason that it involves that one most ghastly and loathsome of all the most ghastly and loathsome images of death and suffering which have ever presented themselves to our imagination—for this very cause do we now the most vividly desire it. And because our reason violently deters us from the brink, *therefore*, do we the more impetuously approach it. There is no passion in nature so demoniacally impatient, as that of him,

who shuddering upon the edge of a precipice, thus meditates a plunge. To indulge for a moment, in any attempt at *thought,* is to be inevitably lost; for reflection but urges us to forbear, and *therefore* it is, I say, that we *cannot.* If there be no friendly arm to check us, or if we fail in a sudden effort to prostrate ourselves backward from the abyss, we plunge, and are destroyed.

(7)   Examine these and similar actions as we will, we shall find them resulting solely from the spirit of the *Perverse.* We perpetrate them merely because we feel that we should *not.* Beyond or behind this, there is no intelligible principle: and we might, indeed, deem this perverseness a direct instigation of the arch-fiend, were it not occasionally known to operate in furtherance of good.

(8)   I have said thus much, that in some measure I may answer your question—that I may explain to you why I am here—that I may assign to you something that shall have at least the faint aspect of a cause for my wearing these fetters, and for my tenanting this cell of the condemned. Had I not been thus prolix, you might either have misunderstood me altogether, or, with the rabble, have fancied me mad. As it is, you will easily perceive that I am one of the many uncounted victims of the Imp of the Perverse.

(9)   It is impossible that any deed could have been wrought with a more thorough deliberation. For weeks, for months, I pondered upon the means of the murder. I rejected a thousand schemes, because their accomplishment involved a *chance* of detection. At length, in reading some French memoirs, I found an account of a nearly fatal illness that occurred to Madame Pilau, through the agency of a candle accidentally poisoned. The idea struck my fancy at once. I knew my victim's habit of reading in bed. I knew, too, that his apartment was narrow and ill-ventilated. But I need not vex you with impertinent details. I need not describe the easy artifices by which I substituted, in his bed-room candle-stand, a wax-light of my own making, for the one which I there found. The next morning he was discovered dead in his bed, and the coroner's verdict was,— "Death by the visitation of God."

(10)   Having inherited his estate, all went well with me for years. The idea of detection never once entered my brain. Of the remains of the fatal taper, I had myself carefully disposed. I had left no shadow of a clue by which it would be possible to convict, or even to suspect me of the crime. It is inconceivable how rich a sentiment of satisfaction arose in my bosom as I reflected upon my absolute security. For a very long period of time, I was accustomed to revel in this sentiment. It afforded me more real delight than all the mere worldly advantages accruing from my sin. But there arrived at length an epoch, from which the pleasurable feeling grew, by scarcely perceptible gradations, into a haunting and harassing thought. It harassed because it haunted. I could scarcely get rid of it for an instant. It is quite a common thing to be thus annoyed with the ringing in our ears, or rather in our memories, of the burthen of some ordinary song, or some unimpressive snatches from an opera. Nor will we be the less tormented if the song in itself be good, or the opera air meritorious. In this manner, at last, I would perpetually catch myself pondering upon my security, and repeating, in a low undertone, the phrase, "I am safe."

(11)   One day, while sauntering along the streets, I arrested myself in the act of murmuring, half aloud, these customary syllables. In a fit of petulance, I remodelled them thus:—"I am safe—I am safe—yes—if I be not fool enough to make open confession!"

(12)   No sooner had I spoken these words, than I felt an icy chill creep to my heart. I had some experience in these fits of perversity, (whose nature I have been at some trouble to explain,) and I remembered well, that in no instance, I had successfully resisted their attacks. And now my own casual self-suggestion, that I might possibly be fool enough to confess the murder of which I had been guilty, confronted me, as if the very ghost of him whom I had murdered—and beckoned me on to death.

(13)   At first, I made an effort to shake off this nightmare of the soul. I walked vigorously—faster—still faster—at length I ran. I felt a maddening desire to shriek aloud. Every succeeding wave of thought overwhelmed me

with new terror, for alas! I well, too well understood that, to *think,* in my situation, was to be lost. I still quickened my pace. I bounded like a madman through the crowded thoroughfares. At length, the populace took the alarm, and pursued me. I felt *then* the consummation of my fate. Could I have torn out my tongue, I would have done it—but a rough voice resounded in my ears—a rougher grasp seized me by the shoulder. I turned—I gasped for breath. For a moment, I experienced all the pangs of suffocation; I became blind, and deaf, and giddy; and then, some invisible fiend, I thought, struck me with his broad palm upon the back. The long-imprisoned secret burst forth from my soul.

(14)   They say that I spoke with a distinct enunciation, but with marked emphasis and passionate hurry, as if in dread of interruption before concluding the brief but pregnant sentences that consigned me to the hangman and to hell.

(15)   Having related all that was necessary for the fullest judicial conviction, I fell prostrate in a swoon.

(16)   But why shall I say more? To-day I wear these chains, and am *here!* To-morrow I shall be fetterless!—*but where?*

First, look at the selection as a whole and make some broad generalizations concerning use of the literary principles.

Meaning

1. What is Poe's purpose?

2. What is the effect of this purpose on the reader?

Form

3. What is the genre?

4. Identify the plot structure. What is the exposition? Complication? Climax? Dénouement?

Narrative Voice and Tone

5. What is the point of view?

6. What is the narrator's attitude?

7. What is the story's tone?

Character

8. How would you describe the narrator's character?

Language (Uses and Meanings)

9. What is the overall irony at work in this story?

10. What is ironic about the narrator's account of his crime when compared to his account of his confession? Be sure to address how this story fulfills the concept of poetic justice in that evil is punished. (See page 234.)

Background

In the very first paragraph, the speaker refers extensively to *phrenology*. A check into reference sources will reveal that phrenology is the study of the lumps and bumps, dips and curves of the human skull in an effort to determine character and the faculties of an individual. This so-called science was popular in the mid-nineteenth century and was practiced well into the twentieth.

To the phrenologist, the shape of the skull and its protuberances can be studied and used to analyze a person's character and faculties. The faculties are divided into predispositions called propensities, emotions are the result of sentiments, and higher reason is the realm of the perceptive and reflective faculties. The phrenologist examines the cranial bumps on a person's head to determine where each of these faculties is located. There are thirty-five faculties in phrenology, and each portion of the brain in which a faculty is seated is called an organ.

In "The Imp of the Perverse," the speaker makes mention of these six organs:

1. *Alimentiveness*—faculty for seeking food

2. *Amativeness*—faculty for sexual desire

3. *Combativeness*—faculty for fighting

4. *Ideality*—faculty for conceiving ideals

5. *Causality*—faculty for determining the causes of effects

6. *Constructiveness*—faculty for constructing

(Johann Spurzheim was a famous German phrenologist.)

Another concept that you may encounter in other writings is *a posteriori* as used in the first paragraph of "The Imp of the Perverse" and its opposite, *a priori,* used in the third paragraph:

a posteriori

▶ Meaning one is based on logic: inductive reasoning (beginning with effects and determining their causes).

▶ Meaning two is based on philosophy: determining something through empirical (observable) evidence or experience.

a priori

▶ Meaning one is based on logic: deductive reasoning (beginning with the cause and determining the effects) from a generalization to specific instances.

▶ Meaning two is based on philosophy: innate feelings and/or ideas determined before empirical evidence has been gathered or experience occurred.

▶ A third meaning is connotative: presuming something is true before knowing the facts.

Next, consider a thorough examination of the first paragraph.

▶ What is the first paragraph about?
▶ What is the attitude of "I" toward phrenologists?
▶ What is the speaker's tone when he says that "We saw no *need* of the impulse"?
▶ How does the speaker characterize the "intellectual or logical" man?
▶ What does the speaker reveal about his own character?
▶ What do the following words mean as used in context?
  1. *prima mobilia*
  2. Kabbala (also spelled *cabala*)
  3. propensity
  4. supererogation
▶ What is the effect of the phrase "will-I nill-I"
▶ According to the speaker, what is the reason that phrenologists and moralists have missed an important "propensity" of man?
▶ What is the difference, as presented in this paragraph, between the unidentified propensity and those propensities that are identified?

▶ What is the speaker suggesting concerning the unidentified propensity when he says that "we could not have understood in what manner it might be made to further the objects of humanity, either temporal or external"?

▶ Based on the context, what does the speaker mean when he says that phrenology and the systems of mind were "concocted *a priori*"?

The following list contains a few points that you might want to think about as you analyze this story.

Paragraph 2

▶ What "(if classify we must)" suggests
▶ Comparison and contrast of two views
▶ Effects of rhetorical devices
▶ Elements of logic

Paragraph 3

▶ Identification of what elements are in paradox
▶ Determination of why an *a posteriori* approach would have revealed perverseness
▶ Meanings of *"mobile"* and *"motivirt"*
▶ Elements of irony
▶ Identification of the compelling force
▶ Use in context of "admit"
▶ Identification of the fallacy
▶ Identification of the motive for combativeness

Paragraph 4

▶ Meanings of "sophistry" and "radicalness" in context
▶ Meaning of "circumlocution"
▶ Characterization of speaker
▶ Use of "one's own heart"
▶ Effect of "tantalize"
▶ Meaning of "laconic and luminous"

Paragraph 5

▶ Effects of using everyday examples
▶ Tone of "It must, it shall be undertaken to-day, and yet"
▶ Implications of "craving"

- ▶ Identification of what is "definite" and "indefinite"
- ▶ Identification of "substance . . . shadow"
- ▶ Meanings of "knell of our welfare" and "chanticleer-note"
- ▶ Irony
- ▶ Effects of change in elements of style (especially syntax and sentence length)

Paragraph 6

- ▶ Emotional impact of example
- ▶ Figurative use of "cloud"
- ▶ Literary allusion
- ▶ Use of "palpability"
- ▶ Figurative use of "chills the very marrow of our bones"—effect
- ▶ Effect of paradox in "delight of its horror"
- ▶ Cause and effect relationship
- ▶ Role of *"thought"*
- ▶ Structural use and effects of italics

Paragraphs 7 and 8

- ▶ Meaning of "Beyond or behind"
- ▶ Identification of the "archfiend"
- ▶ Implication of a silent auditor
- ▶ Speaker's current situation
- ▶ Meaning of "prolix"
- ▶ Effect of "victims" and "Imp"
- ▶ Foreshadowing of "good outcome"—his confession

Paragraphs 9 and 10

- ▶ Plot elements
- ▶ Meaning of "agency"
- ▶ Effect of "fancy" on characterization
- ▶ Effect of "impertinent"
- ▶ Characterization of speaker
- ▶ Use of language: "shadow of clue"
- ▶ Implications of "epoch"
- ▶ Relationship of "harassed" to "haunted"
- ▶ Use of analogy
- ▶ *Speaker's admission* that the murder was a sin

Paragraphs 11 and 12

- ▶ Tone ("sauntering")

- Irony and foreshadowing ("arrested myself")
- Implication of "a fit of petulance"
- Effect of "icy chill creep to my heart" (personification)
- Significance of use of analogy

Paragraph 13

- What occasioned his running
- Emphasis of "to *think*"
- The effect of simile
- What occasioned the chase
- Emphasis of *"then"*
- The effect of hyperbole
- Character revelation of secret bursting from soul

Paragraphs 14–16

- Effect of "They"
- Connotations of "pregnant"
- Contrast of "chains . . . fetterless"
- Meaning of "distinct enunciation"
- Speaker's reference to "hangman and to hell"
- Meaning of "To-day" and "To-morrow"
- Implications of *"here"* and *"but where?"*

This list is only a partial treatment of the many uses of the literary principles that contribute to the writer's style and that affect the meaning of the work. As you study through this list, see how many other uses of the literary principles are at work. Be sure to notice the changing moods of each individual paragraph. Notice how the character changes throughout the story as the speaker progresses to the point at which he begins to recognize the potential consequences beyond death for sins committed during life.

How Can You Use These Ideas in Your Writing?

At the heart of "The Imp of the Perverse" is character development and revelation.

The writer uses some of the obvious and expected ways to reveal character: connotative word choice, actions, and so forth. However, he also reveals character by using an unusual technique in a unexpected way: **prose rhythm.**

The first six paragraphs are lengthy and cumbersome with complex sentence structures. Paragraph 7 is shorter (a structural relief) and concludes the speaker's background discussion of "the spirit of the *Perverse.*" These first paragraphs are like a roller-coaster car going up the rails until it is just at the top. It pauses slightly in paragraphs 7 and 8; then the rapid, unstoppable descent begins as the speaker states "For weeks, for months, I pondered upon the means of the murder." By tiny paragraph 16, the readers are at the bottom of the hill, stunned and exhausted from the ride.

What makes this prose rhythm unusual is that it is not just a structural progression that builds the momentum for the readers, but also a progression of thought. Paragraphs 1–7 contain a complex psychological discussion that requires concentration and insight. At paragraph 8, however, the reader's attention is grabbed by the introduction of a new thought: Some silent auditor has asked the speaker to explain why he is "here." Where is "here"? Why is he wearing fetters? Questions begin to come to mind about the character of the speaker. Paragraph 8 gives the reader a sense of expectation, like that feeling when the car is pausing slightly at the top of the roller coaster and you know the ride is about to get frightening. He announces that he planned a murder. The ensuing story of that murder reveals the character of the speaker and propels the reader to the bottom of the ride where the speaker leaves his readers with a chilling question that lingers.

Lesson: You can develop prose rhythm in your writing through not only progressions of sentence and paragraph structure, but also through progressions of thought, ideas, and emotions. Be sure, however, to keep your audience and purpose in mind. Many of today's readers have limited reading time; therefore, the prose rhythms used in magazine and newspaper articles, for example, generally should propel readers into the mainstream of thought almost immediately. To illustrate, an article on skin cancer prevention might begin with an attention-getting anecdote of a happy ending situation and then begin to describe the hidden dangers progressively until it ends with a call for research and prevention measures.

Do you see any other ideas in this essay? You might want to consider identifying literary uses that you would avoid, such as use of vocabulary without context clues to meaning.

Examining a Sonnet

When I Consider How My Light Is Spent
by
John Milton

line   When I consider how my light is spent
Ere half my days, in this dark world and wide,
And that one talent which is death to hide
Lodged with me useless, though my soul more bent

(5)　To serve therewith my Maker, and present
　　　My true account, lest He returning chide.
　　　"Doth god exact day-labor, light denied?"
　　　I fondly ask. But Patience, to prevent
　　　That murmur, soon replies, "God doth not need
(10)　Either man's work or his own gifts; who best
　　　Bear His mild yoke, they serve Him best. His
　　　　state
　　　Is kingly. Thousands at His bidding speed
　　　And post o'er land and ocean without rest;
　　　They also serve who only stand and wait."
　　　　　(Note: John Milton was blind.)

Sometimes an analysis is a natural progression of ideas. By definition, a sonnet is a 14-line poem written in iambic pentameter. (See page 73.) Consequently, analysis of a sonnet can begin with determining the rhyme scheme *because the point at which the pattern changes may signal a shift in thought:*

Line 9 marks a change in end-rhyme:

Line 1	spent	a
Line 2	wide	b
Line 3	hide	b
Line 4	bent	a
Line 5	present	a
Line 6	chide	b
Line 7	denied	b
Line 8	prevent	a
Line 9	need	c
Line 10	best	d
Line 11	state	e
Line 12	speed	c
Line 13	rest	d
Line 14	wait	e

What changes occur? This two-part structure establishes changes from the following:

▶ Question ("Doth God exact day-labor, light denied?"—line 7) to answer ("God doth not need/Either man's work or his own gifts"—lines 9–10)

▶ Resistance ("my soul more bent"—line 4) to acceptance ("They also serve who only stand and wait"—line 14)

▶ Self-interest ("and present My true account, lest He

returning chide"—lines 5–6) to obedience ("who best/Bear His mild yoke, they serve Him best"—lines 10–11)

▶ Impatience ("When I consider how my light is spent/Ere half my days"—lines 1–2) to patience ("They also serve who only stand and wait"—line 14)

Change indicates possible contrasts. Do you see any? In the context of this poem, light comes to represent Milton's life ("Ere half my days"—line 1) as contrasted to a "dark world" of death, his sight itself as contrasted to the "dark world" of blindness, good (the means "to serve there with my Maker"—line 5) as contrasted to a dark work of evil (that does not serve), and knowledge (understanding) as contrasted to the "dark world" of ignorance.

Contrast can give clues to the intended meaning. What is the main point Milton is making? Whether speeding "o'er land and ocean" (line 13) or standing and waiting (line 14), whether blind or sighted, the best way to serve God is to obey Him in all circumstances (lines 10–11).

Once you have established the meaning, you can examine how the writer uses language to reinforce that meaning:

▶ The phrase "my light is spent" (line 1)—"Spent," as it is used here, can mean something being used up, worn out, tired out, or gone. "Light" can be symbolic of understanding, vision, or happiness.

▶ Personification of Patience (line 8)—Patience answers Milton's question to instruct him spiritually, an edifying role.

▶ "That one talent" (line 3)—"And that one talent" represents natural gifts, abilities, and sight itself that he would use in service. Both his sight and those abilities he would accomplish with and by means of his sight are "Lodged with me useless" (line 4). Line 3 is also an allusion to the "Parable of the Talents" in the Bible, in which the servant who buries his talent is cast into "outer darkness."

▶ "Day-labor" (line 7)—"Day-labor" is figurative, representing work or service (labor) that requires sight (day—the time when the sighted can see with the light).

How Can You Use These Ideas in Your Writing?

Meaning is at the center of a written work. After you have a clear statement of your meaning, the structure (whether in prose or poetry) should either support and explain that meaning or lead up to it as a natural conclusion. Consequently, your word choices (connotative meanings, figurative language, allusions, and so forth) should contribute to the tone that in turn further establishes the meaning. When preparing to write, begin with a clear statement of your intended meaning. What idea do you want to convey to your readers?

Do you see any other ideas in this poem? Consider the writer's use of contrast as a structural device. Turn to the writing discussion on page 355 for more insight into use of contrast in your own writing.

Examining a Lyric Poem
"The Song of the Shirt" by Thomas Hood

stanza

(1)   With fingers weary and worn,
      With eyelids heavy and red,
  A Woman sat, in unwomanly rags,
      Plying her needle and thread—
        Stitch! stitch! stitch!
  In poverty, hunger, and dirt,
  And still with a voice of dolorous pitch
  She sang the 'Song of the Shirt!'

(2)   'Work! work! work!
  While the cock is crowing aloof!
      And work—work—work,
  Till the stars shine through the roof!
  It's O! to be a slave
      Along with the barbarous Turk,
  Where woman has never a soul to save,
      If this is Christian work!

(3)   'Work—work—work
  Till the brain begins to swim,
      Work—work—work
  Till the eyes are heavy and dim!
  Seam, and gusset, and band,
      Band, and gusset, and seam,
  Till over the buttons I fall asleep,
      And sew them on in a dream!

(4)   'O, Men with Sisters dear!
      O, Men! with Mothers and Wives!
  It is not linen you're wearing out,
      But human creatures' lives!
      Stitch—stitch—stitch,
  In poverty, hunger, and dirt,
  Sewing at once, with a double thread,
      A Shroud as well as a Shirt.

(5)   'But why do I talk of Death?
      That Phantom of grisly bone,
I hardly fear his terrible shape,
      It seems so like my own—
      It seems so like my own,
      Because of the fasts I keep;
O God! that bread should be so dear,
      And flesh and blood so cheap!

(6)   'Work—work—work!
      My labour never flags;
And what are its wages? A bed of straw,
      A crust of bread—and, rags.
That shatter'd roof,—and this naked floor—
      A table—a broken chair—
And a wall so blank, my shadow I thank
      for sometimes falling there!

(7)   'Work—work—work!
From weary chime to chime,
      Work—work—work—
As prisoners work for crime!
      Band, and gusset, and seam,
      Seam, and gusset, and band,
Till the heart is sick, and the brain benumb'd,
      As well as the weary hand.

(8)   'Work—work—work,
In the dull December light,
      And work—work—work,
When the weather is warm and bright—
While underneath the eaves
      The brooding swallows cling,
As if to show me their sunny backs
      And twit me with the spring.

(9)   'O, but to breathe the breath
Of the cowslip and primrose sweet!—
      With the sky above my head,
And the grass beneath my feet;
For only one short hour
      To feel as I used to feel,
Before I knew the woes of want
      And the walk that costs a meal!

(10) 'O, but for one short hour!
A respite however brief!
No blessed leisure for Love or Hope,
      But only time for Grief!
A little weeping would ease my heart,
      But in their briny bed
My tears must stop, for every drop
      Hinders needle and thread!

(11) 'Seam, and gusset, and band,
    Band, and gusset, and seam,
      Work, work, work,
    Like the Engine that works by Steam!
    A mere machine of iron and wood
      That toils for Mammon's sake—
    Without a brain to ponder and craze
      Or a heart to feel—and break!'

(12) —With fingers weary and worn,
    With eyelids heavy and red,
    A Woman sat, in unwomanly rags,
      Plying her needle and thread—
      Stitch! stitch! stitch!
        In poverty, hunger, and dirt,
    And still with a voice of dolorous pitch,—
    Would that its tone could reach the Rich!—
    She sang this 'Song of the Shirt!'

Finding the meaning (What is the poem about?), narrative voice (What is the speaker's attitude? What is the woman's attitude?), and tone; these all need to be addressed. Of special note in this particular poem, however, is not just the language and the other literary principles but the *effects* of those uses.

A useful analysis method is to construct a cause-and-effect chart. The "cause" column lists the literary device, with the "effect" column describing its effect on such principles as the meaning and tone. Also, cause-and-effect charts, such as the following one, are useful for writers during the writing process.

Cause	*Effect*
First stanza (lines 1–8) • Alliteration of *w* and *s* • Repetition of *stitch* • Diction: "unwomanly"	A "chain-gang" rhythm that reinforces the sense of the monotony of the labor In stark contrast to the imagery of a "woman"
"dolorous pitch"	In contrast to what one would expect of a "Song of the Shirt"

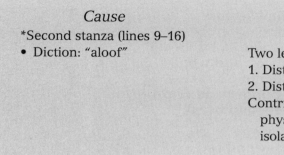

Cause	Effect

*Second stanza (lines 9–16)
• Diction: "aloof"
	Two levels of meaning:
	1. Distant in space
	2. Distant in feeling
	Contributing to a sense of
	    physical and emotional
	    isolation

*Notice that the speaker changes to the woman singing her song in the second stanza.

Continuing with the second stanza, what are the *effects* of these *causes?*

Cause	Effect

• Break in rhythm:
  "It's O!"
• Contrast of "barbarous
  Turk" to "Christian work"	

Hint: In her isolated state of continued work, with whom does she identify? What is the significance of "If"?

Third stanza (lines 17–24)

Cause	Effect
• Imagery: "the brain begins to swim" • Inverting "seam, and gusset, and band" • Sewing "in a dream"	

Now, you identify the cause-and-effect relationships in the remaining stanzas. Here are a few clues to important elements you might want to identify:

Fourth stanza: Addressing an auditor
                       Linen as a symbol

Fifth stanza:	Personification of death
Tenth stanza:	Tears in a "briny bed"
Eleventh stanza:	Simile
	Literary allusion: Mammon
	A brain that ponders and crazes
Twelfth stanza:	"the Rich"

Be sure to address this poem as a literary whole. What are the effects of the repetition of part of the first stanza in the last stanza? Do you see any overall (central) contrasts, themes, or progressions of ideas in the poem? The rich-poor contrast is obvious; however, look at stanza 9 for insight into the woman's change in circumstances. Also, you might want to examine the role of hope/hopelessness in stanza 10.

How Can You Use These Ideas in Your Writing?

Artists (in pictorial art) use a principle called chiaroscuro in which they use the arrangement of light against dark for a variety of effects. When writers paint pictures with words, they also can use contrasts (of words, sounds, meanings, ideas, forms). Contrasts can attract attention, provide transition, establish a point, disprove a position, or produce many other effects. These contrasts can be very direct and provide structure for an entire work, such as in "When I Consider How My Light Is Spent" (page 348) or subtle inferences as in "The Song of the Shirt."

For example, you might describe two geographic regions to shock readers concerning the poor water quality occurring naturally in local wells in contrast to wells in the other region. Readers could be comforted, however, to learn from your article that in contrast to the average community, your city does a superior job in water treatment. Contrasts can educate readers, such as when writers describe and explain by detailing what the item or process is *not*.

Not all contrasts are made directly. Connotations of certain words, word sounds, changes in rhythm, and different uses of figurative language can also produce shades of contrast that you can use to produce your desired effects.

Do you see any other ideas in "The Song of the Shirt"? Consider how symbolism is used; then, think about how you might use symbolic language in your writing.

Examining a Narrative Poem

The Lady of Shalott
by
Alfred, Lord Tennyson

PART I

On either side the river lie
Long fields of barley and of rye,
That clothe the wold and meet the sky;
And thro' the field the road runs by
    To many-tower'd Camelot;
And up and down the people go,
Gazing where the lilies blow
Round an island there below,
    The island of Shalott.

Willows whiten, aspens quiver,
Little breezes dusk and shiver
Thro' the wave that runs for ever
By the island in the river
    Flowing down to Camelot.
Four gray walls, and four gray towers,
Overlook a space of flowers,
And the silent isle imbowers
    The Lady of Shalott.

By the margin, willow-veil'd
Slide the heavy barges trail'd
By slow horses; and unhail'd
The shallop flitteth silken-sail'd
    Skimming down to Camelot:
But who hath seen her wave her hand?
Or at the casement seen her stand?
Or is she known in all the land,
    The Lady of Shalott?

Only reapers, reaping early
In among the bearded barley,
Hear a song that echoes cheerly
From the river winding clearly,
    Down to tower'd Camelot:
And by the moon the reaper weary,
Piling sheaves in uplands airy,
Listening, whispers, "Tis the fairy
    Lady of Shalott.'

PART II

There she weaves by night and day
A magic web with colours gay.
She has heard a whisper say,
A curse is on her if she stay
　　To look down to Camelot.
She knows not what the curse may be,
And so she weaveth steadily,
And little other care hath she,
　　The Lady of Shalott.

And moving thro' a mirror clear
That hangs before her all the year,
Shadows of the world appear.
There she sees the highway near
　　Winding down to Camelot:
There the river eddy whirls,
And there the surly village-churls,
And the red cloaks of market girls,
　　Pass onward from Shalott.

Sometimes a troop of damsels glad,
An abbot on an ambling pad,
Sometimes a curly shepherd-lad,
Or long-hair'd page in crimson clad,
　　Goes by to tower'd Camelot;
And sometimes thro' the mirror blue
The knights come riding two and two:
She hath no loyal knight and true,
　　The Lady of Shalott.

But in her web she still delights
To weave the mirror's magic sights,
For often thro' the silent nights
A funeral, with plumes and lights
　　And music, went to Camelot:
Or when the moon was overhead,
Came two young lovers lately wed;
'I am half sick of shadows,' said
　　The Lady of Shalott.

PART III

A BOW-SHOT from her bower-eaves,
He rode between the barley-sheaves,
The sun came dazzling thro' the leaves,

And flamed upon the brazen greaves
   Of bold Sir Lancelot.
A red-cross knight for ever kneel'd
   To a lady in his shield,
That sparkled on the yellow field,
   Beside remote Shalott.

The gemmy bridle glitter'd free,
Like to some branch of stars we see
Hung in the golden Galaxy.
The bridle bells rang merrily
   As he rode down to Camelot:
And from his blazon'd baldric slung
A mighty silver bugle hung,
And as he rode his armour rung,
   Beside remote Shalott.

All in the blue unclouded weather
Thick-jewell'd shone the saddle-leather,
The helmet and the helmet-feather
Burn'd like one burning flame together,
   As he rode down to Camelot.
As often thro' the purple night,
Below the starry clusters bright,
Some bearded meteor, trailing light,
   Moves over still Shalott.

His broad clear brow in sunlight glow'd;
On burnish'd hooves his war-horse trode;
From underneath his helmet flow'd
His coal-black curls as on he rode,
   As he rode down to Camelot.
From the bank and from the river
He flash'd into the crystal mirror,
   'Tirra lirra,' by the river
   Sang Sir Lancelot.

She left the web, she left the loom,
She made three paces thro' the room,
She saw the water-lily bloom,
She saw the helmet and the plume,
   She look'd down to Camelot.
Out flew the web and floated wide;
The mirror crack'd from side to side;
'The curse is come upon me,' cried
   The Lady of Shalott.

PART IV

In the stormy east-wind straining,
The pale yellow woods were waning,
The broad stream in his banks complaining,
Heavily the low sky raining
    Over tower'd Camelot;
Down she came and found a boat
Beneath a willow left afloat,
And round about the prow she wrote
    The Lady of Shalott.

And down the river's dim expanse
Like some bold seër in a trance,
Seeing all his own mischance—
With a glassy countenance
    Did she look to Camelot.
And at the closing of the day
She loosed the chain, and down she lay;
The broad stream bore her far away,
    The Lady of Shalott.

Lying, robed in snowy white
That loosely flew to left and right—
The leaves upon her falling light—
Thro' the noises of the night
    She floated down to Camelot:
And as the boat-head wound along
The willowy hills and fields among,
They heard her singing her last song,
    The Lady of Shalott.

Heard a carol, mournful, holy,
Chanted loudly, chanted lowly,
Till her blood was frozen slowly,
And her eyes were darken'd wholly,
    Turn'd to tower'd Camelot.
For ere she reach'd upon the tide
The first house by the water-side,
Singing in her song she died,
    The Lady of Shalott.

Under tower and balcony,
By garden-wall and gallery,
A gleaming shape she floated by,
Dead-pale between the houses high,

> Silent into Camelot.
> Out upon the wharfs they came,
> Knight and burgher, lord and dame,
> And round the prow they read her name,
>   *The Lady of Shalott.*
>
> Who is this? and what is here?
> And in the lighted palace near
> Died the sound of royal cheer;
> And they cross'd themselves for fear,
>   All the knights at Camelot:
> But Lancelot mused a little space;
> He said, 'She has a lovely face;
> God in his mercy lend her grace,
>   The Lady of Shalott.'

    An identification of the plot line is appropriate to understanding the meaning of a narrative work. As an illustration, the following analysis models a very simple approach to identifying the plot.

Exposition

Summary, Part I: Shalott is an island up-river of Camelot. The Lady of Shalott lives in a tower; people have not seen her, but know of her existence and have heard her sing.

Complication

Summary, Part II and Part III, Stanzas 1–4: Part II introduces the curse on the Lady of Shalott. She does not know what will happen; however, she does know that she must not look directly out the window toward Camelot. Consequently, she views the world through a mirror and spends her time weaving a magic web in patterns that she sees in her mirror. Part III heightens the complication when she sees Sir Lancelot reflected in her mirror as he goes riding to Camelot.

Climax

Summary, Part III, final stanza: She looks to Camelot and the curse begins.

Dénouement:

Summary, Part IV: After preparing a boat, she casts herself adrift, sings her last song, and dies before reaching the first house in

Camelot. Sir Lancelot, upon seeing her dead form, comments on her beauty.

For more information about plot structure, see page 46.

In examining this poem on a line-by-line basis, make special note of Tennyson's use of **syntax.** (See page 255 for syntax.) Syntax is especially crucial to the climactic stanza (Part III, stanza 5), in which the subject-action verb repetition adds drama to the moment: "She left . . . she left . . . She made . . . she saw . . . She look'd . . . ." Look at the second stanza of Part IV:

> **And down the river's dim expanse**
> **Like some bold seër in a trance,**
> **Seeing all his own mischance—**
> **With a glassy countenance**
> **Did she look to Camelot.**

Do you recognize the sentence structure used here? Its effect? This is a periodic sentence in which the main subject and verb ("she did look") come at the end of the sentence. Periodic sentences project a dramatic building of tension. (See page 256.)

Also, "Shalott" appears in the last line of *every* stanza *except* Stanza 4 of Part III, the last line before the climactic stanza. In this line, not "Shalott" but "Sir Lancelot" appears. What do you think is the significance of this to the poem's meaning?

What other uses of syntax can you find in this poem? What sad irony is at work?

How Can You Use These Ideas in Your Writing?

Syntax, word arrangement, contributes to rhythm, thought progression, and the overall "feeling" of a work, whether prose or poetry. Consider the following awareness exercise to help you discover your natural sense of syntax.

Select one of your works that is typical of your writing. Using a manageable portion (a paragraph, stanza, or entire article if short enough), make a chart identifying the following:

▶ The patterns of the parts of speech used
▶ Types of sentences (loose, periodic, parallel, balanced)
▶ The tenses of your verbs
▶ Independent versus dependent (subordinate) clauses

Is your syntax working for or against you? Consider your

audience and intended meaning; then, experiment with the syntax to see what effects are produced.

Do you see any other ideas in this poem? For example, how do you use ironic relationships in your writing?

Summary

When you read a selection analytically, you look for, identify, and attempt to understand how the writer is using the principles of literature. Also, you examine what effects are produced. Sometimes an analysis includes interpreting what you think the author means and/or expressing what you think the work means and your opinions regarding the work.

Developing analytical skills can help you be a more perceptive reader and expressive writer. However, like most skills, learning how to analyze written works requires experience. You can gain experience through using several different approaches, such as the "Questions to Apply Your Learning" sections that accompany each of the chapters on the five principles of literature in Part I. Another approach is to use the procedures listed in the "Quick Reference Guide" in the Appendix. The models provided in this chapter show you several ways you can analyze a reading selection and should encourage you to develop a variety of approaches that suit your needs.

Remember: The "best" way to analyze a work *varies* with each selection. Just be sure that you *do* address the five literary principles on at least three levels:

▶ *Identify the use of the principle.*
▶ *Recognize the effects of that use.*
▶ *Examine ways the literary principles interact within the work.*

Analysis Skills Are Valuable to You in Your Own Writing

At the prewriting stage, you can use the principles of literature to decide upon the form, develop a statement of intended meaning, identify your speaker (his or her attitudes and so forth), summarize *your* attitudes, and decide upon a setting that projects your intended tone. In other words, you can develop a literary principle-based writing plan.

During writing, you can use the prewriting decisions as a

working guide to keep the principles in focus. As you develop a character, for example, you may find that your setting (because of changes in the character) is now in conflict with the changing tone. Will the setting still work or do you need to remove the character to another location? Perhaps the contrast of the setting to the new tone projected by the character is working, or perhaps you need to abandon that setting and begin again.

After writing, do a quality check of your product against your plan. Maybe you ran into unforeseen problems that required you to change your initial prewriting decisions. If these changes work, fine. If not, revise accordingly. Do not focus just on the structural parts. Also, examine your work as a whole. Does it accomplish what you want?

A talented, "natural-born writer" uses the literary principles, regardless of whether he or she can or does recognize them as such. This situation is much the same as a singer who sings the correct notes but may not be able to read music. However, for those developing their writing skills or readers writing a literary analysis or book review, terms and principles are available and serve to improve the communication of the reader-writer synergy. The goal is to use the principles effectively in your writing.

Analytical Reading Is Also an Attitude, a Frame of Mind

Once you learn the basics of analysis, you can apply the principles to *anything* you read and write. As a result, when you read a magazine article, your mind should be alert for answers to such questions as "What does the writer mean by this?" "Who is speaking here?" "Is this point valid?" "How is this organized and what can I expect?" "What is the author implying by using this or that word?" Analytical thinking may gradually become second nature to you by using this approach.

Writing a Book Review

Writing a book review gives you an ideal opportunity to combine your reading and writing skills to your advantage. Unlike high school book reports that were supposed to prove to your teacher that you *really had* read the assigned book and understood it, book reviews have a different form and purpose.

Background Information

Of the major types of written book evaluations (literary analysis papers, literary essays, critical reviews, critical essays, book reviews, book reports), book reviews occupy a middle-of-the-road position. On one side are literary analysis papers and essays (described on page 324). These evaluations are in-depth examinations on a scholarly basis. (The terms *critical review* and *critical essay* will be discussed on page 377.) On the other side are book reports, a more elementary form. Book reports do not evaluate the book except on a basic level and generally emphasize, for example, a paraphrasing or retelling of the story when the work is narrative. The book review, in contrast, evaluates a book's merits for the average reader within the projected audience for that particular type of book. It contains some elements of literary analysis, expressed in ways that are helpful to the targeted readers. A book review also may include some paraphrasing, but only enough to gain the reader's interest.

Submitting book reviews to newspapers and magazines, especially if you become a regular contributor, can add a new, interactive perspective to your writing activities. Also, you will find that learning to write book reviews can train you to think and read critically and to express your thinking in a clear, concise manner.

When you write a book review, your purpose is to inform your readers about the strengths and weaknesses of a book. Many readers look to reviewers to help them decide what books would be interesting to read. Consequently, publishers and writers generally take reviews seriously.

To be judged fairly, a book should be examined from two different perspectives:

▶ The purpose of the book
▶ The expectations of the readers

What Is the Purpose of the Book?

The answer to this question will dictate the form, tone, and style of the book. If the purpose of a book is to entertain, for example, then the form, tone, and style should serve that purpose. *How* the book entertains is in the hands of the writer. If the purpose clearly is to entertain, to fault a book because the tone is frivolous or the writing style sounds "tongue-in-cheek" might be an unfair judgment.

What Are the Expectations of the Readers?

Each genre of book comes with a body of conventions in the minds of the readers. In other words, readers have expectations about what certain types of books should contain. You *expect* a romance to have love scenes. What would a mystery be without clues for readers to follow? Science fiction readers might look for aliens in space stories, and adventure-story enthusiasts might expect a bold writing style with plenty of action scenes. Reader expectations are not static, but change with society, current trends, and technological advancements.

A book review updates readers on how well the writer crafted the book to serve its purpose and whether the book will meet with the readers' expectations. *Consequently, a book reviewer needs to understand the purpose of the book being reviewed and keep current so he or she can anticipate reader expectations.* (See "The Effects of Understanding the Literary Principles," page 324, and "What Is a Literary Analysis?" page 319.)

Sometimes a book not only fails to meet reader expectations, but actually conflicts with them, such as subjects considered inappropriate for comic forms. Also, readers may react when a writer tries something new or unexpected within a literary form. For example, as reported in the October 4, 1999, issue of *Newsweek*, biographer Edmund Morris's unusual use of fictional narrator in his book *Dutch: A Memoir of Ronald Reagan* was met with debate among reviewers and confusion on the part of readers at the time of its release.

Do You Need to Know Literary Terms?

Suppose, for example, you own an antique truck and begin working under the hood on its engine because some parts are not working properly. You pick up the telephone and call or send an e-mail to someone knowledgeable for advice about truck engines. If you do not know the names of the parts, how will you be able to ask questions and understand the answers? Likewise, a knowledge of basic literary terms allows critics, readers, and writers to discuss works of literature with some degree of common knowledge and understanding.

The Fundamentals of a Book Review

Styles, of course, can vary. The following seven-step method, however, incorporates the fundamentals of developing a book review and can be adapted to suit your situation.

Step 1. Read a Wide Variety of Book Reviews.

You can learn a lot about writing by reading book reviews.

> **To prepare for writing book reviews,** read some recently published book reviews (in newspapers and magazines) to learn how book reviews are structured, the types of books being reviewed, and any current trends of thought among book reviewers.

> **To improve your own writing,** read both recent and historical reviews (found in libraries) to gain perspective and to learn valuable lessons about writing.

Gain Perspective

For many people, a book receives either a "good review" that rec-
ommends it to readers or a "bad review" that extensively criticizes
the book. Some reviewers have gained reputations for their quick
wit and scathing comments, becoming adept at finding flaws that
may (or may not) exist in a work. The cutting tones and forcefully
stated opinions of such reviews often elicit (because of their shock
value and elements of sensationalism) a variety of reader responses,
ranging from agreement to outrage. Surprisingly, extremely negative reviews can sometimes generate greater interest in a book than
it might otherwise attract, thus increasing the numbers of readers.

One thing you can learn from reading such reviews is that a
"bad" review can happen to any writer, no matter how famous or
popular. If you receive a bad review for something you have written, keep the review in perspective. Remember the following
points:

- ▶ A review is based on the opinions of one person who may,
  or may not, be knowledgeable, fair, and accurate in his or
  her judgment.
- ▶ Generally speaking, reviewers want to help their readers
  better understand works and make informed choices.
  However, reviewers usually must follow guidelines. In addition, some reviewers have established or are trying to
  establish reputations concerning attitudes and styles.
- ▶ Reviewers do not always agree with one another. One person's "classic" is another's "worst book of the century."

Finally, examine the negative points as carefully and objectively as possible. Are the comments valid? If you can state objectively why they are not, you have gained writing skill because your
close examination of your work reinforces and helps you clarify
your own thinking. If, on the other hand, the comments are valid,
your writing should improve because you probably will strive not
to repeat your mistakes.

Learn Valuable Lessons

You can learn from other writers' mistakes. If you study both historical and modern reviews carefully, you can learn what uses of
the principles of literature are praised and what uses are criticized
and spot mistakes to avoid in your own writing.

To illustrate this point, excerpts from Samuel Langhorne Clemens's (a.k.a. Mark Twain) review of James Fenimore Cooper's *Deerslayer* and *The Pathfinder* follow. This review illustrates how you can spot timeless ideas and principles in historical reviews to help you improve your own writing today. This review was published in the July 1895, *North American Review*.

Fenimore Cooper's Literary Offenses

The Pathfinder and The Deerslayer stand at the head of Cooper's novels as artistic creations. . . .

. . .They were pure works of art.

Prof. Lounsbury

The five tales reveal an extraordinary fullness of invention. . . .One of the very greatest characters in fiction, Natty Bumppo. . . .

Prof. Brander Matthews

Cooper is the greatest artist in the domain of romantic fiction yet produced by America.

Wilkie Collins

It seems to me that it was far from right for the Professor of English Literature in Yale, the Professor of English Literature in Columbia, and Wilkie Collins to deliver opinions on Cooper's literature without having read some of it. . . .

Lesson 1. Reviewers Can Be Light Years Apart in Their Opinions.

Notice that Twain quotes three other reviewers who give glowing descriptions of Cooper's abilities as a writer and the quality of *Deerslayer*. In direct opposition, Twain begins his negative review by disagreeing with the other reviewers. Readers and writers need to remember that regardless of the views expressed, a review is only one person's opinion.

Lesson 2. Use Superlatives with Caution.

Did you notice the other reviewers' use of superlatives in describing Cooper's work? ("very greatest characters," "the greatest artist") Superlatives are easy to attack and may be difficult to defend.

> Cooper's art has some defects. In one place in *Deerslayer,* and in the restricted space of two-thirds of a page, Cooper has scored 114 offenses against literary art out of a possible 115. It breaks the record.
> There are nineteen rules governing literary art in the domain of romantic fiction—some say twenty-two. In *Deerslayer* Cooper violated eighteen of them. These eighteen require: . . .

Lesson 3. *The Principles of Good Writing Are Timeless*.

Twain lists and describes eighteen requirements:

> 1. That a tale shall accomplish something and arrive somewhere. . . .
> 2. They require that the episodes of a tale shall be necessary parts of the tale and shall help to develop it. . . .
> 3. . . .
> 4. They require that the personages in a tale, both dead and alive, shall exhibit a sufficient excuse for being there. . . .
> 5. They require that when the personages of a tale deal in conversation, the talk shall sound like human talk,. . . in the given circumstances, and have a discoverable meaning, . . . purpose and a show of relevancy, and remain in the neighborhood of the subject in hand, and be interesting to the reader, and help out the tale, and stop when the people cannot think of anything more to say. . . .
> 6. . . . 7. . . . 8. . . . 9. . . . .
> 10. They require that the author shall make the reader feel a deep interest in the personages of his tale and in their fate . . . .
> 11. They require that the characters in a tale shall be so clearly defined that the reader can tell beforehand what each will do in a given emergency . . . .
> 12. *Say* what he is proposing to say, not merely come near it.
> 13. Use the right word, not its second cousin.
> 14. Eschew surplusage.
> 15. Not omit necessary details.
> 16. Avoid slovenliness of form.

17. Use good grammar.
18. Employ a simple and strightforward style.

The preceding excerpts selected from Twain's list include principles of good writing that are timeless; they apply today with as much validity as in the generations past.

> Cooper's gift in the way of invention was not a rich endowment. . . . In his little box of stage-properties he kept six or eight cunning devices, tricks, artifices for his savages and woodsmen to deceive and circumvent each other with, ... A favorite one was to make a moccasined person tread in the tracks of the moccasined enemy, . . . Cooper wore out barrels and barrels of moccasins in working that trick. Another stage-property that he pulled out of his box pretty frequently was his broken twig. . . . In fact, the Leatherstocking Series ought to have been called the Broken Twig Series.
> . . . For several years Cooper was daily in the society of artillery and he ought to have noticed that when a cannon-ball strikes the ground it either buries itself or skips a hundred feet or so, skips again a hundred feet or so, and so on till finally it gets tired and rolls. . . . If Cooper had any real knowledge of Nature's ways of doing things, he had a most delicate art in concealing the fact. . . .—no, even the eternal laws of Nature have to vacate when Cooper wants to put up a delicate job of woodcraft on the reader.

Lesson 4. Know Your Subject.

Twain spotted problems with Cooper's knowledge of his subject, such as how a cannon-ball rolls, mistakes that damage the credibility of the writing. A writer needs to do the research necessary to make the work believable.

Lesson 5. Do Not Overuse or Contrive the Use of Any Given Literary Devices.

Notice Twain's objection to Cooper's overuse of moccasin trails and contrived uses of broken twigs. Today, you can probably make a long list of overused, contrived devices in television sitcoms and dramas: "chance" encounters that you know will happen, a flat tire that leaves the young couple stranded near a monster-filled forest, the song that signals a flashback is coming, and poorly constructed flashbacks that are confusing. Repeatedly relying on devices that have worked in the past or manipulating circumstances as an "easy way out" for a problem in plot structure may be tempting, but also can lead to stories that lack interest because they are too predictable with incidences that are too coincidental.

> **The reader will find some examples of Cooper's high talent for inaccurate observation in the account of the shooting-match in *The Pathfinder*.**

> *A common wrought nail was driven lightly into the target, its head having been first touched with paint.*

> **The color of the paint is not stated—an important omission, . . . for this nail-head is a *hundred yards from* the marksmen and could not be seen by them at that distance, no matter what its color might be.**

Lesson 6. Pay Attention to Details, Especially Those That Affect the Work's Credibility/Validity.

Contrary to the popular saying "Don't sweat the small stuff," a writer should pay close attention to all details that might compromise the work. See "A Validity Checklist" on page 110.

> **. . . He even failed to notice that the man who talks corrupt English six days in the week must and will talk it on the seventh, and can't help himself. In the *Deerslayer* story he lets Deerslayer talk the showiest kind of book-talk sometimes, and at other times the basest of base dialects.**

Lesson 7. Dialogue Must Be Consistent to Setting and Character.

Here Twain is pointing out a problem in character development. For characters to be believable, their speech patterns must be consistent with their background. Also, as discussed on page 196, for character to change (including speech patterns), there needs to be sufficient time, motivation, or some other factor that makes the change seem possible.

Lesson 8. You Do Not Have to Agree with Every Point Made By a Reviewer.

Reexamine Twain's comment concerning a character's speech patterns. Circumstances vary. For example, have you ever listened to someone who adjusts his or her speech pattern to suit the audience? A speaker might use formal English when addressing a large group, but use informal and colloquial English (including slang) when relaxing at home with family and friends.

> **Cooper's word-sense was singularly dull. When a person has a poor ear for music he will flat and sharp right along without knowing it. He keeps near the tune, but it is *not* the tune. . . . you perceive what he is intending to say but you also perceive that he doesn't say it. This is Cooper. He was not a word-musician. His ear was satisfied with the *approximate* word. . . .**

Lesson 9. Consider the Tone of Words (Both Sound and Meaning), Not Only in Poetry, but Also in Prose.

Stories are intended to create images in the mind. Consequently, the words in a story need to have a tone that "sounds" right, yet the words also must have precise meanings.

Lesson 10. The Principles of Literature Provide Guidelines for Readers and Writers, but the Reviewer's Opinion Is Subjective.

You do not have to agree with a reviewer's opinion concerning whether a writer has or has not successfully used the principles of literature. You may, for example, have an entirely different view of Cooper's skill in writing *The Pathfinder* and *Deerslayer*.

Step 2. Select a Newspaper or Periodical.

Once you have a general sense of what is being done in the field of book reviews, select a newspaper or magazine that regularly features book reviews written by freelance writers. Do not overlook the small-town newspapers and smaller periodicals that welcome book reviews.

After selecting a publication, write to the appropriate editor and request guidelines for submitting book reviews. Finally, conclude Step 2 by collecting and studying a sampling of reviews that have already been published by the newspaper or periodical. Make note of types of books reviewed, approaches, patterns—anything that might help your review fit into the slant already established by the publication.

Step 3. Read the Book.

Upon receipt of guidelines from the editor, you should begin your review by reading the book for pleasure. Sit in your favorite quiet place, relax, and enjoy. As you read, make note of your first impressions. After you have completed this "getting-to-know-you" stage with the book, take a moment to write just a few lines summarizing your overall impressions.

Step 4. Reread and Analyze.

Now you will begin collecting and developing the specific body of information you need to draw upon for actually writing the review.

Form (See page 40.)

Look at the book for overall effect. What is the genre? If, for example, the book is a biography, what are your expectations of a biography's form? Is the book graphically suited to the subject and, at the same time, reader friendly? What do you expect to find? Photographs of the subject? A timeline of his or her life? Is there an index? Is an index helpful or necessary? These considerations will vary with the genre.

Toward Writing the Review

The contents of the book will depend upon the genre and may include, as appropriate:

- ▶ Cover design (Is it appealing and suited to the genre and subject?)
- ▶ Readability of print (Look at type size and style and at white space on pages.)
- ▶ Contents Page (Is it easy to use?)
- ▶ Graphic illustrations/photographs (Are they interesting, clear, appropriate?)
- ▶ Index (Is it complete, useful? If none is included, would an index be helpful?)
- ▶ Logical chapter/section divisions and use of organization principles (Check for logical divisions and progressions of thought.)

- ▶ Use of footnotes or textual notes (Are they easy to follow and do they suit the format?)
- ▶ Preface/Introduction (Does it set the stage for the material that follows?)
- ▶ Concluding section (Does it give you a sense of closure?)

Meaning (See page 25.)

Identify the purpose of the work. Of course you should be able to identify and state the work's subject, theme, and/or literal meaning. Beyond that, however, see if you can spot any other meanings (allegorical, symbolic, figurative) for the work, as appropriate.

Dividing the work into sections, can you paraphrase its meaning?

Toward Writing the Review

Make a judgment call concerning the meaning of the work. Has the writer communicated his or her meaning well, or does the work lack a clearly expressed meaning? Be able to cite specific examples or a logical basis for your opinion concerning the work's meaning. Remember that meaning can be expressed directly or indirectly.

Voice and Tone (See page 116.)

Are the attitudes revealed convincingly presented? Do you agree with or share the attitudes expressed and the opinions upon which they are based?

Toward Writing the Review

- ▶ Decide upon the effectiveness of the writer's handling of voice in relation to tone. Determine the point(s) of view, the speaker(s), and all major attitudes expressed (either directly through statements made or indirectly through the tone and those elements that contribute to the tone). Remember that attitudes can be expressed by the speaker, the author, and characters.
- ▶ Evaluate the overall tone of the work. Identify what you think the overall tone is (such as bold, amusing, embittered, tranquil, and so forth). Then see if any of the following work toward or detract from that tone: the subject, denotative or connotative word choices, syntax and diction, the

sound (prose rhythms and the sound of the words used), and the setting (if involved).

▶ Is the style of writing appropriate to the audience? Keep in mind such factors as age and interests.

Character(ization) (See page 174.)

Character involves two distinct levels:

1. A *character* can be defined as a person, including his or her traits or characteristics. This definition involves *characterizations* as the methods used to reveal the character's personality.

2. *Character* can also be defined as the distinguishable features of a written work, place, or thing. *Characterization* is a statement that summarizes the qualities or features that give the work (place or thing) its "character": "The story can be characterized as . . . ."

Toward Writing the Review

▶ Identify the major and minor characters (as appropriate). Then select the main character and briefly sketch a character analysis, using the information about character on pages 174–181. Look at the effectiveness of the writer's revealment of character. Can you spot any strengths or weaknesses in the characterizations?

▶ What are the distinguishable features of the work as a whole? Make a statement that, in your opinion, characterizes the work. For example, "This biography can be characterized as an attempt to provide new insight into the woman's life by dramatizing her years prior to taking public office."

Language (Uses and Meanings) (See page 203.)

Figurative language, diction, syntax, denotations, connotations, implications, even a writer's selection of what verb tense to use and whether the writing is in the active or passive voice contribute significantly to the effects the work has on the reader.

Toward Writing the Review

Systematically look at the language used in the work, using Chapter 5 for reference. Make a list of those elements of language use that are outstanding. Make note of those that in any way detract from the work. For example, does the writer overuse passive voice, lessening the impact of the action? Perhaps the syntax is a strength in the writing. Include some examples.

Step 5. Identify the Author.

Check the brief biographical sketch of the author (usually found on the back jacket cover of the book). Try to find any other biographical information you can that might relate to his or her writing the book. Can you discover any of the circumstances under which the work was written? Has the writer given interviews or written articles explaining motivation for writing the book, how the idea came about, or perhaps the purpose in writing it?

Step 6. Establish a Context.

▶ Determine the audience. For whom is the book written? Is it a romance aimed at junior high school girls or is it a political analysis written for professional women and men of the baby-boomer generation? Has the writer effectively aimed the writing at the audience?

▶ Examine the contemporary expectations of the work. Naturally, if the work were written during, for example, the English Romantic Period, it would have to be judged based upon the standards and expectations of that historical period. The same principle applies to today's works. How does the work fit into recent trends in writing? Does it take an outdated approach? Is it too "trendy"? Would you say that it is on the cutting edge? These questions should lead you to examine both the form and the content of the book.

▶ Before writing your own review, look at what other critics and reviewers have said or written about the book (if available). Because, by this point, you should have already established your own opinions based on solid evidence, a look at other reviews should help you gain new perspectives and/or reinforce your thinking without compromising your position as a reviewer. This step can be valuable as you find yourself agreeing or disagreeing with the views expressed; however, *your review should express your opinions.* Also consider asking someone else to read the book and share impressions with you. Did he or she like it? Why?

Step 7. Write Your Review.

The guidelines from the publisher that you received during Step 2 and the study you made of other reviews written for that publisher will help you determine the form and tone of your review.

A review or criticism? A rose by any other name. . . has just as many thorns.

You may discover in your preparation that some editors and writers refer to *book reviews,* some to *critical reviews,* and others to *critical essays.* What are the differences among these three forms? In a perfect situation, each term would be defined absolutely with concrete guidelines for how to write each, and everyone would adhere to those definitions and procedures exactly. Meanwhile, in the real world, practice has made these terms just another part of the body of writing jargon. Sometimes they are used precisely, with each used to mean a specific type of review. At other times, however, they are used interchangeably.

Very generally speaking, book reviews deal with currently published books, evaluated for their popular appeal for the purpose of acquainting readers with the book and influencing them on whether they should read it. Consequently, book reviews are of vital interest to everyone who has a financial interest in the success of a book. In contrast, critical reviews look at more scholarly works, are written for the purposes of stimulating discussion among literary scholars, and are published in literary journals. Critical essays may or may not be published and also are aimed at scholarly literary discussion. However, these definitions are not universally used. You will find scholarly journals with a "book review" section, for example. In some circumstances, a "reviewer" refers to one who writes reviews of popular works for newspapers and magazines; and a "critic" is a literary scholar who reviews works for their literary merits over their commercial value and general appeal.

Basic Elements of a Book Review

Book reviews, critical reviews, and critical essays, depending upon the style and guidelines of the editor and expectations of the readers, may contain combinations of some of the following elements:

- **A brief overview of the book** The overview might include one or more descriptive, summary statements concerning the book's physical appearance (if unique) and/or contents. The overview may identify the book's theme (or purpose) and how the author handles the theme or meets the purpose.
- **Statements that either directly address or allude to the quality of the book** These statements may be part of the overview of the book as a whole or be interlaced throughout the review, as different key features are discussed.
- **Biographical information about the author** Readers sometimes are curious about writers. For example, the region the author lives in might relate directly to the work and be of interest to readers.
- **A comparison/contrast to other similar works** Here you will look at such elements as style, approach, scope, readability. Identify how the book excels or falls short of expectations when compared to other books on the market that are written in the same genre.
- **Opinions and comments from a personal perspective** These statements may include such things as a personal anecdote that in some way relates to the book or simply a description of how the book affects you as an individual.

In addition to these major elements, book reviews can include:

- Brief quotations from the work as illustrations
- Use of literary jargon (usually if aimed at a scholarly audience)
- Observations concerning public reaction to the book
- Evaluation of the book's timeliness
- A reality check of the book's accuracy and completeness

Some Do's and Don'ts

Do use a professional tone when expressing opinion.
   Don't make unsubstantiated criticisms regardless of how witty they may sound.

Do use a style suitable to your readers.
   Don't use professional jargon unless your audience is in the profession. For example, if you are reviewing a book on airplanes for a flying magazine, your audience probably will understand such terms as *aileron* (a movable part of an airplane wing); however, if the review is for a general circulation newspaper, avoid such terms unless you define them. Is the book aimed at pilots or the general public? If it is for the general reader, you might want to examine the author's use of professional jargon. Has he or she explained the terms adequately for the audience? Your comments concerning the book's readability in regard to jargon might be very helpful to readers. Also, how you discuss the writer's use of the principles of literature will depend upon the makeup of your audience. Is your review a scholarly literary discussion? Then include literary terms as needed. Use such terms judiciously, however, in a general circulation newspaper.

Do use brief quotes to illustrate your points.
   Don't give away the plot.

Do give enough detail to represent the book fairly.
   Don't generalize or use superlatives. For example, avoid such generalizations as "Everyone loves his style" or such superlatives as "This is the best book ever written on this subject."

A Book Review Should Be a Useful Tool for the Reader

Ways to Organize a Book Review

With this distinct purpose in mind, following are just a few of the structural ways a review might be organized. These are based on actual reviews.

▶ Book Being Reviewed: A collection of short stories.

Paragraph 1: Introduces the title, author's name, and type of book (a collection of short stories) being reviewed.

Paragraph 2: Makes a general statement of the theme that binds the stories together (or a comment concerning the lack thereof).

Paragraph 3: Introduces title of first story and describes main characters and subject. Compares approach to previous works by author.

Middle: Briefly touches on other stories, summarizing without revealing climax.

Conclusion: Establishes some of the book's strengths. Postulates possible causes of its main weakness.

▶ Book Being Reviewed: Nonfiction account of historical event.

Paragraph 1: Links historical event to attitudes or events today, making readers care about subject of the book.

Paragraph 2: Describes historical event's main significance.

Paragraph 3: Introduces title of book and author's name.

Middle: Summarizes event's highlights as presented in the book.

Conclusion: Describes dramatic moment of the event and ends with a general statement of the book's length, style, and value to readers.

▶ Book Being Reviewed: Memoir.

Paragraph 1: Consists of brief, dramatic quote that introduces speaker.

Paragraph 2: Establishes main character, setting, and situation.

Middle: Describes plot to turning point in speaker's life. Comments concerning readability. Makes observations, such as that readers will learn to care about the people in the book.

Conclusion: Summarizes author's writing background and current biographical information, including marriage and occupation.

▶ Book Being Reviewed: Historical biography of well-known figure.

Beginning paragraph: Points out popular conceptions about subject of biography, then makes statement about how this biographer reveals new information and takes a new slant.
Middle: Describes highlights of the book.
Conclusion: Expresses opinion concerning whether author's treatment of subject is fresh and interesting.

As you can see, book reviews can be very simple in their construction, but still give readers insight about the book.

Common Writing Mistakes

When reviewing a book, watch for these common misuses of the principles of literature and the possible effects.

Errors in Meaning

▶ The writer's purpose is not clear.

Result: Readers come away asking "What was *that* all about?"

▶ The approach is boring.

Result: There is no emotional impact on readers or the work is not "impressive." (This is especially important if the topic or theme is one that has been overworked.)

> ▶ The writer fails to help the readers make a connection with the subject.

Result: Readers do not care about the subject.

Errors in Form

▶ The work lacks organization.

Result: Confusion for the readers.

▶ The writing violates or falls short of the reader's expectations for that genre.

Result: Confusion and a sense of dissatisfaction, such as when a drama lacks sufficient conflict to justify the consequences presented.

▶ The work contains elements of faulty reasoning, logical fallacies, distortion and misinformation, inconsistency of thought, and so forth.

Result: Readers question the validity of the work and the credibility of the writer.

Note: Be sure to read "A Validity Checklist" on page 110 for examples of ambiguous thinking and distortions of fact to watch for in your reading and writing.

Errors in Voice and Tone

▶ The story suddenly changes point of view, narrators, or the narrator's role without sufficient transition.

Result: Confusion for the readers.

▶ The writer misuses panoramic or scenic methods.

Result: Effects can range from confusion to boredom.

▶ The writer's attitude is at odds with the evidence presented.

Result: The author's credibility comes into question.

▶ The tone shifts without transition or justification.

Result: A "jarring" feeling of dissatisfaction for the reader.

▶ The sound of the language (prose rhythm) conflicts with the subject and projects a dissonant tone.

Result: Distraction that detracts from the meaning of the work.

▶ The setting creates a tone (mood, feeling, atmosphere) that is at odds with some other aspect of the work.

Result: The reader detects an unwanted sense of unreality.

▶ The writing style is not appropriate to the subject and/or the audience.

Result: Readers might feel confused or offended.

Errors in Character

▶ The writer fails to develop the characters' attitudes, emotions, response mechanisms, and intrinsic values, causing them to be flat rather than round characters.

Result: The story lacks realism, and readers do not learn to care about the characters.

▶ The story is overloaded with stock, type, or stereotypical characters.

Result: A boring, unbelievable story.

▶ A character undergoes change in personality without sufficient probable motivation or a realistic amount of time.

Result: Readers fail to connect with characters.

Errors in Language (Use and Meaning)

▶ The work contains technical errors in language, such as anachronisms (violations of time and space) and malapropisms (words inappropriate to context).

Result: These mistakes damage the work's validity.

▶ The work contains obscure figures of speech.

Result: Confusion over meaning.

▶ The language (diction and syntax) used by a character is inappropriate to his or her education, background, and region.

Result: The character becomes unbelievable.

▶ The language used carries with it connotations that do not fit the circumstances.

Result: Such connotations can make readers feel confused or offended.

▶ The work contains overuse of general, abstract (rather than specific, concrete) descriptors and passive (rather than active) verbs.

Result: Dull writing.

By studying Part I of this book and by drawing upon your own reading experiences, what other common writing mistakes can you add to this list?

A Sample Book Review

A Brief Review of *Beauty*

Even if you have seen the movie of Susan Wilson's *Beauty* (Crown Publishers, Inc.) with *Northern Exposure's* Janine Turner in the leading role, you can expect something different when you read the book. The movie version's feel-good conclusion stops short of the ending that gives *Beauty* its deeper meaning and makes Wilson's modern version of the *Beauty and the Beast* tale more than just another pretty face.

Circumstances throw Leland Crompton, a wealthy recluse deformed by advanced acromegaly, and Alix Miller, a talented portrait painter, together in Crompton's mountain home. In the main body of the book, Alix tells the story of how their relationship begins, grows, and undergoes the struggles you might expect of two people learning to see and love inner beauty despite physical and societal ugliness. Alix's love story does, however, contain a few surprises. Wilson handles the illness and eventual death of Alix's father with descriptive detail that helps readers form an emotional bond with Alix and greater understanding of Lee. Also, Wilson skillfully weaves the Beauty/Beast contrast throughout the book. The setting is the dangerous, cold beauty of rugged mountains. Alix's handsome, but selfish boyfriend makes Lee even more desirable. Perhaps the most intriguing contrast is in Alix's own personality. Alix's dialogue and actions at points are too coarse for idealized Beauty. Her thoughts, in contrast, reveal sophisticated vocabulary and emotional insight expected of Beauty in a fairy tale.

The comfortable size to hold, short length, and traditional romantic elements make this book ideal to curl up with at bedtime. However, don't nod off too soon. The real message of this book comes at the end when Lee takes over from Alix as the narrator of their story. The conclusion is unexpected, thought provoking, and sets the story apart.

In the language of his day, Edgar Allan Poe wrote that he liked a story that is short, with vivid effects and a conclusion that goes beyond what readers expect, endings that touch the soul. He believed that of Passion, Truth, and Beauty, only Beauty can bring a soul to tears. Poe probably would have liked Susan Wilson's *Beauty*.

Appendix
A Quick Reference Guide
to the Five Literary Principles

Definitions

Meaning involves the subject, theme, and purpose of a work on literal and figurative levels, as well as the *effects* of the work on the reader.

Form is the genre, organization, sequence, and structure of a work.

Voice includes the identities of the speaker, author, characters, and the attitudes or perspectives of each. **Tone** (of voice) is how the speaker and characters sound (playful, serious, angry); the "atmosphere" projected by the subject, setting, and author's style; and how these elements combine to project a feeling from the entire work that produces an *effect* on the reader.

Character involves the people in a work and the means by which their attitudes, emotions, response mechanisms, and intrinsic values are revealed to the reader (a characterization). In addition, places, things, and literary works can have character. A written work is characterized by a description of its distinguishing features.

Language (Uses and Meanings) involves the use of figurative language, imagery, and diction to produce an effect and how the context affects and is affected by denotation and connotation of words.

Uses

When reading a selection for **meaning**, determine:

1. Purpose (descriptive/expressive, expository/informative, narrative, or argumentative/persuasive)

2. Effect (such as the work is entertaining, disturbing, interesting)

3. Literal meaning
   a. State the subject in a word or phrase.
   b. State the theme/thesis or hook in one sentence.
   c. Paraphrase each logical division (paragraph, subsection, stanza).

4. Any other possible levels of meaning, such as allegorical, symbolic, figurative

When reading a selection for **form**, determine:

1. Basic form (prose, poetry, or drama)

2. Method(s) of organization used (analogy, cause and effect, comparison/contrast, definition, description, analysis and classification, example, induction, deduction, narration, process analysis, or other)

3. Sequence used (chronological, climactic, deductive, inductive, problem-solving, spatial, topical, mixed, or other)

4. Nonfiction prose genre, such as essay (formal, informal), (auto) biography, criticism, informational, or other

5. Prose narrative by length (novel, novelette, short story, anecdote, or other)

6. Prose structure
   a. Outline nonfiction prose.
   b. Plotline prose narrative.

7. Prose narrative effects (tragedy, comedy, satire, romance, realism, or other)

8. Prose narrative genre, such as picaresque, stream of consciousness, bildungsroman, regional, social, detective, novel of character (incident, manners, sensibility,

the soil), psychological, problem, propaganda, western, gothic, epistolary, science fiction, suspense, utopia, tale, tall tale, fable, folktale, parable, legend, myth, mystery, romance, or other

9. Structure of the poem by identifying
    a. Rhythm patterns, rhyme scheme, and physical form (prose poetry, free verse, blank verse, qualitative verse)
    b. Stanza form (ballad, elegiac, terza rima, rime royal, ottava rima, Spenserian)
    c. Genre, such as epic poem, dramatic poem, lyric poem, elegy, ode, sonnet (Italian/Petrarchan, English/Shakespearean, Spenserian), haiku, song, ballad, aubade, parody, limerick, epigram, epitaph, epigraph, shaped verse, satire, metaphysical poem

10. Dramatic structure of the play by identifying
    a. Plot (exposition/introduction, conflict/exciting force, rising action/complication, climax/turning point, falling action, resolution/dénouement)
    b. Length (acts, scenes, episodes) and audience format (stage production, television, movie)
    c. Use of dramatic elements, such as foreshadowing, flashbacks, in medias res, double plots, reversals, dramatic conventions
    d. Dramatic genre, including tragedy (such as classical, romantic, revenge, domestic), comedy (such as high or low, as well as romantic, realistic, comedy of manners, sentimental, burlesque, operetta), or tragicomedy

When reading a selection for **voice and tone,** determine:

1. Point of view of the narrator (first person, third person limited, third person unlimited) and decide if:
    a. Third person narrator is intrusive or unintrusive
    b. Narrator is self-effacing, using the scenic method, or if the narrator uses the panoramic method
    c. First person narrator is credible

2. Relationship of the narrator/speaker, writer, and main characters

3. Narrator's/speaker's, writer's, and main characters' attitudes

4. Speaker's tone (of voice), such as formal, informal, playful, sincere

5. Tone of the work by describing
   a. Tone of the subject, the subject's treatment, and the setting
   b. Tone(s) projected by the characters
   c. Style, such as high, middle, low; demotic, hieratic

When reading the selection for **character,** determine:

1. Each character's distinguishing traits and describe:
   a. Attitudes (such as positive, negative, kind, unkind), emotions (such as love, hate, stable, attached), and response mechanisms (such as fury, nonchalance, self-confidence)
   b. Intrinsic values, including a generalization of "what kind of person" he or she is

2. What techniques are used to reveal character and examine
   a. Each character's identity, such as hero or stock
   b. Any stereotypes
   c. Character revealed through exposition, actions, dialogue, and thoughts (if revealed)
   d. Motives of each character
   e. Impact (if any) of setting on character

3. Character changes (development) in terms of motivation, time, and insight

4. The "character" of the setting (if applicable)

5. The distinguishing features of the work as a whole

When reading a selection for **language (uses and meanings),** determine:

1. Literal meaning of the work by section, paragraph, sentences, phrases, words, or other

2. Figures of speech based on analogy (such as simile, metaphor), rhetoric (such as rhetorical questions,

amplification, aposiopesis), syntax (such as antithesis, apostrophe), and the *effects* of each figure of speech used

3. Diction in terms of isolated word choices (such as Germanic source, puns, connotations)

4. Levels of diction in terms of dialect, purpose, or other

5. Denotative meanings of all unknown words

6. Overall degree of specificity and concreteness

7. Syntactical patterns and their effects on meaning

8. Subordinated ideas

9. Who does the action and when the action takes place

10. Connotations and implications

Index

Numbers of pages containing primary definitions are in **bold**. Additional literary terms can be found on pages within the larger indexed entries.